RECONFIGURING ISLAMIC TRADITION

Cultural Memory

in

the

Present

Mieke Bal and Hent de Vries, Editors

RECONFIGURING ISLAMIC TRADITION

Reform, Rationality, and Modernity

Samira Haj

STANFORD UNIVERSITY PRESS

STANFORD, CALIFORNIA

Stanford University Press
Stanford, California

Printed in the United States of America on acid-free, archival-quality paper

Library of Congress Cataloging-in-Publication Data
Haj, Samira, [date]
    Reconfiguring Islamic tradition : reform, rationality, and
        modernity / Samira Haj.
        p. cm.
    Includes bibliographical references and index.
    ISBN 978-0-8047-5250-3 (cloth : alk. paper)
    ISBN 978-0-8047-7860-2 (pbk. : alk. paper)
    1. Islamic modernism.   2. Islamic renewal.   3. Islam and reason.
    4. Muhammad ibn 'Abd al-Wahhab, 1703 or 4–1792.   5. Muhammad
'Abduh, 1849–1905.   6. Philosophy, Islamic—History.   I. Title.

    BP166.14.M63H33 2009
    297.8—dc22   2008011825

Typeset by Westchester Book Group in 11/13.5 Adobe Garamond

Chapter 2 is a revised version of "Reordering Islamic Orthodoxy," *Muslim World*, v.
92 (Fall 2002).

*In memory of my mother,
herself a bearer of the tradition*

Contents

Acknowledgments   xi

Author's Note on Transliterations   xiii

1. The Islamic Reform Tradition   1

2. Rethinking Orthodoxy: Muhammad ibn 'Abdul Wahhab   30

3. An Islamic Reconfiguration of Colonial Modernity:
   Muhammad 'Abduh   67

4. Governable Muslim Subjects   109

5. Love and Marriage   153

6. Conclusion   188

Notes   207

Bibliography   265

Index   275

Acknowledgments

The research and writing of this book were made possible by fellow-ships from the Fulbright-Hays Scholars Abroad program, the American Research Center in Cairo (funded by the National Endowment for the Humanities), the Center for the Critical Analysis of Contemporary Culture at Rutgers University, New Brunswick, and a College of Staten Island Presidential Research fellowship award.

Over the many years that it took to complete this book, various colleagues, friends, and family members have read portions of the various versions of this text. I want to thank them all. Special thanks for the critical advice and insightful comments of Nadeem Haj, Charles Hirschkind, Omnia el-Shakry, and Nadia Abu El-Haj. Special thanks to Nadeem Haj for his early contribution to the formation of many of my intellectual insights and for his constant probing of the philosophical foundations underlying these insights.

Of course I could not forget those who helped to make my stay in Cairo not just comfortable but also pleasant. I want to thank my sister Amal Abuel-Hajj, her husband Edmund Hull, and the staff of their household in Cairo for their sustenance and generosity, for giving me free access to their home and especially their pool, not to mention the many fabulous meals (of Muhammad) and the many challenging but animated discussions over the dinner table generated by Edmund and family friends. Nor do I want to forget the immeasurable pleasure I derived from the company of my then two young nieces, Leila and Lena. I am especially indebted to their mother and my sister Amal Abuel-Hajj and her assistant, Isma'il Solaiman, at the Library of Congress branch in Cairo for helping me find rare sources, for facilitating access to archival material and libraries, and for finding out-of-print books. It is also with pleasure that I recall the kindness and support I received from many friends and colleagues that I came to know and admire while in Cairo. Among the many who helped on the way, I want to thank Saba Mahmood for her friendship and 'Abdul Wahhab al-Masiri, who, in addition to engaging my work, introduced me to many of his intellectual colleagues and friends.

My greatest debt, however, is owed to Joseph Bohorfoush, whose caring and loving companionship made the completion of this work possible. To my loving friend and lifelong intellectual comrade, Johanna Brenner, who read every page of this book several times over and whose constant support and critical prompting helped bring this work to completion, I reserve my greatest thanks and gratitude. Lastly, I pay tribute to my mother (*teta wasileh*), the Muslim matriarch who taught me so much about life. Only after my many years of resistance and then study did I come to appreciate her and to understand the Islamic tradition that she practiced and lived. This book is dedicated to her and to all those who came to know and love her as dearly as did her grandson Nadeem.

Author's Note on Transliterations

All the translations from Arabic are mine, except when otherwise noted. I have tried to combine simplicity and consistency in the transliteration of Arabic words and names, most often following the system used by the *International Journal of Middle East Studies* (*IJMES*).

The Islamic Reform Tradition

Like a specter haunting the Western mind, Islamic revivalism appears in distorted forms, rarely conceptualized on its own terms. Instead, Islam is framed through a particular reading of the experience of post-Reformation Europe, an uncritical self-understanding of the emergence of European modernity. Western definitions of the "modern," which inform the larger body of scholarship on Islam, presume a necessary qualitative break with the traditional past.[1] The modern is defined in terms of European conceptual and institutional arrangements in which religion has been marginalized from civil society, state, and politics. Accordingly, the modern becomes the site of a progressive emancipatory historical unfolding, whereas tradition, its conceptual opposite, is the locus of tyrannical politics and social stagnation. And the political subject who inhabits this space of the modern is necessarily an autonomous, self-constitutive, and tradition-free individual. These categories do not adequately comprehend Islamic imaginaries or the forms of subjectivities that might possibly emerge in a modern Muslim world. Once the institutions and practices of Western liberal societies are conceptualized as the measure of the modern, it is not surprising that across the scholarship on Islamic movements today, Islam is often depicted (either explicitly or implicitly) as a major, if not the principal, contemporary force threatening democracy and individual freedom.

The oppositional construction of modern versus traditional, secular versus religious, humanist versus antihumanist, and rational versus irrational

was assumed in early orientalist scholarship. The orientalists characterized their "cultural synthesis" of Islam as traditional and nonrational
and hence inimical to modernity. Framing their analysis within the universal humanism and rationality of the post-Enlightenment period,
early orientalists presumed that autonomous political subjects alone are
capable of exercising reason. Consequently, most orientalists found
Muslim reformers, with their claim of a divine origin and their conception of a collective subject, to be romantically defective and backward
looking.[2]

The orientalists' conception of Islam as a cultural monolith was
critically analyzed in the 1960s by nationalist and Marxist scholars who
characterized this body of literature as imperialist, essentialist, and ahistorical.[3] But it was only after the landmark publication of Edward Said's
Orientalism (1978) that this discourse was seriously challenged, both conceptually and institutionally, within and beyond academia. Drawing on
Foucault's concept of power/knowledge and Gramsci's notion of the "or-
ganic intellectual," Said explained orientalism as a discourse of power
founded on the dichotomization of East and West, one that served a critical function in the articulation and the unfolding of imperial empires, in
both the colonial and neocolonial periods.[4]

Under the influence of *Orientalism*, a new generation of scholars
produced a far more complex and historically nuanced body of knowledge
on the Middle East. This revisionist literature varied in approach and
method. Whereas some sought out political economy, others embraced
Marxism and or the "new" social history of the time.[5] There were also
those who turned to the postmodernist critiques to contest the cultural
essentialism and modernist assumptions favored by orientalist scholarship.[6] Although this highly theoretical and self-consciously critical scholarship represents a refreshing break from the essentialist, ethnocentric,
and racist writings of older orientalists, the new discourse on Islam continues to reproduce key aspects of earlier arguments. Although Islam as a
whole may not be depicted as backward looking or portrayed as traditional and nonrational, contemporary radical Islamists are drawn that
way. A good part of this revisionist scholarship on Islam assesses contemporary Islamic movements as modern only to the extent that they employ
modern material and institutional resources; however, the scholarship
implies that these movements embrace modern resources only to attain

nonmodern ends—that is, to establish theocratic and authoritarian regimes. In searching for aspects or instances of Islamic tradition and practice that are commensurable with modernity, the yardstick of analysis remains the modern West.[7]

The reproduction of central aspects of the older arguments on Islam in this revisionist scholarship is rooted in the discursive framework of Said's landmark book. While striking a powerful blow to the essentialist totalizing methodologies and arguments of orientalist scholarship, *Orientalism* fell short of a more radical critique of liberal humanism and, in particular, its intrinsic connection with the expansion of Western hegemony worldwide from the eighteenth century on. Rather than viewing orientalist discourse as inherent to the Western humanist tradition, Said considers it a deviation from that tradition's grand narratives and emancipationist politics.[8] Critical of the abuses committed in the name of the Enlightenment, Said nonetheless remains faithful to the secular liberal humanist tradition. Although he draws on the work of Foucault, a trenchant critic of Western humanism, to expose "the deep complicity of orientalist forms of knowledge with institutions of power," Said never follows this critique to its logical conclusion in which the universalist claims of European humanism are fundamentally contested.[9]

This methodological tension can be clearly detected in the revisionist historiography on Islam that followed Said's path. Many of the recent works on contemporary Islam continue to invoke the humanistic, secularist, and anti-traditionalist assumptions of the post-Enlightenment period, in their effort to analyze modern Islamic thought and politics. Fidelity to the tradition of secular progressive humanism and its human liberationist project drew the revisionist scholars, as I will discuss in a later context, to analytical frameworks that tend to assess the modernity of Islam in terms of how closely it conforms to Western cultural and institutional arrangements. The continuing strength of the liberal humanist discourse within scholarship on Islam is especially striking, given the trenchant and now long-standing critiques that have been brought forward by scholars in many different disciplines.[10] It is this body of work on which I draw, particularly the works of Alasdair MacIntyre and Talal Asad, to create new ways for conceptualizing Islamic reformers and their movements.

Islam: A Discursive Tradition

Rather than accepting the counterposition of tradition and modernity, I suggest that we pursue Alasdair MacIntyre's conceptualization of tradition as an ever-changing set of socially embodied arguments extended through time. MacIntyre, a moral philosopher and an eminent critic of liberalism, posits tradition as "an argument extended through time in which certain fundamental agreements are defined and redefined in terms of two kinds of conflict: those with critics and enemies external to the tradition who reject all or at least key parts of those fundamental agreements, and those internal, interpretative debates through which the meaning and rationale of fundamental agreements come to be expressed and by whose progress a tradition is constituted."[11] This definition provides a useful framework for understanding how the function and the meaning of Islamic arguments change over time and in response to both internal and external challenges facing the tradition.

Elaborating on MacIntyre's concept of tradition, Talal Asad, an anthropologist of religion, suggests that a more effective way of addressing Islam is to approach it the way Muslims do—namely, as a "discursive tradition" consisting of historically evolving discourses embodied in the practices and institutions of communities. To Asad, Islamic tradition is a set of

discourses that seek to instruct practitioners regarding the correct form and purpose of a given practice that, precisely because it is established, has a history. These discourses relate conceptually to a *past* (when the practice was instituted, and from which the knowledge of its point and proper performance has been transmitted) and a *future* (how the point of that practice can best be secured in the short or long term, or why it should be modified or abandoned), through a *present* (how it is linked to other practices, institutions, and social conditions).[12]

Thus, tradition is more appropriately conceptualized as discourses extended through time, as a framework of inquiry rather than a set of unchanging doctrines or culturally specific mandates. To put the same point in another way, what appears to scholars as a commitment to fixed, essentialized tenets that must be preserved at all costs is rather a framework of inquiry within which Muslims have attempted to amend and redirect Islamic discourses to meet new challenges and conflicts as they materialized in different historical eras. From this starting point, a tradition-constituted inquiry is viewed as an embodied continuity, as having long-term temporal structures built around kinds of arguments that conventional Western scholarship has been unable to recognize. What distinguishes this definition of tradition from the standard formulations of "traditional" is that tradition refers not simply to the past or its repetition but rather to the pursuit of an ongoing coherence by making reference to a set of texts, procedures, arguments, and practices. This body of prescribed beliefs and understandings (intellectual, political, social, practical) frames the practices of Islamic reasoning. It is these collective discourses, incorporating a variety of positions, roles, and tasks that form the corpus of Islamic knowledge from which a Muslim scholar (*'alim*) argues for and refers to previous judgments of others, and from which an unlettered parent teaches a child. It is from within this tradition of reasoning that claims are made and evaluated and are either rejected or accepted as Islamic.[13]

This analytical framework allows us to move away from the counterposition of Islamic tradition and liberalism in conventional literature. For, notwithstanding its claim of breaking with tradition, liberalism itself, as MacIntyre further explains, evolved to become a tradition: "liberal theory is best understood, not at all as an attempt to find a rationality independent of tradition, but as itself the articulation of an historically developed and developing set of institutions and forms of activity. . . . Like other traditions, liberalism has its set of authoritative texts, and its disputes over their interpretation."[14] If Islamic reformers have sought support for their contemporary arguments by referring back to foundational texts of the past, they are little different from liberal theorists who go back to authoritative texts to resolve contemporary incoherencies, nor are they different from American jurists and lawmakers who seek to determine what the forefathers intended in the foundational documents of the Constitution and the Bill of Rights or who argue their different positions through competing interpretations of these foundational texts.

By failing to approach Islam on its own terms and by being unable to imagine Islam as inhabiting a modern world, scholars are often led to wrongly conclude that "fundamentalist" Islamic movements that violently reject Western modernity embody the essence of Islam, whereas Islamic thinkers who seek to redefine a modern Islam are viewed as inevitably borrowing from liberal political thought. My intention is to highlight the problems of these notions by analyzing the work of two significant Muslim reformers whose work many consider to have inspired the two major strands of contemporary Islamic political thought. The first is the eighteenth-century Arabian reformer Muhammad ibn ʿAbdul Wahhab (1703–87), who is often referred to in the literature as the legendary mastermind of a "fundamentalist," "ultra-right," and "violent" political movement and, concomitantly, as the inspiration for present-day militant Muslim groups (like al-Qaʿida) in their struggle against modernity. The second is the nineteenth-century Egyptian reformer Muhammad ʿAbduh (1849–1905), who has been designated a liberal humanist and described as having "underlined the essence of Muslim humanism" for the modern world.[15]

Dissenting from these views, I propose that both reformers' ideas be addressed not simply in terms of their political goals and especially not in terms of either their "fundamentalist" or "liberal" inclinations.[16] Rather, their work should be evaluated in terms of the manner in which they engage with and speak from a historically extended, socially embodied set of arguments that have their own internal standard of rational coherence. We can accordingly then grasp their "intellectual" production not simply in its proximate political function but also in its relation to a set of enduring arguments that have been central to Muslim scholarship in general and thus to the two reformers' conceptual formation.

In approaching the works of these two reformers, who come from different historical periods and social settings, my goal is to provide a way of conceptualizing the Islamic tradition that is different from that proposed by conventional scholarship.[17] I also want to illuminate some aspects of how Muslims view modernity, as these views have been overshadowed by Western scholarship and because they problematize assumptions founded on the oppositional dichotomies of modern versus traditional, secular versus sacred. In other words, I want to demonstrate that a tradition is not simply the recapitulation of previous beliefs and practices; rather, each successive generation confronts its particular problems via an engagement with a set of ongoing arguments. In constructing their arguments, Muhammad ʿAbduh and ibn ʿAbdul Wahhab had to argue from within the tradition. This does not mean they were mimicking the past. Rather, they were attempting to make persuasive arguments for the present by referring to a past and to an authoritative corpus that determined the epistemological, cultural, and institutional limitations and possibilities within which their claims could make sense. Not every claim that relates itself to the past is therefore part of the tradition, as tradition is being adjudicated and re-adjudicated over time through consensus. As such, Islamic tradition is not fixed but is constantly changing, albeit within a long-standing framework that impinges on the direction and form of that change. Viewed from this perspective, these two reformers can no longer be counterposed as "fundamentalist" and "liberal" but should instead be understood in terms of the differences in the worlds they inhabited. And any discontinuities in their thought may be apprehended as part and parcel of a discursive break dictated by the circumstances of a changed world.

Discourse of Reform and Revival

As many scholars have already noted, contemporary Islamic revivalism is neither an innovation nor a novelty, for it is deeply embedded in the Islamic tradition, which conceptualizes human history as a continuum of renewal, revival, and reform (*tajdid, ihya', and islah*).[18] These concepts are understood within the tradition as imperative for safeguarding and ensuring the continuity of a moral community. As a corrective form of criticism, renewal, revival, and reform involve going back to the authoritative corpus to evaluate whether current norms and beliefs fall within the institutional and conceptual boundaries authorized by the Qur'an and the Sunna (the Prophet's sayings and practices). The return to the authoritative texts, far from a reassertion of already agreed upon tenets, requires a particular form of reasoning through which existing interpretations of the texts are challenged and new understandings put forward. The moral critic who takes up the task of redefining the true faith and reasserting anew its authority is called a revivalist. Revivalists, as Abdolkarim Soroush, a contemporary Muslim scholar from Iran, explains, "are not lawgivers (*shari'un*) but exegetes (*sharihun*)" in that they correct "defects" in this body of Islamic knowledge, which "abound[s] in exegeses," and in so doing they bring new insights and understanding to this incomplete form of human knowledge.[19]

Critical to the Islamic historical memory is the notion of the Prophetic age as the exemplary and revered era for all times. Under the guidance of the prophet Muhammad, the early community of Muslims is envisioned as having attained the highest and purest form of faith possible in this world. From within this historical imaginary, moving forward in time is conceived as fundamentally dangerous because as the archetypal era recedes, Muslims are bound to become more prone to corruption (*fasad*) and degeneration. This impending retreat (*taqahqur*) from piety is detected in a laxity about and deviation from the exercise of relevant virtues and authorized practices. To circumvent this tendency toward a progressive degeneration of the community over time, Muslims devised a mechanism in the form of corrective criticism and renewal to be carried out by the pious and the learned. Over time, the practice of reform and revival became a defining feature of the Islamic tradition, an authorized practice founded on the Quranic verse, which repeatedly instructed pious Muslims to "promote the good and prevent the evil."

The genealogy of this concept of impending retreat (*al-taqahqur*) is traced back in conventional Islamic histories to the third Islamic century and in particular to the work of al-Jahiz (d. 255 A.H./868 A.D.), a prominent Muslim thinker and man of letters. Al-Jahiz's chronicle of Islamic history identifies three successive stages of retreat, as Muslims slowly backed away from the highest and most virtuous stage (the era of *tawhid*) to "the age of depravity," moving toward the third stage, what he described as a virtual repudiation of faith.[20] Although this theory of "progressive retreat" (*aswa'*) seems pessimistic, al-Jahiz drew a different conclusion. As a fellow Mu'tazila committed to the practice of corrective criticism, al-Jahiz put his trust in pious and faithful Muslim scholars, such as himself, who through ceaseless effort of "promoting the good" would lead the community toward that "right path" of impeccable faith (*tawhid*).[21] Two generations later, the role of reformers as bearers of truth and justice was firmly established. A normative act, revivalism came to be seen by the twelfth century, as the most eminent reformer of that age, al-Ghazali (d. 505 A.H./1111 A.D.), revealed, a practice authorized by none other than the Prophet himself when he said, "God will send to this Community at the head of each century those who will renew its religion for it."[22] Al-Ghazali not only reconfigured Islamic orthodoxy by extending Aristotelian methods of reasoning into the Islamic idiom and semantics; he also infused features of mystical Sufism into the orthodox discourse, creating a "vital nerve between the inner and exterior aspects of religion."[23]

Later generations of reformers continued to elaborate and expand on the practice of revivalism, attempting to ensure the effectivity of reform as a corrective to moral and social backsliding. As it evolved, reformers came to invoke the right to *ijtihad*, reasoning independent of precedent, to reestablish the authority of the Qur'an over a consensus based in precedent (*taqlid*) and to challenge taqlid as authoritative practice in order to contest those who, abiding by consensual precedent, defended the status quo. Most reformers invoked the concept of ijtihad to challenge the authority of the religious leadership in their respective communities. Going back to the original authoritative sources, the Qur'an and the *Hadith*, revivalists claimed to want to free Islam from the dead weight of ineffectual and harmful accretions. They considered the conventional religious authority, which imbued taqlid, as unable either to recognize the serious problems raised by current practices or to provide proper guidance to the community. The seventeenth and eighteenth centuries, as recent historians' work demonstrates, abounded with Muslim revivalists who were greatly alarmed by what they saw as a pervasive moral laxity and decadence ailing their respective communities and who, accordingly, sought their renewal and revival by invoking the practice of ijtihad.[24]

In support of ijtihad, several of the early reformers, referencing the authoritative sources, extended the argument to say that "God has conferred His Gifts on later generations as He did on the earlier ones," thus making the claim that God authorized all generations, regardless of how close or far they were from the era of Revelation, with the right to make their own judgments over what they considered to be the "good" of society.[25] Many of these reformers located their argument for ijtihad in the work of the fourteenth-century Hanbali thinker ibn Taymiya, for it provided them with sound and effective arguments against the infallibility of consensual precedent (taqlid) as espoused by established religious authority.[26] Moreover, in making their claim for the right to practice ijtihad, eighteenth-century reformers came to understand degeneracy as the failure of human knowledge and the dereliction of a feeble religious authority rather than the consequence of an innate regression over time.[27]

Reformers in Distinct Social Settings

As reformers, ibn 'Abdul Wahhab and Muhammad 'Abduh both relied on this long-standing discourse of Islamic revival but with a difference demarcated by their different historical contexts. Whereas ibn 'Abdul Wahhab belonged to a world defined primarily by religion and Islamic knowledge, 'Abduh was born into a scientifically oriented new world in which the preservation of "the eternal message of religion in the course of such an invasive torrent of change and renewal constitutes the core of the struggles and sacrifices of the reformers" of his time.[28] Unlike ibn 'Abdul Wahhab, who, like earlier revivalists, had dedicated his life to rescuing Islam from the clutches of the ignorant and the "unenlightened," modern reformers such as 'Abduh confronted a much greater challenge, one of reconciling, as the philosopher-poet Iqbal put it, "eternity and temporality."[29] Safeguarding Islam against "the perilous path of the temporal world and bestowing proper meaning and relevance upon it in an increasingly turbulent secular world," as will be discussed in the course of this book, was not a simple task for most reformers of this period, especially because Muslims were "conscripted" rather than having freely and willingly volunteered for this project called modernity.[30]

Confronting the perils of a secularizing world, nineteenth-century reformers found themselves drawn to the argument that God has equally bequeathed upon later generations the right to direct interpretation of the two most authoritative sources and thereby the right to set new norms when needed. This claim helped to release this new generation of Muslims from what they came to label as the "fetters" of obsolete rulings and practices, thus allowing all learned Muslims to interpret the primary sources and evaluate for themselves what is and what is not appropriately Islamic in light of the particular social needs and concerns of their communities. A few, including 'Abduh, went a step further by extending this understanding to say that God bestowed upon each and every faithful Muslim (*fard 'ayn*, or *individual duty*) armed with proper education and knowledge of the religion the right to participate in making authoritative judgments regarding the good of society. The extension of this duty to individuals opened a new terrain in which all capable and educated lay Muslims could engage Islamic forms of reasoning and reach judgments independently of consensual authority, a stance which in a roundabout way and over time came to subvert the power of the 'ulama who claimed to be the sole interpreters and guardians of Islam.[31]

However, I would not read this conceptual alteration as a politically premeditated or conscious act by reformers intent on undermining the authority of the established 'ulama. The alterations and amendments in conceptions and structures of Islamic authority were more the product of complex, changed, and changing conditions and of new opportunities (affecting both reformers and adversaries) rather than the outcome of a calculated act or idea. In Egypt, the two conditions that facilitated these conceptual changes were the recent extension of education to a larger public and the emergence of print culture, which broadened public access to Islamic classical texts—conditions that did not exist in the age of ibn 'Abdul Wahhab and the earlier generation of reformers, for whom manuscripts and manuals were the prevailing form of textual culture. Although eighteenth-century reformers extended the right to interpret and judge beyond the established religious authority to include Muslim scholars, it would never have occurred to them to extend that right to a general public, even a limited one as 'Abduh did. In a manuscript culture, lay Muslims with no access to higher learning or printed texts depended on learned scholars ('ulama) to transmit and interpret Islamic knowledge for them. In contrast, the modern era of public education and print culture opened new avenues for lay educated Muslims to access Islamic knowledge directly through printed texts, without interpretation being mediated through or approved by a higher authority. These conditions facilitated the emergence of Muslim subjects capable of judging for themselves, enabling lay Muslims to engage in public discussions over the nature of religious authority that previously were confined to the scholarly class of 'ulama. It is out of these structural and circumstantial changes that the notion of an educated, rational Muslim subject who was responsible for his or her actions became, by the turn of the century, a constitutive feature defining a "good" Muslim. A proper Muslim was now expected to participate responsibly and effectively toward the cultural and material advancement (*ruqqy*) of his or her society.

Both ibn 'Abdul Wahhab and Muhammad 'Abduh were Muslim scholars ('ulama, singular 'alim) trained in Islamic knowledge and hermeneutics—a genealogy of authoritative texts beginning with the two original sources (or *usul*, singular *asl*), the Qur'an (Revelation) and Sunna (practice of the Prophet), as well as *fiqh* (*shariʿa*, or jurisprudence), a constructed corpus of human knowledge made of interpretive elaborations of the foundational two sources. Their training in Islamic discourses followed older forms of instruction that relied on memorization and recitation, which in the predocumentary past were regarded not just as simple thoughtless repetition but as a learned skill to enhance memory and the set of virtues for which memory is instrumental. Through these techniques of learning, centered on recitation, an acute memory, and the creation of commentaries, students acquired the skill to debate and question. The recitation paradigmatic, as Brinkley Messick puts it, is integral to the Islamic discursive tradition because Muslims believe the Qurʾan, the spoken word of God, to be a "recitation text" that was received orally by the Prophet, who could neither read nor write.[32] In this sense, recitation is not confined to the learned and the jurists alone but is a practice that is part of the daily ritual life of ordinary Muslims as well. Early Muslim cultures, argues Messick, were primarily "logocentric," as they privileged the spoken word (over the written), with institutional implications that were especially significant.[33]

With the emergence of modern scientific culture and its emphasis on intuition and original discovery unfettered by older ideas, the attitude toward early memorial cultures changed. Different from the past, when retentive memory was regarded as a celebrated virtue, under modern documentary culture it came to be vilified as superfluous, nonrational, and traditional. The privileging of documentary culture over a memorial one was bound to create tension within this logocentric Islamic tradition. This tension is clearly evident in the life narrative of Muhammad ʿAbduh, described below, but not in that of ibn ʿAbdul Wahhab. Although both reformers had their early training in the Islamic discourse of memorization and recitation, ibn ʿAbdul Wahhab, the product of a memorial culture, embraced it as a given; ʿAbduh, produced by an Islamic culture that is becoming profoundly documentary, rejected it as ineffective and redundant.

In looking at the prescientific world that produced ibn ʿAbdul Wahhab as a scholar and a reformer, my purpose is to delineate what is distinctive about modernity itself, particularly the uniqueness of the modern condition and its relation to religion. Whereas in the world of ibn ʿAbdul Wahhab, little distinction was drawn between morality and social structure, in the modern world of 'Abduh, morality was slowly being separated from social structure and privatized. Keeping this difference in mind, I now turn to a brief narrative of their lives in order to convey how the social, political, and cultural environment into which they were born and lived as Muslims helped to inform and shape their reform projects.

The Life Narrative of Ibn 'Abdul Wahhab

Ibn 'Abdul Wahhab was born in 1703 in a tribal social setting to a Najdi scholarly family of Hanbali jurists and theologians.[34] His father, sheikh 'Abdul Wahhab ibn Sulaiman, was the residing *qadi* (judge) as well as a leading *faqih* (jurisprudent scholar) of the town of al-'Uyaina, in central Najd, when ibn 'Abdul Wahhab was born.[35] The father was a respected judge, appreciated for his *'adl* (justness), modesty, and virtuousness. He taught Islamic jurisprudence, hadith studies (Prophetic tradition), and Quranic commentaries (*tafsir*) in the *madrassa* of the local mosque and wrote several exposés (*rasa'il*) on these same subjects. His father's brothers all practiced jurisprudence and taught theology in the surrounding villages and oasis of central Najd, as did other members of this clan. One of his uncles, Ibrahim ibn Sulaiman, for example, was identified by eighteenth-century biographers as an eminent Hanbali scholar and a writer, as was his son 'Abdul Rahman, who authored several religious works on the Hanbali tradition.[36] But the most renowned within the clan was the grandfather, Sulaiman ibn 'Ali, whose authoritative writing and knowledge of Hanbali thought had attracted from afar many Muslim scholars who sought his advice whenever they encountered difficult problems in fiqh or other theological questions relating to the Hanbali school. His mother, too, as the daughter of distinguished Sheikh Muhammad ibn 'Azzar and as the sister of a well-known scholar who taught and wrote on Islamic fiqh, came of a learned family.[37]

From early on, Muhammad ibn 'Abdul Wahhab led the privileged life of a scholar, constantly surrounded and challenged by learned members of his extended family who provided him with a lively scholastic environment. Under the tutelage of his father, both Muhammad and his brother Sulaiman started their training as children reciting the Qur'an and memorizing basic hadith studies, fiqh, and Quranic exegesis. Of the two, however, Muhammad, as recorded by his chroniclers, proved to be the faster learner. Not only did he memorize the whole Qur'an before the age of ten; he also showed a keen inquisitive mind that did not refrain from questioning the logic of certain jurisprudential rulings and interpretations.[38] In awe, 'Abdul Wahhab Sulaiman confessed in a letter to one of his brothers that even he "learned few significant tips about the fundamental principles of the faith."[39] Ibn Bishr, as the chronicler of the movement, in anticipation of Muhammad ibn 'Abdul Wahhab's future as a Muslim critic and reformer, depicted Muhammad's early virtuosity as a timely inspiration from God: "God Almighty expanded his breast for him, enabling him to understand those incongruous matters that led men astray from His Path."[40] It was not a view shared by all, including "anti-Wahhab" polemicists who later on portrayed Muhammad's inquisitive youthful mind as an early sign of religious deviancy, which alarmed his father and other members of the clan.[41]

By the age of ten, Muhammad ibn 'Abdul Wahhab in addition to having memorized the whole Qur'an had basic knowledge of other required subjects, thus completing the first instructional phase of his life. His father, following the norms of his day, arranged a marriage for Muhammad when he turned twelve. At the same time, 'Abdul Wahhab ibn Sulaiman initiated his vocation as a scholar by arranging for young Muhammad to lead prayers in the local community. As with all promising young scholars, Muhammad was then sent off on his first learning trip to the holy city of Medina, which housed the largest Islamic learning center in Arabia as well as the tombs of the Prophet and his early companions. It was during this visit, as recorded by his chronicler, that Muhammad began to observe firsthand what he considered to be deviant behavior by Muslims during their visitation to the Prophet's tomb. Once back in his hometown, he began to grapple with the notion of Islamic monotheism (tawhid) and to engage members of his family and community in discussions of certain local practices that he considered in violation of the fundamental principles of monotheism. He began to verbally urge the people of 'Uyaina to abandon their excessive reverence to people and to saints and their tombs, and he appealed to them to combat magic and sorcery, for fear of committing polytheism (*shirk*). Although some members of the community obliged him, many disregarded his message, driving ibn 'Abdul Wahhab in the end to depart his town to seek further knowledge on the doctrine of *tawhid* and on its relationship to practice.[42]

Still in his youth, ibn 'Abdul Wahhab took up residence in a madrassa attached to the local mosque in Medina. While there, he sought guidance from several distinguished scholars and critics; the most renowned among them were the Hanbali 'Abdallah ibn Ibrahim al-Saif (d. 1183 A.H.) and the Hanafi critic and revivalist (*mujaddid usuli*) Muhammad Hayat ibn Ibrahim al-Sindi (d. 1165 A.H./1751 A.D.).[43] Under ibn Saif's tutelage, ibn 'Abdul Wahhab expanded his knowledge of Hanbali fiqh and hadith studies, but as he acknowledged later on, Saif's greatest influence was in instilling the idea that knowledge and not violence is the best weapon to combat degeneracy (fasad) and ignorance:

On one occasion when ibn 'Abdul Wahhab was in the company of ibn Saif, his tutor suddenly turned to him and asked: "do you want to see the weapons I amassed for al-Majma'ah?" When the student enthusiastically urged his tutor over and again to show him his collection, ibn Saif led him to a house of his that was filled with books and said, "this is what I collected to take back to my town."[44]

Upon completing his studies with ibn Saif, ibn 'Abdul Wahhab was given a license (*ijaza*) that authorized him to teach in the surrounding mosques. While teaching, ibn 'Abdul Wahhab sought out his second tutor, a renowned Hanafi scholar and moral critic, M. Hayat al-Sindi. Al-Sindi had a widespread reputation as a keen critic of popular practices such as the veneration of tombs, including that of the Prophet and his companions.[45] As recorded by ibn Bishr, ibn 'Abdul Wahhab told the following story of his mentor:

One day ibn 'Abdul Wahhab was standing beside the Prophet's chamber which contained his tomb in the great mosque of al-Medina; a crowd of people gathered about, praying to the Prophet, beseeching and entreating his forgiveness (asking shafa'a). While watching, al-Sindi came along and joined his pupil, who asked his mentor what he thought of these people's conduct. The teacher's reply was: The Prophet is absolved from their actions and little do they know that their actions are fallacious and untrue [to God's path].[46]

Al-Sindi was known to have been especially harsh in his criticisms of established religious authorities for their lax attitude toward what he regarded as "un-Islamic" practices. Emboldened by his teacher's criticisms and views, ibn ʿAbdul Wahhab began in his own teaching circles to openly criticize Muslims "prostrating themselves before the tomb of the Prophet and rubbing their cheeks against it," condemning these practices as un-Islamic and contrary to monotheistic teachings authorized by the tradition (*ahl al-kitab wal-sunna*).[47]

It is worth noting that ibn ʿAbdul Wahhab's search for answers to his inquiries were not exclusively limited to the Hanbaliya, the school of thought to which he, his family, and most of the Najdi population belonged, as is evident in his seeking out of al-Sindi as his tutor. Of all the tutors, it seems that al-Sindi had by far the greatest sway on ibn ʿAbdul Wahhab's life as reformer, for al-Sindi is often described in popular Wahhabi literature as "the spark that lighted ibn ʿAbdul Wahhab's path."[48] His chroniclers disclosed that it was under the tutelage of al-Sindi that ibn ʿAbdul Wahhab came to understand the relationship of ijtihad (reasoning independent of precedence) to taqlid (consensual precedence) and to appreciate the Hanbali's idiosyncratic insistence on ijtihad as a necessary measure for all times. Although a Hanafi, al-Sindi both in his writing and teaching constantly referred back to the works of the Hanbali scholar ibn al-Qayim to support his arguments in favor of ijtihad and against the only authorized form of reasoning among his contemporaries, that of set precedence or taqlid. As he engaged al-Qayim's work, ibn ʿAbdul Wahhab became more curious about al-Qayim's mentor and source of his thought, ibn Taymiya. This new interest drove ibn ʿAbdul Wahhab to leave Najd for *bilad al-sham* (Syria), where Hanbali studies were being revived and energetically pursued by local scholars in Damascus. On his way, he stopped in the town of Basra.[49] While there, he delved into the study of Arabic linguistics and the life narrative of the Prophet Muhammad (*al-sirah al-nabawiya*), two of the ancillary disciplines that were essential to his formal education as a scholar. For a tutor he sought out a distinguished linguist by the name of Muhammad al-Majmuʿi al-Bisri, a revivalist scholar most renowned for his mastery of tawhid, a particular branch of Islamic thought that examines the long-standing arguments within the tradition regarding the concept of God's oneness.[50]

The more confident in his views ibn ʿAbdul Wahhab became, the harder the line he took against the cult of saints, a practice that was most rampant among the Shiʿa Muslim population of Basra and southern

Mesopotamia. He targeted in particular the pilgrimage to the Shi'a shrines of 'Ali at Najaf and al-Hussain at Karbala, where offerings to and prayers over these shrines were common. Declaring these popular practices unauthorized innovations (*bida'*), he denounced them as a form of polytheism (shirk). Turning their tombs into worshipping shrines, Muslims, he argued, were in actuality denying or rejecting monotheism. Ibn 'Abdul Wahhab's harsh criticisms of these activities and his call for a return to monotheism eventually led to his forceful expulsion from Basra. Left with little money and no support or protection, he abandoned his plan to travel to Damascus and headed home instead. He took residence in the town of Huraymila, where his father now lived and was its designated qadi. By then, ibn 'Abdul Wahhab was a man of thirty some years. As soon as he settled down, he began pointing out to residents the error of their ways and exhorting them to change. According to some sources, this troubled his father, who rebuked his son and asked him to stop. Providing few details, ibn 'Abdul Wahhab's biographer ibn Bishr says of this incident simply that "words were exchanged between him and his father."[51]

The fact remains that ibn 'Abdul Wahhab restrained himself until his father's death in 1153 A.H./1740 A.D. before formally declaring his call (*da'wa* for *tawhid*) to Islamic monotheism. This call was met with strong resistance from local residents and surrounding tribes, which forced him to leave the town of Huraymila and seek refuge in his birthplace, 'Uyaina, where again his success was short-lived.[52] It was in the town of Dar'iya, where the powerful Sa'ud clan (*Anaiza* tribe) ruled, that ibn 'Abdul Wahhab finally found protection and a haven for his cause. In 1744 A.D., an alliance forged between ibn 'Abdul Wahhab and Muhammad ibn Sa'ud, head of the tribe, gave birth to the reformist movement known among its members as *al-Muwahidun* (Unitarians). In return for his physical protection and support for his revivalist call, ibn 'Abdul Wahhab agreed to support the rule of ibn Sa'ud and his descendants over Najd and its surrounding regions. Explicit in this arrangement was the delineation of roles between ibn 'Abdul Wahhab in the domain of religion and ibn Sa'ud in the domains of politics and the military. Although he authorized the military campaigns undertaken by the Sa'udi *amirs*, which led to the extension and consolidation of their power across Arabia, 'Abdul Wahhab, as the imam with the sole authority to declare jihad (holy wars), refrained from endorsing them as jihad. The call for jihad was restricted to Muslim activities he defined as un-Islamic.[53] Thus does recent Wahhabism scholar Delong-Bas make the following argument against the conventional literature that conveys ibn ʿAbdul Wahhab as a warmonger:

Although observers and historians have assumed that any and all military activities undertaken by the Saʿudis after the 1744 alliance were *jihad* activities, ibn ʿAbdul Wahhab's teachings and writings do not support this contention. His behavior—his tendency to withdraw from Saʿud's company during such arrangements and his ultimate withdrawal from his position as *imam* in 1777—further makes it clear that he did not actively support all Saʿudi military action.[54]

The fact that following his official retirement, ibn ʿAbdul Wahhab went into seclusion and led the life of a recluse until his demise in 1792 is read by some scholars, including Delong-Bas, as an indication of his disapproval of the Saʿudi rulers' political ambitions.[55] Regardless of whether one agrees with this interpretation, the more pertinent question relates not to whether ibn ʿAbdul Wahhab was violent per se, nor to whether violence was an inevitable outcome of his views, but to how the social, political, and cultural environment in which he lived as a Muslim informed and shaped both his ideas and actions, whether violent or nonviolent.

The forged alliance between the kin of Wahhab and Saʿud, which resulted in the creation of the first Saʿudi dynasty, is often described in the literature as the first Wahhabi state, which fused religion and politics and set a precedent for future generations and movements. In actuality, this arrangement was not that novel, as it followed earlier models (the Ottoman state included) in delineating in the agreement the specific roles for each party, delegating politics and the military to the prince and religion to the imam.[56] Although it is true that the boundaries of the religious and the political were more fluid and therefore harder to ascertain at this time, it is wrong nonetheless to assert that a segmented tribal dynastic formation, founded on alliances between tribes, is analogous to a centralized modern state system that consolidates its power through modern regulatory and governing technologies unavailable to eighteenth-century Arabia. It is also wrong to presume that contemporary political Islamists' insistence on the inseparability of state and religion were inspired by this religio-political alliance that gave birth to the Wahhabiya dynasty. The descriptor *secular* (describing a separation of state and religion) and its binary other (fusion of state and religion) were concepts unavailable to the world of ibn ʿAbdul Wahhab and his interlocutors. It was not part of their idiom or semantics, nor was it on the forefront of their actions. As philosopher Ian Hacking (among others) contends, human actions depend on the possibilities of description for their action: "acts are acts under description. . . . If new modes of description come into being, new possibilities for action come into being in consequence."[57] The fusion of state and religion as a concept that enabled action emerged in response to secularism, with its insistence on the separation of state and religion, as a necessary condition under modernity. These new modes of description have little to do with this eighteenth-century Arabian dynastic formation. Today's Islamists and their actions have to be simply explained in the context of modern politics and institutions rather than as having originated in Islam or the Wahhabiya dynasty. To portray ibn ʿAbdul Wahhab as the legendary mastermind of a "violent" political movement that has inspired present-day violence and intolerance among contemporary extremists is not that useful because doing so blurs the history of the Wahhabiya movement more than explaining it or its relations to radical Islamic movements today. The point is not to deny either the zealotry or the violence of any of these movements but to try and understand their violent actions not as something fixed or inevitable but as the product of historical events and social and political forces.

The Life Narrative of Muhammad ʿAbduh

In contrast to ibn ʿAbdul Wahhab, with his tribal background, Muhammad ʿAbduh was born in 1849 A.D. to a peasant family of middling income in a small village, Mahallat Nasr, in the Egyptian Delta. His background was more modest and less erudite than ibn ʿAbdul Wahhab's scholarly genealogy. In his autobiography, ʿAbduh speaks of a family of respectable social standing, of a father of Turkish origin, and of an upright Arab mother of peasant stock. He describes his father as a "pious stern man of few words," who insisted on "taking his meals apart from his wife and children," in deference to his patriarchal authority at home and as a sign of his social status in the village.[58] As the head of the family, the father assumed full responsibility for running the household and for disciplining and educating his children. For 'Abduh, the youngest child, his father chose the vocation of an 'alim (Muslim scholar) and not farming. The father's aspiration for a learned son is best understood in light of his recently acquired modest wealth as a small landowner and the new opportunities it opened to him and his family. As a middling landowner, the father was a beneficiary of the modernizing measures introduced under Muhammad 'Ali, the ruler of Egypt (1805–1848), which resulted in a radical restructuring of the rural economy in the Delta. To accelerate the commercialization of agriculture, the Ottoman *iltizam* or tax-farming land system, now considered obsolete and inefficient, was discarded for a form of land tenure founded on private property and formal registration of land. The confiscated iltizam land was in turn either distributed in the form of grants or sold for a token sum of money, mostly to Muhammad 'Ali's immediate family and his loyal entourage but also to poorer Egyptian rural notables (*ayan*) and village heads (*umda*, or *sheikh al-balad*) who were appointed as the new representatives of the government in the countryside. The economic and political power granted to them enabled many members of this middling class to consolidate and enlarge their holdings, turning them into large commercial *latifundia* by the second half of the century. The leaders of the Egyptian nationalist movements (both secular and Islamic) that led the 'Urabi revolt and the anticolonialist struggle in Egypt were by and large recruited from the ranks of this "notable peasantry" class that came to wield great power by the turn of the century.[59]

'Abduh's father, a member of this new middling-class peasantry, had both the ambition and the means to gain middle-class respectability. One guaranteed path to social mobility was to educate his youngest son, 'Abduh, for the profession of a learned scholar. Rather than sending his son to a poor local school, the father hired a private tutor to teach 'Abduh the preliminaries of reading and writing at home. Once 'Abduh reached the age of ten, he was sent off to the home of a well-known local sheikh to memorize and recite the Qur'an. Completing the task within two years, 'Abduh demonstrated a natural aptitude for learning while at the same time validating the father's ambitious goals on behalf of his son. Unlike ibn 'Abdul Wahhab, whose singular passion was learning, learning was not all that consumed 'Abduh in his youth. In his autobiography, 'Abduh declares his passion for sports, particularly horsemanship, target shooting, and swimming. Horsemanship, which he excelled at, offered an alluring distraction from his studies and a natural escape from the harsh demands of his teachers and the great expectations of an ambitious father. After he finished memorizing the Qur'an, twelve-year-old 'Abduh was sent off to the Ahmedi Mosque in Tanta to continue his studies. The Ahmedi center was regarded then as the second greatest Islamic learning center after al-Azhar in Cairo. In the first two years of his training, 'Abduh encountered no difficulties with the first subject of his study—perfecting the art of recitation and mastering the power of the spoken word. However, he became disillusioned in his third year when he was initiated into his second subject of study, mastering the science of the Arabic language. Frustrated by what he described later as a deadly, uninspiring teaching environment, in which instruction depended primarily on memorization of commentaries of "arcane and pedantic texts without comprehension," 'Abduh was brought to the brink of despair.[60] Determined to leave learning for good but reluctant to face his father's disapproval and reprimands, 'Abduh ran away from school and went into hiding at his uncle's house. After three months there, he went back to his village with the intention of giving up his studies altogether and taking up farming, following in the footsteps of his brothers. With this goal in mind, he arranged to get married. He was then sixteen years old. His father, however, refused to give up on him and forty days after the marriage demanded that 'Abduh go back to Tanta. Unable to stand up to his father, 'Abduh again ran away, this time to one of the surrounding villages where his father's uncles resided. 'Abduh recalls his "good times" with the youth of the village, while he was there participating in their life of amusement and leisure.[61] These times were brought to an end, however, when he came into contact with one of the uncles, Sheikh Darwish, who "inspired and transformed his life forever." Darwish was an erudite Sufi ascetic with a wide range of knowledge that included learning in the Islamic sciences and jurisprudence but primarily in the sciences of asceticism (*'ilm al-tasawwuf*). He had acquired this knowledge while traveling (in Libya and Morocco) as a youth, before settling back in his village to engage in agriculture.[62]

As 'Abduh related later in life, Sheikh Darwish's spiritual approach to the faith proved decisive to 'Abduh's future as an effective Muslim scholar and critic. From Darwish 'Abduh learned how to receive Islamic knowledge through the "heart" and by means of "inner discernment" (*fiqh al-batin*). ʿAbduh describes this experience as an "enlightened space of knowledge that freed me from the prison of ignorance, from literalism and its bonds of *taqlid* to *tawhid* (unity of God) with its emancipating power. . . . He was the key to my happiness . . . [for] he gave me back the part of myself which has gone astray, uncovering an innate spirit that lay hidden deeply within me."[63] After his spiritual enlightenment, ʿAbduh went back to Tanta to complete the scholastic year and from there moved to al-Azhar in Cairo, where he stayed eight years, dedicating himself completely to his studies. In his earlier years at al-Azhar, ʿAbduh lived the austere life of an ascetic, avoiding any human contact to such an extreme that he "would ask God's forgiveness following an inane or mundane tête-à-tête." His interest drew him to study Islamic philosophy, logic, history, and other subjects that were neither acknowledged nor taught at al-Azhar. After the end of every scholastic year, he would go back to his village to spend July and August with his family, which now included Sheikh Darwish, who continued his instruction in "Qurʾanic studies and Islamic sciences."[64] Year in and year out, ʿAbduh relates, "the sheikh would ask me of the subjects I studied during that year and when informed, his response was 'have they not taught you logic, mathematics and geometry?' to which I would reply, 'these are subjects not accredited nor studied in al-Azhar,' and his repeated response would be, "knowledge seekers never despair, they search out knowledge wherever they find it."[65]

Whether ʿAbduh's personal narrative of his childhood happened as told or is simply the complicated workings of a recovered memory by ʿAbduh later in life is not our concern here. What is important, rather, is that these accounts chronicle an evolving ethos, one that reflects a change in societal attitude toward what is and what is not authoritative and useful in Islamic knowledge and how best to disseminate this knowledge. The "recitational logocentrism," with its focus on memorization of classical texts once considered an inspiring and creative way of learning the tradition is now conveyed by ʿAbduh as rigid, ineffective, and moribund. The retentive mind of the memorial culture that produced ibn ʿAbdul Wahhab a century earlier is now in ʿAbduh's age dismissed as pedantic and arcane and as a poor substitution of the original authoritative sources.

The change in attitude toward what is useful knowledge, in general, and what is "authoritative" Islamic knowledge, in particular, can be hardly understood outside the context of nineteenth-century Egypt and its social and economic restructuring, first under Muhammad ʿAli and later under the British. These changes dictated the replacement of existing decentralized multiple systems of education with a unified system that necessitated besides Islamic knowledge the inclusion of useful knowledge of secular and scientific subjects. These educational and instructional innovations introduced under Muhammad ʿAli first targeted the military establishment and its elite officers and were only later on expanded to include a newly created field of public education.[66] As is to be expected, the creation of a centralized public education system did not spare the existing Islamic learning centers, from al-Azhar university all the way down to the *kuttab* (Islamic madrassa), from its all-embracing and comprehensive program of modernization. Throughout the nineteenth century, the process of modernizing education became a focal point of conflict between various modernizing forces (both secular and religious) and their varied oppositions (from the secular to the religious). Muslim reformers and educators, from the early-century ʿAttar to the mid-century Tahtawi to the turn-of-the-century ʿAbduh, considered the restructuring of existing Islamic learning institutions and their instructional and pedagogical approaches—focused on what does and what does not constitute an authoritative text—to be the key to reforming Muslims. ʿAbduh's negative youthful memories and conflicted feelings about his training as a Muslim scholar were not unfamiliar themes in narratives of the discourse on Islamic reform in the nineteenth century. To many a reformer in this era, the cause of Muslim "backwardness" and "decline" was a stagnating and sterile Islamic education centering on memorization of medieval scholastic texts with little relevance to the Islamic faith and of no value to the daily lives of Muslims. Considering that Islam "is a way of life," leading reformers and educators lamented the disarrayed state of Islamic education and its disconnectedness from the daily experiences of Muslims.

As ʿAbduh put it, the world he inhabited required that he reverse or undo what he had learned at al-Azhar and before that at Ahmedi. His first mentor, Sheikh Darwish, showed ʿAbduh the path of unlearning by teaching him to receive knowledge through the heart, whereas Jamal al-Din al-Afghani, his second and greater mentor, taught ʿAbduh to integrate the knowledge of "inner discernment" with the outer power of the spoken word (*parole*) and reform politics, putting an end to his commitment to the austere life of an ascetic. In their first encounter, al-Afghani struck the young, impressionable student with awe, admiration, and love. 'Abduh relates their meeting as follows: "He [al-Afghani] began by asking us questions of certain verses of the Qur'an, and of their interpretations by exegetes and mystics. But when he began to give his own interpretation, my heart was instantly filled with wonderment and love, because Qur'anic exegesis and mysticism were his two great passions (*qurat 'ayneh*) or the key to happiness, as he used to say."[67]

After this encounter, 'Abduh became one of al-Afghani's most devoted students and followers. Under his tutelage, he continued his studies of philosophy (ibn Sina's *Isharat*), mysticism (*Kitab al-Zawra'* by Jalal al-Dawani), history (ibn Khaldun), logic, and theology (al-'Iji). Al-Afghani also taught 'Abduh to master the art of writing as well as the arts of *parole* and oration (*khitaba*). Upon completing his degree at al-Azhar, 'Abduh's career as a Muslim critic and reformer was launched at the school, as it was there that he began to campaign for reform among the students who sought out his teaching circles. He introduced the students to texts in theology that were not acknowledged or taught at al-Azhar, including the commentary of al-Taftazani (d. 1350 A.H.) on the creed of al-Nasafi (d. 1142 A.H.), who shared views with the Mu'tazila—which immediately put him in conflict with the established 'ulama of al-Azhar. His campaign for reform included writing articles for popular journals in which he addressed concerns relating to Islam as well as to political, economic, and cultural issues.

Social Context

The narratives of these two reformers' lives make clear that they occupied strikingly different worlds and thus different terrains, both discursive and nondiscursive, on which they came to stage their revival projects. To fully understand their actions requires that we move away from explanations that impute causal force directly to their ideas, to their particular interpretations of Islamic texts, without any consideration of the historical context within which their Islamic reform projects came to unfold.

Once we place ibn 'Abdul Wahhab in the context of the tribal social setting in which he lived, we can appreciate the complex factors that shaped the evolution of his reform project. Although Najdi tribes were highly specialized, with considerable variation in their economic and social organization, kinship was the prevailing principle of social organization among them, which also meant that an individual's bonds lay with his or her blood lineage.[68] To lose the solidarity of one's kin or the protection of a tribal chief was to be condemned to the life of a pariah that neither ibn ʿAbdul Wahhab's father nor he would choose or want. Given the importance of kinship relations, it might be that even if ibn ʿAbdul Wahhab's father had agreed with his son's ideas, he would have silenced rather than fostered his son's reform project. One might attribute the father's "exchanging words with his son" as a consequence of his obligations, according to tribal custom, to the ruler of Huraymila, who took the father in, designated him his qadi, and gave him a safe haven in the town after his dismissal and strained departure from ʿUyaina.[69] It may also be the case that the son and father clashed over doctrinal matters. However, to attribute their dispute to the son's "extremism" is to disregard other factors that might have weighed quite heavily in the father's response. Complex actions (as all human actions are) are not reducible to a single consistent motive. The same argument can be extended to the choices the son himself made. Given his circumstances, it is at least probable that the driving force behind ibn ʿAbdul Wahhab's forged alliance with ibn Saʿud of Darʿiya was accidental rather than inevitable, considering his desperate desire to find tribal protection. His life was literally in danger once he was declared an outcast and forced out of the last of his many residences, his kin town and birthplace, ʿUyaina. The willingness of ibn Saʿud, a member of the tribal nobility, to use his combined wealth and power to protect ibn ʿAbdul Wahhab and spread his message is similarly complex. Was it only his political ambition to control all of Najd that drove him to make the pact with ibn ʿAbdul Wahhab, as some argue? Or, was it his true commitment to Wahhab's monotheistic message, especially after his own wife came into the movement's fold, as others maintain? How we explain the acts of violence committed in the name of the movement is another complicated question that cannot be reduced simply to one of intolerance. Raids against other tribes (*ghazwa*), often more violent than not, were hardly atypical to this culture. To imagine raiding as a useful instrument of corrective power against what the Wahhabis considered "un-Islamic" practices is not an implausible option.

By contemplating these various questions and possible explanations, it becomes apparent that the arrangements into which ibn 'Abdul Wahhab entered can make sense only within the general context and in light of his particular circumstances. The options available to him and the course of action he took were, in other words, bounded and shaped by the tribal setting, on the one hand, and his particular life narrative, on the other. The arrangements he made were hardly premeditated acts, nor were they intended with a clear vision and awareness of their future effect. To understand better the history of ibn 'Abdul Wahhab is also to try and consider the constraints on as well as the opportunities for actions available to him under these particular conditions and the impact of his personal history in shaping his choices. As a process that is neither fixed nor inevitable, history, to borrow the words of Jonathan Sheehan, is "built on the insight that people participate in larger processes of which they are individually quite unaware."[70]

Although the social relations that helped in the making of ibn 'Abdul Wahhab were predominantly tribal and dominated by tribal custom, these relations were, at the same time, mediated through Islam, a system of belief embedded in social practice. Unlike our contemporary world, with its numerous zones of knowledge and meanings, the world of ibn 'Abdul Wahhab, as will be explained later, was primarily dominated by Islamic semantics and knowledge. Islamic knowledge was the prerequisite for what constitutes norms, and it was the guiding framework for what good moral Muslims should and should not do. Central to this knowledge is the concept of tawhid, or the commitment to the oneness of God. As the principal source of religious knowledge, tawhid was the concept on which the logic of many of the beliefs, tasks, and practices depended and made sense only in light of it. Ibn 'Abdul Wahhab's call for tawhid needs to be understood in light of what he perceived to be the chief threat to this embodied system of belief—that is, the widespread practice of the "cult of saints" and the worship of their relics. The question of whether these practices are authorized became the platform of his reform campaign (da'wa) and the ground on which he fought other Muslims over what is and what is not Islamic.

Although the Wahhabiya movement aimed to correct practices and sometimes did so by force, it was not a modern state armed with its own agencies and technologies of power. Nor was it confronting a hegemonic imperial system of power located in the West. Most of the struggle in the Wahhabi movement occurred within the context of the Ottoman Empire, an empire already weakened and under threat by newly emerging powers in Europe. As a revivalist movement, it was not contesting external power but struggling against an internal threat posed by the profusion of practices and beliefs threatening to overwhelm the Muslim community.

This was not the world, nor the discursive terrain, that Muhammad 'Abduh occupied and engaged. Arriving more than a century later, 'Abduh's was a world radically changed from that of ibn 'Abdul Wahhab. Older ways of structuring and seeing, now regarded irrelevant, yielded to newer ways of seeing and arranging the world. These changes, marking a discursive break, created a semantic and structural shift that left a dramatic and long-enduring imprint on 'Abduh's life from his childhood—as his autobiography bears witness—all the way into his adulthood. The uncompleted project of "modernizing" Egypt went through ebbs and flows in the nineteenth century, culminating in military occupation and colonization by the British in 1882. Already an outspoken reformer and political activist, 'Abduh found himself compelled to engage the new semantics of change dictated by colonial modernity, including key questions of what constitutes a modern society and how far can one go in drawing new conceptual and institutional boundaries that define the public and private, the profane and sacred, the individual and society, without abandoning Islam as embodied practice. Engaging Western discourses, however, did not make 'Abduh a lesser Muslim nor necessarily a liberal.

Under the rubric of Europe's civilizing and modernizing project, 'Abduh's Egypt was undergoing dramatic changes requiring the restructuring of society and polity. The extensive transformation of Egypt entailed the dismantling of older arrangements and institutions and their replacement with new ones modeled after those of Europe. Out of this colonial reorganization of cultures and economies, the ideology of polarity between the modern and traditional worlds was erected. This in turn produced a new analytical and conceptual framework that came to vilify older social forms as traditional and nonmodern and to valorize newer forms as progressive and modern. Under this binary construct, religion was inscribed as superfluous and nonrational. It was in response to this new prescriptive vision of modernity, which constructed the modern as the site of libratory and historical unfolding and tradition as the locus of tyrannical religiosity and social backwardness, that ʿAbduh's project of an Islamic reform emerged and acquired its shape and meaning.

Although best understood within the context of the British takeover of Egypt (in 1882), one should not lose sight of the fact that ʿAbduh's project of reform was firmly rooted in the Islamic discursive tradition and was not a mere ideological weapon, a ruse, or a reaction to European power. For him, the reform of Islam was necessary to guarantee the survival of the Muslim community in the modern world; it was also the way to effectively ward off European aggression and expansion. ʿAbduh approved of the nation-state and its modernizing agencies and institutions but wanted to translate them into Islamic terms. Although he endorsed this modernizing project, he had misgivings about its liberal prescriptions of replacing an order founded on a moral community with one organized around the autonomous individual. The moral survival of the community is what ʿAbduh feared was at stake. In contrast to the view that proclaims ʿAbduh a liberal, I argue that he was in fact most fearful of the liberal viewpoint and its celebration of the modern self-constitutive subject.[71] What he resisted was not modernity—indeed, he understood the necessity for Egypt to grasp hold of modern political and economic institutions in order to challenge colonial control. Rather, he resisted the specific configuration of modernity as it had developed in the West—and particularly, secularization as practiced in Europe, where religion and morality were banished from the public sphere and, concomitantly, individual interests were enshrined as the fundamental social determinant. As a Muslim, his conception of modernity incorporated a view of the relationship between the individual, the community, and the state that differs from the European liberal humanist tradition while being no less modern. To recognize this central difference in European and Islamic conception of modernity, I maintain, might shed light on the current conflicts unfolding in the Islamic world. The conflict between these two visions of the modern, bearing as they do on every feature of social life from the individual and the family to the nation, might possibly explain the violence wracking the Muslim world today. I am therefore arguing that Islam is not intrinsically violent. Rather, it is the conflict between two visions of the modern, each of which is inscribed in and regulated by a system of power that accounts for this conflict.

Grasping these two reformers' strategic choices as the inevitable outcome of their commitment to the fundamentals of the religion is to mischaracterize Islamic thought as unitary and unchanging. Reasoned arguments led Muslims to agree or disagree with each other over the most effective strategies and practices for sustaining a moral community of believers. These arguments, however, were founded on premises different from those that inform Christian and/or Western forms of reasoning, concepts of morality, and individual virtues. In the Islamic framework, disciplined practices are fundamental for seeking individual virtue, which is attained in and through a moral historical community. Thus, the focus on practice and obligation is argued for and grounded in a set of shared beliefs and understandings, which assumes an individual belonging within the community. It is only within this light that one can understand these reformers' moral criticisms and reform policies. The Islamic tradition engages a conception of truth, reason, and ethics different from those proposed by the traditions of the West. It also implies a conception of moral accountability that is inseparable from a socio-political and historical community living by God's *shar'*. These concepts, beliefs, and practices are perceived not as serving some independently definable interest of an individual or a group occupying a particular social role. Rather, it is only through the community sustained by compliance with a set of beliefs and practices that the good receives its definition. A Muslim as a member of the community is conceived of as a self that cannot attain its own good except in and through achieving the good of others and vice versa.

2

Rethinking Orthodoxy

MUHAMMAD IBN ʿABDUL WAHHAB

> I do not—thanks be to God—conform to any particular Sufi order or jurispru-
> dent [faqih], nor follow the course of any speculative theologian [*mutakalim*] or
> any other Imam for that matter. . . . I summon only God, only Him, and observe
> the path laid by His prophet, God's messenger.
>
> ibn ʿAbdul Wahhab, *Tarikh najd*

> The faith that drives Osama bin Laden and his followers is a particularly austere
> and conservative brand of Islam known as Wahhabism. . . . Throughout the sect's
> history, the Wahhabis have fiercely opposed anything they viewed as bidʿa, an
> Arabic word, usually muttered as a curse, for any change or modernization that
> deviates from the fundamental teachings of the Qurʿan.
>
> *New York Times Magazine*, October 7, 2001

Introduction

Notably absent in Western Islamic scholarship is a serious study of
the eighteenth-century Muslim reformer Muhammad ibn ʿAbdul Wahhab. This lacuna, I believe, is not accidental. Rather, it reflects the scholarly consensus that ibn ʿAbdul Wahhab's thought is simply unworthy of
serious consideration.[1] Ironically, however, he does not suffer from anonym-
ity, for he is celebrated as this legendary mastermind of a "puritanical,"
"fundamentalist," "violent" movement that fuels the passions of present-day
Islamic militants in their "war" against modernity and democracy. Early

orientalist scholars depicted the original Wahhabi movement as "conservative" and "ultra-right-wing," given to violence and fomenting discord, and reminiscent of the Kharijite revolt in early Islam. Like the Kharijite rebels, the followers of Wahhab sought to impose their views through intolerant and fanatical methods that instilled in the minds of coming generations the conviction that change was feasible only through violent means. The master orientalist Gibb contends that even though the Wahhabis' zealotry shocked "the conscience of the Muslim community by the violence and intolerance which they displayed, its example was the more eagerly followed in other countries as their Muslim governments fell more and more patently under the European influence and control."[2] The Wahhabi influence, he goes on to argue, contributes to the outbreak of militant movements, wherever one finds a Muslim community. Even the revivalist anticolonialist movement of the late nineteenth century, led by the famous reformer Jamal al din al-Afghani, was swayed by the "revolutionary *theocratic* impulse" of the Wahhabis.[3] Although the contemporary scholar of Islamic studies Hamid Algar agrees with the early orientalists' depiction of the violent nature of the Wahhabiya movement, he raises doubts of its connection with the nineteenth-century *Salafiya* movement, in spite of some commonalities. Despite their shared elements, including their "rejection of Sufism and the abandonment of consistent adherence to one of the four Sunni *Madhhabs*," the differences are far greater, as the Salafiya movement never branded Muslims who disagreed with its views as apostates nor did it rely on coercion to rally Muslims to its cause.[4] Short of casting it as un-Islamic, Algar characterizes this "crude violent non-Sunni movement" as "an exception, an aberration, or at best an anomaly," because in essence it "denounced all the practices, traditions and beliefs that have been integral to Sunni Islam."[5]

The other factor contributing to disinterest in understanding Muhammad ibn 'Abdul Wahhab is the pervasive belief that his thought is simply worthless. In the words of Algar, his thought is "crude" and "extremely slight, in terms of both content and bulk."[6] Portrayed as intellectually inferior, ibn 'Abdul Wahhab is written off as an unoriginal thinker who reproduced a simplistic and distorted version of the medievalist works of ibn Taymiya. The French orientalist Laoust, for example, describes ibn 'Abdul Wahhab as an imitator, not an innovator, and considers his doctrinal premise as prosaic and as a pedestrian reproduction of early "scripturalists" belonging to the Hanbali sect, a school of thought that rejected reason in favor of a "literalist" and stricter reading of the Qur'an and the Sunna.[7] The affinity between the two, adds Montgomery Watt, a disciple of Laoust, lies not in the quality of thought but, rather, in the "conservative" disposition in which their thought is anchored.[8] He, too, maintains that ibn 'Abdul Wahhab mimicked ibn Taymiya's harsh and conservative views, especially on monistic Sufism and the cult of saints, which ibn Taymiya labeled as heresies in need of redress, by force when necessary.

The problem with the larger part of this body of scholarship is that it inappropriately imposes modern and secular analytical categories on a pre-scientific culture and a premodern context. One such assumption is this natural (rather than a naturalized) opposition between religion and reason—a feature unique to the modern age. The proposition that this religion is necessarily nonrational and is therefore violent, for example, informs Gibb's and Brockelmann's conclusions. Both associate the "violence" and "radicalism" of the Wahhabiya with the movement's attempt to order society in line with its religious worldview—the only view available to ibn 'Abdul Wahhab and his movement then. From these scholars' secular vantage point, religion and politics do not—or, at any rate, ought not to—mix. And when they do, the inexorable outcome is manifested, in the disparaging terms of the scholars, in "fundamentalism," "violence," and "irrationality." The same exact descriptions are often doled out to explain present-day radical Islamists, whether in Afghanistan, Algeria, or Lebanon, among others, without any consideration of the social and historical contexts that contributed to their making or to the differences between these movements and this eighteenth-century movement. Violence emptied of its political and social meaning is simply presumed rather than accounted for in its historical context. One example of the difference between the contemporary movement and the Wahhabiya should suffice in this context: Today's radical Islamists' strongest weapon is suicide bombing, which most equate with martyrdom, regarding it a duty (fard 'ayn) bestowed on all able-bodied Muslims.[9] Ibn 'Abdul Wahhab, however, opposed all forms of suicidal martyrdom and condemned it as a forbidden rather than a commendable act. He registered his disapproval by citing a number of hadiths that explain that a Muslim's duty is to value and prolong his life, one granted to him by God for the purpose of doing good deeds by participating fully toward creating this community of righteous Muslims. Sacrificing oneself for religion shortens that life and the opportunities to do good—thus, lessening the rewards in the afterlife. Ibn ʿAbdul Wahhab clearly differentiated between those martyrs killed in battlefields defending their country against an invading army from those who commit suicide in the name of religion. The martyrs will be rewarded, the others punished.[10]

Another unexamined assumption leading to this negative assessment of ibn ʿAbdul Wahhab's thought is that "religious reasoning" is fundamentally "unoriginal" and "uncreative," for original thinking can be demonstrated only by the radically different, and not by repetition.

This understanding of creativity as original thought unfettered by older arguments was foreign to ibn ʿAbdul Wahhab (and his mentor, ibn Taymiya) because any "novel" idea (*bidʿat dalal*) that breaks from this discursive tradition is simply regarded as an unauthorized practice. We should not lose sight of the fact that the concept of creativity as original thought has to begin with its own recent history and is itself a novel concept even to the West. Creativity as original thought unattached to older forms of reasoning is itself related to the emergence of scientific forms of knowledge and to their fetish of facticity.[11] It was only once scientific rationality became authorized as the sole universal form of reasoning— singularly allowed to conceptualize the temporal world we live in and to regulate its economies and societies—that religious forms of reasoning became irrelevant and nonrational. Different from our scientific modern culture, this early culture of memory was no less creative. As the scholar of medieval literature Mary Carruthers eloquently argues, intricate reasoning and originality is expressed in a "retentive memory; a trained and disciplined memory rooted in a past. The distinction lies in the techniques of learning and styles of reasoning, not in the creative act itself."[12] She contrasts the conception of creativity in memorial culture with the modern, where understanding of creativity instead stresses original discovery unfettered by older arguments. This delineation of creativity predominant in documentary modern culture is imposed on a culture that was profoundly memorial, that is, where memory was a celebrated virtue. Although the conception of the activity of intellect and thought are strikingly different between the modern and the premodern, the idea of creativity itself remained essentially the same. Both express intricate reasoning and original discovery. Carruthers challenges the distinction often drawn between oral societies, which are often seen as primitive, and literate societies, which are viewed as civilized. Learning by hearing and reciting aloud, she argues, should not be confused with ignorance of reading and with illiteracy. She suggests instead that the privileging of memory in certain cultures should be addressed independent of orality and literacy, as these terms came to be defined in the modern social sciences of today. It is misleading "to speak of literacy culture as a version of literacy at all[;] the reason is that this concept privileges the physical artifacts, the writing-support over the social and composition by an author and its reception by an audience."[13]

A more useful way of explaining ibn 'Abdul Wahhab is to approach him as a Muslim, one who was formed and informed by the Islamic discursive tradition in general and by the specificity of his tribal context and personal circumstances in particular. A discursive tradition, as stated earlier, conceptualizes Islam not as a commitment to a fixed and essentialized set of tenets, but rather as historically evolving discourses with long-term temporal structures built around certain authorized arguments and counterarguments regarding the "goods" that are constitutive of a Muslim community. From this standpoint, ibn 'Abdul Wahhab's reform project is not presumed to repeat the past or copy older ideas but to seek coherence by making reference to a discursive tradition made up of a set of texts, arguments, and practices. It is only from within this tradition-constituted discourse that ibn 'Abdul Wahhab is able to make claims about what is and what is not Islamic. He is evaluated in terms of how his ideas and practices engage with and articulate themselves within this long-standing socially embodied set of arguments and counterarguments that have their own internal standard of rational coherence. Put differently, rather than view his thought in terms of its proximate political function or for its "inflexibility" or "crudity," we should judge it in its relation to a set of enduring arguments that have been central to Muslim scholarship in general and to ibn 'Abdul Wahhab's intellectual and social formation. His reform views are also addressed as integral to his intention and belief-informed activities at the same time that the political aspects of his work are situated in relation to his scholarly intentions and beliefs.

In sum, dissenting from the conventional scholarship that interprets ibn 'Abdul Wahhab's reform project as politically motivated, using religion as a screen to attain political power, I argue that it was not political expediency that drove him to take his critical stand against practices informed by the cult of saints. Nor were his criticisms of these practices simply forged to inspire "his followers and [to] ma[ke] their sleepless passion for feud useful to his causes," as the orientalist Brockelmann alleged.[14] Rather, ibn ʿAbdul Wahhab, like other reformers before and after him, was engaging long-standing arguments within the tradition over the Islamic or un-Islamic nature of these practices.

Reform and Tajdid

As all Muslim reformers do, ibn ʿAbdul Wahhab located his criticisms within the discourse of critique and reform (islah and tajdid), which is viewed within the tradition as a necessary deterrent against the impairment of religion (*taʿtil al-din; khalal fil-al-din*) and the corruption of the living community, caused by failure to exercise relevant virtues and authorized practices. Etymologically, islah, derived from the Arabic term *sulh*, describes a condition that is virtuous, just, and good and refers to the activity of insuring this state of virtue and incorruptibility by enacting a set of authorized practices. Its binary other is fasad, an "altered state of decay and degeneration," caused by a breakdown in the virtues and practices associated with the *din* (Islam).[15] In Islamic literature, the concept of islah (reform) is used interchangeably with the term tajdid (renewal), the latter suggesting a recurrent effort of Muslims to redefine and reconfigure the religion (din) in light of the two most authoritative sources, the Qurʾan and the Sunna.

Ibn ʿAbdul Wahhab's call to return to the fundamentals of the faith (guided by the two most authoritative sources) is often misconceived to mean a literal reading of these sources. But approached from within this discourse of reform, it is understood as moving away from centuries of historical interpretations and accretions in favor of a direct and unsullied examination and interpretation of the foundational sources in regard to problems that continue to plague Muslim communities. As moral critics (*muslih* or *mujaddid*), the task of reformers like ibn ʿAbdul Wahhab is to identify and diagnose the problems and defects (*khalal fi al-din*) in society by returning to the authoritative sources, because part of a reformer's role is to inquire as to whether these concerns were addressed within the corpus and, if so, how. This method of critique and juxtaposition is part of what constitutes tajdid. It was only through comparison of his contemporaries' practices (in this particular case, the cult of saints) to precedent and the authoritative sources that ibn 'Abdul Wahhab was able to make a reasoned evaluation of whether a particular belief or practice is correct.

Monotheism

Moral laxity and religious corruption caused by the profusion of superstitions linked to the cult of saints was the setting that prompted ibn 'Abdul Wahhab's call for reform and his summon to tawhid, or monotheism. As a system of belief embodied in practice, Islamic monotheism is conceived to be fundamentally performative in character, as belief in the oneness of God is to be realized through the enactment of a set of authorized practices. As such, Islamic monotheism is conceived as relational in the sense that it is embodied in human activities and embedded in social structures. Tawhid presupposes the individual's belongingness in a corporate setting—that is, an *umma* consisting of individuals who have agreed to live by a set of authoritative texts and practices.[16] It also means that an individual who belongs to the collective has to accept the moral and institutional boundaries that define the community.

As understood by Muslims in general and by ibn 'Abdul Wahhab in particular, monotheism is not a detached set of abstract doctrinal statements about the nature of God and man's relation to God, but a set of practices constitutive of the scholarly, political, and day-to-day life of the community. Thus, the structure of authority and the way Muslims live will make little sense detached from and independent of this set of authorized practices and virtues, embodied in monotheism.

It is only in this light that one can understand ibn 'Abdul Wahhab's call for monotheism and assess his work, *Kitab al-tawhid* (The Book of Unity), that laid the conceptual foundations for his critique. In this short treatise, his criticisms target the commonly held beliefs in the power of saints and pious men and the practices consequent upon these beliefs—worship of saints' tombs, reliance on the intercession of the Prophet and the saints, and other such popular practices. This criticism, however, was not confined to popular practices; it was also directed at the blind acceptance of religious authority (taqlid) and, by implication, the ʿulama (established Muslim scholars), whom he criticized for confining independent reasoning (ijtihad) and for their uncritical acceptance of medieval Islamic sources as the final authority on these questions. He maintained that the final authoritative sources are the Qurʾan and the Sunna of the Prophet, along with the examples set by the early Companions, who considered a precedent-free ijtihad necessary for the continuous interpretation of the Islamic shariʿa. By upholding the absolute supremacy of the Qurʾan and the early Sunna, ibn ʿAbdul Wahhab's intention was to undercut the hegemonic authority of taqlid (unquestioned precedent) as practiced by the ʿulama of his age and instead to extend the practice of independent reasoning as against precedent. It is precisely this approach to the tradition that explains his appeal to later generations of Muslims.

In reasserting the finality of the authoritative texts, ibn ʿAbdul Wahhab located his arguments for reform in the works of another Hanbali, the medieval scholar ibn Taymiya (1263–1328 A.H.), who was also renowned for his devastating critique of pantheistic beliefs and practices and the ways in which they threaten the fundamentals of Islam. One of the chief problems confronting ibn Taymiya's age was monistic Sufism, accompanied by the spread of heretical practices, such as the worshipping of saints and their relics and the pilgrimage to their shrines. Along with these commonalities in their concerns, it was ibn Taymiya's relevant ideas on the subject that persuaded ibn ʿAbdul Wahhab to turn to ibn Taymiya's work, rather than the mere desire to emulate or mimic him. What triggered his interest in ibn Taymiya was the latter's specific arguments against the cult of saints and their relics and, concomitantly, against popular practices—deviations, in his eyes, from tawhid. Contrary to the dismissive assessment of ibn ʿAbdul Wahhab for his selective appropriation of ibn Taymiya's thought, I suggest instead that selective references are typical within any tradition. Almost all scholars at one point or another go back to earlier authoritative works and select specific arguments in terms of their contemporary relevance. Ibn ʿAbdul Wahhab's case is not any different. There were specific arguments put forward by ibn Taymiya that were not only relevant but proved instrumental to ibn ʿAbdul Wahhab's reconfiguration of the concept of tawhid, the key to his reform project.

Ibn Taymiya

Ibn Taymiya lived in a period of confusion and uncertainty, marked by the devastating havoc caused not only by the Mongol invasions but equally by monistic Sufism and a marked growth of what he considered deviationist behavior that threatened to dismantle the fundamentals of Islam from within.[17] But as ibn Taymiya maintained over and again, the ascendance of these heretical practices and beliefs was only a symptom of a much larger problem facing the tradition—that of discursive incoherence. Conceptual incoherence in the dominant discourse, he argued, paved the path for moral degeneration and the growth of heretical practices as patronized by extremist Sufis, including those who profess the will of God but are not compelled to follow his commands (shar'). This incoherence he attributed in particular to the confusion of speculative theology and its understanding of tawhid—the concept that informs beliefs and governs correct Islamic practices.

Ibn Taymiya's strongest criticism against speculative theology (*ilm al-kalam*) was directed toward its endeavor to separate theology from law and morality, by postulating that *al-naql* (tradition transmitted orally [by *sama'*] and ordained by God; also, another term for Revelation) and *al-'aql* (human reasoning) are oppositional rather than complementary, as had been understood by the early generation of Muslims. This faulty methodology led to a separation under which law and ethics came to be assigned to the domain of the *shar'* (Divine Commandments) and the authority of *naql* in contrast to theology and metaphysical issues that were assigned to the domain of *'aql* (human reasoning). This separation resulted in the birth of a conceptual distinction to be drawn between the domain of the shari'a and that of the din (religion). As such, theology and metaphysics came to be incorporated under the discipline of *usul al-din* (primary principles of religion), whereas the legal came to fall under the rubric of shari'a (*usul al-fiqh*).[18] This separation, according to ibn Taymiya, encouraged the ascendance of extreme Sufist attitudes that a Muslim who acknowledges God was not obligated by his commands. The ascendance of such currents stripped the shari'a of its moral character and created a tradition in which usul al-fiqh came to be regarded instead as a formal code of particular precepts and practices that were detached from the inner or spiritual foundation of the din.

Although it is true that ibn Taymiya defined his main objective to be the refutation of the conceptual foundations of speculative thought (*ahl al-kalam*), his fiercest attacks were directed against monistic (*Ittihadi*) Sufism and zeroed in on ibn ʿArabi (1165–1240 A.H.) and his doctrine of the Unity of Existence.[19] According to ibn Taymiya, this doctrine basically voided the distinction between God and his creation by positing that God is indistinguishable from reality, which in turn led to the heretical concept that it is possible to attain unity with God. Ibn ʿArabi's doctrine of the Oneness of Existence, according to ibn Taymiya, represented a break from the dominant discursivity of Islamic monotheism, because it posited an absolute being that is not transcendental, that is nameless and without attributes, except for that of self-existence. Ibn Taymiya's main objective was to shake the conceptual foundation of monistic Sufism and expose its relationship to the degeneration of the Islamic moral order. He did so by demonstrating how these notions, which obliterate the distinction between God and the temporal created world, had in effect revoked the two most elemental aspects of Islam: first, the concept of tawhid (the oneness of God), which is imbedded in the notion of a transcendental God; second, the objective validity of a Muslim moral community founded on the sharʿ—which presumes the existence of a God that commands (*amr*) and of subjects that are the object of such commands. Going back to the authoritative sources of the Qurʾan and the Sunna, ibn Taymiya reaffirmed the absolute dissimilarity of God (the creator) and man (the ʿabd, or slave) and reasserted that the worship of the one God is realized only through the observance of commands prescribed by the sharʿ. In so doing, he arrived at a new way of conceptualizing tawhid by discerning that tawhid embodies two interlinked meanings: *tawhid al-rububiya* (an omnipotent, willful God) and *tawhid al-uluhiya* (one God to worship). Whereas the first was essential for belief, the second was pivotal to belief as practice. By drawing this distinction between *tawhid al-rab* (God the Creator), which was central to later speculative theological debates (of ahl al-kalam), and *tawhid al-ilah*, which was what he interpreted to be the true meaning understood by the early generation Muslims, ibn Taymiya's aim was to validate a moral community living by sharʿ. And by interlinking these two meanings of tawhid, his aim was to refute monistic Sufism and its claim that if an individual professes the Will of God, he or she is no longer bound by the command of God, and to reestablish the fundamental connection between belief and practice.[20]

Ibn ʿAbdul Wahhab's interest in ibn Taymiya lies in the latter's exposure of pantheistic Sufi practices and the ways in which they came to threaten the core of the moral order. He was less enthralled by ibn Taymiya's intricate examination of speculative philosophy and theology or his critical assessment of monistic Sufism. All that mattered to ibn ʿAbdul Wahhab was ibn Taymiya's redefinition of tawhid; the manner in which it accentuated God's Will as the Creator, Commander, and shariʿa giver; and the ways in which it relinked belief to practice. By making reference to these particular issues, ibn ʿAbdul Wahhab, therefore, was not either misappropriating or repeating old arguments for nostalgia's sake, but seeking them out because they shed light on how to understand and approach these suspected practices in the context of his own community. They also provided him with the conceptual, cultural, and institutional boundaries to the claims he was making for the present. Moreover, considering the different worlds they occupied, it is important that we recognize the ways in which ibn Taymiya's arguments as utilized in the context of ibn ʿAbdul Wahhab came to acquire a new meaning and function.

Kitab al-Tawhid

Al-tawhid, the article of faith that defines what it means to submit (*islam*) and bond (*ibada*) oneself to the one God, is the setting of ibn ʿAbdul Wahhab's critical inquiry. It is also the ground from which he fought to reconfigure and reassert orthodox discursive dominance. For tawhid, as discussed earlier, presupposes a concept of an Islamic orthodoxy, one that consists of concepts and moral precepts that rely for their authority on there being a set of shared beliefs about what is good for the individual and the community. These shared beliefs are understood as obligations that are fundamental to the cultivation and attainment of a morally virtuous Muslim community. In this manner, tawhid is understood less as a doctrine (*aqida*) or a statement to be proven true or false and more as a set of shared beliefs and understandings that are deeply imbricated in the social and institutional making of the community (that are constitutive of the individual and the community).

Ibn 'Abdul Wahhab's *Kitab al-tawhid*, as noted by his contemporary biographer and companion ibn Ghannam, identifies and criticizes those problems and unauthorized practices ibn 'Abdul Wahhab encountered firsthand in his travels. It describes a state of corruption (fasad) in the community: pantheistic practices at the holy sites, praying at the tombs of saints, talismans and bewitchment, and sorcery to ward off evil spirits, among other superstitious practices. Ibn 'Abdul Wahhab records what he witnessed of Muslims forsaking the worship of God for the worship of others and criticizes these practices as violations of the principal article of tawhid, that of the worship of the one God and no other but him.

Kitab al-tawhid belongs to a genre of Islamic writings called *mutun* (singular *matn*, meaning text), which are instructional abridged texts that privilege the recited oral word over the written texts. In spite of their "modest literary quality," these manuals, as Messick points out, "became the most widely disseminated of the shari'a texts." As abridgments of foundational texts, these instructional manuals intended for memorization did not have the eloquence or lucidity of written manuscripts, and subsequently "their authority as a written text is both subsidiary and secondary."[21] Written in the form of a matn intended for recitation and teaching, *Kitab al-tawhid*, consists of sixty-seven short chapters, each of which comprise a set of Quranic verses and some hadiths plus an abbreviated interpretive summary of the moral lessons to be drawn from them.[22]

Tawhid as Embodied Practice

Embracing ibn Taymiya's conceptualization of tawhid, ibn 'Abdul Wahhab goes on to explain it as more than the concept of God being One (tawhid al-rab), because embedded in it is the notion of *tawhid al-ilah*, which involves the submission to (*islam*) and the worshipping ('ibada) of him to the exclusion of all others. These two interrelated concepts—*islam*, the act of surrendering to God, and 'ibada, its implementation in life through worship and obedience to God alone—are crucial components of tawhid. Entrance into Islam is dependent on an outer act, that of uttering the *shahada* (I bear witness that there is no god but God and Muhammad is his prophet), which grants the speaker admission into the community. *Islam* also means the inner act of submission and surrendering oneself through worship (*'ubudiya*), for to surrender one's whole self to God is to render to him the worship that is his due. In this manner, the act of *islam* (surrendering) is intertwined with the act of bonding oneself (*'ibada*) to God. [23]

It is important to stress in this context that the term *'ibada*, which has its root in *'abd* (slave), means the act of enslaving oneself to God, rather than simply being the servant of him. Unlike modern Western usage in which slavery is seen as a negative and immoral act, the bonding of oneself to God in the Islamic tradition is a virtue.[24] To bond with God is meant to free the self (both inwardly and outwardly) from enslavement to temporal allurements and material things, such as power, prestige, ambition, and money. As noted by ibn Taymiya, "a slave is one who worships with the heart, hence the saying: 'the slave is a free man as long as he is content; the free man is a slave as long as he is greedy."[25] It is in this sense that *'ibada* is linked to virtues and the act of purifying one's inner self from worldly vices. In this sense, the concept of "slave" is meant to clarify the distinction between God and his creation and to emphasize man's essential difference from him, for a principal feature of the Islamic conception of monotheism is that God shares no essence with his creation and that man's association to God, as explained by ibn 'Abdul Wahhab, is one confined to *'ubudiya*, a relation of unconditional obedience and worship.[26] Additionally, and central to ibn 'Abdul Wahhab's definition of tawhid, this unconditional obedience and worship of the one God is to be socially embodied rather than a private act or statement detached from a living community. A crucial component of *islam* and *'ibada*, he explains, is a system of morality that presumes the presence of community and of virtuous members held accountable for each other's moral state of being.

Worship and the Morally Good

As I mentioned above, ibn 'Abdul Wahhab relies solely on the sacred texts, the Qur'an and the hadith, to make his arguments against shirk (associationism), the act of forsaking God for the worship of saints and other living and nonliving things. In so doing, he is seeking to also restore what he conceives to be the orthodox view on tawhid. By situating his argument within the authoritative corpus that set the limits for his claim, he is not trying to extract and resuscitate fixed social practices congealed in the texts as much as attempting to interrogate and criticize what is being said and done among his contemporaries. To make his argument persuasive, he selects Quranic verses and hadiths with long-standing authority among the early-generation Muslims. The significance of these verses, he points out, lies not just in their prohibition of *kufr* (denial of the oneness of God) but in their moral injunctions. As the *al-ayat al-mukhamat*, these command verses conclusively convey the fusion between the concept of the oneness of God (tawhid) and the moral precepts governing relations of Muslims to each other and to the community at large. To put the same point in another way, tawhid speaks not of faith but of the act of faith (*iman*) and/or the act of worship ('ibada)—for having faith is not just about uttering or professing that God is one, but about acting in a way that confirms this belief.

To practice tawhid is to exercise the moral obligations demanded by God. Illuminating this point, ibn 'Abdul Wahhab makes reference to authoritative verses from *surat al-isra'*, *al-an'am*, and *al-nisa*, regarded within the tradition as the guiding principles for this set of moral codes. By referring to these verses, ibn 'Abdul Wahhab sought to make a reasoned argument that correct moral practice constitutes an act of worship ('ibada).[27]

In all his works, ibn 'Abdul Wahhab stresses that intrinsic to the concepts of submission and worship is the execution of God's moral commands, which are relational, embedded in social structures and embodied in daily social interactions. In making this argument, ibn 'Abdul Wahhab wants to demonstrate to members of his community that the worship of gravestones and saints is unauthorized because it betrays the Islamic notion of tawhid as explained in the Qur'an and the Sunna. The same is true of popular customs, such as sorcery and magic, which, as styles of life, endanger the moral foundation of the community by distracting Muslims from practicing the specific authorized practices and virtues that enhance and enrich the community.

Virtues (*fada'il*) Are Acts of Worship ('*ibada*)

In his exegesis, ibn 'Abdul Wahhab seeks out surat al-isra', known in the tradition as the Quranic *sura* of the "eighteen commands" (*muhkamat*).

These commands clearly state that tawhid and the worship of God are linked to a structure of virtues comprising a wide range of practices. These include the cultivation of mental and bodily aptitudes, as well as kindness, sound judgment, justice, generosity, responsibility, lovingness, modesty, and truthfulness.[28] They commence with the Quranic command "Set not up with God any other god (O man) lest thee sit down reproved, forsaken" (17:23), and close with "And set not up with God any other god, lest thee be cast into hell, reproved, abandoned" (17:39).[29]

Although these Quranic commands begin and end by commending tawhid and warning against belief in other than God (ishrak), it is the middle verses that are most illuminating, because they affirm that disciplined virtues are components of worship. They also take for granted the individual's belonging to a particular community where individuals are identified and constituted in and through certain roles and assigned tasks.[30] Different from our modern conception of the self, the cultivation of an independent, rationally detached individual is not what Muslims like ibn 'Abdul Wahhab strive for; they strive instead to nurture disciplined virtues through a living community. A Muslim cannot attain these virtues except as a member of a community. To surrender to God (*islam*), as explained by ibn 'Abdul Wahhab, necessitates practicing tasks that comprise a set of virtues.[31] To utter the shahada is not just a verbal acknowledgment of the oneness of God; it is an affirmation that grants entry into the community (umma), which concurrently means a commitment to pursue that which is socially good and to reject that which is harmful and abominable (*al-amr bil m'aruf wal-nahiyi 'an al-munkar*).

Within this system, there is a hierarchical ranking of virtues. The highest on the scale, as explained by ibn 'Abdul Wahhab, is the honoring of parents, as the following Quranic verse from *al-isra'* proclaims: "Thy Lord hath decreed, that ye worship none save Him, and (that ye show) kindness to parents" (17:24). Linking in the same breath worship and kindness is meant to underscore worship as an embodied practice: honoring one's parents is an act of worship. Failing to honor one's parents is a form of shirk (associationism)—it signifies a rejection of what is due God. Whereas the Qur'an states that honoring the parents is a kind of worship, the Sunna elaborates on this statement by conveying the social responsibilities embodied in this act of kindness—that is, obedience to them, caring for them in old age, treating them well, and showing them compassion and respect. The Sunna also enumerates what is prohibited, including the acts of rebuking, striking, injuring, and speaking badly to them. Not even the slightest reproach (*fie*) is permitted.[32] With each command, it becomes more evident that all activities converge with 'ibada (worship) and are therefore essential components of tawhid (monotheism). This also means that surrendering to God necessitates the actualization of that surrender through its integration into life through these daily activities (*amal*).

As a set of practices founded on the notion of the oneness of God, tawhid is apprehended as an integral worldview in which human life, too, is conceived as a unity. In this sense, tawhid implicates every aspect of one's life, including hopes and failures, passions, happiness, marriage, family, and community. A pious Muslim therefore cultivates the inner qualities of compassion and remorse. These qualities are translated socially, outwardly, through such deeds as paying dues to needy kinsmen and alms to the poor. Piety also signifies the practice of sound judgment, as does charity. To be charitable, for example, is to be generous by displaying a concern for the welfare of the poor while simultaneously elevating the good in the community. It also mitigates social inequality, which is at the heart of social discord.

Built into this system of Islamic morality is the assumption that men and women are weak by nature, always tempted by corruption and frequently "falling into decadent ways." Hence there is the need for this ceaseless effort (*juhd*) on behalf of the individual and his community to seek the good, as authorized by the Quranic verse that repeatedly instructs pious Muslims to "promote the good and prevent the evil." Different from the notion of atonement in Catholicism (i.e., that Christ suffered to wash away all previous sin) or the notion in Calvinism that once saved, it is not possible to fall from grace, Islam, unencumbered by either the doctrine of original sin or the notion of salvation, is instead "inspired by the Quranic image of a world created for human usufruct as well as temptation"—that is, a world made of both good and evil and of women and men entrusted to seek the good and to avoid evil.[33] The quest for the right balance between embracing the temporal world and shunning its evils without a categorical rejection of the world is at the core of the Islamic ethos.

Whereas the practice of disciplining the passions and desires is conceptualized within the tradition as central to the attainment of standards of Islamic excellence, failing to exercise them is seen as endangering the moral and social fiber of the community. And inasmuch as the weakening of the moral community is assumed to be a natural propensity, it is imperative that the virtuous actively prevent this degeneration by constantly dissuading, criticizing, and impeding those who are weak and morally confused. Thus, moral critics are considered necessary at all times to teach and correct members of the community in order to prevent their backsliding into decadence. In this respect, constant moral criticism and islah are not simply privileges but obligations, because the survival of the community depends on the constant effort of its members to seek the Islamic good. And as these commandment verses conclude, once a Muslim acknowledges that God is one, he or she must act accordingly. A good Muslim is therefore one who aspires to a morally good and just society consisting of Muslim members who, like him or her, are bound to a God who commands good and forbids evil.

In sum, then, the good cannot be sought in the exercise of these virtues independent of or detached from the tasks (social, political, and personal) required of a living community. By stressing the interrelationship of tawhid, *islam* (surrendering), ʿibada (worship), and their embeddedness in social relations as disciplined virtues, ibn ʿAbdul Wahhab tried to teach his contemporaries that being a Muslim is not simply a matter of utterance or mere belief; it is a way of life. By returning to these Quranic verses and explaining what they mean, ibn ʿAbdul Wahhab was seeking to demonstrate not just that, in the orthodox view, worship of the one God is compatible with this structure of morality but that cultivating each and every one of these virtues was integral and internal to tawhid.[34] Monotheism, as embodied practice, is a concept that encompasses a comprehensive set of tasks, roles, and acts, each of which is insufficient without the others and each made sufficient only through all of them.

The unity of these acts is next demonstrated in the interconnectedness of speech and movement with inner conviction. Ibn ʿAbdul Wahhab conceptualizes tawhid as embodied practice through three interrelated principles: utterance (*qawl*), performance (ʿamal), and inner conviction (iman). Utterance, as the crucial intermediate link between faith, on the one hand, and action, on the other, has been, and still is, central to this sustained argument within the tradition, about what constitutes a good Muslim. Good Muslims constantly strive to synchronize their thoughts and outward behavior with their inner convictions. The relationship of the outer domain of saying (aqwal [plural of qawl]) and doing (ʿamal) and the inner domain of faith (iman) figured centrally in the debates in the age of ibn ʿAbdul Wahhab. Whether speech is a signifier of the outer domain of action (ʿamal) or the inner domain of intention (*niyya*) has been and still is essential to Islamic discourses. In contrast to the Protestant Christian tradition, in which inner belief is directly linked to action and not mediated through speech, utterance as the link between action and intention (niyya) is pivotal within the Islamic tradition. The question of whether utterance of the shahada (witnessing) signifies simply an external act of submission (*islam*) or an internal conviction—iman, for example— was and still is an unresolved question within the tradition.

Disputes over whether *islam* (submission) is the precondition for iman (inner faith), whether iman is identical to *islam*, or whether *islam* is wider than iman perhaps seem abstract at first sight. Yet, they have considerable practical implications for law and morality. This discourse, needless to say, is neither exclusive to Islam nor particular to ibn ʿAbdul Wahhab's age, for the relationship of action to intention has yet to be resolved in our modern secular world. This tension affects us today: it influences the way we address the legal and moral issues of culpability and, in particular, the question of what constitutes guilt: (inner) intention or (outer) action.

The Making of a Good Muslim

Although most Muslims do not question the compatibility of *islam* and iman (inner faith), there is a long-standing argument among Muslims over whether there is a distinction between the two and, if so, what the connection is between them. For instance, the Muʿtazila represents one tendency within the tradition that draws no distinction between iman and *islam* by maintaining that verbal expression of the shahada is one and the same as inner faith (*tasdiq bil-qalb*, or sincerity with the heart). This also means that intention, or niyya, is a necessary condition for action and that "actions are valid only through the intentions."[35] The implications of this interpretation are considerable, including the suggestion that committing a grave sin results in the loss of one's status both as a *muʾmin* (a pious Muslim) and as a Muslim.[36]

The *Ash'ariya*, on the other hand, differentiates between *islam* and iman. It regards *islam* as larger than iman in that "all *islam* is not faith." Later Ash'ariya followers extended this understanding to include an understanding of how one could be a Muslim without being a mu'min and a mu'min without being a Muslim, which carries the implication that in the former case, individuals are culpable because they are hypocrites; in the latter, they are not.[37]

A third school of thought, the Hanbaliya, differed from both the Mu'tazila and the Ash'ariya. While distinguishing between *islam* and iman, this tradition also proposed that one must be a Muslim before becoming a mu'min. Hence, uttering the shahada is a prerequisite for attaining faith. *Islam* is hence understood as the guarantor of iman, with the intimation that faith is to be affirmed by both utterance (*qawl bil-lisan*) and action (*bil-'amal*). Although intention or inner faith was conceived by this school as inseparable from *islam*, this interpretation stresses the importance of the outer domain of speech and action. Pointing to ibn Hanbal's saying that "God only knows what is in one's heart," the Hanbaliya argues that, in the temporal world, a Muslim's testimony of what was in his or her heart was action.

These varied interpretations were central to the conflicts arising between ibn 'Abdul Wahhab and those who opposed him. Adopting the Hanbaliya position allowed ibn 'Abdul Wahhab to make the claim that Muslims' status in this temporal world is defined by what they say and do, by aqwal and 'amal. An understanding that allowed him to criticize the rampant corruption of the community he witnessed and of Muslims who were no longer saying or doing is right in accordance with his interpretation of the authoritative sources. Through all his works, ibn 'Abdul Wahhab stresses that inner faith (iman) is integral to tawhid. However, inner faith, he insists, must be preceded by the utterance of the shahada because to actualize iman is to understand and recognize God's commands, which were revealed to humankind through a series of prophets, the last of them being the prophet Muhammad. A *mu'min* is therefore one who professes that there is no god but God and that Muhammad is his last but not only prophet.

Islam is therefore indispensable to iman. To affirm by utterance (*bil-lisan*) is an obligatory step to attain inner iman.[38] Yet, because no created human can know what is in one's heart, the only expressive testimony of one's faith is outward action.[39] A mu'min, says ibn 'Abdul Wahhab, is one who bases his worship ('ibada) on knowledge of God, the Prophet, and the Prophet's teachings (Sunna) and who actualizes that knowledge through deeds ('amal). To translate this knowledge into a living practice is the true meaning of iman. What ibn 'Abdul Wahhab seems to be saying is that iman is integral to action. For to be a true mu'min entails the activation of this inner commitment into conscious action, a process that is transformative as it involves both exertion (juhd) and discipline (of desires) on behalf of the individual believer to become a good Muslim. In this sense, the English translation of *iman* as "faith" fails to capture its true meaning, for more than faith, iman is, as Talal Asad describes it, a "virtue of faithfulness towards God, an unquestioning habit of obedience that God requires of those faithful to him (*mu'minin*), a disposition that has to be cultivated, and that links one to others who are faithful, through mutual trust and responsibility."[40]

Although the Western scholar of religion W. C. Smith does not approach iman as a virtue, he nonetheless does recognize that iman, which means "to acknowledge" and "to accept," is altogether different from belief, a modern concept that has its historical foundation in the European Enlightenment. "Faith is not belief," he notes, because the prevalent modern meaning for the term *belief* alludes to a subjective skeptical form of knowledge rather than the true and absolute knowledge presumed in faith. The modern concept of "believing," as against "knowing," is understood as common-sense belief that stands in contradistinction to objective knowledge, founded on "certitude" and "correctness" in what one knows. Built into the term *belief* is both a "lack of certitude" and "open neutrality as to the correctness . . . of what is believed." [41]

On the contrary, the Islamic notion of iman presupposes that knowledge—which is provided by God—is absolutely and invariably true. Therefore, the validity of this knowledge is never in doubt. This is because, as Smith elaborates,

implicit in the Qur'an, and also explicit in it, is the view that the truth is given, is clear, is known. If the truth is known, then men and women's beliefs may be categorized in terms of it—whereas this is precisely what the modern Western concept of believing explicitly does not mean. On the contrary, modern "believing" as a concept inherently implies, or even postulates, that truth, in the religious field, is not known.[42]

Unlike the skepticism built into the modern understanding of belief, iman refers to an affirmation and appropriation of this absolute truth combined with a resolution to live in accord with it. This truth is constitutive of the self, a conscious and continuous effort at disciplining one's desires through practices of certain deeds and rituals. The repeated performance of the act involves this continuous effort in the making of the self.

Once this truth is acknowledged and accepted, it follows that the attitudes, roles, conduct, and thoughts of men and women are to be assessed in its light. Consequently, the issues and concerns that arise relate more to the position one takes toward this knowledge rather than in trying to establish its truth or falsity. One can either accept this knowledge and become a mu'min or disacknowledge or "conceal" it and turn into a *kafir*. In the classical Arabic dictionaries, *iman* (like *tasdiq wa-tahdhib*) is a term analogous to sincerity, moral excellence, and purification. A mu'min is a Muslim, one who willingly accepts and submits to God (*al-khudhu' wal-qubul*), is never doubtful or skeptical (of this knowledge) (*qhayr murtab wala shaak*), and is cognizant of his or her obligation to God and his commands.[43]

Even with the concept of kufr, the counterpart of iman, knowledge is also presupposed. *Kufr* literally means "veiling" or "concealed in blackness" (*satara al-shay'*—e.g., *wasf allayl bil-kafir li-satrihi al-ashkhas*), thus signifying *juhud al-ni'mah*, the rejection of God's favors and trust. To deny God's benefits is apprehended in Islamic discourses as an act of kufr, whereas a kafir is one who not only disacknowledges God, but who also lacks the virtues that define a faithful Muslim. A kafir or an infidel is also an ungrateful, unthankful, and scornful individual. In sum, then, to explain kufr as "disbelief" is as misleading as translating iman into "belief." Kufr, as the repudiation of what one knows to be true, presupposes knowledge. Both these concepts, as C. W. Smith points out, "equally imply a preceding conceptual framework within which the one designates active acceptance, the other, active rejection. (That rejection is not of the framework, but of something conceived also within it.)"[44]

According to ibn 'Abdul Wahhab, faith is judged by what Muslims do rather than just by what they say. To strive to be closer to God is more than to have said (*qawluhu bil-lisan*) that God is one; it is to apprehend it inwardly and outwardly through absolute devotion to God, the Prophet, and the community (*bil-qalb wal-ʿamal*). To be a muʾmin, as the Prophet has said and done, is to seek none other than God's face. To seek God's "face" is the quest to attain *ikhlas*. Literally meaning "sincerity," ikhlas is not the same as sincerity; indeed, it presupposes sincerity. The concept of ikhlas always refers to iman and as acknowledgment and devotion by the tongue and the heart (*ikhlas bil-qalb wal-lisan*). This form of sincerity is conceived in the Islamic discourses as the virtue of all virtues. It is the exercise of exclusive and pure worship of and absolute devotion to God, the Prophet Muhammad, and his community of believers. Inasmuch as it combines the inner virtue of an unadulterated pure heart totally devoted to God with the outer virtue of impeccable conduct, ikhlas is the most profound virtue to be attained by a muʾmin.[45] To attain it and become a *mukhlis* is to arrive at inner and outer excellence, to attain perfection, the highest status expected of a faithful Muslim.[46]

It is important to stress in this context that, contrary to what C. W. Smith sometimes implies, the adherence of the heart (*qalb*) does not correlate with feeling with one's heart as against grasping with the intellect. Acceptance by the heart, as I argued earlier, refers more to the attempt to attain excellence or to the virtue of total devotion, both inward and outward.[47] Moreover, the term *al-qalb* as employed in the Arabic dictionaries refers generally to one's innermost core, which includes both intellect and feelings.[48] Rather than feelings, the term *qalb* signals inner purity not detached from mental effort.[49] This point deserves emphasis to distinguish between, on the one hand, the modern Western dualism founded on the opposition between intellect and feelings, mind and body, and, on the other, the assertion of this unison and synchrony in Islamic discourses.

As elaborated by ibn ʿAbdul Wahhab, embracing God with one's heart is inseparable from saying (bi-lisan) and doing (bil-ʿamal), for to say one thing and to do another is the way of a hypocrite (*munafiq*).[50] In his exegesis of al-Israʾ, ibn Kathir explains that these verses (referred to by ibn ʿAbdul Wahhab) were meant to establish the distinction between the truly faithful and the hypocrite (munafiq). The faithful are those who combine the virtues of *ihsan*, iman, and *ʿamal saliha*—that is, excellence, sincerity, and immaculate conduct. To exercise ihsan is to do "good" or "act well," by "giving more than one owes and making less than is owed to one."[51] The concept is synonymous with ikhlas, the virtue that frees the faithful from hypocrisy. Ibn Kathir adds the quality of *shafaqa* to his definition of iman: the faithful individual is one who integrates ihsan with shafaqa. Shafaqa, which literally means caring mixed with a sense of awe, signifies vulnerability and weakness conjoined with trepidation of doing evil. In the context of iman, it means that to cultivate excellence requires not just an accepting heart and good deeds but tenderness and affection, and always the fear of falling into harmful or evil deeds.[52]

The polar opposite of a virtuous mu'min is the hypocrite: one who acknowledges with the tongue but rejects with the heart that God is one. *Nifaq* (hypocrisy) is the shirk (or *kufr al-nifaq*) of the heart: it is the joining of iman with wrong deeds (*jama'a isa'tan wa-amnan*).[53] But this form of kufr (*shirk al-nifaq*) is only one of four. The other three are *kufr al-inkar* (disacknowledgment, the gravest sin), or one who denies what he knows is true (the oneness of God) and refuses to admit it; *kufr juhud* (ingratitude), or one who accepts with his heart but declines with his tongue; and *kufr al-mu'anada* (stubbornness, abstinence), or one who accepts God with his heart and admits it with his tongue but does not practice it.[54]

In Kitab al-tawhid and the chapter entitled "Fear of *Shirk*," ibn 'Abdul Wahhab describes these different forms of infidelity by citing the Quranic verse that says that there is no mercy for those who commit the gravest sin, kufr al-inkar. Although God might forgive other sinners, he will not pardon those who deny and refuse him. The danger of hypocrisy lies in how it translates into a debased quality of life and a vice that threatens the moral cohesiveness of the community. This concern is central to ibn Abdul Wahhab's criticism. He wants to demonstrate that to avow faith, on the one hand, and to worship dead saints and living holy men, on the other, is to live a lie.[55] Hypocrisy is predicated on *kidhb*—"to lie," "to be untrue." It also signifies an intent to deceive, a quality that is antithetical to ikhlas, the virtue associated with inner iman and integrity. In this way, like the complementary virtue of iman, hypocrisy (or kufr al-nifaq) is a vice that entails both intent and action. Unlike a hypocrite, a true mu'min is a *siddiq* (*allathi ussadiq qawluhu bil-'amal*) who says and practices the truth, thus combining the inner virtue of ikhlas with the outer virtue of living an exemplary life.[56]

Muslims are charged with shirk when they deny the truth by not practicing it, elaborates ibn 'Abdul Wahhab. They do not know that ikhlas is to say and do what one holds to be true (*al-iman: qawl wa-'amal*), as instructed by the Prophet who says, "call on them to actualize the unicity of God. If they obey inform them that God has imposed upon them to pray five times a day. If they obey you in this, then inform them that God has laid upon them the duty of charity to be levied for their rich and distributed to their poor."[57]

In stressing over and again the dangers of committing shirk, ibn 'Abdul Wahhab's goal is to dissuade Muslims against committing wrong acts by putting their trust and faith in false powers rather than in the powers of the only God. To be devoted to God, he sermonized, is to trust (*tawakul*) only in him, and trusting God is another virtue that leads to the path of true iman. A true mu'min is one who depends on and entreats God and no other.

It bears emphasis in this context that ibn 'Abdul Wahhab stresses these particular virtues and not others because he wants to confront certain dysfunctions (*khalal*) and social problems afflicting and weakening the community as a whole. By emphasizing the notion of *al-tawakul* in God, for example, he is targeting such popular malpractices as the conjuring of trees and stones, sorcery, and magic. Indeed, there are innumerable accounts from this period of women seeking good fortune from trees and stones, of men and women making pilgrimages to the same tree to get its blessing by performing rites—for example, hanging bits of cloth when a boy is born to protect him from the hand of death. These practices were not incidental but widely spread. One infamous story is that of a revered Taj (b. Shamsaan) of Najd, a blind man worshipped by ordinary locals and feared by their rulers for conjuring "miraculous feats." His renowned powers led locals to pray for and make offerings to him.[58] Such wrongful acts of seeking refuge in other spiritual or human powers, even in times of predicament, ibn 'Abdul Wahhab explained, were a breach of faith (*khiyana*) and by implication a form of shirk.[59]

At the same time, one needs to have a more nuanced understanding of how ibn 'Abdul Wahhab came to implement or enforce his criticisms. After all, as a moral critic, ibn Abdul Wahhab's task was not limited only to intellectual persuasion of those who erred. It extended to a determination to correct these wrongdoings—if necessary, by force.

A relevant incident that one can relate in this context is of his personal lapidation of a confessed adulteress, which as interpreted by Algar has put ibn ʿAbdul Wahhab on the map because it resulted in his expulsion from his birth town and led to the eventual formation of his alliance with the powerful prince ibn Saʿud, who happened to also be the principal political rival of the tribal chieftain who instigated ibn ʿAbdul Wahhab's expulsion. It is also the story commonly cited to point to the movement's misogynistic and violent character. When approached in its fuller context, as Delong-Bas research concludes, the incident reveals a far more complex picture than the one presented by the opposition. As reported, a woman approached ibn ʿAbdul Wahhab and freely admitted to having committed adultery (*zina*). The first time she confessed, rather than condemning her on the spot, he gave her the benefit of the doubt, rebuked her for her ignorance, and warned her of the severe punishment awaiting her if she did not repent. After repeated confessions, he thought her to be either insane or coerced, which would then exonerate her from the responsibility. But upon investigation, he found her to be of a sound mind, freely and unrepentantly engaging in forbidden sexual acts in spite of his many warnings. Realizing that she was testing his authority and power, ibn ʿAbdul Wahhab was subsequently compelled to pass the judgment that condemned her to death by stoning, as authorized under the law.[60] His initial reluctance to pass judgment on the woman seems to also complement his general views on the question of "fornication": in his discussions of sexual relations outside marriage, he, on account of the unequal relations between the sexes, held men largely responsible for sexual violations and expected them to maintain order by controlling their desires. He considered women, as the weaker sex, to be more at risk of being forced or coerced into submission.[61]

When ibn ʿAbdul Wahhab began to put his criticisms into effect, felling sacred trees, razing tombs, and destroying revered sites, it was not his violent and radical temperament that inspired his action but, rather, his duty as a moral critic and a muslih. To explain these acts apart from their animating intention, reason, and purpose is to reduce them to mere psychological or moral aberrations. A more illuminating approach is to situate them within his social context and his scholarly convictions. Ibn ʿAbdul Wahhab used force to correct what he considered to be a breach of the religion, thus putting into effect his criticism of what he defined as proper Islamic behavior. Although most of his contemporaries agreed with him that correction was a necessary measure, many disagreed with

him over what ought to be considered a breach of the religion. His interpretation, as many of his contemporaries explained, left little space for
Muslims who act erroneously but not knowingly or consciously, a counterclaim embedded in the internalist argument rather in that of ibn 'Abdul
Wahhab's externalist argument of what constitutes Islam.

Issues in Dispute

As argued earlier, Muslims do have fundamental disagreements over
the interpretation of the authoritative corpus and by implication over the
meaning of orthodoxy and religious authority. Muslim disagreement re-
volves around how to realize Islamic practices and virtues, whether they
conform to or violate the core of the religion, and, if so, how. In general,
the tasks and obligations of Muslims are appraised in light of five categories: (1) mandatory (*wajib*), (2) recommended (*mandoub*), (3) deleterious
(*makruh*), (4) permissible (*mubah*), and (5) prohibited (*haram*). Whereas
the mandatory and prohibited practices that are explicitly stated in the
Qur'an are for the most part closed to litigation (*qat'i*), the larger body of
rules and practices governing the community are not and as a consequence
are open to interpretation as well as subject to debate and dispute.[62] To resolve the controversy, each side in the debate usually goes back to original
texts to show how its position is supported in the authoritative texts. In its
process, although not in its content, this form of disputation is analogous
to Western jurisprudence, in which new laws are judged in terms of their
relationship to the system, as expressed in founding documents, such as
the United States Constitution, and whether they violate the system itself.
In the Muslim case, disagreements are usually over rules governing daily
practices, over what is implied by a certain practice, and whether they are
binding or optional, whether they are permissible, harmful, or forbidden.

As an unresolved tension within the tradition, these disagreements
are bound to recur over and again. Sometimes this tension moves center
stage, whereas at other times it remains in the wings. It all depends on
context, time, and place. In ibn 'Abdul Wahhab's epoch, for example, the
conflict moved center stage. Indeed, it became the platform of his reform
campaign (da'wa) and the ground on which he fought other Muslims over
what is authoritative and orthodox.

The cult of saints is a crucial point of contention within the tradition. Some Muslims, headed by the medieval jurist ibn Taymiya, regard these as *bid'a*, which translates literally as "anything made, done, or produced newly" and is understood in the Islamic discourses as signifying an "addition to religion." It is condemned as an innovation that has "swerved from the right path" (*bid'at dalal*) and is external to and independent of authorized beliefs and practices, which in turn can lead to an "impairment of the din"(*t'atil al-din*). However, not all innovations are regarded as forbidden (*bid'at dalal*), for there are permitted innovations (*bid'a mubuha*), such as *bid'at huda*, an innovation intending to promote the good. The question of what constitutes an un-Islamic innovation as against an Islamic one is the point of contention between ibn 'Abdul Wahhab and his opponents.

Here is also where the difference lies with the modern secular interpretation of "good" as a novelty that "effects a change in the established order" and breaks from precedents and traditions. This negative valuation of tradition, stemming from a valuation of the new—of not being bound by tradition—is what distinguishes a humanist Western view from an Islamic one. For Muslims arguing within the tradition, it is the authoritativeness of these precedents that define merit, not inventions that mark a rupture with the past. In this sense, when a Muslim such as ibn 'Abdul Wahhab critically evaluates these innovations, it is not on account of his "regressive" outlook. Rather, his criticism of such practices as innovations (bida' as plural) is part of an engagement in a long-standing argument within the tradition. He is thus simply attempting to locate his criticisms within an authoritative corpus in order to make an intelligible and persuasive argument to his audience. This position, however, does not necessarily make him right, as many of his contemporaries noted; some disagreed with ibn 'Abdul Wahhab as to whether all the practices he condemned were indeed un-Islamic.

The debate over the practices relating to the cult of saints is a case in point. Although most Muslims would agree with ibn 'Abdul Wahhab that a bid'at dalal that breaks from the fundamentals of Islam is a form of shirk, many would deny that visitations to tombs, in particular, are bida' or un-Islamic. Instead, they interpret the practice not as worship but as a visitation (*ziyara*) to seek a blessing (*baraka*) from the virtuous and pious. To make the claim that these practices are permitted (*mubaha*) and even commended, those who disagree with ibn ʿAbdul Wahhab are as compelled to situate their inquiry within this long-term argument that defines the conceptual and institutional limitations and possibilities of what is and is not Islamic. Needless to say, there is much more at stake in these disagreements than the mere act of visitation, as these disputations do express fundamental conflicts among Muslims over visions of life.

In this concluding section, I will discuss how this discursive framework shaped the debate between ibn ʿAbdul Wahhab and other Muslims who disagreed with him over whether visitation to tombs and the practice of supplication of the pious to intercede with God on behalf of the believers (*shafaʿa*) were authorized practices.

The Cult of Saints

Visitation to Tombs and Veneration of the Dead

As mentioned earlier, visitation to tombs and veneration of the dead and pious was a subject that stirred harsh criticism from ibn ʿAbdul Wahhab, who deemed visitation to be the equivalent of worship (ʿibada) and the substitution of the saints for God. These practices are un-Islamic because they negate true *tawhid*, which is established not only by professing the unity of God (*tawhid al-rab bil-qawl*) but by enacting this unity through worship and action (tawhid al-ilah). A true testimony of faith is to synchronize the acknowledgment that God is one through inward devotion to God extended outwardly through virtuous disposition toward the community. But because it would be difficult to establish one's intention, faith is measured mostly by performance. To worship the righteous and their tombs is a breach of faith. Because tawhid is to practice what one holds to be true, one cannot, at the same time, believe in the absolute power of God and venerate any other power.

Ibn ʿAbdul Wahhab regarded visitation to cemeteries as permissible (mubah), even desirable (*mustahab*), for it displays deference to and fear of God as well as love and respect for the dead. What he harshly criticized and objected to was visitation and pilgrimage to selective graves, particularly those of the Prophet and the pious. He maintained that these practices, which included making offerings, turned the graves into sites of worship despite strict warnings against such actions by the Prophet and his companions. The Prophet, as ibn ʿAbdul Wahhab pointed out, had tried to preempt such behavior by categorically banning the future use of his grave as a mosque or site of prayer. He repeatedly forewarned Muslims of the dangers of associating him with God, as did the "People of the Book" and others before them. He cites the following *hadith sahih*: "Malik reported the Prophet saying: 'O Lord, May my grave never become an object of worship. God's fury is directed towards those who make their prophets' graves into mosques."[63]

Thus, it is not visitation per se but the practice of turning these graves into sites of worship that ibn ʿAbdul Wahhab regarded as a prohibited innovation, invented under the Umayyads. He points out that after his death, the Prophet was buried in ʿAisha's quarter with no tomb to commemorate his grave for fear of the grave turning into a worshipping place. No one was allowed to enter, touch, or pray at his burial site. His grave remained detached from *al-madina* mosque until the Umayyad caliph Walid ibn ʿAbdel Malek expanded the mosque by incorporating ʿAisha's quarter and the Prophet's grave into its grounds. It was from that point forward that visitation came to be permitted.[64] Ibn ʿAbdul Wahhab condemned this activity as a bidʿat dalal, an invention that has "swerved from the right path." Accordingly, he sought to disbar it.

But other Muslims, contemporaneously and otherwise, disputed ibn ʿAbdul Wahhab's interpretation. They did not regard "everything that was not practiced by the early generation as a deviation from the right path" (bidʿat dalal). They argued that there is also desirable innovation *bidʿa mubaha*) and innovations (*bidaʿ huda*) that instill the good in Muslims. Visitation and prayer over the tombs of the Prophet, the companions, and the pious (awliyaʾ), they argue, can be of the second type, a desirable and permitted practice. Such a practice, they maintain, is not an act of worship but an act of visitation to seek the wisdom of the virtuous and pious (ziyara to seek the baraka and *ittʿaz*). This blessing from the pious is justified by the hadith that says, "whoever visited me after my death is like visiting me when alive." It is also recounted in another Prophet's saying that commends visitation: "Do visit the graves, it is a good omen to visit the dead."[65]

Hasan ibn Hasan Khuzbak, a harsh critic of the Wahhabiya movement, disagreed with ibn ʿAbdul Wahhab's portrayal of visitation of the pious as the worship of other than God (ʿibada). Rather, it was a worthy and recommended practice (mandoub) because it cultivated piety in the believer (*itt'az wal-i'tibar*). Visitation to the Prophet's tomb to honor his ascendance and greatness (*wujub ta'zim al-nabi*) as an exemplary Muslim was especially to be encouraged. But ibn Hasan Khuzbak, too, insisted on a set of rules to govern the ritual of visitation (*adab ziyarat al-qubur*). Practitioners, for example, are instructed to refrain from the following:

> bowing when visiting living or dead sites, kissing the ground or the site of a tomb, touching or rubbing the back and the front of the body against the tombs of the prophets or the pious (awliya'), or circling these sites. . . . [H]onoring the dead and the pious has its rules that have been stated in the shari'a. The 'ulama disapprove of the act of touching, whether of the walls of the Ka'aba or the walls of the mosque, even the kissing of the Qur'an. To honor the Prophet and the pious is to make them your exemplary, which means following what they have practiced as cited in the Quranic verse (3:31): "Say [O Prophet]: 'If you Love God, follow me, [and] God will love you and forgive you and forgive you your sins; for God is much-forgiving, a dispenser of Grace."[66]

Although many of the most distinguished 'ulama of his age agreed with ibn 'Abdul Wahhab's harsh criticisms of the abuses committed at the graves of the pious, they disagreed with his *takfir* (accusation of apostasy) adjudicating those transgressors as infidels. A later Muslim scholar-historian, Mahmud Shukri al-Alusi, who wrote approvingly of the Wahhabiya movement and of its religious leader, nonetheless cited his own grandfather's serious objections to the condemnation of those practitioners as infidels (*kuffar*). The grandfather, who was also a Muslim scholar and a contemporary of ibn 'Abdul Wahhab, opposed the latter's pronouncement of the wrongdoers as apostates. Basing his argument on the issue of intentionality, he pointed out that the larger body of transgressors acted that way not because they intended to do so but because they were ignorant and confused. When "worship of tombs is perpetrated due to ignorance on the part of the practitioner and when these practices are condoned and not corrected by the learned scholars, then no one should nor has the right to pronounce them apostates."[67]

In a similar vein, the prolific and prominent Indian reformer Wali Allah (1703–62 A.H.) would also disagree with ibn 'Abdul Wahhab's characterization of the transgressors as infidels on the basis of the argument that Muslim transgressors—those who unconsciously commit prohibited acts—do not lose their status as Muslims because they have not de-nounced *islam*. Although such acts might be prohibited (haram), they are not proof of apostasy or associationism (shirk or kufr), precisely because they are not predicated on intention. Wali Allah's interpretation rests on a particular understanding of iman (faith) that locates itself within a ten-dency in the tradition that embraces external performance as a perfection of faith, rather than as an integral part of faith (iman). His interpretation, in other words, hinges on the long-term argument that assigns intentions (niyya) a central role in adjudicating who is and who is not a Muslim. He goes on to argue that the charge of apostasy (takfir) is justifiable only when the individual performing such prohibited acts publicly proclaims them as acts of worship and openly acknowledges obedience to creators other than God.[68]

Sulaiman ibn ʿAbdul Wahhab, ibn Abdul Wahhab's brother, dis-puted him on the same ground as Wali Allah—that a wrongdoer is not necessarily an infidel (kafir) or an associationist (mushrik). Anyone who uttered the shahada is a Muslim and remains so until he or she recants. This is what Muslims have adjudicated (*ijmaʿ*); to say otherwise is to ne-gate the consensus of the *ahl-kitab wal-sunna*. What is remarkable about Sulaiman's position is that he argues against his brother from within the framework of the Hanbaliya, the school to which both belonged. Not only that, Sulaiman draws on ibn Taymiya and his student ibn al-Qayim's arguments in his endeavor to effectively dismiss his brother's arguments.

Sulaiman, like his brother, also situates his claim in the most au-thoritative sources, the Qurʾan and the hadith. Quoting particular verses and hadiths, he draws on ibn al-Qayim's argument that it is the shared belief among all Muslims that "once an infidel acknowledges that 'there is no God but God and that Muhammad is his prophet' he becomes a Mus-lim." Once individuals say they are Muslims, they remain Muslim until they state otherwise. As far as the popular practices of visitation to graves and the touching and the seeking of good fortune (*tabarruk wal-tamassuh bil-qubur*) are concerned, Muslims tend to disagree. Some have disap-proved of it and classified it as deleterious (makruh), others forbade it as a *muharam*, but none have ever renounced it as *kufr* nor named those who practiced it as infidels (or *murtaddin*).[69]

It bears stressing that all the disagreements with Muhammad ibn ʿAbdul Wahhab were primarily over the assessment of the seriousness of these transgressions and the best strategy to remedy the wrongdoings of Muslims. In contrast to ibn 'Abdul Wahhab, Sulaiman emphasized the need to inform and educate members of the community who had gone astray. Sharing ibn 'Abdul Wahhab's belief that some of these practices violated the basic principles of tawhid, Sulaiman disagreed with his brother that those who committed the violations were apostates and should suffer severe punishments.

Intercession

Intercession is a theological term that originally referred to the Day of Judgment, when the Prophet Muhammad would be called upon to intercede on behalf of his community. Numerous Quranic verses describe the Prophet prostrating himself and beseeching God to forgive those believers who have sinned. Over time, however, the term *intercession* adopted a wider purpose as it became incorporated into daily life and into the ritual of praying. Intercession came also to refer to the practice of performing prayers to beseech God for the forgiveness of the sins of the dead (*salat al-istighfar*). Although supplicating God for forgiveness (shafa'a) was recognized as an acceptable practice (mubah) by all Muslims (*bil-ijma'*, that is, by consensus), there was fundamental disagreement over whether the practice of supplicating anyone other than God is permitted.[70]

In this dispute, ibn 'Abdul Wahhab agreed that intercession is permitted (mubah); however, he condemned his contemporaries for abusing it in practice. He criticized believers, as did his predecessor ibn Taymiya, for habitually entreating pious men and saints to plead on their behalf as well as to carry out favors for them. He distinguished this solicitation from the practice of honoring the pious and acknowledging their charismatic and sometimes extraordinary powers, which he considered to be a *karama* and a good virtue. In contrast, he argued, to practice the rituals of supplication and solicitation at the graves of the pious (*tawasul wal-istigatha*) in order to seek favors from God is both ineffective and heretical. The practice is ineffective because each individual is ultimately responsible for his or her acts. And it is heretical and un-Islamic because it makes idols out of the pious by worshipping them. In support of his claim, he recounted the authoritative *hadith sahih*, which he interprets as condemnatory of the practice of seeking assistance at the gravesites of the pious.[71] To pray at the site of the pious is considered by the Prophet to be the worship of other than God and hence a rejection of God (shirk). In *Kitab al-tawhid*, ibn 'Abdul Wahhab elaborates, over several chapters, the conceptual and institutional limitations of this practice. Primarily he points to the danger implicit in this practice, especially in exaggerating the power of the virtuous and pious, the Prophet included. To demonstrate the limited powers and humanity of the Prophet, he cites the famous Quranic verse in which the prophet is rebuked for attempting to intercede on behalf of his apostate kin: "Verily, thou canst not guide aright everyone whom thou lovest: but it is God who guides him that will [to be guided]" (28:56). Ibn 'Abdul Wahhab then proceeds to warn against the aggrandizement of the pious, including the prophet. He makes reference to numerous Quranic verses and hadiths that warn Muslims of the dangers of turning humans into deities. All of these references point to Muhammad's humanity by accentuating his slave status, despite his special role as the apostle of God. They all warn Muslims against making their Prophet into God, as did those others before them (referring to Christians).

In this context, it should be underscored that the intercession of the prophet (*shafa'at al-nabi*) has a long-standing history in the tradition, precisely because it relates to the subject of the Prophet's status and how far Muslims may aggrandize him without transcending his humanity. Although Muslims revere the prophet as the most virtuous and acknowledge his unique and superior status (for the divine word flowed through his heart), they also insist on his humanity. All agree that what distinguishes Islam from other revealed religions is this unequivocal distinction drawn between God and his creation, including his prophets. As the slave of God, man shares no essence with God, his creator. Because the prophet is also the slave of God, he may not be associated with God or any of his features. The Qur'an categorically and firmly states this. So does the Sunna, in which Muhammad and the early-generation Muslims repeatedly prohibit associating the prophet with God and consider this act the gravest sin.

It is within this long-term argument and, more specifically, with his long-term interlocutor, ibn Taymiya, that ibn 'Abdul Wahhab situated his claim against the rituals of supplication and solicitation at the graves of the pious. He stressed the distinction drawn in the tradition between God's nature and that of a slave. As the slave of God, ibn 'Abdul Wahhab argues, to claim that man shares an essence with his creator is to reject God and become an associationist. To act as if humans have the power to intercede—a power that is exclusively God's—is to endow them with divine attribution, which is also a shirk.[72]

To prove that intercession is exclusively God's and is effective only upon God's permission, ibn ʿAbdul Wahhab quotes Quranic verses from different suras that stress the idea that "unto God belongeth all intercession." In his interpretation of these verses, he points out that although the Qurʾan does not conclusively exclude intercession, it makes it contingent on God's willingness to allow the prophet to intercede and God's necessary approval of the person being pleaded for. Intercession is conditional, as it holds good only for the truly faithful, those who ascribe no association with God. And as for the grave sinners or those who associate God with another, no one can intervene on their behalf, not even the prophet.

To summarize, although ibn ʿAbdul Wahhab emphasizes that "no one denies the interceding of the prophet except those of *ahl al bidaʾ* and the unrighteous," he nonetheless insists that "intercession is only possible with the sanction and the blessing of God."[73] Thus, ibn ʿAbdul Wahhab concluded that the practice of intercession, restricted to the prophet and no other, was allowed, but with limitations.

Those who disagreed with ibn ʿAbdul Wahhab argued that within the tradition, the practice of praying and supplicating at the graves of the pious is not considered worship (ʿibada) nor can it be described as shirk (associationism) within the tradition. Disputing the Wahhabis, a nineteenth-century sheik of al-Azhar, Muhammad Hassain Makhluf, argues that the authoritative sources approved (mubah) and "looked positively on beseeching, entreating the prophet, his family, as well as the righteous."[74] To entreat the intercession of the righteous, according to him, is regarded by most Muslims, including the established authority of the four schools, as a blessing, as *karama wa-tabarruk*. In fact, it is an esteemed practice. Within the tradition, the pious are exemplary and should be revered by other Muslims who ought to emulate them. In making this claim, Makhluf agrees that one should not extend to the pious the power of intercession. What goes beyond the boundary of the permissible is asking the prophet or the pious to perform miraculous acts on behalf of the believer. Such practices were indeed reviled (*makruh*) in the tradition, Makhluf argued, because they endowed the prophet and his pious (awliyaʾ)

with powers that equaled those of God. Notice that he classified such practices as loathsome and sinful (*makruh*) and not as forbidden (haram) and heretical, as did ibn ʿAbdul Wahhab. In addition, Makhluf saw no harm in entreating the prophet to intercede on individual Muslims' behalf, regardless of whether these Muslims were truly virtuous or were sinners. Because the prophet Muhammad is the intercessor (*shafi*ʿ) between God and his community, the prophet is allowed to call on God to show mercy and to forgive his followers as well as to grant their wishes.[75] This form of supplication and praying for forgiveness is authorized by the authoritative corpus, according to Makhluf. There is no danger of deifying Muhammad in this form of practice, because it only acknowledges his right (*haqq*) to intercede without bestowing on him the authority to forgive or reward. Although all Muslims accept that the power to forgive and reward is the prerogative of God alone, there is no harm in asking aid of others in a time of predicament. This act signifies not worship (ʿibada) but the virtuous act of one slave (ʿabd) seeking the assistance of another (ʿabd).[76]

Moreover, Makhluf contests ibn ʿAbdul Wahhab's interpretation of the Quranic verse "Who is there that could intercede with Him, unless it be by His leave?" arguing that he mistook its meaning and failed to place the verse in its proper context. Makhluf maintains that the verse is an allegorical (*taʾwil*) argument for God's absolute power rather than a discussion of intercession. This interpretation, Makhluf argues, makes sense only in the context of the verse, which is revealed to address not Muhammad but non-Muslim idolaters. To support his claim, Makhluf draws on an earlier interpretation put forward by the philosopher al-Razi, who argued that the verse was a response not to Muhammad but to the pantheists who prayed to their idols as their intercessors. Consequently, this verse cannot be employed to adjudicate the Prophet's right to intercede with God on behalf of his followers.[77]

In a similar vein, Wali Allah saw no wrong in seeking the blessing (baraka) and intercession (shafaʿa) of pious people, as long as the practices did not deify them. But the strongest response to ibn ʿAbdul Wahhab's condemnation of intercession and seeking the blessing of the pious dead came from Shiʿa scholars, whose tradition (*shiʿism*) was often blamed by ibn ʿAbdul Wahhab for spreading the cult of saints and its relics.

In a treatise entitled *Manhaj al-Rashad*, the Shiʿa scholar Jaʿfar Ka-shif al-Ghita (d. 1813 A.D.) refuted ibn ʿAbdul Wahhab's claims by draw-ing exclusively on Sunni books of hadith. *Istighatha*, or appealing to sacred and pious personages for help, al-Ghita maintains, is a well-established custom that is firmly grounded in both Shʿia and Sunni devo-tional discursive practice. He argues that "neither belief in the permissibility of such practices nor the rejection thereof is integral to faith in Islam."[78] Al-Ghita, though agreeing that invoking people dead or alive as agents "independent from the Creator (*faʿil mukhtar*) is indeed a species of unbe-lief," dismisses the daily practice of reliance on friends and the seeking of refuge (*iltijaʾ*) in others as a simple harmless part of human daily activities.[79]

Conclusion

There is no doubt that ibn ʿAbdul Wahhab differed from other Muslims of his age in how he approached the profusion of superstitious practices linked to the cult of saints and the level of harm they inflicted on the living community. This said, one cannot ignore how much of his fears were also shared by his contemporaries. Many of the reformers of his age were as concerned as he with the "degeneration" of the Muslim com-munity. Like ibn ʿAbdul Wahhab, they looked back to previous scholars, including the Hanbaliya, to help them understand how harmful and dan-gerous these practices were to the survival of the moral community. From this perspective, it should be clear that to associate ibn ʿAbdul Wahhab's particularly restrictive and condemnatory approach with his supposed intellectual rigidity and dogmatic reliance on "strict" interpretation com-pletely mischaracterizes the meaning of his reform project and his claims. Ibn ʿAbdul Wahhab's method of disputation, his insistence on a return to the original sources, and his selective use of those sources and utilization of arguments made by scholars of an earlier age were all part of the long-standing tradition that constitutes Islamic reform. His approach was no different from other reformers, not only those of his own age, but also those who came before and after him. Ibn ʿAbdul Wahhab differed from other reformers both in his condemnatory attitude toward certain practices and his reliance on force to correct them. However, neither his alliance with the Saʿudi tribal chiefs nor his restrictive attitudes can be attributed, as mainstream scholarship does, to a violent, fundamentalist, or traditional strain in Islamic thought. Why he thought as he did, why he allied himself with the Saʿudis, and whether he did or did not withdraw his support of them at the end of his life are all certainly interesting questions worthy of pursuit. As to why (and, more significantly, how) his arguments have been recently taken up by modern politico-religious movements is also an equally important question to explore. But none of these questions can be explained by invoking an inherent tendency within Islamic thought itself, nor, for that matter, by his dismissal as a pariah, unrelated to Islam. Ibn ʿAbdul Wahhab, like other Muslim scholars, worked within an established discursive tradition, with its own methods of disputation and rules for making and adjudicating claims. As a reformer, he turned to the originary corpus in order to challenge the authoritative consensus and interpretations based on precedent. Perhaps there is no better explication of this approach to understanding ibn ʿAbdul Wahhab, than to consider the work of another reformer who is constituted by conventional scholarship as his opposite—Muhammad ʿAbduh. Where Wahhab is said to express the irrational, inherently antihumanist, and antimodern currents within Islam, ʿAbduh is often invoked to represent a Europeanized humanist rational Islam. Contrary to this depiction, ʿAbduh's reform project, his methods, and his intellectual engagement are as centrally located in the Islamic tradition as is ibn ʿAbdul Wahhab. The way they approached their reform projects expresses the difference not in their relationship or commitment to the Islamic tradition, but in their historical context, in the political, social, and economic conditions of their age, and in the challenges facing the Muslim communities of their times.

An Islamic Reconfiguration of Colonial Modernity

MUHAMMAD 'ABDUH

Life takes precedence over religion in Islam.

'Abduh, *A'mal kamilah*

Since I am critical of unreasoned obedience (taqlid) to al-Ash'ariya creed, why would I then champion that of the Mu'tazila? I do not abide by any authoritative consensus (*taqlid al-jami'i*) for the sake of abiding by authority. I defer only to reasoned evidence.

'Abduh, *Tarikh al-Imam*

[I]f I am to be REALLY saved—what I need is *certainty*—not wisdom, dreams or speculation—and this certainly is faith. And faith is faith in what is needed to my *heart*, my soul, not my speculative intelligence. For it is my soul with its passions, as it were with its flesh and blood, that has to be saved, not my abstract mind.

Wittgenstein, *Culture and Value*[1]

Introduction

In contrast to the scholarly consensus reached regarding ibn 'Abdul Wahhab's "blatant" fundamentalism, Muhammad 'Abduh is by and large depicted as a liberal humanist, a liberal *salafi*, and sometimes as an agnostic who cloaked himself in the mantle of religion for political expediency. And although he might occasionally be referred to as a traditionalist, he is never regarded as a fanatic or a fundamentalist in spite of his insistence on the letter of the Qur'an and the shari'a, the two defining features of "fundamentalism" in this literature. What demarcates 'Abduh from the "fundamentalists," most argue, is his tolerance for and general amenability toward European progressive principles and culture.[2] In this regard, many highlight his noble yet futile attempt to introduce rationality and Enlightenment humanist concepts into an essentially immutable religion.

A good example is the orientalist Vatikiotis's celebration of 'Abduh's "Islamic humanism." 'Abduh, notes Vatikiotis, "underlined the essence of Muslim humanism" by preaching an Islam "free of rigid traditional formulation and invigorated by rational and historical methods of criticisms."[3] 'Abduh's Islamic humanism is seen as advocating "belief in Man as a part of the greater belief in God, on the assumption that human values are largely formulated by earthly experience."[4] 'Abduh is praised here for being a unique kind of Muslim. Unlike the romantic who sought solace in mysticism, the conservative with his defensive and dogmatic posturing or the unreconstructed secularist who alienated the masses by adopting wholesale Western ideas, 'Abduh sought to create a rational Islam grounded in a novel notion that Islam is fundamentally a social religion—a religion, to be exact, that complied with "an ethical system favorable to progress and strongly influenced by rational processes."[5] In spite of all these commendable qualities, 'Abduh's attempt to render Islam modern was destined to fail because, according to Vatikiotis, "humanism of any kind in Islam" faces insurmountable obstacles inherent in the religion itself.[6]

Vatikiotis's account of 'Abduh's vain quest for a humanist Islam is a familiar one since it represents the traditional orientalist view that Islam is irredeemable, that intrinsic qualities, such as the fusion of religion and politics, will inevitably prevent its rehabilitation for the modern world.[7] What is clearly embedded in this view is the assumption that modernization will inevitably lead to the retreat of religion from the public into the private nonpolitical domain, as it did in the Western hemisphere. Hence, any criticism of this exclusivist vision of modernity was interpreted as a rejection of modernity *toute courte* and, by extension, as a retreat into the nonrational, traditional past. Equating modernity with this particular vision of secularism is what Muslims, including 'Abduh, I argue, found most troubling. Questioning this singular humanist secular image of modernity was in fact a central feature of 'Abduh's reform project. Delineating the boundaries of secularism and determining how far religion can be extricated from the domains of polity and economy without dismantling its authority altogether was a crucial issue for 'Abduh and continues to be today for contemporary Islamists.

Viewing 'Abduh through the prism of this exclusive European version of secularism led Albert Hourani, in his often-called master-piece, *Arabic Thought in the Liberal Age*, to give 'Abduh the enigmatic label of a "liberal salafi"—that is, one who combined a liberal sensibility and an openness to Western positivist thought with a salafi temperament and a yearning to retrieve the purity of early Islam. Aware that there was no escape out of the modern age, 'Abduh, in contrast to other Muslim scholars, was less concerned with whether "Muslims could accept the institutions and ideas of the modern world" and more with how to convert Islam, a revealed religion, into a valid framework of life for the modern world. To Hourani, 'Abduh differed from other traditional Muslims because he was interested less in proving to Muslims "the truth or falsity of Islam" and more in wanting or wishing them to be modern.[8] While admiring 'Abduh for his attempt to reconcile Islam and modernity, Hourani argues that 'Abduh's effort was destined not only to result in eclecticism but, more seriously, to also lead him to distort the "authentic" Islam for future generations. 'Abduh's eclecticism generated more confusion in following generations as disparate and conflicting positions emerged. Whereas some of his followers (like Rashid Rida) used his work to stress a more fundamentalist and rigid line, others (like 'Abdul Raziq) adopted some of his positions to promote a more secular vision of society.

Hourani judged 'Abduh as an unsystematic and muddled thinker for selecting some Islamic ideas and discarding others not because they made sense but because they served his political ends.[9] His eclecticism, Hourani argues, led many of 'Abduh's close friends and critics to suspect him of agnosticism and of feigning a commitment to Islam for the sake of expediency. As Hourani put it,

there were some, even among those who knew him well and liked him, who doubted whether he was himself convinced of the truth of Islam. Such statements, taken literally, cannot stand against the evidence in his own writing and of those who knew most intimately the movement of his thought. . . . But in another sense the doubts had certain validity. They point to an aspect of his thought which, for his critics, might very well be a sign of weakness: a sort of eclecticism.[10]

From Hourani's perspective, even more reprehensible than the suspicion of 'Abduh's feigning commitment to Islam is his invention of a fictitious Islam, one that essentially stripped the religion of its true and authentic meaning. Conjuring new meanings and attaching them to old Islamic concepts, 'Abduh, according to Hourani, infused Islam with liberal and democratic qualities that it simply never had. Traditional religious concepts like *maslaha*, *shura*, and ijma' in 'Abduh's hands came to falsely embody the modern political meanings of utility, parliamentary democracy, and public opinion. Rather than seeing 'Abduh's engagement with the past as a constitutive and necessary element of Islamic revivalism, Hourani read it as a fabrication of what is truly Islamic:

It was, of course, easy in this way to distort if not destroy the precise meaning of the Islamic concepts, that which distinguishes Islam from other religions and even from non-religious humanism. It was perhaps this of which his conservative critics were uneasily aware: there was bound to be something *arbitrary in the selection and the approximation.* Once the *traditional* interpretation of Islam was abandoned, and the way open to private judgment, it was difficult if not impossible to say what was in accordance with Islam and what was not.[11]

Ironically, Hourani's statement (even if unintentional) seems also to echo Lord Cromer's famous remark that "Islam cannot be reformed; that is to say, reformed Islam is Islam no longer; it is something else."[12] In retrospect, however, Hourani was bound to arrive at this conclusion, considering the analytical framework he utilized—that of an inverted version of the "invented tradition," an analytic moreover that came to acquire great popularity and authority in postorientalist scholarship on Islam. Although this more recent scholarship tries in general to break away from the classical orientalist polarity of modern/traditional by making the claim that the Islamists are a product of the modern age, this approach remains implicitly, if not explicitly, committed to the notion that changes in the tradition are inventions of the original and not truly "authentic."[13] Assuming a break from an authentic depiction of the past might also explain the continual popularity of *Arabic Thought in the Liberal Age* among contemporary scholars loyal to the invented-tradition analytic in spite of Hourani's disavowal of it later in life.[14]

Departing from these views, I read 'Abduh as neither a traditionalist nor a liberal, but as a Muslim reformer who was critical of both traditionalist religious authority and colonial modernity. As a Muslim reformer, 'Abduh, like ibn 'Abdul Wahhab before him, was seeking to reconfigure Islam in order to both challenge and accommodate the changes in his age—in this case, to ensure the continuity of Islamic authority in the context of an overpowering colonial modernity. Accordingly, he sought out the Islamic discourses to assess the past and make it relevant to the present by rethinking on the basis of Islamic criteria what is and what is not of value in Europe's project of modernity. Taking into account the colonial context, 'Abduh's concerns were bound to differ from those of earlier reformers, including ibn 'Abdul Wahhab, because 'Abduh was confronting the task of securing control over a reality increasingly taken over and regulated by the more powerful discourses centered in Europe. Deeply imbricated in the struggle against Europeanization, 'Abduh's project of revivalism can hardly be understood outside the context of colonial aggression and its project of transforming Egyptians into "non-Muslim" Muslims. Though motivated by the British takeover of Egypt, 'Abduh's reform project was at the same time firmly grounded in the Islamic discursive tradition and was not undertaken simply for political or ideological reasons, as a scam to appeal to a traditional sector of society, nor as a defensive reactive measure against European power. In fact, 'Abduh took for granted that the spirit of Islam was consonant with and amenable to change. He took issue with the orientalist assumption that Islam is incompatible with "progress," which he differently construed as advancement (ruqqiy) in the material and moral sciences. For him, the Islamic revivalist project was crucial to guaranteeing the continual survival of the Muslim community in a changing world, and it was a way to effectively ward off European colonial aggression and expansion without necessarily rejecting all it offered.

By situating 'Abduh's reform project within an intellectual genealogy of *tajdid-Islah*, a form of reasoning internal to the Islamic discursive tradition, I demonstrate that 'Abduh's rationalism was indigenous. By tracing his engagement with colonial modernity, I show that Abduh's thought was situated within the historical parameters of his time. This duality—the Islamic basis of his thought and its construction within colonial modernity—is clearly illustrated in his conceptualization of "degeneracy" as both taqlid (unreflective following of consensual precedent) and *taghrib* (Europeanization). This duality is also evidenced in his engagement with the Islamic question of *'aql* (sound human reason) and its relationship to ijtihad (reasoning independent of precedent). The dual nature of his critique of degeneracy distinguishes 'Abduh from ibn 'Abdul Wahhab. Although both utilized the same concept, Islamic degeneracy unfolding in nineteenth-century colonial Egypt no longer was thought of, nor did it function, in the same way as in the tribal context of premodern Arabia. Degeneration under colonial modernity, in other words, came to acquire a totally different meaning.

Aside from the difference in their historical settings, the distinction between the two reformers is quite evident in the way in which each approached the Islamic discourses and hence the different ways in which they came to conceptualize orthodoxy. 'Abduh's conception of orthodoxy, different from ibn 'Abdul Wahhab's, was translated into a *mean* (balance) between taghrib and taqlid. And whereas ibn 'Abdul Wahhab sought ibn Taymiya's doctrine of tawhid to reorder orthodoxy, 'Abduh's reliance on al-Ghazali's doctrine of the mean (*mizan*) and the Mu'tazila's notion of 'aql, along with ibn Taymiya's right to ijtihad, enabled him to reconfigure orthodoxy as a space within which he could integrate elements of colonial modernity (e.g., the nation-state and agents) and remain within the parameters of the Islamic tradition. Far from a simple process of emulating earlier historical moments and discursive arguments or fabricating a new Islam, 'Abduh drew on multiple tendencies and arguments within the tradition in order to establish a counter-discourse that could vie with established Islamic orthodoxy, on the one hand, and Europeanization, on the other.

This conception of orthodoxy as a relation of power (rather than a commitment to fixed, essentialized tenets) will help us rethink the conventional view on this topic. In reconfiguring orthodoxy, 'Abduh was trying to subvert the status quo rather than break away from the tradition. In probing the question of what constitutes a Muslim, 'Abduh brought forth the importance and significance of disagreement within Islam—an issue generally ignored or disregarded in mainstream scholarship. In fact, throughout the history of the religion, by using reasoned arguments different Muslims have disputed one another over strategies and practices most effective for sustaining a moral community of believers.

Abduh's Project of Tajdid

It is simply not possible to arrive at a proper understanding of 'Abduh's reformist project outside the Islamic discursive tradition of corrective criticism and renewal. Like all other traditions, including liberal humanism, the Islamic tradition consists of a set of authoritative texts, beliefs, and practices from within which Islamic forms of reasoning are usually made. It is from within these discourses, which embody particular arguments and forms of thought, that a Muslim is able to make reasonable and persuasive arguments. In this sense, 'Abduh did not actively shun speculative or abstract thought nor did he seek to retrieve the pristine past. Rather, he sought new insights to contemporary questions and concerns from within the set of discourses that frame Islamic reasoning.

In saying this, I want to refute in particular the popular view that 'Abduh's reasoning originated in Enlightenment thought or that his rationalization for reform was, as Hourani describes, "constructed on a framework of Comtean positivism."[15] Such a claim is flawed because it is grounded in an invalid oppositional construction between the sacred as nonrational and the secular as rational and the assumption thereof that Islamic discourses are inherently nonrational. Instead, we need to recognize that forms of reasoning different from those of the Enlightenment govern Islamic discourses and that Muslims like 'Abduh can make reasonable claims only within the confines of this tradition-informed rationality. Accordingly, 'Abduh's arguments for Islamic reform originated not in Comtean positivist logic but rather in a long-standing argument internal to the Islamic tradition. This argument engages the place of human reasoning ('aql) and independent judgment (ijtihad) in relation to revealed knowledge (*nass*) and the authority of consensual precedent (taqlid). 'Abduh asserted that the primacy of the authoritative texts was compatible with human reasoning and revelation, rejecting taqlid in favor of ijtihad as the basis for revival and the restoration of religious authority.

Because my approach rests on the premise that an Islamic-bounded inquiry seeks coherence by making reference to a variety of authoritative arguments and texts, 'Abduh's thought here is not judged by Western liberal standards of rationality as much as by how they relate to Islamic rationality. Indeed, the rational merits of his arguments do not rest on facts or the merits of proof (positivist rationalism), but rather on how his views engage with historically extended, socially embodied arguments that have their own standards of coherence.

Within this analytical framework, it would be of little value to consider 'Abduh a "liberal" for he never saw a need to break from the Islamic tradition, nor did he ever seek an alternative to or replacement for religious authority. To the contrary, his main goal for reform, as he asserted repeatedly in his writings, was to restore Islamic orthodoxy by reordering Islamic knowledge for the sake of informing and regulating social practices under the new modern condition. Put differently, the two defining polarities (liberal and conservative) within the political spectrum of liberalism have little bearing on his thought or the coherence of his arguments, because 'Abduh saw himself engaging with Islamic discourses that seem to be founded on radically different presuppositions, some of which were even incommensurable with Western liberal values.

A good case to exemplify this point is the presumption within the liberal tradition that tradition and modernity and religion and reason are incompatible, a presupposition utterly unreasonable from the perspective of 'Abduh and his Islamic reformist project. 'Abduh's position is not unreasonable considering that the opposition between the modern and the traditional, as the German conceptual historian Reinhardt Koselleck argues, is ideological rather than descriptive. The conceptualization of history as always moving, and moving forward toward the future and away from the past, presupposes a natural, rather than a naturalized, opposition between the modern and the traditional. A recent development, this progressivist ideal originated between 1760 and 1780 with the articulation by European Enlightenment thinkers of the uniqueness of historical process and the possibility thereof of progress. This new concept, as Koselleck explains, is very much connected to the act of breaking away, both intellectually and materially, from the "traditional" past and its theological conception of the world. In this sense, the European or Western understanding of history becomes inseparable from the notion that tradition and modernity, religion and reason, are irreconcilable.[16]

Although 'Abduh's reform project was firmly rooted in the tradition of Islamic revivalism, his project was also contemporary, rooted in the social setting within which his ideas for reform came to materialize. More specifically, 'Abduh's project originates in the 1870s, a politically active period in Egyptian history marked by the expansion of European imperial power and the rise of indigenous oppositional groups intent on obstruct-ing the extension of European colonization over the region. In the after-math of Muhammad 'Ali's military defeat (1840), Egypt was integrated into the world economy as a primary producer of raw goods and cash crops, mainly cotton. Its integration required that Egypt intensify the modernization of its economy as well as the rationalization of its institu-tions. However, lack of necessary capital to implement these changes forced the Egyptian government to borrow money from Europe at a high interest rate. Eight years after the opening of the Suez Canal in 1868, the government, its treasury coffers practically empty and on the verge of bankruptcy, conceded to a settlement that provided the European powers the "legitimate" pretext to expand their control over the finances and economy of the country. Under the agreement, an Anglo-French financial control team was set up to monitor Egypt's treasury, while other Europe-ans were placed in the various ministries, a guise to safeguard their own financial interests. During this period, there emerged overlapping opposi-tional groups, consisting primarily of middle-class intellectuals (both secular and nonsecular Muslims), who saw a subservient khedive acceding to the loss of Egypt's political and cultural independence, constitutional-ists calling for measures to curb the khedive's absolutist power, and Egyp-tian army officers angered at their exclusion by the Turco-Circassian ruling bloc from high positions in the army. This multifaceted opposi-tional movement culminated in the well-known popular revolt of 1881–82, the 'Urabi revolt, which in turn gave the British the excuse they were looking for to justify a military takeover of Egypt, which they carried out in September of that year.[17]

'Abduh was one of the leading Muslim nationalist intellectuals of this period. Although trained in al-Azhar, 'Abduh's ideas on reform and his wide knowledge of the Islamic tradition started, as he put it, when he unlearned all he had learned at al-Azhar. His education took place in dis-cussion circles around al-Azhar and in the hands of various mentors, the most prominent among them being Jamal al-din al-Afghani. 'Abduh's career as a public critic started in al-Ahram, but his intellectual mark was not felt until he became the chief editor of the *Official Gazette* (*al-Waqai' al-misriya*). The *Gazette* became his platform for disseminating his ideas about reform. In various articles, he described the degenerate and igno-rant state of Muslims and the ways that this state made them easy prey to

Western aggression. He held accountable for this state of vulnerability an established religious authority that, because it was imbued with taqlid, was rendered powerless in the face of the forceful rearrangement of society and polity under colonial modernity.[18]

His writings emphasized the importance of modern sciences and technology to the advancement of Egyptian society. He advocated public education and the refurbishing of Islamic courts as a way of promoting social reforms, which included the improvement of women's status and changes in current family and marriage practices. Although he was critical of the 'Urabi revolt, he nevertheless lent his support to it, calling on all Egyptians to put aside their differences and to unite to resist the British military assault and later occupation. After the collapse of national resistance against British occupying forces, 'Abduh was jailed for three months and then exiled for three more years. During his exile, 'Abduh's influence did not abate. He, along with his mentor, al-Afghani, formed a secret society in Paris and published *al-'Urwa al-Wuthqa*, a journal that continued to publicize the idea of Islamic revival as central to fending off European aggression and as a necessary condition for the progress of Muslim societies. However, although both 'Abduh and al-Afghani agreed that reform was essential for the advancement of Muslims, they disagreed over the means to that end. Whereas al-Afghani hoped by political means to unite all Muslim countries under one Islamic state, 'Abduh doubted that political strategies from the top down would bring the desired results. This is where he broke ranks with his mentor. As a reformer, he depended more on methods of persuasion and the slow transformation of Muslim subjects through education and the law than on political agitation and revolution. After his fallout with al-Afghani, 'Abduh settled in Beirut and began teaching Islamic theology in one of the local schools founded by the Muslim Benevolent Society. As in Cairo, his home became a meeting ground for discussion and debate, attracting young scholars and writers of Muslim, Christian, and Druze background.[19] Upon his return to Cairo in 1888, 'Abduh became a judge in the native courts, set up by the British in 1883 to "dispense the new codes of positive law." This experience strengthened his recognition of and commitment to the need to reform the legal system without the abandonment of its Islamic foundation. From 1899 until his death in 1905, 'Abduh occupied the highest and most prestigious religious rank a Muslim scholar can attain, that of the mufti of Egypt.

Transpiring within the context of European colonialism, 'Abduh's project of regeneration, though deeply entrenched in the struggle against British colonial rule, with its Europeanizing and secularizing mission of Egypt, was simultaneously embedded in the Islamic discursive tradition. The Muslim communities, as described by 'Abduh, were not just undergoing moral degeneracy but were also suffering from cultural and material stagnation, which made the Ottoman Empire (of which Egypt was a province) vulnerable and easy prey to European aggression and expansion. In this sense, 'Abduh's reformist project was not simply a "defensive retrenching" movement, attempting to retrieve the essence of Islam, nor was he an agnostic using Islam as a mantle merely for political expediency. Instead, 'Abduh is approached here as a Muslim reformer, one committed to the idea of uplifting Muslims from their calamitous state of moral and social decline in order to fend off further Europeanization. And because 'Abduh's beliefs are constitutive of his tasks, as stated in an earlier context, it would not be possible to identify his actions prior to, or independent from, his intentions or beliefs. Nor, for that matter, can one detach his beliefs, intentions, and actions from the particular historical context from within which all these combined elements came to operate.

Taqlid and Taghrib: Two-Sided Features of Degeneracy

'Abduh's project of renewal was double-faceted, engaging an internal front as well as an external one. The internal involved reconstituting Islamic orthodoxy by reordering Islamic knowledge to inform and regulate modern social practices; the external was to fend off the colonizing and Europeanizing mission of Europe and its singular vision of modernity. Within the tradition of Islamic revivalism, 'Abduh saw himself as a reformer with a duty to revitalize a morally decadent, socially stagnant Muslim community on the verge of collapse under pressure from an invasive colonial Europe. From his perspective, the Muslim community was left unattended by an unreflective traditional religious authority immersed in taqlid and unwilling to confront the new problems and concerns arising from the extension of capitalist modernity through colonization and taghrib (Europeanization)—an Arabic concept with a double-edged meaning: (1) the adoption of European ways of life; and (2) estrangement, alienation (*tanfir*), and repulsion from one's own.[20]

One theme pivotal to ʿAbduh's renewal project, which engaged both the internal and the external fronts, is his critique of the concept and practice of taqlid, or "unreflective obedience to authoritative consensus."[21] ʿAbduh condemned taqlid in whatever form it might take: whether blind following of "traditional religious authority" or Europeanization (*taghrib*) and unreflective acceptance of all Western norms and values. He deemed "unreasoned following of authority" the "enemy of Islam" regardless of whether that authority was Islamic or European. His criticism of taqlid, of both religious and Western authorities, became the vehicle through which he defined his Islamic revivalist project. In essence, it became the framework from within which he debated Muslims and Europeans over what was and was not orthodox and authoritative in Islam and what was and was not appropriate in European modernity. This was evident in all his writing, including his most commonly cited work, *The Unity of Theology* (*Risalat al-tawhid*), in which he described his objective as one of "freeing the minds of Muslims from the chains of belief on authority," because God, as he explained, "has not created humankind in order to be led by a halter."[22]

Considering that ʿAbduh located his arguments for reform within the discourse of revivalism, it is not surprising that he would condemn taqlid and commend ijtihad and the right thereby to make rulings and set norms free from earlier precedent. One of his arguments against those who practiced taqlid was that they failed to factor in the element of current historical time and of changing social circumstances that created concerns neither encountered nor addressed by previous generations. In making the Qurʾan consensual precedent rather than the primary source for his inquiry, ʿAbduh's motivation was to free the religion from the dead weight of earlier accretions, which were, as he described, cumbersome and less essential to Islamic practices in his age. Freeing the religion from earlier accretions, however, did not mean dropping all precedent but to sift through this large body of knowledge by maintaining only those elements that were of relevance and discarding those that were irrelevant.[23] Ijtihad, he further argued, was a necessary and constitutive feature of this discursive discourse of revival because Muslims at all times need this investigative form of reasoning to cope more appropriately with new problems as they arise in different historical times and contexts. That is why he regarded the unreflective acceptance of the authority of others a disease that had "vitiated the *din*," infecting the hearts and minds of Muslims and making the religion immaterial and useless.[24]

'Abduh's crusade against taqlid, though not sparing the larger community, targeted mostly the established 'ulama, whom he accused of "wasting the best of the *din*" with their endless quibbles "over superfluous semantics and obsolescent phonetics," leaving unattended a community in a dire state of degeneration and stagnation. 'Abduh made the claim that the Islamic tradition "abhors and forbids *taqlid*," charging those contemporary scholars who championed it with committing virtual blasphemy, because they acted not out of ignorance (as digressers do) but willfully and deliberately. His novel Commentary on the Qur'an, in particular, and his other work, in general, abound with scathing criticisms and denunciations, presenting a religious authority that had deviated from orthodoxy, misleading the community into a downward path of peril. Imparting a new interpretation of verses (168–69) from *surat al-Baqara* ("O Mankind! Partake of what is lawful and good on earth, and follow not Satan's footsteps: for, verily, he is your open foe"), 'Abduh invokes the image of Satan to describe scholars who by ascribing to this "reprehensible practice of *taqlid*" issue quasi-religious ordinances of their own that end up misleading the lay public to the wrong path. These verses, he warned Muslims at large, made it abundantly clear that taqlid and following forefathers and customs sanctioned not by conviction and reason but by ancient usage are forbidden as well as dangerous.[25] Further on in his commentary, he says that whereas the Qur'an forbids Muslims from submitting to taqlid, the 'ulama commands them to

follow their words blindly; and if one follows the Qur'an and the Hadith, they oppose him with denial, supposing that in so doing they are preserving the religion. On the contrary, nothing else but this has vitiated the religion; and if we continue to follow this method of blind acceptance, no one will be left who holds this religion. But if we return to reason to which directs us in this verse, and other verses like it, there is hope that we can revive our religion.[26]

In his war against taqlid, 'Abduh was engaging his contemporary interlocutors, the heads of the four legal schools, who forcefully attacked 'Abduh for violating authorized precedence (taqlid) and for reinventing

the practice of ijtihad, because it had not been practiced since the third
Islamic century. One of 'Abduh's most aggressive interlocutors was his
ex-teacher and contender from his al-Azhar days, Sheikh Muhammad
'Ilish (d. 1882), who sanctioned taqlid precisely because he considered it
to be the most compelling and effective mechanism to fight against
Europeanization. In response to the argument used by 'Abduh that the
Qur'an unequivocally condemned the following of the forefathers in error, 'Ilish drew on the work of the famous Maliki jurist al-Shatibi (d. 790
A.H./1388 A.D.), who made a distinction between the legal definition and
the Quranic reference to taqlid. Whereas the intent of the Quranic verse
was to warn against the following of corrupted inherited customs of forefathers who had deviated from the right path, the legal purpose of taqlid
was to constrain jurists from ruling on a whim and under the influence of
worldly desires and interests. From a legalistic perspective, therefore,
taqlid was meant to be a preventive measure against the corruptions of
worldly power. In his disputation with 'Abduh, 'Ilish rested on this view
that taqlid is the only safe mechanism by which contemporary Muslims
can maintain the fabric of their community and guard against the corruptions of power produced by Europeanization and colonial modernity.

To undermine 'Abduh's credibility, 'Ilish accused 'Abduh of inno-
vating and bastardizing Islam. To discredit the legitimacy of practicing
ijtihad, 'Ilish—in his capacity as the mufti of the Maliki school—passed
a legal opinion (*fatwa*) rejecting unequivocally the claim made by Muhammad ibn 'Abdul Wahhab that Muslims were allowed to go back to
the Qur'an and sound hadith to arrive at their own rulings, which in turn
challenged the infallibility of authorized consensus (ijma') of the early
jurists. No one, he opined, has that right, except for "God and those who
were thoroughly versed in religion," meaning the early Muslim community and the founders of the four legal schools, because they had direct
access to the Prophet and his companions and were therefore able to interpret the Qur'an without danger of falling into error. His opinion, moreover, warned of the dangers posed by untrained laymen practicing ijtihad,
especially in the context of contemporary times and the dangers posed by
Europeanization, and concluded with the legal opinion that it was "not
permissible for a layman to abandon *taqlid*."[27]

As the disputation between 'Abduh and his nemesis 'Ilish makes
clear, the issue of whether taqlid or ijtihad is the more authoritative is far

more complex than is commonly granted, with a long-standing history that is not reducible to a simple choice of either one or the other. When approached genealogically, it is clear that these two concepts are inseparable and completely dependent on one another for their definition. This, however, does not mean that their meaning and function over time do not change. For example, taqlid, as the acceptance of legal precedence (i.e., consensus) and the adherence to a legal authority (*madhhab*, or school of thought), rather than being a "sign of declining glory of Islam" as ʿAbduh maintained, was a sign of growth and development of the Islamic legal system, "a development that was not ineluctable . . . but rather symptomatic of a more fundamental and monumental event, namely the rise and final coming to maturity of the *madhhab*."[28] As the "reenactment of *ijtihad*," taqlid, as the legal expert Wael Hallaq demonstrates in his latest work, *Authority, Continuity, and Change in Islamic Law*, denoted "an intelligent application of principles."[29] The transition from a case-by-case style of ruling—founded on forms of ijtihad reasoning—as was the practice in the early stages of Islam, to rulings based on taqlid, or principles and methods of generalization, was conceived within the Islamic discourses as an expression "of the internal dynamics that came to dominate and characterize the *madhhab* as both a doctrinal entity and a hermeneutical engagement."[30] In its highest form, taqlid, Hallaq argues, "did not simply signify a reiteration of older statements or rulings" but was rather "a creative activity" involving a rigorous evaluation and contemplative examination of a practice before it was authorized. Put differently, ijtihad and taqlid, as categories of analysis, were not always considered as antagonistic or oppositional as they came to be visualized and represented in the modern age. Far from being a blind following of authority, as modern reformers contend, taken historically taqlid represented the emergence of a new style of discourse, which though different both in kind and quality from its predecessor was a note of maturity in the legal system.[31] The practice of taqlid, as Hallaq also demonstrates, did indeed change in meaning and significance as it evolved over time in response to different circumstances and contexts. By the nineteenth century, however, rather than the creative activity it was meant to be, taqlid, as ʿAbduh maintained, became defensive and unreasonable, inept and ineffective in the hands of his contemporary jurists.

Revisiting the question of the ʿulamaʾs ineffectiveness in his short essay *al-fiqh wal-fuqahaʾ* ("Jurists and Jurisprudence"), ʿAbduh points out how leading jurists of his time in addition to wasting "their mental effort on inconsequential linguistic problems" had managed to pass rulings founded on taqlid that breached the fundamental principles of the law.[32] This was exemplified in a ruling on prayer, which, although unanimously approved by the leading jurists of all four schools in Egypt at that time, blatantly violated the principles laid by the Qur'an and the hadith. The ruling accepted prayer as a religious injunction even when it was performed, "without humility without mental and spiritual perspicacity. This is certainly an invalid rule as it violates every Quranic verse relating to prayer."[33] These jurists justified their ruling under the rubric of intention. Some even backed it up "by distorting the *hadith* that says: 'actions are valid only through the intentions' . . . when the Prophet meant that acts should be unaffected and genuine . . . Do they mean when I get up to walk, what I do intend in fact is to sit and not walk? What kind of nonsense is this?"[34]

What the hadith meant, he explained further, was actually the opposite of what these schools had concluded, as proper intention is necessary in order for prayer to be valid, and proper intention must include the "seeking of God's face," which can be accomplished only through the virtue of humility and with complete devotion of mind and heart to the worship of God. Those who do not seek God, he explained, are deemed hypocrites and their prayers are to be rejected. The abuse of religious knowledge and the falsification of its stipulations were rampant because "jurists and theologians have brazenly made their books the final authority on principles of the religion and have shamelessly enforced their rulings even when these blatantly contradicted the Text and the Sunna."[35] This laxity and state of degeneracy was created by "Muslims who turn away from the Qur'an and the Hadith, following instead jurists who are in the habit of making poor arguments and authorizing incorrect rulings."[36]

In this same article, 'Abduh advances a two-pronged attack on the leading jurists and scholars of his age for their sloppy prescriptions, on the one hand, and their obtuse and formalistic rulings, on the other. Again, he attributed these extremes to ignorance and a lack of understanding of the true spirit of Islam. Below I give two examples of cursory and unreflective rulings that 'Abduh criticized as inessential to the din and incongruous with modern norms. The first targeted a prominent Azhari scholar, al-Anbabi, for a "preposterous" ruling on what was and was not permissible in the enactment of ablution:

What would inspire a [hard working] commoner to waste precious time to learn intricate convoluting rules of ablution and other such rituals from convoluted and loquacious works as those taught at al-Azhar? What need is there for these obsolete and rambling works that describe in minute details what water to use for ablution in preparation for prayer? Why not follow the path of the Prophet who explains in few simple words what he meant by "Pray as you see me pray." . . . Any drinking water would do to cleanse and wash the body for ablution.

Where did they come up with the idea that rose or orange blossom water is not permitted in ablution? . . . Why would they forbid cologne water when [as a purifying substance] it is known to kill germs? Shaykh al-Anbani declares cologne impure because it contains alcohol (medicinal spirits) and alcohol causes inebriation. This is such a weak and unreasonable argument because no sensible human being would drink that stuff knowing for certain that it will cause physical harm such as the serious burning of the throat.[37]

One of his strongest arguments against taqlid and the "unreasoned" following of authoritative opinions, one can surmise from 'Abduh's criticisms, was that these practices failed to consider the social circumstances and changes (place and time) that invariably occurred, producing problems and issues that had not yet been considered or ruled upon previously. Accommodating new circumstances was not, after all, a novel or unfamiliar idea to the legal Islamic tradition, as Wael Hallaq, its most prominent contemporary scholar, discloses. Muslim jurists considered as agents of change within the legal Islamic system recognized that "change was a distinct feature of the law," expressed through such maxims as *taghyur al-fatawi bi-taghyir al-Zaman* (legal opinions change with changing times) and the rubric of "necessity (*darura*)" and "custom (*urf khas*)."[38] The early-generation Muslims (salafiya), as 'Abduh also recognized, considered ijtihad not only admissible but a public duty (*fard kifaya*) incumbent upon all learned Muslim scholars.[39] Thus, contrary to what the 'ulama of his day claimed, ijtihad was an indispensable tool to investigate and address more effectively the problems facing Muslims in a changed and changing world.

'Abduh's arguments against taqlid hinged on the practice of ijtihad to reconfigure Islamic norms and practices through the prism of historical time and in light of the societal and structural changes produced within colonial modernity. As circumstances changed, he argued, so did the habits and practices of Muslims, a condition denied by the leadership at that time, to the detriment of both society and religion. On occasion, 'Abduh ironically posed the following question to his interlocutors: "what are we to do when there is no precedent to follow? Are we to stop the clock so that your books and rules remain valid?" Because suspending time is impossible, "people, commoners and rulers alike, are instead compelled to abandon Islamic practices in favor of other practices that are equally unacceptable," meaning European.[40]

In contrast to an "unyielding Islam" espoused by the established authority, 'Abduh presents one that is far more flexible and responsive to particular societal needs. Drawing on the works of the twelfth-century al-Ghazali and the fourteenth-century al-Shatibi (the scholar invoked by his opponent, 'Ilish, to refute him), 'Abduh posits that Islam was designed to benefit humanity and to facilitate man's welfare and happiness on this earth and beyond. In the prologue to his commentary (tafsir), he stressed that the principal purpose (*maqsad*) of the Qur'an was to "lead mankind to the path of happiness by offering guidance and benevolence (*hidaya wa-irshad/hidaya wa-rahma*)."[41] His commentary stressed over and over again that the Qur'an was the guiding light to religious practices and the primary source for all believers seeking to attain happy and virtuous lives in this world and the afterworld.[42] Bypassing the Qur'an, he repeated, was a reprehensible act because it elevated jurists and scholars above the authority of the Qur'an and the Prophet.[43] The vitality of the Qur'an to the good life, he said, was not wasted on the early master jurists when they ruled that "the Qur'an is the final authority (*hujat*) for all believers until the Day of Judgment," nor did they misconstrue, as contemporary jurists did, the meaning of the Prophetic hadith on which they based the following ruling: "the Qur'an is the final arbiter for you and against you."[44]

'Abduh's statement that "life takes precedence over religion in Islam" revisited the view within the tradition that considered Islam to have been created for the benefit and preservation of humankind and in turn was more concerned with people's lives (how people live and conduct themselves on a daily basis) than with fixed abstract statements detached from human action and condition. For Islam to be a way of life, a diligent and continuous rethinking was vital to keep Islam viable and accessible for Muslims to follow. It was over this question that 'Abduh came to clash with the ʿulama of his age, for the jurists in power had failed to carry out their public duty (fard kifaya) that involved the reordering of Islamic knowledge to satisfy societal needs and ward off, at the same time, the further Europeanization of culture.

ʿAbduh argues the impotence of the establishment and the detrimental effect of the establishment's inflexibility by making reference to a particular case on usury (*riba*) on which it ruled in the context of the Egyptian Treasury's declaration of bankruptcy. He compared the response of an early generation of the Bukharan Muslim community to an economic crisis with the Egyptian jurists' response to a similar crisis in Egypt. Unlike the Muslims of Bukhara, who ruled in favor of a generally forbidden practice, riba (usury), to mitigate the economic suffering of their community, the jurists' response to the 1870s crisis in Egypt was to

irrevocably prohibit rich Muslims from lending money [to their government] on the basis that if they permit it, it might weaken further an already weakened religion. The Egyptians instead were forced to borrow from foreigners who lent them the money at exorbitant [interest] rates with the long-term effect of bleeding the country dry and turning over its wealth and natural resources to foreigners to exploit. These jurists should be held responsible before God not only for incurring distress upon the people of Egypt, but also for violating Islamic law. What they have not done is take into account the particular circumstances and present state of affairs [in Egypt] to pass reasonable judgments that people can respect and abide by. . . . What they could have done is to set up counseling or advisory associations (*jamʿiyyat*) or committees where jurists come to investigate and probe more thoroughly [issues of this kind] so that jurists may be able to reach sensible decisions [that people can] conform to. . . . [Such inquiries] might have alerted our jurists that forbidden acts under special circumstances are sometimes permitted even though in general and as universal principles [*al-hukm laysa ʿamm*], they remain reprehensible.[45]

Drawing on the works of earlier Muslim jurists, ʿAbduh refers to a prevailing concept within the Islamic legal discourse, that of suitability (maqsad), which states that the aim of Islamic jurisprudence has been to constantly and consistently promote benefit (the good) to the exclusion of harm (*munkar*). This concept was derived from the Quranic vision of a world created for human benefit, enjoyment, and temptation. Unencumbered by the Christian doctrine of original sin and its extended view that a religious life demands a categorical rejection of this "fallen" world, Islam holds the view that the primary intention of Revelation is the protection and the preservation of humankind in both this world and the afterworld. Consequently, one of the principal goals of the Islamic shari'a under this suitability clause, according to the medieval jurist al-Ghazali, was to protect "life, property, mind, religion and offspring."[46] The concept of suitability, as Wael Hallaq vividly illustrates, was later elaborated on and extended by al-Shatibi so that it included the practice of alleviating hardships under particular circumstances in which actions generally and universally prohibited are in turn deemed permissible under the rationale of suitability.[47] It is clear from the above quote that 'Abduh is making an argument parallel to al-Shatibi's: usury in the Bukharan case, he asserted, was deemed valid under this legal principle of suitability and for the specific reason of alleviating hardships that would have endangered the welfare of the community (maslaha). According to this legal argument, a universally prohibited act (*kulliyat*, or universal categories) may be permissible only in partiality (*juzi'yat*), that is, within a particular context, time, and place with the stated condition that its practice be confined to this limited time and circumstance to ensure that it will not infringe on its universality and disable it permanently as a forbidden act. To persist in the practice of riba beyond its particulars, in other words, would constitute a violation of a universal Islamic principle. Put differently, Islamic law allows for the modification of prohibited acts by making them valid only under a specific circumstance (e.g., to mitigate hardships) and for a limited period of time. Were these practices to persist, then and only then would they be regarded as a violation of shari'a principles.

'Abduh blamed the jurists not only for bringing the country to its knees economically but also for its colonization, which resulted in the legalization of riba (interest) by the British, thus leading Muslims to commit a graver sin than they would have had they been initially permitted to do so within the confines allowed by the shari'a under the clauses of alleviating hardship and suitability.

Mizan and Islamic Orthodoxy

'Abduh embedded his definition of orthodoxy within the doctrine of the mean as put forth by the Ash'ariya, a school of which al-Ghazali was among the most convincing theorists. Al-Ghazali conceived of ortho-doxy as attaining equilibrium between undue difficulty ('*usr*) and extreme ease (*yusr*) and viewed the goal of the law as the enactment of this golden rule through the creation of a balance or a synchrony between these two extremes. Identified in Arabic as *al-mizan* (the scale), the middle-of-the-road doctrine (*al-wasat*) was viewed as integral to the principle of justice ('*adl*), labeled by al-Ghazali as the balance of all virtues.[48] Within this analytical framework, a Muslim community was regarded as healthy and virtuous only when it was in a state of balance and equilibrium; otherwise, it was diseased and degenerate. The mean (*wasat*), according to al-Ghazali, was the "straight path" (*Sirat al-mustaqim*) and the orthodox way, as this bal-ance would be impossible to attain without divine intervention.[49] Mus-lims seek out this straight path, he maintained, in order to reach happi-ness and virtue, a condition that, contrary to the Greek philosophers' belief, was not simply a natural phenomenon but a continuous effort on behalf of the individual and community to strive toward a balance that is informed by and in conformity with the revealed commands (shar').[50] That is also why al-Ghazali recognized, as did Aristotle, that the mizan was only a relative mean because it was dependent on the circumstances (time, place, and context) and the moral conditions (on a scale to perfec-tion) for its definition, with the difference from Aristotle's view being that al-Ghazali believed that this balance was unattainable without divine guidance.

One might say that 'Abduh sought out al-Ash'ariya's doctrine of the mean, not because he was fundamentally traditional, as Malcolm Kerr has argued, but because of its relevance to 'Abduh's times. Orthodoxy, in his view, was striking a balance between two extremes. The two extremes that he and his age were struggling against were taqlid and a religious es-tablishment hostile to change, on the one hand, and Europeanization (taghrib) or the embracing of all the norms and values of European mo-dernity, on the other. The mizan analytic, one can even argue, enabled 'Abduh to reconfigure a discursive terrain that would allow for linguistic and structural changes dictated under colonial modernity without aban-doning the boundaries necessary to maintain an Islamic community. I suggest that it was the search for a balance between taqlid and taghrib, and not, as some claim, a nostalgia for a pristine past, that drove 'Abduh to seek out the Islamic doctrine of the mean.

Moreover, his appeal to and selective reference to specific arguments within the Islamic tradition is not read here as either a distortion of the "authentic" or the product of an eclectic mind, as selectivity of arguments is a typical practice in and a fundamental feature of all traditions, including Islam. As argued in an earlier context, scholars from all traditions, including liberalism, at one point or another go back to earlier authoritative works to harvest particular arguments that are useful to resolve or address contemporary conflicts. Every tradition at each stage of its evolution, as Alisdair MacIntyre has argued, is bound to face new challenges and problems that need addressing. Sometimes the resolution of a genuine crisis involves improvising and amending concepts and practices, but without abandoning fundamentals. No living tradition can forever remain closed and unchanging because revisions and adjustments of arguments and norms are constantly needed in order for a tradition to stay alive. This is what I would suggest happened in the early stages of the Islamic tradition. Through the process of injecting and rejecting different knowledges, cultures, and practices that accompanied the opening of new lands to Islam, the tradition was able to both survive and remain Islamic.

From the perspective of many Muslims, including ʿAbduh, *baraʾit al-ashʿariyyun* (the innocence of the Ashʿaris), the advent of the Ashʿariya was a successful creative outcome of a crisis rather than a bleak moment in the history of the tradition, as it is often narrated by orientalists. Within the tradition, the Ashʿariya is viewed as a synthesis of early Islamic beliefs and Muʿtazila thought and practices rather than an ending of rationality. By redefining Islamic orthodoxy as a compromise between these extremes, al-Ashʿariya was able to transcend the crisis and gain prevalence. A similar resolution occurred in the classical age. By al-Ghazali's period, the Islamic tradition was confronting another conceptual and spiritual predicament due to the popularity of new ideas and practices (Greek philosophy and Sufism), defined by the religious authority then as alien (*bidʿa*) and forbidden. Instead of rejecting all forms of philosophical knowledge as utterly un-Islamic, the Muslim theologian al-Ghazali Islamicized Greek logic and extended its usage to Islamic law and theology, thus making logic an integral part of Islamic reasoning. He also integrated some Sufi beliefs and practices into the mainstream orthodox discourse, thus transcending a split between two strong opposing currents threatening to rip apart the tradition. The author of the *Incoherence of the Philosophers* was not opposed on principle to any possibility of learning from other traditions and bodies of knowledge. Just the contrary, al-Ghazali's willingness to profit from and engage with non-Islamic thought and practices enabled the Islamic tradition to overcome incoherence and reassert its religious authority.[51]

Like 'Abduh, al-Ghazali engaged in reform at a time when most established theologians were antagonistic to all foreign imports, referring to them as forbidden innovations and bida'. Going against the current of his time, al-Ghazali made the argument for innovation by drawing on the Shafi'i school of thought that made a distinction between "good and permissible" (*bid'a mubaha*) and reprehensible and forbidden innovation (*bid'at dalal*). The integration of new practices and concepts as amendments and additions to the religion was acceptable when their purpose was to promote the good within the confines of what was authorized. Although he criticized the philosophers, al-Ghazali nonetheless appreciated the exactness of logic and its efficacy in reconstructing the religious sciences on firmer ground. He also utilized logic in his refutation of some Sufi practices and beliefs as heretical and unauthorized (e.g., self-mortification) while using the same logic to lend his approval to other practices, including the interiority of faith (*zuhd*), which helped to enhance faith by facilitating a more intense and disciplined religious experience.

In 'Abduh's age, the Islamic tradition was experiencing a different crisis and perhaps a more serious predicament, conceptual and circumstantial. In al-Ghazali's time Muslims were at the peak of their power; in 'Abduh's times, by contrast, Islamic discourses were experiencing difficulty retaining control over a (social, political, and economic) reality being rapidly taken over by more powerful discourses centered in Europe and armed with stronger modalities of power. Egypt conscripted to Europe's colonizing and modernizing project was undergoing dramatic transformation, including the reorganization of its political and social structures. Along with these new arrangements, a new idiom articulating this change emerged denigrating earlier forms and social structures as old, nonrational, and nonmodern and the newer norms and ways of life (market economy, secularism, nation-state, nuclear family, etc.) as rational, progressive, and modern. With this new articulation, religion came to be defined as primarily nonrational and inconsequential. It is in the context of colonialism and Europe's prescriptive definition of the modern as the site of universal rationality, progressive history, and emancipatory politics and of tradition as the locus of autocratic religiosity and backwardness that ʿAbduh's reform project came to unfold and acquire its particular meaning and significance.

In light of what has been said thus far, it would be difficult to conceive of ʿAbduh as a liberal humanist intent on breaking away from both tradition and orthodoxy. ʿAbduh's scathing criticisms of the ʿulama and his condemnation of their authority, as I have argued so far, were driven by the desire to reaffirm religious orthodoxy rather than find an alternative to it. In place of the European vision of *reform* as the replacement of religious authority with secular liberal humanism, I suggest instead that ʿAbduh's conception of reform hinged on giving religion a substantive role, albeit a different one from earlier eras, in regulating moral and social relations in the modern age. In order to do so, like all reformers ʿAbduh had to seek out the authoritative sources and to utilize Islamic arguments and forms of reasoning in the effort to redefine norms and practices in light of modern arrangements.

An Islamic Critique of Taghrib and Secularism

It is my argument that the concept of equilibrium or the doctrine of the mean proved germane to Muslims, including ʿAbduh, because it opened a discursive terrain to amend and revise Islamic norms and practices in light of modern knowledge and power. The concept of orthodoxy as a moderation between two extremes allowed ʿAbduh to reassess in Islamic terms what was and what was not of value in colonial modernity, thus integrating certain features of European modernity considered beneficial to the community and discarding others that were harmful and incongruent with the authoritative sources. ʿAbduh accepted the modern nation-state and its disciplinary and regulatory forms of power, yet he rejected outright the binary construct that consigned religion to a world of the past and perceived Islam as uniquely nonrational, tyrannical, and antihumanist.

These views were implicit in his writings in general and explicitly stated in two renowned replies. The first, which came to be known as *Islam and the Reply to Its Critics*, was in response to an article, published in a French journal and written by Gabriel Hanotaux, the French minister of foreign affairs, which criticized Islam as backward, despotic, and insistent on the inseparability of state and religion. The second, *Islam and Christianity and Their Respective Attitudes Toward Learning and Civilization* (*al-Islam wal-nasraniya bayna al-'ilm wal-madaniya*), responded to the essay written by a Europeanized Christian Arab, Farah Antun, the chief editor of the Arabic magazine *al-Jami'a*, which described a backward Islam intolerant of philosophy and science as against a Christianity that encouraged learning and knowledge and opened the gate for the birth of an enlightened and civilized Europe. In these replies, 'Abduh criticized the polar analytic used by both authors to describe a backward, despotic, and intolerant East in contrast to a progressively humanist and tolerant Christian West. The potent and incisive replies to the two outspoken defenders of Europe's modernizing mission with its prescription of liberal secularism won 'Abduh fame throughout the Muslim world as well as Europe. These articles also generated passionate arguments and counterarguments engaging the front pages of various Arabic and non-Arabic newspapers and journals. The fiery response was, in fact, not surprising, considering the Eurocentric and racialist content of the articles, which were produced at the height of the imperial age and deeply implicated in the rationalization of Europe's civilizing and colonizing project.

On the whole, Gabriel Hanotaux's article, which endorsed the view that the backwardness of the East was due to an inherently despotic and antihumanist Islam, reiterated the orientalist binary constructions prevalent in that era to justify French colonizing practices in Algeria.[52] Drawing on the racialist discourse then prevalent, Hanotaux attributed the differences between the Islamic and the Christian "civilizations" to an essential difference between the two religions, one Semitic and the other Aryan. The two oppositional but interrelated features that produced the difference between the religions were (1) the immanence of the Christian God in human life as against a transcendental God in Islam; and (2) the presence of the notion of free will in Christianity and its absence in Islam, where "predetermination" prevails. These doctrinal features, he maintained, contributed to the development of opposed cultures and attitudes, marked by self-reliance and independence in the West as against dependence and blind submission in the East. Additionally, the unity of politics and religion that is characteristic of Islam, he further opined, rendered the progress of the East impossible.[53]

Upon reading the translated version of the article printed in *al-Mu'ayid*, 'Abduh was outraged by its content, which he considered to be a frontal and explicit assault on Islam. He wrote a potent and incisive response that was printed in the same newspaper. His powerful reply elicited a response from Hanotaux followed by a rejoinder from 'Abduh.[54] In his long reply, which stretched over six articles, 'Abduh, though essentially agreeing with Hanotaux's description of the current inferior state of Muslims, contested, nonetheless, its attribution to Islam. He criticized Hanotaux for his lack of knowledge of Islamic history as well as for concocting an Islam foreign to most Muslims. That Muslims were antagonistic to sciences and scientific forms of knowledge clearly did not resonate with Islam or its history, as Muslims had made tremendous contributions to humanity in this field. He disclaimed Hanotaux as a *muqalid* (labeling him both an imitator and amateur) for displaying ignorance and repeating unfounded claims akin to those made by Muslim scholars whom he vilified as perilous imitators (*muqallidun*).[55]

In his powerful rhetorical response, 'Abduh points to Hanotaux's uneducated claim that Europe's present civilization and culture was purely Aryan, which by implication imparts a potent critique of the prevalent binary and racialist analytic—a Semitic East versus an Aryan West—utilized by Hanotaux and many orientalists and colonial administrators of his age.[56] Hanotaux, according to 'Abduh, seemed to overlook that even his forefathers, the Greeks, had to borrow from earlier great cultures and build on the knowledge and arts of other civilizations in order to construct their own. All civilizations and nations, he judiciously reminded Hanotaux, borrow from one another according to need. The Muslims were not any different, for they, too, were inspired by the Persians, the Greeks, and other civilizations, incorporating some of their arts and sciences and rejecting others in the process of making them their own. So Aryan Europe could not have ascended to its greatness had it not borrowed and built on the knowledge, cultures, and experiences passed on to it by earlier civilizations, including the Islamic, or so-called Semitic, civilization.[57]

His most potent criticism, however, was reserved for Hanotaux's assertion of the egregious fusion of religion and politics in Islam and its contribution to Muslims' backwardness. He reminded Hanotaux not only of his ignorance of Islamic history but also of his own history by pointing out that Europe's trajectory toward secularism was primarily a product of a long-standing war among Christians, rather than a constitutive feature of human progress. In historicizing the specificity of Europe's path to secularism not only does 'Abduh criticize Hanotaux's assessment of his own history; he also challenges Europe's prescription of secularism as a necessary condition for Muslims' advancement. Though agreeing with Hanotaux's appraisal of the benefits accrued to Europe as a result of the separation of state and church, 'Abduh dismissed Hanotaux's advice that Muslims follow the same trajectory for "their own good." Why do Europeans insist that Muslim societies follow their path, he constantly asked, when Muslims have never experienced theocracy as Christians did, and when the separation of worldly and religious powers in Islam had already been put into effect long before the arrival of the Europeans? Muslims, he explained, "never encountered at any stage in their long history something that resemble[s] the power wielded by the Papacy of Europe, nor were they ever exposed to a Pope-like figure who could and did exert power to remove Kings and banish princes, extract taxes and decree Divine laws, all on behalf of the Christian communities."[58] And contrary to Hanotaux's contention, temporal and religious powers under Ottoman Islamic jurisprudence have always been delineated as two separate entities, with allocated tasks assigned to each:

As accorded by the shari'a, the rights and obligations of temporal and civic power are vested in the figure of the *Khalifa* or *Sultan*, and not in the figure of the *Qadi*, the representative of religious authority. The sultan is in charge of managing the internal as well the international affairs of the empire. He is responsible for its defense, for waging wars and for its foreign affairs. The [sultan] has no say over religious matters other than hiring and firing. Those in charge of religious affairs wield no power over any of his affairs nor can they ever intercept or seize political power. Religious authority can only lend advice to and oblige the sultan to abide by the laws and rulings commanded by the *shar'*.[59]

As 'Abduh pointed out, there was no way to predict or guarantee that the separation of the two powers would necessarily induce progress. In spite of the historical separation in Islam, contemporary Muslims had yet to advance and show progress. Perhaps, he mockingly remarked, the reverse might have served Muslims of his day, for they might have been better off "had their rulers combined the two powers of state and religion because these [political] rulers would not have been able to openly breach the religion in acts of oppression, excess and prodigality that brought woe to Muslims and deprived them of their dearest possession—their independence."[60] In another context, 'Abduh again ridiculed the notion that the separation of state and religion would lead to the advancement of Muslims as too simplistic by pointing out that the British colonists had already created a legal system made up "of Mixed and National courts that are unattached to religion (shari'a), and where civic law reigns uncontested exactly as Hanotaux proposed; yet this arrangement has yet to shepherd progress or improve the condition of Muslims. The reverse seems to have transpired instead."[61]

In disputing the orientalist discourse of power, I want to suggest that 'Abduh shrewdly turned these arguments on their head by proposing that the causes for the sorrowful condition of Muslims lay in a weakened rather than a strong-holding Islam, thus rerouting the argument back to an internal condition of incoherence that lies primarily within the Islamic discursive tradition. Locating the disease of backwardness in the moral degeneracy of the Muslim community, 'Abduh deemed a revived Islam (rather than its demise or confinement) a constitutive feature to Muslim advancement. As against the Europeans and Europeanized Arab intellectuals who were adamant that breaking away from Islam, in particular, was necessary to become modern and find equal footing with Europe, 'Abduh maintained that a reconfigured Islam in light of the confusion produced by colonial modernity was the only solution for faithful Muslims seeking advancement.[62] The Islamic reform movement, he further insisted, was not simply a political tool created to wage a war against the Christian West and its values but an internal revivalist movement intending to summon Muslims to reform themselves and their present condition through the only means that would secure success, namely, a renewed Islam. The aim of Islamic revivalism starting from the mid-eighteenth century on, he reminded Hanotaux and his Europeanized allies, was meant to

correct the faith by removing the errors that have crept into the religion. Freeing the fundamental principles of the din of all these harmful innovations (*bida*) will free Muslims from disorder and confusion. . . . Seeking true and proper knowledge, both religious and secular, is the only path open for Muslims to re-gain their moral "good character" (*malaka salima*) and once again be virtuous and enlightened members; only then could the "good" flow through to the com-munity as a whole.[63]

ʿAbduh delved once again into the issue of whether political power should be civic (*madani*) or religious in nature in his engagement with yet another of his interlocutors, a Europeanized Egyptian by the name of Farah Antun (1874–1922). A Francophile Christian Arab intellectual, Farah Antun defended Europe's civilizing mission, especially its secular rationality. He owned and edited *al-Jamiʿa al-ʿUthmaniya*, which propa-gated French Enlightenment and its secular views, especially universal reason, opposition to superstitions (equated with religion), and the French revolutionary notions of liberty and equality. In one article, Antun claimed that the twelfth-century Spanish Muslim philosopher ibn Rushd (1126–98 A.D.), known as Averroes, was a nonbeliever because his central theory was founded on the efficacy of secondary causes, condemned as un-Islamic by authoritative Islamic discourse. Antun maintained that all religions are essentially alike and the prophets were no more than mere philosophers born with special gifts at conveying the "truth" through religious sym-bols. He proclaimed prophecy obsolete because rational individuals no longer need prophets and religion to access the truth once they can attain it on their own by using "reason."[64]

Essentially, Antun's article recapitulated Hanotaux's views by mak-ing the claim that the fusion of state and religion in Islam made it intoler-ant of philosophy and scientific knowledge, leaving Islamic civilization festering in stagnation and backwardness. In contrast, Christian tolerance and openness toward philosophers and scientists allowed for the triumph of learning over religious persecution in Europe, setting in motion the emergence of the greatest of all civilizations, namely, modernity. ʿAbduh disputed Farah Antun's remark that the separation of temporal and reli-gious powers that inheres in Christianity's notion of "Give Caesar what is Caesar's and give God what is God's" has no equivalence in Islam. ʿAbduh argued that Islam did not ever champion political sovereignty nor did it need to seek political power because, unlike the Christian Church, the Qur'an categorically prohibited coercion (*ikrah*) in anything that pertains to faith, as is evidenced in the two following verses: "There Shall be no coercion in matters of faith," and "And say: the truth [has now come] from your Sustainer: let then, him who wills, believe in it, and let him who wills, reject it."[65] All Muslim jurists without exception held the view that forcible conversion (through political power) was under all circumstances null and void and that coercion of faith as such is regarded a grievous sin. Islam as a way of life, he argued, provides moral guidance rather than seeking political power. Religious authority "lies not in its political power but in its moral guidance and in calling upon the faithful to summon the good and prevent harm. God has bequeathed this moral authority equally to all Muslims regardless of their social position in society. He bequeathed the lowest in status to rebuke those above him as He bequeathed the highest in status to correct those beneath them."[66]

He reiterated again the fact that there never was a religious sovereign power in Islam that might parallel the power of the Christian Church, in which a pope proclaiming divine right ejected kings, disinherited princes, and decreed divine laws. In Muslim societies, a Muslim political ruler represented worldly power and never ruled by "divine right"; therefore, it was wrong of Antun to "confuse an Islamic caliphate form of government with theocracy, a divinely derived government."[67] Drawing a distinction between worldly power and religious authority would not necessarily mean that temporal power should automatically accompany a separation of din and shar'. Political sovereignty did not, nor should it ever, exert its power beyond those civic tasks assigned to it, which also meant that temporal power should also refrain from exerting its control over the tasks assigned to religion.[68]

What becomes distinctly clear from these writings was that 'Abduh objected less to secular forms of power than to the Europeans' insistence that Muslims follow the same trajectory of secularization (*al-'ilmaniya*) as theirs when that historical experience itself was alien to Muslims. The relegation of religion to the nonpolitical sphere in Europe, as 'Abduh recognized and Western scholars have recently confirmed, was, after all, the outcome of a particular history that belonged to Europe. More specifically, one of the more important events in that history was the papacy's forced abdication of its political and divinely legitimized power after a century of violent religious wars that ended only with the peace of Westphalia in 1648. Out of these circumstances, religion came to be seen by the ensuing generation of Europeans as the source of unruly passions, an institution to be neutralized to safeguard the well-being of the communities.[69] Because of these circumstances, religion came to be slowly stripped of its power in Europe and relegated to the private sphere. ʿAbduh, in fact, was not ignorant of that violent history, nor was he unaware of the long bitter wars that ensued between absolutism and the papacy.[70] In response to Antun's claim of a tolerant Christian Europe, ʿAbduh mockingly remarked:

Is it valid to characterize surrender to the victorious tolerance? Is it correct to equate powerlessness with leniency? Are we to liken the prohibition of "evildoing" by sheer force with munificence and kindness? Is it right to describe the cohabitation in one town of both the Pope and the King of Italy and the presence of these two seats of power, that of the King and the Pope, in the same capital, a sign of Papal tolerance (*tasamuh*) towards sovereign power? Is it not more plausible that the King is likely the one to be the more tolerant [of the Pope] given that his political worldly power and military might which secured him supreme authority [over the land] could [easily] strip the papacy of the skeletal [*thumala*] power left in its name? Wouldn't it be more truthful to explain the [present state of] tranquility between science and religion as the upshot of political toleration of religion rather than religious [or Christian] tolerance of temporal political power and scientific forms of knowledge? [Would it be honest to] call the triumph of science over Christianity after what happened between them and after the monarchical usurpation of power in most of Europe's kingdoms and religion's acquiescence to trail behind, tolerance?[71]

Contrary to Antun's conclusion, ʿAbduh argued, it was the intolerance of Christianity (the Catholic Church) that ultimately led to its disempowerment and not the other way around. He substantiated his analysis with evidence drawn from European history that demonstrated the intolerance of the Church to both science and philosophy, contrary to the claims made by Antun.[72] The separation between the two powers and the privatization of religion as a result emerged out of a particular history of Christianity, one that was confined to Europe. As with Hanotaux, ʿAbduh again questioned the wisdom behind the suggestion that Muslims follow Europe's prescribed path when their history and experience of religion was strikingly different. Muslims had neither been exposed to anything like the religious violence experienced by the Christians of Europe, nor had they encountered an institution as formidable as the church that ruled Europe by combining temporal and divine powers for centuries on end.

It is important to note that 'Abduh was not rejecting the secular authority (*al-sulta al-madaniya*) of the modern state, as some might conclude, but was putting forward the idea that it was for Muslims to define the boundaries of civic power as they saw fit and in accordance with their needs and historical experience. In other words, he raised the issue of the social and historical particularity of Muslim societies. For change to be effective, he maintained, it had to take into account the history and culture of the region, thus making the point that secular power (al-'ilmaniya) was historically and culturally specific rather than predetermined or universal. In the case of Muslims, who did not see a contradiction between the preservation of a social role for religion and the modern condition, the more pertinent question was how to limit an intrusive secular power that intended on regulating all features of life, including morality. This, I would argue, is not by any means an unreasonable position considering that even in the Western hemisphere, as recent scholars of Europe have postulated, secularism was neither self-evident nor universal. The view of religion as antithetical to European Enlightenment has been revised if not reversed in this recent literature, which suggests not that the resurrection of religion in eighteenth-century Europe was an outcome of the limits of European modernity but rather that religion was at the "heart of the project of modernity itself [and] a constitutive element of its very shaping."[73] Moreover, the extent of separation between state and religion tended to vary from one Western society to another, depending on the particular historical context and social arrangements within each, which, in turn, formed how these different communities came to negotiate and define the boundaries of the separation most suitable to their conditions. The different forms of secularism, in other words, were the product of historical processes and the outcome of arrangements arrived at by different societies and not an inevitable or uniform outcome of modernity.[74]

For 'Abduh, then, the burning question was how to safeguard religion as the defining authority on morality in the context of an all-intrusive modernizing colonial state seeking to reshape the norms and beliefs of Muslims in accordance with post-Enlightenment humanism and the principles of progress and reason, which were conceived as irreconcilable with attitudes and practices founded on religious beliefs. It is clear that 'Abduh objected to the coercive universalization of European modernity and to an all-encompassing modernizing state insisting on governing all features of human life, including the functions previously governed by religion, those of morality and law, as will be discussed in the following chapter. What he was searching for was a discursive terrain with a more balanced boundary between worldly power and religious authority and where the latter, rather than being marginal and ineffectual, continues to authorize norms that govern Muslims' lives. This explains why 'Abduh opposed the wholesale Europeanization of society as propagated by a class of Western-educated Egyptian intellectuals, the likes of Farah Antun, who became indifferent toward religion as they came to acquire European secular values and norms. Although he accepted the need for Egypt to change, he objected to the colonial rearrangements of norms and values along the ideological bifurcation of the world into modern and nonmodern and the denigration by extension of religion. He also recognized that the key to maintaining the authority of religion in a changing world lies in the restructuring and reforming of the one institution he considered most pivotal to the revival of the Muslim community and most crucial for warding off Europeanization, al-Azhar.

al-Azhar: 'Abduh and His Interlocuters

'Abduh believed that the task of rejuvenating Egyptian society lay in the reform of the Islamic educational system, starting with al-Azhar. This was not surprising, considering that al-Azhar, the university that trained and graduated Muslim scholars, judges, teachers, and preachers for Egypt and beyond, was the seat of religious knowledge, authority, and orthodoxy. He regarded the reform of al-Azhar and the revival of the religion as two features of the same activity. The reform of al-Azhar, he once remarked, "would be the greatest service to Islam; its reform signifies the reform of all Muslims as its decadence is a clear sign of their depravity."[75] It was also necessary because reordering the religion in light of the modern condition would be an impossible task without reorganizing and restructuring the site of religious power that defined and authorized what was Islamic and what was orthodox. This issue—who claims the right to define what is truly Islamic—was a matter of contention from the early nineteenth century in Egypt, causing the rift between the established 'ulama of al-Azhar and those reformers before 'Abduh who spearheaded the revivalist movement. This movement began with the famous scholar Hasan al-ʿAttar (1776–1834) whose modernizing suggestions, to borrow the words of the historian Afaf Marsot, were "the first breeze of the wind of change that was to blow half a century later."[76] The endeavor was pursued by the next generation that included Rifaʿa Rafiʿ al-Tahtawi, al-ʿArusi, and al-Mahdi, among others, and culminated by the end of the century in the reform headed by ʿAbduh himself.

More specifically, the rift between the old ʿulama and this new generation of reformers can be historically traced back to the social, economic, and political restructuring of Egyptian society starting from the late eighteenth century all the way up to ʿAbduh's age and beyond. Egypt's reorganization in the nineteenth century mandated the creation of a unified system of education that expanded knowledge beyond the religious to include "useful" and "applied" secular scientific and technological forms of knowledge, which were deemed necessary to the modernizing project under way. These changes in turn induced a shift in societal attitudes toward what constitutes "useful" and "authoritative" Islamic knowledge and how best to propagate it. The logocentrism of the old system of disseminating Islamic knowledge through recitation and memorization of classical texts, once accepted as creative, was now dismissed as disorderly, ineffective, and moribund by a younger generation of scholars socialized under the new order.[77] To these young Muslims keen on change, the "decline" and vulnerability of Muslims were blamed primarily on this sterile arcane system of Islamic learning centered on memorization of medieval scholastic texts that were neither relevant to the din nor applicable to Muslims' lives. Considering that Islam "is a way of life" was more the reason why many of these reformers came to lament what they perceived as the chaotic and dilapidated state of Islamic learning and its remoteness from the daily experiences of Muslims.

That explains why for these upcoming Muslim reformers, including ʿAbduh, the restructuring of al-Azhar and its instructional and pedagogical approach became their platform for revival and the ground on which they came to challenge the established ʿulama of al-Azhar over what is and what is not "useful" and "authoritative" in Islamic knowledge, and by implication what is and what is not orthodox in Islam.[78]

ʿAbduh, to recall our earlier discussion, accused the religious authority seated at al-Azhar of being steeped in unreasoned traditionalism (taqlid), condoning the blind following of earlier precedence at a time when the Muslim tradition was facing a crisis and was in dire need for a dynamic and knowledgeable team of scholars, jurists, and teachers un-afraid of using ijtihad and the Qur'an to sensibly evaluate what was not of value in Western modernity.

As described by reformers, al-Azhar university, once the leading center for enlightened learning and the archetypal mosque for training refined and learned Muslims, had now lost its vitality and was reduced to such a state of decadence that it could hardly play any role in the regeneration of the Muslims at this time. The poverty of knowledge, opined 'Abduh, was clear in a program reduced to a stifling repetition of the transmitted sciences (*al-'ulum al-naqliyya*) and medieval scholastic dogma that had little relevance to the new and changing realities. While theology, jurisprudence, and Sufi orders were the primary topics of study, philosophy, Islamic logic, rhetoric, and astronomy were invariably relegated to the background. In addition, no secular subjects like history or algebra were allowed, nor were any of the modern sciences, as they were considered worldly subjects that could veer students away from the study of religion.[79] Even the original authoritative sources were hardly studied, instead substituted with medieval sources whose content was reproduced by more recent explanatory works and pedantic arcane commentaries carried to the extreme. This was especially the case with theology, a subject that was primary to the training of Azhari scholars.

The study of theology, as 'Abduh and other critics noted, consisted mostly of a couple of mutun (manuals) that students were expected to memorize. 'Abduh recalled an incident during his student days at al-Azhar that is worth retelling as it captures the apparent "intellectual atrophy" of the institution, as experienced by the younger 'Abduh. The story goes as follows: as the new young instructor at al-Azhar, 'Abduh introduced to students in his reading circle Islamic texts on logic, theology, and history that were not commonly studied or even acknowledged at al-Azhar. One of the readings that happened to anger the master scholars was al-Taftazani's (1322–1389 A.D.) commentaries on Islamic doctrines (*sharh al-'Aqai'd al-Nasafiya*). When summoned by Sheikh 'Ilish, who accused him of divisiveness and radicalism for advocating Mu'tazila doctrine against Ash'ari orthodoxy, 'Abduh's response, which "made 'Ilish fume with anger," was to deny the accusation on the principle that he would never condone any creed without reasoned evidence. His exact words were as follows: "Since I do not condone obedience (taqlid) to the Ash'ari creed, why would I then champion that of the Mu'tazila? I do not abide by consensus (*taqlid al-jami'*) just for the sake of abiding. I defer only to guided evidence."[80]

Besides complaining about the poverty of education, 'Abduh depicted the institution itself as being in a deplorable state of disorder, faction-ridden with various competing sects (Hanafi, Shafi'i, Maliki, and Hanbali) as well as Sufi orders, each seeking out the seat of power that would guarantee its discursive dominance. Because the seat of power inhered in the position of the Sheikh al-Azhar, he who occupied that seat in accordance with the old customs now seen impractical favored his sect and supporters, leading to infighting over the discrepancy in the allocation of resources.[81] Put simply, the old ways of organizing al-Azhar rendered the institution in the eyes of the reformers of the nineteenth century a redundant, inefficient, and unruly institution in dire need of reform and order.

When 'Abduh was put in charge of reforming al-Azhar in the 1890s, he was aware that reforms should be effected gradually and continuously and better still with the conviction of influential 'ulama from within the institution.[82] This sort of change, as he often stated, had to be implemented from below and from within in order to be effective and successful. Although he truly distrusted the efficacy of existing power and its use and abuse from all parties concerned, he did on occasion have to resort to its use.[83] In this particular case, however, as quoted by Rashid Rida, his biographer and most trusted friend, 'Abduh did not trust the khedive, the British administration, or, least of all, the old-guard Azharis. He accused them all of corruption as well as of abuse of power to serve their selfish interests:

I intend to reform al-Azhar by convincing the Muslim scholars in charge of the institution of the need for change and not through the powerful hand of the government and its laws. There is really little difference between the corrupt (rotten) rules that govern al-Azhar and the present government, whose rules are passed by a dictator, the Khedive himself.

I would not call on or let a foreign hand infiltrate this institution. I will not permit the government interceding in matters relating to this institution since this government itself is run by a foreign power.[84]

As it transpired, the reform plan was to engineer change over several phases and to include from the beginning several prominent old-guard Azhari scholars to represent the different legal schools on the advisory council, which was set up immediately after ʿAbduh took over.[85]

The first measure toward its centralization was the creation of an administrative council (*majlis idarat al-Azhar*) made up of three selected Azhari scholars and two outside officials (one was ʿAbduh and the other a friend of his, ʿAbdel Karim Salman). The council was to meet twice a month to discuss and recommend measures regarding all affairs relating to the institution, both administrative and pedagogical. At the same time that the council was set up, Hassuna al-Nawawi, a renowned Hanafi scholar open to the idea of reform, was appointed as the rector of al-Azhar. In 1895, to boost the power of the council, al-Nawawi was then appointed chairman.[86]

Briefly summarized, the most important modernizing measures considered by the council were the following:

1. Rectifying the huge discrepancy in wages by regulating the salaries of teachers and staff on the basis of qualification, merit, and length of service.

2. Thoroughly restructuring al-Azhar's principal source of income, the religious endowment funds, which resulted in a quadrupling of its revenues.

3. Rearranging of the curricula and method of teaching, requiring all students to take courses in the primary subjects (ʿ*ulum al-makasid*) of tawhid, tafsir, fiqh, usul al-fiqh, and *akhlaq* (morals) and in instrumental linguistic subjects (*wasaʾil*) that included algebra and arithmetic. Secular subjects such as history, geography, philosophy, social economy, and natural sciences were also introduced in the form of electives. To secure a diploma, students were required to pass an examination in all core subjects and some of the electives. The new curriculum was intended to discourage students from studying extensive glosses and commentaries and commended the acquisition of the essentials of religious sciences, stressing the importance of cultivating moral character.[87]

4. Creating a library with branches in the various loggias and in the main mosques in Cairo, Alexandria, and other towns and villages, where preparatory schools were set up.

Other rules were also passed to regulate the loggias, *riwaq*, that housed students surrounding the mosque, securing additional dormitories, improving sanitation, installing a new system of running water, and installing petroleum lights to replace oil lights formerly in use. A physician was placed in al-Azhar and a modern dispensary was created to provide students with medicine free of charge. Later on a hospital was also established.[88]

Notwithstanding the council's ceaseless effort to effect change in al-Azhar, the actual implementation of these measures, especially in the curricula and pedagogy, was by contrast meager. In spite of the plan to reform the institution gradually and through the strategy of including the 'ulama in the planning and implementation of the new program, the old guard, according to 'Abduh and his allies, continued to rebuff ideas of reform. The dispute between the reformists and the old guard spilled over into the newspapers and journals and to the public at large. Both sides turned to the new print media to make their case. The 'ulama linked the reformers to Europeanization (taghrib) and condemned them as harmful to the community and to religion. They looked upon the new curricula and the inclusion of secular subjects as being in violation of the spirit of the institution and as a way of alienating the students from the study of religious subjects. The secularization of the curricula, they argued, would subvert the very purpose of al-Azhar because the majority of students, if only for the pragmatic reason of employment, would automatically be driven away from the study of religious subjects and sciences.[89] The objective of al-Azhar, according to the newly appointed rector of al-Azhar, Sheikh 'Abdul Rahman al-Sharbini, was to preserve the religion through the exclusive dissemination of religious knowledge rather than engage in politics and the study of "worldly subjects." In an interview solicited by the newspaper *al-jawa' ib al-misriya*, he objected to the teaching of secular modern subjects, saying that it "would transform al-Azhar mosque from a great religious institution into a school of liberal arts (*adab*) and philosophy aimed to fight religion and extinguish its light."[90] He also denounced 'Abduh's attempted reforms for producing "chaos among the students, who are now displaying signs of disrespect and contempt towards their honorable teachers [and,] deceived by what they hear, highly extolling Spencer and his philosophy while concomitantly mock[ing] with contempt what the great early Muslim Masters have to offer."[91]

In his rebuttal, 'Abduh responded to al-Sharbini's dismissal of philosophy as a secular subject irrelevant to religious studies by pointing out that not even al-Sharbini himself can avoid touching on philosophical concerns and subjects, such as phenomenology and logic (*ilm al-mantiq*), when teaching speculative theology (*ilm-kalam*), syntax, and rhetoric. The notions of being and existence, or contingent and noncontingent existence, are essential features of Islamic speculative theology and of the doctrine of tawhid. As primary religious subjects, tawhid and theology are closely connected to worldly questions regarding the universe and cosmological truths. 'Abduh accused al-Azhar teachers, including Sharbini, of wasting many of their years on instrumental subjects consisting of superfluous enunciations and obsolete eloquence of language instead of teaching primary religious subjects. Years were spent in detailed investigation of Taftazani's diction (*bayan*) to such an extreme that such works were now placed above the Qur'an. What would al-Sharbini say of the great master theologian-philosophers, including al-Razi, who made it a habit of theirs to engage in worldly subjects, including cosmological sciences, because they were essential to the establishment of religious truths? Why, then, does al-Sharbini reject these "worldly subjects" as unprecedented innovations? Is arithmetic then to be considered a secular subject unrelated to religious knowledge, when in actuality it was an acknowledged component of Islamic jurisprudence (fiqh), one that is key to the study of inheritance and statutory sciences?[92] Are we to reject mathematics, he says, "even when the Prophet himself commanded his scholars to teach it as an essential feature of Hadith studies? Is not the science of religious obligations and morals (*ilm al-adab al-diniya wal-akhlaq*) an essential part of studying [Islam], the true fiqh and foundation of all shari'a sciences? . . . Are these the [secular modern] sciences that *al-ustaz* [al-Sharbini] refers to as philosophical subjects?"[93]

Moreover, 'Abduh wondered how students could avoid the study of the primary religious subjects when the new laws at that time stated that these primary subjects (*ulum al-din*) were compulsory and that students had to spend the maximum time in pursuing these studies, while lesser time was allocated to the instrumental subjects and electives that include the secular subjects. Denying that students had lost respect for their heritage and teachers, 'Abduh refuted al-Sharbini by pointing out the difference between disrespect and the art of criticism. He recalled that throughout the forty years of his teaching at al-Azhar, although students had been in the habit of criticizing their teachers, they were never disrespectful. Rather than being disrespectful of the tradition, the reform, he reminded al-Sharbini, reintroduced the students to the original works of the early masters: "When have al-Azhar students studied the original works of al-Shafi'i, for example?"[94]

The 'ulama successfully campaigned against the reform by making the claim that these changes were nothing but measures to diffuse foreign ideas, values, and practices, with the aim of corrupting the religion and its symbol, al-Azhar. These changes, they insisted, were Western innovations to undermine the power of the religion in the society. They did not refrain from accusing 'Abduh of hypocrisy and of faking commitment to Islam. They even denounced him for the length of his hair and for wearing European shoes. One of the leading figures opposing his reform, Salim al-Bishri, became the rector of al-Azhar between 1899 and 1903 and during his tenure froze many of the measures passed by the council and suspended the annual exams required by the new program. Opposition groups were formed within al-Azhar under the leadership of Muhammad al-Rafi'i, another influential 'alim who opposed the reform and was now backed by the khedive.[95] The opposition to 'Abduh intensified as these groups began to put pressure on the government and the British colonial administration to intervene and remove 'Abduh from the council. The fact that Lord Cromer continued to back 'Abduh as a political statement against the khedive was used by the Azhari critics as further evidence of 'Abduh's links to colonial power and its secularizing agenda.

The deep polarization of the al-Azhar community, combined with the dismissal of 'Abduh's friend and supporter, Hassuna al-Nawawi, as rector, and al-Nawawi's replacement with old guard rectors who refused to implement the reforms, forced 'Abduh to resign in 1905 from the advisory council he had created and led. Many read this as a triumph of the old guard and as a setback for reform. But as 'Abduh pointed out to his friend and follower, Mustafa 'Abdul Raziq, the wheels of change are already in motion:

They imagine that by departing from al-Azhar, I have given them a free hand to regard the institution as a fertile pasture for their beasts to graze as they wish; not at all. I have kindled a fire within the precincts of al-Azhar, which no hand can put off. . . . If it does not blaze forth today or tomorrow it would do so in three decades; and then it would be more than a simple blaze.[96]

The above debates between the established Azhari scholars and Mu-hammad 'Abduh centered on the maintenance or the reconstitution and reorganization of the institutional apparatus of al-Azhar and the trans-mission of Islamic knowledge therein. These two oppositional positions represented two different Islamic responses to what was then perceived as the assault of colonial modernity upon religious authority. Both sides en-gaged the Islamic discursive tradition to make their arguments for or against change as a way of maintaining religion. Thus, whereas the Azhari 'ulama sought to uphold the status quo (through the practice of taqlid, the maintenance of the curriculum, and organizational hierarchy), Mu-hammad 'Abduh sought to reorder Islamic knowledge and its attending institutional apparatus. Central to this debate, therefore, is the question of orthodoxy. The old guards based their claim on the defense of ortho-doxy, which they equated with discursive maintenance of the tradition—for example 'Ilish's defense of taqlid as the best measure to prevent further taghrib. In contrast, 'Abduh sought to reconfigure orthodoxy by drawing from within the parameters of the Islamic discursive tradition and mobi-lizing the Ash'ari concept of the mean (mizan) as well and ibn Taymiya's concept of ijtihad to negotiate a space between taqlid and taghrib. Drawing on multiple tendencies and arguments within the tradition, 'Abduh was able to generate a counterdiscourse that could vie with the established Is-lamic orthodoxy, as presented from the viewpoint of the Azhari scholars.

How was this contest to establish discursive dominance over the definition of orthodoxy carried out? The Azahri scholars defending the status quo attempted to undermine 'Abduh's religious authority by mak-ing the case that he transgressed the conceptual and institutional bound-aries of communal consensus, ijma'. Their smear campaign was also meant to delegitimate his claims to orthodoxy by insinuating his alliance with Lord Cromer and the British colonial authority. 'Abduh also mobi-lized all the resources at his disposal, making excellent use of the new medium of print to reach a wider Islamic public. Nor did he refrain from utilizing his prominent institutional placements as a judge, Azhari ad-ministrative council member, and grand mufti of Egypt to try and insti-tute discursive dominance. The debates as well as the political and institutional maneuvering of both sides clearly demonstrate how power (political, intellectual, institutional) is central to the constitution of orthodoxy.

The reconfiguration of orthodoxy entails the conceptual rejecting or marginalizing of some elements and the reintroducing or revitalizing of other elements, such as ijtihad and mizan. More important, it entails the ability to actualize one's understanding of orthodoxy, which is fundamentally related to power. Accordingly, we should dispense with the conventional understanding of orthodoxy as solely an attempt to reproduce the status quo because Abduh's reconfiguration of orthodoxy involved subverting the status quo at multiple levels, at the Azhari level, at the governmental level, and within the Europeanized elements of Egyptian society, all of which were specific to late nineteenth-century Egypt, thus demonstrating that orthodoxy, as a social and historical process, is constituted rather than a given. Conceived as a relation of power, orthodoxy here is not quite the same as the hegemonic and fixed orthodoxy of conventional scholarship. As demonstrated, there were fundamental disagreements among Muslims over the meaning of orthodoxy and, by extension, over the strategies and practices most effective for the preservation of a moral Muslim community in the shadow of colonial modernity.

Governable Muslim Subjects

And had thy Sustainer so willed, He could surely have made all mankind one single community: But [He Willed it otherwise and so] they continue to hold divergent views.

The Qur'an, 11:118

[Ghazali] devised a hybrid concept, conjuring two ideas: he combined intelligibility and understanding with the self—that is, *fiqh* plus *nafs*—in order to produce self-intelligibility (*fiqh al-nafs*).

Moosa, *Ghazali and the Poetics of Imagination*

Introduction

At the turn of the century in Egypt, orthodoxy, a contested terrain, was being reconstituted through an intellectual, social, and political process. Contestation ranged over many issues and concerns but was first and foremost linked to the question of what it meant to be a moral Muslim in the context of colonial modernity. In his disputation with the local Muslim scholars over the definition of orthodoxy, on the one hand, and with European colonialism over the nature of the modern, on the other, 'Abduh, I suggest, opened a terrain for the emergence of "a concept of 'the subject' that has a new grammar."[1] This grammar allowed for a Muslim subject to be civil, but in ways that were different from those that define a Western liberal subject.[2]

In what follows, I delineate from 'Abduh's writings how he envisioned the construction of a new Muslim subject to depend on reform of the institutions of education, law, and the family. In this vision, the new subject was to be not only self-regulating and self-disciplining but also orderly, productive, rational, and healthy in body and mind—that is to say, a modern subject capable of being incorporated into the fabric of modern structures of power and governance. At the same time, this subject was to be created through the inculcation of various Islamic rituals and disciplinary practices, such as tasdiq (inner conviction), *tahdhib* (disciplining), and *tarbiya* (education), thereby stressing the construction of the new subject as also fundamentally moral with a concern for the public good. In this regard, 'Abduh's vision of a Muslim modern self was not the liberal modern self of Europe. Different from those who categorize 'Abduh as a liberal for injecting the European idea of interior subjectivity into Islam, I suggest that because "subjective interiority" has had a long-standing history within the Islamic tradition and has always been a key concept for the constitution of a Muslim subject, 'Abduh was less compelled to draw on the European liberal tradition to define a modern subjectivity.[3]

'Abduh engaged the Islamic discursive tradition to delineate the institutional and legal as well as the moral boundaries from within which he could then redefine a Muslim subject. His project of reform, as stated earlier, rested on the Islamic notion of ijtihad and on freeing Islamic discourse from what he considered the fetters of traditionalist religious leadership by encouraging Muslims to employ their own conviction and reasoning ('aql) independent of set precedent (taqlid). 'Abduh, for example, relied on the Mu'tazila's conception of rationality and, in particular, on their understanding of knowledge as being objectively verifiable so that he could make the argument that objective knowledge is not foreign to the tradition and that the body of modern scientific knowledge is not necessarily incommensurable with Islamic knowledge.[4] He also drew on the Mu'tazila's notion of 'aql (reasoning), which accentuated practical reasoning, to reconstitute a moral self that is more self-reflective and self-regulatory, within the boundaries defined by the Islamic tradition. In defining a Muslim subjectivity, 'Abduh, I argue, could draw on arguments internal to the tradition without having to resort to liberal Europe. For the concept of subjective interiority, for example, 'Abduh relied on al-Ghazali's "ethics of the self," as developed in the *Balance of the Deeds*

(*Mizan al-Aʿmal*), to make the argument for subjectivity and the importance of self-contemplation and self-realization to the making of a morally responsible Muslim subject. The notion of the "hermeneutics of the
self," as Ebrahim Moosa so brilliantly demonstrates in *Ghazali and the
Poetics of Imagination*, rather than being a European import, has, in
fact, a long-standing history within the tradition, starting with al-
Ghazali himself. In contrast to the earlier generations of Muslims who
conceived of ethics (*ʿilm al-akhlaq*) as an inseparable feature of positive
law (*ʿilm al-fiqh*), al-Ghazali, influenced by Sufism, initiated the idea of
a different discourse of ethics (*adab*), one that he regarded as the heart
of the law (fiqh). This discourse of adab, providing the norms for righteous living, involved the cultivation of proper ethical conduct through
a slow process of educating and disciplining the self (body and soul)
until a set of virtues, or fadaʾil, become interiorized. The process of cultivation of an inner disposition along with the disciplining of the outer
self (the body) is identified within the discourse as *malaka* (habitus)—
describing a state in which virtues come to inhabit both the soul and the
body, enabling the moral subject to reach a stage of equilibrium and
happiness.[5]

Al-Ghazali's contribution toward the development of an Islamic
subjectivity altered Islamic views on the law by establishing a more coher-
ent and nuanced understanding of law's relations to the individual subject, in particular. As Moosa argues, by creating a dialogical terrain
between positive law (fiqh) and virtue (*fadila*), al-Ghazali was able to ce-
ment relations between the law and the individual through this medium
called adab or ethics. And through this discourse of adab, al-Ghazali redefined the law (fiqh) as the "embodiment of virtues through practice."[6]
In so doing, al-Ghazali initiated the idea that the efficacy of earthly law
(fiqh)—when in synchrony with God's revealed law—depends on the
development first of self-understanding, disciplined moral subjects.[7] In
Moosa's words, "for the law to have an effect on the conduct of the ethical
subject, something had to occur before the law: the cultivation of the self
through the disciplinary practices of adab education (*taʾdib*) and moral
cultivation (*taʾaddub*)."[8] Al-Ghazali's "hermeneutics and technologies of
the self" became central to ʿAbduh's reformation project and in particular
to his attempt at reconfiguring an Islamic subjectivity more consonant
with the modern condition. Although at certain points ʿAbduh might

seem to be replicating al-Ghazali's ideas, in fact, within the context of colonial modernity, the Islamic notion of interiority acquired a meaning different from how it had been understood and structured in al-Ghazali's times.

Considering the analytical framework stated above, this chapter questions the view that 'Abduh was among the first of the modern Islamists to initiate the privatization of religion and to draw a distinction between law and morality for the purpose of making Islam more amenable to modern liberal subjectivity. One can clearly conclude from 'Abduh's work that he did not construe the privatization of religion as a necessary precondition for modernity, nor that he proposed to separate law from morality.[9] On the contrary, 'Abduh advocated that the law continue to derive its authority from Islamic law (fiqh) and that religious authority ipso facto extends beyond the individual and the private sphere. 'Abduh presumed, as any Muslim would, that religious duties (*ibadat*), as embodied practices, were constitutive of social relations, and he took for granted that interactive transactions (*mu'amalat*) were integral to the constitution of a Muslim subject. Accordingly, the understanding of a Muslim subject as a constitutive part of the collective community is bound to be different than the liberal understanding, in which a clear distinction is drawn between ethics and law, and ethics and religious belief are delineated as private and interior, in contrast to a public domain that is concerned with regulating people's actions and not their beliefs.

Construction of the Modern Muslim Subject

Other than the two defining features of Islam—acknowledging the oneness of God and giving credence to his messenger, Muhammad, through whom the Qur'an was revealed—Muslims, as I have noted elsewhere, have fundamental disagreements over the interpretation of the authoritative corpus and by extension over what constitutes religious orthodoxy and the defining attributes of a good Muslim. Hence, the search for orthodoxy does not foreclose debate or contention among Muslims.

Disagreement among Muslims, as 'Abduh disclosed, was not just permitted but encouraged by Revelation, as the Qur'an stressed the unceasing differentiation in men's outlooks and understandings not as incidental but as God-willed: "Differences in interpretation, judgment and comprehension are innate features of humankind," as was acknowledged in the following Quranic verse: "And has thy Sustainer so willed, He could surely have made all mankind one single community: But [He Willed it otherwise and so] they continue to hold divergent views."[10] Otherwise, ʿAbduh explained, humankind would have been devoid of free will and the ability to discern right and wrong as well as the capacity to think and make judgments, the features that distinguish humans from other forms of life.[11]

Disputes among Muslims, as stated in an earlier context, bear on many issues and activities, some of which become more visible than others depending on time and circumstance. In the age of ʿAbduh, the issue that took center stage was how to rethink Islamic orthodoxy in light of colonial modernity. As we saw in the debates with Hanotaux and others, one issue Muslims of this age were forced to face was how to reconfigure modern forms of power and, more specifically, how to delineate anew the boundaries governing relations between civic power and religious authority and their functions as regulators of social norms. Another concern was how to rearrange a space for the formation of a moral Muslim subject more attuned to colonial processes of governance without the total privatization of religion—that is, how to foster the development of a self-regulating subject capable of making political and social decisions who would not be the tradition-free subject of liberalism but a subject rooted in the Islamic tradition. Put another way, the challenge was to configure a new idiom that would allow for a more balanced arrangement between individual civil "rights" required of a productive political subject-citizen and duties and moral obligations essential for upholding a moral Muslim community.

ʿAbduh, I maintain, did not have to search far to explore the various possibilities available to conceptualize such a subject. One such source was the Ashʿariya, a dominant school within the Islamic tradition that stressed interiority and the cultivation of the inner self as essential to the formation of a moral subject. In particular, al-Ghazali's "ethics of the self" seemed to offer an Islamic notion of subjectivity that is compatible with modern institutions and disciplinary practices.[12] As I argued in an earlier context, there is a long-standing argument within the tradition over the interiority or exteriority of religion and by extension over whether a Muslim subject is to be judged by inward faith or outward action. Such disagreements obviously are more than a simple quibble over semantics, for they concern legal and moral issues with considerable implications for the quality and vision of people's lives.

Seeking the Islamic discourses that engaged this question, ibn 'Abdul Wahhab, for instance, drew on the Hanbali argument that adjudicated a Muslim's testimony of what is in his heart to be through its external enactment. Choosing this externalist interpretation of the religion, ibn 'Abdul Wahhab in turn judged a Muslim through the lens of his exterior actions, thus strictly reading all wrongful acts (regardless of their intention) as a breach of faith and a form of shirk and correcting them accordingly. In contrast, 'Abduh opted for interiority, with its counterclaim that external acts were not a reliable measure of a true moral self because there were those who performed acts without sincerity or truthfulness. Hence, different from ibn 'Abdul Wahhab, 'Abduh conceived of a Muslim self as one who interiorized conviction in God (tasdiq) through pedagogy and the inculcation of a set of disciplinary practices (tarbiya, tahdhib) until that truth was transformed into permanent principles of action.

In line with al-Ghazali's analytic of equilibrium, 'Abduh continuously identified the Muslim community of his age as suffering from an imbalance and a disease of the soul caused by deficiency in knowledge (religious and otherwise) and poor understanding of the true spirit of the religion.[13] As a physician of the soul, 'Abduh believed that the cure lay in cultivating interiority by searching for truth and knowledge within oneself, measures that required training the self to seek out the voice of reason ('aql) within one's inner soul (*nafs*, or seat of subjectivity) until that knowledge comes to be attained, integrated, and converted into principles of action. The cultivation of interiority, while engaging inner sentiments and desires (*qalb* and *wijdan*, or heart and experience), must simultaneously bring these emotions under the guidance of a contemplative intellect ('aql).[14] 'Abduh stressed reason and reasoning many times in his writing but especially in his exegesis of *al-Baqara*, quoted below, in which he condemned obedience to religious authority without intelligibility or deeper conviction by pointing to how the Revelation discloses otherwise:

[Quranic verse:] And so, the parable of those who are bent on denying the truth is that of the beast, which hears the shepherd's cry, and hears in it nothing but the sound of a voice and a call. Deaf are they, and dumb, and blind: for they do not use their reason. (2:171)

['Abduh's commentary:] Faith on authority and devoid of contemplative understanding (*'aql*) and [inner] discernment (*hidaya*) describes the virtual state of the godless (*howa sha'n al-kafirun*) rather than one of faith. For the faithful is one who arrives at his faith through an inquiring intellect (*'aqqala dinuh*) and by probing one's inner soul (*'arifahu bi-nafsihi*) until one is completely convinced by that truth (*hatta iqtana'a bihi*). Those who act out their faith without [this form of] understanding—even when doing good deeds—are not truly faithful. . . . Faith is not servility of man (*yuthalil al-insan*) to do good work like a servile animal, but an arrived at state-of-consciousness and recognition. . . . That is why the Qur'an has referred to unbelievers as "deaf, dumb, blind" for not hearing, saying, or seeing the truth as one of [inner] discernment, reflection and intelligibility (*taddabur, fihm, 'ilm and tabayyun*).[15]

'Abduh's reference to this interior process as *al-tasdiq bil-wijdan*, or conviction through inner experience involving both the heart (qalb) and reasoning ('aql), thus stressed the point that the realization of truth is an active process as well as a contemplative one. 'Abduh converts the concept *sidq*, or conviction, into a performative act (tasdiq)—a process of active engagement in acquiring the truth, which includes participation in pedagogy and training (tahdhib and tarbiya) until the inner self acquires the truth and then turns that truth into principles for daily action. Through a set of practices and rituals that aim to discipline the body and train the inner self, a Muslim subject comes to inhabit these virtuous qualities and act on them. 'Abduh's description of interiority as the acquisition and assimilation of the truth, though influenced by al-Ghazali, seems also to be analogous to Foucault's notion of the "subjectivization of truth," a process requiring constant examination and prodding of one's inner self until the truth is inwardly realized. 'Abduh's approach to truth also is predicated on the notion that the realization of the truth lies within oneself. Although the interiority of religion as proposed by 'Abduh is obviously soul-oriented, the body figures highly in its realization because the mastery over one's inner self can come only by training (*riyada*) and disciplining the body through a set of rituals and practices.

'Abduh repeatedly stated that Islam was not about shallow utterance and empty rituals, as then condoned by the Azhari 'ulama; rather, it was about the cultivation of interiority through reflection and training. Rituals, he explained, were the means to train and discipline the Muslim to come closer to God in both inner life and external action. The ritual of prayer, involving repeated bending and prostration of the body, was intended to train the body, mind, and soul simultaneously to surrender oneself to God, to engage in the act of surrendering to the truth by devoting oneself totally to God.[16] The objective of praying was to instill the virtues of modesty and piety in a Muslim. Other ritual acts, such as almsgiving (zakat), which were more external than prayer, had a similar purpose—in this case, to inculcate another cardinal virtue, that of justice ('adl). Pointing out that the commands for almsgiving were almost always attached to verses commanding prayer, 'Abduh emphasized that rituals functioned to create the capacity for virtue in the individual and, by extension, in the community. Whereas the goal of prayer was to discipline and improve the inner self, almsgiving was to cultivate righteousness and to attain social justice. In sum, the authorized rules and practices are meant to cultivate the truth within oneself through continuous self-discipline (training the body through repetitive rituals) until these virtuous qualities (*husn al-khulq*, or good morals) come to inhabit the inner self and become inseparable from one's outer demeanor. 'Abduh described this process of self-realization and self-improvement involved in the creation of a moral thinking Muslim subject as malaka (acquire or possess), a concept equivalent to habitus. The development of these dispositions clearly has a bearing on all aspects of one's life, whether private or public.[17]

Although 'Abduh's interpretation resonates with al-Ghazali's cultivation of the moral self, the contours of the self and the setting were profoundly modern, changing the perception and function of the original construction. For example, al-Ghazali, in contrast to 'Abduh, developed his doctrine of interiority in response to the didactic rationalism of speculative theology (*kalam*) and, in particular, its formalism and externality. Drawing on Sufi beliefs and practices, al-Ghazali introduced sentiments and inner experience and knowledge of the self, which he called *fiqh al-nafs*, into mainstream orthodox discourse. Al-Ghazali's motivation was to inject spirituality into positive law (fiqh) by "infusing mysticism and ethics" and taking law "out of the narration of justice" to inscribe it "in mystical authority." Though not rejecting the exteriority of positive law (fiqh), he made inner disposition a necessary condition for the efficacy of the law and for the attainment of equilibrium and happiness in this world and the next. Although he rejected as un-Islamic and unauthorized certain aspects of Sufism, such as union and incarnation with God, he nonetheless integrated the mystical experience and inner awareness of Sufism into the mainstream definition of a true Muslim.[18] In ʿAbduh's age, the concept of the self had a different function and acquired a different meaning. Unfolding within the context of a secular colonial order that insisted on describing religions as fundamentally "irrational," ʿAbduh's response was to prove that neither the Islamic tradition nor Muslims are inevitably nonrational and accordingly that Europe's model of secularism was not necessary for Egypt. Located in this setting, ʿAbduh, one might conclude, was compelled to give more credence than did al-Ghazali to reason (ʿaql) in the cultivation of the inner self.[19] While stressing the significance of interiority by engaging al-Ghazali's hermeneutics of the self and the cultivation of inner disposition, or *tasdiq bil-wijdan* (conviction through inner experience), ʿAbduh at the same time injected the Muʿtazila formulation of ʿaql—with its view that rationality was an equal source to nass (Revelation) in ascertaining worldly truth, making laws, and judging right from wrong—into his understanding of interiority.[20] By incorporating the Muʿtazila concept of reasoning into al-Ghazali's "hermeneutics of the self," ʿAbduh gave interiority a different meaning than did al-Ghazali. Moreover, ʿAbduh's objective is clearly different, as he was compelled to reconceptualize an Islamic subjectivity compatible with capitalist modernity and its institutions and attitudes, rather than to challenge the formalism and positivism of speculative theology.[21] Unlike al-Ghazali, who used the metaphoric term *fiqh al-nafs* (discernment of the self), linking law (fiqh) and inner self (nafs) and describing the act of discernment of the self as one of *taffaquh* (ability to discern), in ʿAbduh's lexicon ʿaql (reasoning), *ʿaqqala*, and *taʿaqqala* replaced *fiqh*, *faqqaha*, and *taffaquh* to explain the process of interiority and self-intelligibility and its relation to sharʿ (law).[22]

It is worth noting at the same time the difference between ʿAbduh's view of interiority of the subject and a European liberal understanding. Within the European liberal tradition, subjectivity or the interior domain of the private (emotions, individual experience, belief) is conceived of as separate from the exterior public domain of polity and economy (citizenship, self-interest, and universal reason). Within this binary construct, relations between free and sovereign individuals within the public (exterior) domain are contractual and governed by law in contrast to the private (interior) sphere of the family and religion, where relations are governed by obligation and duty. In contrast to the construction of the private/public spheres as oppositional and separate in modern Europe, private/public relations in 'Abduh's imaginary are more nebulous than distinct, more hybrid than binary. This, I argue, is because interiority in the Islamic discourse assumes that the essence of the law is located within the self, which also means that whereas subjectivity allows a space for the private self of a subject, ethics (integral to the law) binds the subject to the community through the subject's external actions (*mu'amalat*). Coming from this perspective, it is simply not possible for a Muslim subject, even a modern one, to cultivate a moral self as an autonomous agent. A Muslim realizes his or her righteous self through a living collective, an umma bound together by agreed upon authorized rights and social obligations. Only through a Muslim community sustained by the acceptance of authorized practices and beliefs can the good be identified and pursued. Unlike the dominant conception of the good life within liberalism, where acts are conceived atomistically and where the separation between the self and social roles is assumed, a community is essential for the realization of a Muslim subject.

As a Muslim, 'Abduh would never have assumed that an individual could realize his or her moral self outside the context of the Muslim collective, the community. As with other Muslims, he, too, presumed the individual's embeddedness within a community of believers. The principal driving force of Islam, as he repeatedly argued, was the establishment of a harmonious moral community through the promotion of public good and the shunning of public harm. Though sharing earlier reformers' concept of an embedded self, 'Abduh's proposed Muslim self was necessarily different, for, as a product of the contemporary age, this self had to be capable of incorporation into modern institutions of power and governance. On the other hand, this modern subject would also have to be fundamentally different from the one propounded by colonial modernity.

'Abduh's strategy for reform shaped his approach to modernizing Egyptian society. The strategy emphasized the transformation of individual values and dispositions through the institutions of education, the courts, and the family. This strategy was very much in line with the concept of interiority and the cultivation of a new Islamic subjectivity. His approach to change, starting at the micro-level of first cultivating a new generation of Muslim subjects, led him to break with his mentor, al-Afghani, for advocating reform from the top down, primarily through political means. To ʿAbduh, reform of politics and government should follow from the revival first of the individuals of the community. He thus claimed that his own reform strategy predicated on the Quranic verse (13:11) "Verily, God does not change men's condition unless they change their inner selves" would produce change that was far more solid and long-lasting.[23]

In what follows, I will exemplify the two-sided nature of the attempt to construct a new Muslim subject by looking at ʿAbduh's reform project in regard to three institutions that he thought were crucial for putting this vision of a revived Islam into practice: education, the family, and the Islamic courts. I will conclude by discussing ʿAbduh's activity as a grand mufti and head of the institution of *dar al-iftaʾ*, which opened a new space for him to introduce his own rulings and to set precedents through his legal opinions—that is, his *fatawa*. Other than contributing to an expanding rich literature on Islamic fatawa, the discussion of his legal opinions will help shed further light on how the *fatawa* evolved into an effective instrument for inserting Islamic law into the public domain and for institutionalizing a reformed Islam as a regulator of social relations. Finally, as "radical" *fatawa*, they present a tangible example of how Muslims, like ʿAbduh, came to (unintentionally) subvert the workings of both older forms of religious authority and new forms of colonial power.

Education and Pedagogy: *al-taʿlim wal-tarbiya*

Like those reformers who preceded him, ʿAbduh considered education the only way to lift up Muslims from their state of degeneration and decline. In a series of articles on education and pedagogy (*al-taʿlim wal-tarbiya*) in Egypt, he linked religious training and knowledge to the newer forms and structures of learning. He advocated centralizing the existing multiple systems of education, placing them within a unified system that combined the teaching of religious as well as secular and scientific subjects.

Again, working from the Islamic analytic of the mean (mizan), ʿAbduh identified the predicament of education in Egypt (and other

Muslim countries) to lie in extremes: ineffective religious schooling headed by al-Azhar, on the one hand, and Europeanized education in missionary and government schools, on the other. The religious schools, he complained, were producing a class of uneducated, unrefined Muslim subjects whose close-mindedness (as practitioners of taqlid) rendered them ineffective and useless in the face of changing conditions. The missionaries teaching Muslim students Christianity, foreign curriculum and foreign languages led them to be dependent on foreign culture and nations and to be estranged from their own. The public educational program was the worst, because it reproduced European educational models that taught only secular subjects, thus failing to train the students in basic moral standards (which had at least been taught by the missionaries). The outcome, he thought, was as disastrous as the religious schooling system, because it produced Europeanized Egyptians, aliens to their culture, history, and religion. Even more detrimental, these two diametrically divergent systems of education created a deeply bifurcated and divisive culture.[24]

The cure for such a polarized culture was to create a more balanced and harmonious society through educational reform in which these extremes would be modified and then unified. Public education, ʿAbduh suggested, must integrate religious studies and Islamic pedagogy in its secular curriculum because the construction of a judicious productive Muslim of a refined character was possible only through the framework of religious training and through the acquisition of Islamic virtues. The validity of Islam, he stressed, was not a principle detached from social life but a potent factor in the collective activities of the community. As a way of life, religion must be part of public education.

It is important to note that ʿAbduh could not have envisioned the construction of a Muslim self outside the context of modern formal education and forms of pedagogy. Public education was the road to building an Egyptian nation on equal footing with the European nations. To play its role in creating a large educated public, education, he insisted, must be free and available for every member of the society, poor and rich. Without free education, it would be most difficult to modernize Egypt and elevate its subjects to the political and productive levels required of an advanced nation.[25] Every force, he argued, should be employed to install free education. In his criticism, he targeted the British administration and Lord Cromer, in particular, for first instituting and then raising tuition, making

it difficult for the poor as well as women to have access to proper education.[26] Though not objecting to private education, he strongly recommended that public education go back to being free, as it was before the
British came to Egypt. By comparison, the current conditions were described as pitiful, with "the spectacle of fathers and mothers of families
bringing their little boys to the ministry of education asking as a favor
that they may be accepted free, invoking their poverty . . . hoping always
that Providence or pity will relax the rules for once" and ultimately forced
to return to homes and villages "deceived, disheartened and discontented
not knowing what to do with their little children for whom they had
dreamed so many things."[27]

'Abduh was cognizant of the difficulty of attaining cultural and
educational regeneration under the shadow of a colonial power that sought
to restrict education. He also blamed the ruling khedives of Egypt for
initiating this decentralized secular pedagogical system that was incompatible with Egyptian culture. In his writings, he repeatedly raised doubts
about the qualification of the teachers and the methods of pedagogy, and
he criticized the educational program for offering only secular subjects.
His earlier writings in *al-Waqai' al-Misriya* stressed the need for centralization, better supervision, and inclusion of religious studies in government schools. He proposed that the government create a special supervisory
board, consisting of local educators, to inspect the schools and take measures to improve education. It is therefore not surprising that when the
Higher Council for the Department of Education was created to implement the centralization of general education, 'Abduh was one of the first
recruited to serve on its advisory subcommittee. Nor is it surprising that
one of the earliest submitted recommendations of this committee was the
placement of all schools, including missionary schools, under the supervision of the Department of Education. The recommendation generated
strong objections from the missionaries, the British, and local supporters
and was, as a result, never taken up.

'Abduh was particularly concerned with extending education beyond the privileged and the rich (*al-khawas*) to include the commoners
(*al-'amma*), the larger part of the population, and to prepare them to participate more effectively in modern economy and polity. Whereas specialized higher education targeted the middle classes and the rich, the
objective of elementary schools was to educate and civilize the laboring

classes by lifting them up from their state of material and moral poverty and depravity. It becomes clear from his writing that ʿAbduh extended the Islamic concept of cultivating proper Muslims to also include educating and training individuals of the "laboring classes" to become self-directing and capable not only of managing their own affairs but also of participating more effectively in the new economy and in the decision-making processes expected of them as members of the new nation. Different from the *madrasa*, the objective of public elementary education, other than inculcating Islamic values, was to teach the preliminary reading, writing, and basic math that would enable a peasant, for example, to keep a written record of his accounts (buying, selling, etc.) and encourage him to become less dependent on others in the management of his daily affairs.[28]

In the several articles addressing this topic, ʿAbduh connected the Islamic reform project of educating and improving the lower classes (peasants, workers, and craftsmen) to the efficacy of a national economy. He was convinced that educating the lower classes would marshal higher productivity in agriculture as well as encourage the development of industry and trade. Other than Islamic pedagogy and training, he stressed the need for teaching modern subjects that would include secular topics such as the humanities as well as science and technology. In "What Is the True Cause of Poverty in Egypt?" he depicted a country rich in resources but poor in resourcefulness and scientific expertise to effectively exploit its wealth. He attributed the poverty of Egypt to the absence of Egyptians learned in modern sciences. What contributed to the economic stagnation of Egypt, he explained, were the overwhelming levels of general ignorance as well as the absence of appropriate training in the aforementioned fields. Therefore, education—including elementary, secondary, and higher forms of specialization—must include modern Western sciences and technologies, for all were essential in bringing forth the development and advancement of Egypt.[29]

In addition to these important material benefits, as ʿAbduh stated in a public speech, proper educational and Islamic pedagogical training would cultivate the minds of commoners by improving their mental abilities (*irtiqaʾ al-ʿaql*), enabling them to rationally distinguish the good and beneficial (maslaha) from the harmful (*mufsid*) and destructive. The peasants would gain from developing self-reflectivity and sound judgment, especially when settling conflicts and hostilities familiar to the countryside.

Normally, he explained, these hostilities would lead to vengeance, blood-shed, and destruction of wealth and property, all because the wronged parties lacked the ability to think calmly and rationally and discern the difference between what is right and what is wrong. That is why, he con-cluded, secular education (*ta'alim*) must be "accompanied with religious training (tarbiya and tahdhib) and the cultivation of good morals, includ-ing piety and truthfulness (*al-sidq wal a-amana*), the two virtues essential for constructing a healthy and harmonious community."[30]

In the introduction to his tafsir, or commentary, on the Qur'an, 'Abduh states that although the Qur'an was revealed at a particular time, its message was not to the "few and the select" but to all humankind, as indicated in the verse that started *surat al-Nisa* (Women): "O [Hu]man-kind! Be conscious of your Sustainer" (3:1):

Is it not obvious from this verse that God has intended that we comprehend for ourselves the meaning of the Revelation rather than follow or depend on others to explain it to us? It is the duty of every individual (*wajaba 'ala kulli wahid*) to try and grasp the Words of God on his own—notwithstanding his abilities. [The Qur'an] does not differentiate between a '*alim* and unlettered person. It is sufficient [for God] when a commoner understands His [transparent] words: "Truly, to a happy state shall attain the believer: Those who humble themselves in their prayer." (23:1–2)[31]

'Abduh raised a similar point in his exegesis of *juzu' 'amma*, in which he called it the duty of every faithful Muslim to pursue the right to reason independently of others: "A Muslim should exert the greatest effort in search of the truth in this world and to investigate thoroughly and re-lentlessly all avenues within his reach and in accordance with his ability. It is the duty of a rational Muslim to present his argument (for or against) coherently by giving clear and precise evidence."[32] Promoting public good (maslaha) was an individual duty (fard 'ayn) mandated on every member of the community and was not a general duty (fard kifaya) to be suffi-ciently discharged when performed by certain members of the commu-nity (i.e., the 'ulama) on behalf of the rest. Although this duty presupposed a certain degree of religious knowledge, he argued that this knowledge could be obtained by the individual directly from the Qur'an and the Sunna and did not require a specialized knowledge in law and theology (Islamic jurisprudence), as claimed by the established authority. Rather, it was the duty of every able Muslim subject to take the initiative to be informed and to seek directly the authoritative sources to make judgments about what would promote the good and prevent harm. Muslims, including commoners, according to ʿAbduh, are responsible not just for their own actions but also for decisions over the "goods" of the community. The one condition was that they be educated.

ʿAbduh's advocating the right of Islamic reasoning and decision making be broadened to include a wider public is often understood in the literature as a novel idea that was either created or imported. Clearly, I suggest that ʿAbduh's course of action became possible only with the extension of education to the general public as part of the process of restructuring Egyptian society. Without public education, Muslim thinkers and even most "liberals" would not have thought it acceptable or feasible to extend the right to interpret Islamic knowledge beyond the small clique of learned ʿulama, let alone envision its further extension to include women generations later.

Even though the extension of individual obligations (fard ʿayn) opened up the space for the emergence of a *modern* Muslim subject capable of reasoning and judging for him- or herself, it would be wrong to assume that ʿAbduh was seeking a liberal understanding of the self, in which an individual is seen "neither as a moral whole, nor as part of a larger social whole, but as an owner of himself."[33] The rights extended to individual Muslims are meant to promote and benefit the community as a collective, rather than to advance the selfish interests of its individual members. As members of the community, individuals are accountable not only to themselves for their beliefs and actions. Rather, they must also be accountable to others, while, by the same token, also putting others' beliefs and actions into question. It is with this context in mind that ʿAbduh made reference to the term *maslaha* to explain the communal feature of the good life within the Islamic tradition.

It should not surprise us, therefore, that ʿAbduh would mobilize a modern yet Islamically imbued concept of public benefit (*al-nafʿ al-ʿamm*) to refer to the moral well-being of the Muslim community as well as the well-being and progress of the Egyptian nation. Love of one's nation, as he put it, is closely connected to Muslim virtue, for a good Muslim seeks to advance himself or herself only insofar as personal advancement contributes to the uplifting of the nation.[34] He defined *al-wataniya* (nationalism) not as "meaningless rhetoric and emotional nonsense" but as "a balanced world view, one [that values] good morals (*akhlaq*) and mores (*'adat*), healthy bodies, and cherishes and uplifts the nation . . . [and where] every virtuous individual (*sahib fadila*) is one who has the public good (*nafa' 'amm*) in mind."[35]

Nevertheless, in keeping with his view of morality, 'Abduh's definition of *wataniya* rejects the utilitarian concept of public good. Individuals seeking only their own self-interest cannot achieve the greatest good. Instead, Egyptians must be able to consider their own good within the context of the general good. The theme of this correlative relationship between the individual and the community is repeated again in "Pedagogy Is What Makes a Person a Muslim and a Community an Umma," a speech delivered in front of the Benevolent Muslim Society and later published as an article in *al-Manar*. In it, 'Abduh discusses the role of Islamic pedagogy in the construction of moral subjects as a means toward building a virtuous, productive nation.[36] His central thesis is that because morality is learned and not a natural phenomenon, Islamic pedagogy and training should be an essential feature of public education.[37] An enlightened healthy person, he says, "is one who is trained to be honest, sincere and loving, first of himself and then of others. To love others, one has to start by loving and appreciating oneself."[38] All agree that only through [religious] learning is "a person able to attain happiness and share it with others. Yet today we are living in a state of mind where each and every one of us feels despondent and miserable within ourselves and toward others, where trust has dissipated into thin air leaving behind feelings of misgivings, of uncertainty and distrust."[39] Despite all its richness and natural wealth, Egyptian society, he maintained, is suffering from the worst poverty of all, poverty of education and poverty of morality (*faqr al-'aql wal-tarbiya*)—a condition, he insisted, that is not correctable simply by the enforcement of legal and criminal laws that neither educate communities nor reform living conditions.[40]

It is not state laws but Islamic pedagogy, 'Abduh emphasized, that trains individuals, males and females, to become upstanding subjects with refined characters. Islamic education teaches Muslims, regardless of gender, to bond with one another and trains them to develop strong feelings for each other: "God has created us as social beings desirous of creating social bonds with one another; these bonds start in families and branch out to other parts of the society until they are rooted in the nation and the larger Community of Muslims."[41] The relationship of the individual to the community is analogous to "a fruit-bearing tree where the roots, branches, leaves and trunk together come together to produce the fruit." The same is true for Muslims desiring to produce a morally guided community, because without individual and collective effort, "all hope becomes hopeless and all wishes become illusionary dreams."[42]

It is clear from the above that 'Abduh regarded religion as the key for defining individual and communal morality. 'Abduh was vehemently against the dismantling of religion as a regulator of social morality (via the institutions of the family and education). He opposed the colonial administration for intending to dislodge religion from its public functions and insisting on creating a civic society in which morality is a private matter. To 'Abduh, religion provided the moral foundation for the creation and advancement of a modern independent Egypt. The task of lifting the Egyptian nation from a state of "backwardness" to a higher level of advancement, he maintained, was not simply a matter of imitating the West, but one involving the moral regeneration of the people based on the enduring values of religion.

What 'Abduh opposed, in other words, was liberal secularism and its confinement of religion to the private sphere. In particular, he had misgivings about the replacement of an Islamic order founded on a moral community with a European one organized around autonomous political subjects and a society driven by material interests detached from a system of Islamic ethics. This is understandable considering that the Muslim conception of life and selfhood is strikingly at odds with that of a liberal self. Rather than aspiring to be autonomous and self-constitutive, a Muslim subject strives to be good and virtuous by belonging to a particular community where individuals are identified and constituted in and through a set of given beliefs and assigned practices.

To put it somewhat differently, the survival of a moral community was what 'Abduh and other Muslims of his age feared was at stake. What they resisted was not Europe's modernizing features (e.g., nation-state, science and technology, and capitalist economy) but its banishment of religion to the private sphere and its separation of morality from law.[43] To seek an alternative to the secular liberal tradition, 'Abduh relied not only on the Islamic discursive tradition but also on a plan to modernize the institutions most responsible for making this new subject, Islamic courts and the family.

Family and Morality

In line with his strategy of first reviving a Muslim subject, 'Abduh placed huge importance on the family as a site for moral development. Of course, within the Islamic tradition, the family has always played an important role in the inculcation of religion, as parents were expected to take responsibility for their children's religious training. However, in Abduh's view, much more was now required. In particular, the relationships among family members would have to be rearranged so that the younger generation of children would now learn how to be civil, rational, and meritocratic individuals not only by direct teaching but also through their experiences within family relations, by observing how parents relate to each other, and through the example set by their parents in how they interact with their children.

Children's moral development—the inculcation of self-reliance, self-regulation, and concern for the public good—similarly requires that parents model these key aspects of modern subjectivity. Inscribed within new familial relations, children would come to internalize new norms and dispositions that, although remaining Islamic, would enable them to participate more fully under the new social order.

'Abduh's ideas for family reform were not novel to his times, as the reorganization of the family had occupied the minds of other reformers since the dawn of the nineteenth century. The restructuring of Egyptian society and economy under Muhammad 'Ali in the first half of the century required family arrangements and norms more sensitive to the mores and desires of a newly rising middle class. Preceding 'Abduh's age, for instance, the Muslim reformer and educator Rifa'a al-Tahtawi had tackled some of these issues in a series of articles that appeared between 1874 and 1875 in the journal *Rawdat al-Madaris*. Al-Tahtawi discussed a variety of subjects, including the right of girls to public education, the importance of romantic love in marriage, new approaches to parenting, the right of women to work, and the interiority of modesty as a virtue to be inculcated by both females and males alike rather than as an external form of action enforced through sex segregation and veiling.[44]

Companionate Marriage

As older forms of family life—of extended households, arranged marriages, and polygamy—were no longer envisioned as suitable for the present state of affairs, 'Abduh imagined the future family to be both nuclear (*aila*) and monogamous; marriage would be founded on love (*mahaba*), compassion (*rahma*), and mutual respect between two adult individuals. Although his vision of the family might conjure up images of the companionate marriage that came to define "modern" European family life in the early twentieth century, 'Abduh's arguments for changed marriage relations were not rooted in claims about the abstract and "natural" rights of individuals. Although he argued for women to have rights, he explained these rights as congruent with the teachings of Islam, which he maintained give women equal rights when properly interpreted and enforced.

'Abduh invoked the Qur'an and the Prophetic Sunna to rebut current rulings and practices, some of which he considered appalling digressions, such as the "legal" designation of marriage as a "contract under which a man comes to possess a woman's genitalia."[45] As against contemporary practices, the Qur'an, he suggested, commended companionate marriage in the following verse: "God creates for you mates out of your own kind, so that you might incline towards them, and He engenders love and tenderness between you" (30:21). Although Revelation sanctioned a marriage of compassion and love, the jurists endorsed instead marriages that "permitted men to seek pleasure in women's bodies."[46] These beliefs and practices, he added, not only degraded the inviolability of marriage, but also robbed women of their humanity and stripped them of the categorical rights given to them by the shar'. Hence, Islam was not to blame for the present sad state of women, as the Europeans and Europeanized Egyptians claimed. Rather, it was these conventions and inherited customs, sanctioned by uninformed and ignorant jurists, that perpetuated women's degradation, ignorance, and oppression. To restore more balanced and harmonious relations between spouses, these practices and rulings would have to be abrogated and replaced by rules and regulations that promote marriages of loving companions, as authorized by the Qur'an and the Prophetic Sunna.

As one of the prerequisites for a marriage of loving companions is that partners not commit themselves to marriage before being sure of their feelings for one another, 'Abduh recommended that the practice of arranged marriage be discarded, because it presumed that couples do not have to know or love one another before marriage. A marriage contracted without the partners ever having a chance to meet, speak, or approve of one another would inevitably lead to a marriage full of misery and unhappiness, where "arguments and quarrels prevail all the time, with or without a cause, day or night, and even in bed."[47] A natural consequence of constant fighting in a loveless marriage was that both wife and husband would neglect their duties toward one another and toward their children.

It is clear from his writing that 'Abduh's argument against arranged marriage hinges on the notion that arranged marriage was utterly and completely incompatible with modern subjectivity, as a sensible Muslim subject is expected to take responsibility for his or her own life. He strongly criticized the practice of arranged marriage as "unreasonable," especially because the parents or extended kin, not the individuals involved, make this crucial decision. How can any reasonable person, he asked, expect a man and a woman to wed for life "without being acquainted or even faintly attracted to each another?" Yet, custom had dictated that even the wisest of men who would ordinarily "not purchase a sheep or a donkey before seeing and carefully examining it . . . flippantly, recklessly, and unreflectively enter into a long-term marriage arranged by others. . . . Such [conduct] is indeed stupefying."[48] Arranged marriage discourages the young from taking control over their lives by enforcing the custom of obeying received authority instead of holding themselves responsible for their actions.

Reflecting on changing attitudes, 'Abduh acknowledged the spread of dissatisfaction among the younger generation of professionals and educated men with the state of loveless, arranged marriages. Having acquired different tastes, desires, and expectations, an increasing number of this educated and refined young generation of men

prefer bachelorhood to marriage because they recognize that the institution of marriage in its present state would not be able to fulfill their dreams. Many of them have refused to marry because they would not allow themselves to be committed to a wife that they have never seen. What they desire in a wife is a companion and a friend, one who they would love and have her love them back. They are not searching for a woman to serve them at all times, but are in want of a wife who is educated and experienced and is capable of being a good mother for their children, to raise physically and morally healthy, well-mannered children.[49]

Though recognizing the grave effects on men, 'Abduh was most critical of older arrangements for disciplining women into submission and compliance with authority. Young women, he admitted, were much worse off than men, because they were married off without even their knowledge, let alone their consent.[50] These old customs discouraged a young woman from "disclosing what she feels deep in her heart, instructing her against having an opinion of her own. For people considered it improper for a young female to have a voice even when the decision is crucial for her life. It authorized even her kin relations, both close and far, to have an opinion on this matter but not her."[51] Such attitudes and practices, 'Abduh maintained, were in stark violation of [Islamic] law since women were granted rights equal to those given to the men in such matters, for the Qur'an states that "in accordance with justice, the rights of wives [with regard to their husband] are equal to [the husbands'] right with regard to them" (3:228); "and consort with your wives in goodly manner (in kindness)" (4:19). In contrast to established conventions, the Qur'an has high regard for women and urges Muslims to respect their rights and be kind to and thoughtful of them.[52]

'Abduh recommended new courting practices that would facilitate situations in which young partners could meet and come to know each other before marriage, so that they could decide "whether they are physically attracted to one another to begin with."[53] Although physical or emotional attraction was fundamental to successful married life, physical attraction alone, he warned, would not be enough to sustain a happy, long-lasting relationship. The couple must ensure their compatibility, because *tawafuq* (suitability) or having matching tastes, preferences, and temperaments is also essential for solidifying the bonds of marriage and enabling the couple to become friends and companions for one another, especially with the natural waning of sexual passion due to age and familiarity.[54]

At the same time, 'Abduh recognized that as long as women persisted in their present state of ignorance, the current inequitable gender structures would continue and "men and husbands will continue to tyr-annize their women and wives."[55] The inferior status of women would change only through education, for "women have to learn to take them-selves seriously, educate themselves of their rights, and fight for their equality. Only then would marriage become the institution that can bring happiness and sustain a loving marital relation based on physical, intel-lectual, and spiritual attraction."[56] The source of women's empowerment, he argued, was education. It was only through education that a woman could acquire her voice and become an independent thinking person, able to make the right decisions over who she wants to marry and live with. Education (i.e., formal education) would enable this younger generation of women to "earn the respect they deserve from their respective families over who they are to marry without fearing their anger or criticism."[57]

Although it was the individual's right to decide whom to love, marry, and live with, such a right had to be enforced, and regulated, by the shari'a court. Accordingly, 'Abduh recommended formalizing mar-riage contracts and requiring couples to appear in court and to bear wit-ness in front of a judge or marriage officer, verifying their desire to marry. This reform represented a shift from private and familial to public and legal regulation of marriage; requiring the couple's testimony as to their wishes and transferring marriage contracts to the courts undermined cus-tomary parental authority and increased the authority of the law and the courts in regulating family and personal affairs.

Polygamy and Sex Segregation

The new companionate marriage founded on love was also to be monogamous. 'Abduh argued against polygamous marriages and consid-ered "co-wife-ing" intrinsically incompatible with the nature of marital love because neither a man nor a woman is able to love more than one other person at a time. He called for the banning of this practice on the basis that it was disruptive of the social order, creating discord and con-flict within the family and beyond, while simultaneously precipitating the further degradation and humiliation of women.[58] Although the four legal schools allowed polygamy, 'Abduh justified its prohibition on the basis that the practice of polygamy is counter to public welfare (maslaha).

His argument goes as follows: in the Qur'an, polygamy is, to begin with, a conditional right; a man is permitted to marry more than one wife and up to four, contingent on the fact that he can love and provide for them equally, a task impossible for any man to attain no matter how just, loving, and caring he may be. From 'Abduh's perspective, the shari'a privileges monogamy and forbids polygamy except in very exceptional circumstances, as when a wife is barren (and only with her permission). 'Abduh maintained that Muslims had been misled by their jurists when they were told that polygamy was permitted, for the Qur'an emphatically warns against it: "marry from among women such as are lawful to you—two, or three or four: but if you have reason to fear that you might not be able to treat them with equal fairness, then [only] one" (4:3); "and it will not be within your power to treat your wives with equal fairness, however much you may desire it" (4:129). It is clear that these verses "intend not to encourage but discourage and restrict [polygamy's] practice."[59] In the first verse, "God [allowing up to four wives] restricted marriage to one for fear of injustice. In the second verse, He declared justice impossible to attain in a polygamous situation. Thus, one can easily conclude from reading these verses that polygamy should be prohibited."[60] The master jurists permit it, but only when justice is guaranteed. However, due to the laxity in enforcing the second half of this ruling, 'Abduh maintained, the practice had led instead to the spread of abuse and to the degenerate state of marriage at this time.[61]

The practice of polygamy, he argued, was especially degrading to women because it pitted women against one another. It also implied contempt and disrespect for them because no "respectable and reasonable woman would want to share a husband with another, just as no man would ever allow the love of another man for his wife."[62] Moreover, polygamy had always been a source of conflict among wives or between husbands and wives, producing misery for the immediate family as well as the extended family. Whoever claimed that women were accepting of this practice seemed to be ignorant of their suffering and pain. Even when a woman appears to be content, rare as this is, it is only because she has internalized the idea that she is the property of her husband, to do with her as he wishes.

Considering the individual and collective harm incurred by the practice of polygamy, 'Abduh called for the prohibition of polygamy on the basis of its harmful effects on the social fabric of society. As he explained:

This ruling paralleled many others in the shariʿa where rulings were evaluated in terms of relative harm and benefit to the community. But when injustice becomes paramount, leading to general discord and to the moral degeneracy and collapse of families, as was clearly the case in our contemporary culture, it would be permissible for those in charge to legislate laws to prohibit the continuous practice of polygamy conditionally or unconditionally under the principal Islamic rule of protecting public welfare (*riʿaya lil-maslaha al-ʿamma*).[63]

Although ʿAbduh did not emphasize the connection between marital reform and reformed child-rearing practices in his own work, the link between the two was made by others, including Qasim Amin, as will be discussed in the following chapter. Just as ʿAbduh considered that companionate marriage would work only when women as well as men were educated, self-reliant, and self-governing, he suggested that proper mothering required women who could think for themselves, for only such women would be able to inculcate civility and self-reliance in their children.

Considering what has been said so far, one would hardly be surprised to learn that ʿAbduh argued against sex segregation and veiling (*niqab*) as incompatible with sensibilities at this time. ʿAbduh rejected the traditional justification for veiling and segregation as measures necessary to ensure modesty. In his view, to rely on separation to promote modesty implied that women and men were not capable of internalizing modesty and of disciplining and training their bodies and desires. In the context of the present, he argued, the public good could be secured only by individuals capable of exercising self-control, individuals who would be guided by an internalized moral system and who understood the connection between their own self-discipline and the achievement of a good society. Segregation and veiling worked in the opposite direction, relying on external power rather than on internal disciplining of desires. To support his stance against segregation and veiling, ʿAbduh argued that in the Qurʾan the injunction to be modest was addressed in identical terms to men and women: "tell the believing men to lower their gaze and to be mindful of their chastity: this will be most conducive to their purity [and], verily, God is aware of all they do. And tell the believing women to lower their gaze and be mindful of their chastity, and not display their charms [in public] beyond what may [decently] be apparent thereof; hence let them draw their head coverings [*khimar*] over their bosoms" (24:30–31).[64]

Divorce

'Abduh approached divorce reform with the same principles that infused his attitude toward marriage. He argued that divorce should be a formal process regulated by the courts, forcing men to be responsible and giving women protection from arbitrary decisions by their husbands. Further, he proposed that women had an equal right to divorce, arguing that this right should be inscribed into all marriage contracts.[65]

Commenting on the current abuses, 'Abduh noted the following:

We live in a time when men have made a joke of the divorce statement. They play with the chastity of their women as though it was a toy in their hands to do with it as they wish. Such men show no respect for the legal system nor do they have any regard for their wives. It is not uncommon to hear a man in public disputation with another threaten him with: "my wife is divorced if you do not do such and such . . . [in the meanwhile] the wife having no knowledge of or say in the matter finds herself divorced."[66]

'Abduh gives examples of many divorces occurring by the mere utterance of the word *divorce*, without true intent on the part of the husbands. Why, he asks, is "divorce without the intent to separate" so prevalent when the Prophet has clearly stated: "Intentions are the basis for evaluating actions"?[67] Why is it that when our men suffer from moral corruption, unreflective foolishness, and irresponsible behavior, "no heed is paid to intentions, should we not try to understand the ideas of our religious leaders, who declare that there should be witnesses in order for divorce to be legitimate, just as in marriage. Al-Tubrusi mentions this idea, and it appears in the Qur'an in the verses of the chapter on divorce, which advise: and call to witness two just men among you."[68]

To regulate and formalize divorce, 'Abduh suggested the following procedures: every husband must appear in court to state his intent; the judge or the *mazun* (equivalent to a marriage minister) advises him on what the Qur'an and the hadith have to say and reminds him that divorce is a deleterious act. He then is given an extra week to decide. If the husband persists, the judge or the marriage official picks an arbitrator from each side of the family or assigns outsiders to arbitrate between husband and wife in an attempt to reconcile them. If arbitration fails, then divorce procedures may go forward. No divorce would be legal until a judge or marriage officer has signed the divorce papers with witnesses present, and divorce will not be enacted without this official document. These regulations, he maintained, "would agree with the verses in God's Book and would take into consideration the welfare of the people involved. How do we know that God, may He [be] praised and exalted, did not see the kind of society our nation would become and reveal this precious verse to provide us with a rule to which we could refer when necessary? Our present condition necessitates the application of this rule."[69]

Although regulating men's access to divorce would improve women's status in marriage and in society, 'Abduh argued, the better guarantee of women's position would be to grant them the right to initiate divorce. Again, he suggested two approaches that would be possible within the boundaries of Islamic shari'a. Following his method of analyzing the four legal schools to develop what he considered might be a sensible regulation more suitable to modern conditions, 'Abduh explored the Maliki position, which explicitly granted women the right to divorce by decreeing that a woman could appeal to the judge on evidence of harm with or without her husband's permission, with or without the clause in the marriage contract giving her the power to divorce. The second possibility would be for all marriage contracts to include a conditional clause giving women the right to initiate divorce, a condition already accepted by all four schools. Of the two approaches, 'Abduh preferred the second, because it gives the woman the power to exercise the right of divorce instead of placing it in the hands of a jurist, as in the Maliki position. According to the Maliki law, a woman cannot complete a divorce without the approval of the judge who either signs the divorce papers on her behalf or else has her sign it herself. In either case, however, the woman is still at the mercy of the judge and dependent on someone else to exercise decisions over her life. Another problem with the Maliki rulings, 'Abduh disclosed, was that it would not allow a woman to claim harm (and hence the right to divorce) on the grounds of the husband taking another wife.[70]

By inscribing the woman's right to end the marriage in the marital contract, the courts would allow a woman to initiate divorce whenever she

wishes or when her husband marries another woman. Allowing women
the right to divorce supported 'Abduh's idea of a companionate marriage
by giving women the capacity to make their own judgments about their
relationships and granting them more control over their lives. Thus, even
if extending the right to divorce to women had the potential to increase
divorce rates, he pointed out, the benefits to public welfare far outweighed
this potential harm. As 'Abduh put it, "entrusting women with the right
to divorce is to bring about a just and humane condition to women who
have suffered great injustice at the hands of a great number of men. My
hope is that my not so popular voice would move honorable and powerful
men of my nation to come to the rescue of these weak, long-suffering and
oppressed (*maqhurat*) women."[71]

It is important to note in conclusion that many of the suggestions
'Abduh made regarding formalizing marriage and divorce and regulating
polygamy were later instated into the family court system. In 1897, the
Egyptian Code of Organization and Procedure for Shari'a Courts officially instated written documentations in marriage, divorce, and certain
inheritance claims, thus invalidating oral contracts.[72]

Reform of the Islamic Family Courts

In 1899, the same year he was appointed grand mufti, 'Abduh submitted to the government a report based on a year's investigation of the
Islamic courts. His recommendations on modernizing the shari'a courts
largely focused on issues relating to centralizing, standardizing, and pro-
fessionalizing the court system. On the surface, the reforms he suggested
appeared to be procedural and technical in nature, dealing with issues
that ranged from providing better housing conditions for the courts, to
improving the standard of education of all court employees, including
judges, increasing and standardizing salaries, expediting the hearing of
cases, improving records, and simplifying the language and structure of
litigation. Yet, far from being superficial, these recommendations were
part of a larger process of modernizing the system of justice and rule of
law, centered on the standardization, unification, and consistent application of codified legal principles. In fact, the creation of a system to police
and enforce the law lay at the heart of 'Abduh's proposed legal reforms

and his attempt to create Muslim subjects more consonant with conditions required under modernity.

In approaching the reform of the family courts, 'Abduh made clear his distance from some of the basic tenets of the liberal judicial system. It is worth noting, for example, that 'Abduh's critique of the status quo and his recommendations for change did not question the importance of shari'a law for the advancement of Egypt as a modern nation-state. Indeed, 'Abduh argued that the shari'a was essential to the regeneration of Egyptian society, because only a highly moral community would be capable of resisting colonization and of charting its own national path. Thus, 'Abduh did not assume that the application of the shari'a was in any way antithetical to the institution of the modern rule of law.

'Abduh begins his report by describing how social life is in danger of moral collapse and asserting that the restoration of morality depends on reforming and strengthening the family, especially among the lower classes. The Islamic courts should play a crucial role in regulating social norms through their influence on the family. It is precisely because the shari'a is so critical to creating and maintaining a moral Muslim society that reforming and strengthening the court system is so important.

Thus, it makes sense that 'Abduh hardly challenged the content of the shari'a other than suggesting the need for its codification. Instead, he brought forward compelling criticisms of the way the courts were administered and run. Egypt in its present state, 'Abduh proclaimed, was "a society without law." As with education, the existing legal system had deepened the polarization of the society by imposing two unsuitable and incompatible systems of justice: an archaic and cumbersome shari'a-based legal structure on one side and an alien imported European legal system on the other. Rather than dispensing justice, the present systems of law had instead induced a state of confusion and bigotry.

Historically, as a province of the Ottoman Empire, Egypt had been governed by an assortment of laws and institutions, which included, other than the Islamic law and courts that presided over the urban Muslim population, the *'urf*, or customary law, in the rural and tribal areas; the non-Muslim courts (*millet*) that ruled over the different Christian and Jewish sects; and the Ottoman imperial law (*qanun*) presiding over worldly and administrative matters ranging from security, land taxation, and surveillance of the markets to overseeing *al-mazalim* courts (nonreligious grievance courts). In an attempt to centralize and tighten its control over the empire, the Ottoman Porte in the nineteenth century embarked on a reorganization and modernization of its governance rules and modus operandi under what is commonly referred to in the literature as the *tanzimat*. Under this centralized system of governance, new civic and penal codes were introduced in the 1850s to replace the multifaceted legal systems in existence. The new codes were by and large modeled after European legal systems (mainly Swiss and French). The reform of the Islamic courts came later, between 1870 and 1877, when the Ottoman Porte attempted to codify and systematize the Islamic legal system by issuing a series of regulations and laws in the *majallah*. Although the newly codified Islamic law was implemented in many of the provinces of the empire, it was not applied to Egypt, as Egypt by then was in effect an Ottoman province in name only. At the same time, while this was happening across the Empire, Egypt was already undergoing change under European influence and political pressure. In the same year that the institution of the Caisse de la Dette Publique (1876) was set up in Egypt, the European powers also established the mixed court system, founded on the Napoleonic code, to adjudicate criminal and civic cases among Europeans residing in Egypt and between Europeans and Egyptians.[73] A year after occupying Egypt, the British set up native national courts (*al-Mahakim al-ahliya*) modeled after the mixed court system to rule over civil and criminal cases that previously had fallen under the jurisdiction of the shari'a courts. So by the time 'Abduh addressed the subject of reforming the Islamic courts, the shari'a was confined to family law and the administration of religious endowment, or *waqf*, which constituted the subject matter of his report.[74]

Though not absolving the British for employing European civil law, 'Abduh from the beginning focused his criticisms on the ruling khedives for initiating the transplant of European institutions and laws into Egypt prior to the arrival of the British. Laws brought from Europe, he insisted, were ineffective because no one understood them and very few abided by them. In the report, he even makes the claim that few Egyptians seek out the national (*ahliya*) courts and that most Muslims continue to go to Islamic courts to resolve their civil disputes, demonstrating that the shari'a continues to govern Egyptian lives.[75]

Arguing against the universal applicability of European laws, 'Abduh maintained that for a legal system to be effective and just in

Egypt, its laws must be able to relate to the conditions, standards, and culture of the society to which they apply. Otherwise, they fall short of fulfilling their essential function—regulating and disciplining human action and behavior. While stressing the need for a shariʿa-based law, ʿAbduh acknowledged that the present state of the Islamic courts deterred rather than imparted justice. His recommendations for reform, though largely procedural and technical, focusing on issues regarding centralization and homogenization of the courts and the professionalization of its staff, did nonetheless aim to change people's attitude toward the law. For the Islamic courts to become more effective within the new framework of the nation-state, it was necessary to establish a centralized hierarchical system with written fixed rules and regulations that would apply to all the courts. However, although ʿAbduh acknowledged that state intervention was required to put forward and administer these new regulatory policies, he insisted, at the same time, on the autonomy of Islamic jurisprudence and its independence from state control. While recommending the reform of the courts, ʿAbduh could not have imagined a shariʿa-derived law to be antithetical to modernity nor could he have embraced the idea of discarding it altogether.[76] Nor did he question the content of the shariʿa or its authority as a regulator of social morality. In his investigation, he focused primarily, as Asad argues, on the functionality of the courts rather than on the body of the law to which they ascribed. His suggestions had mainly to do with the codification and condensation of Islamic law, similar to the approach of the Ottomans in the majallah. Codification, he argued, would make the law more accessible and easier to comprehend and follow for those who practiced it as well as for those who enforced it. By upholding the Islamic view that the shariʿa is the source of the law, ʿAbduh, differently from what Skovgaard-Peterson and others conclude, was implicitly discarding the liberal European view that the state ought to be the source of law.[77] From ʿAbduh's perspective, the state's authority should be confined to administering and managing the courts but not to formulating the law.

Describing the appalling condition of the Islamic courts, ʿAbduh's report called upon the Egyptian state to undertake the initiative in a thorough-going program of restructuring the court system.[78] Horrified by the physical condition of the courts he visited, ʿAbduh bitingly states:

for the whereabouts of provincial courts, look for the poorest, most debilitated neighborhood and that is where you will find the court. . . . Judges and court employees are mostly housed in shabby houses with unpaved dirt floors that turns into mud once the staff splash it with water to contain the dust. . . . Some of these buildings are so run-down that they barely have a roof to speak of or a road to safely walk on. . . . I observed while people teetered over a palm tree branch to get to court. . . . How does one expect justice or fair judgments to be reached under these appalling conditions?[79]

He recommended that the government take charge of housing and managing the appropriate buildings of the courts. These buildings, he suggested further, must be spacious enough to include a large courtroom for litigation in addition to private quarters for the judges to retire to before and after their court sessions. A healthy working environment is the responsibility of the local government and the condition on which the judge, the scribe, and the plaintiff are guaranteed to respect and enforce the law.[80]

Other than improved buildings to house the courts, 'Abduh identified a need to standardize the qualifications and regulate the employment of all court employees. In the case of scribes who register a plaintiff's complaints, he suggested the following: (1) proper knowledge of the Arabic language, including the skills of clear writing, proper editing, and bookkeeping; (2) basic or preliminary knowledge of Islamic jurisprudence; and (3) that all applicants must pass a standard exam and that those who scored the highest be the ones selected for employment. For each of these points, 'Abduh stressed the connection between the reform of the courts and the reform of the general educational curricula in both the public school system as well as al-Azhar, where training students in such vital skills as composition, clear scribing, and basic math along with religious studies must be put into effect. He also called for the creation of specialized but different programs for training judges, scribes, and marriage officials. 'Abduh suggested new arrangements whereby scribes would be housed in offices with windows open to the public, which would ensure more formal relations by minimizing contact between the scribes and their public.[81] Additionally, 'Abduh gave a detailed account of what he considered to be the responsibilities of scribes and recommended the creation of a clear job description defining the responsibilities of scribes according to rank. Clearly written regulations and rules would create a work ethic that was absent in the courts at this time, as it would make the yearly evaluation of the employees much more feasible and just. Finally, he recommended that scribes become full-time government employees with a regular and reasonable monthly salary suitable to their rank.[82]

The creation of similar rules and regulations to monitor the judges and improve and centralize the administration of the courts was also recommended. Once again, the report described a state of disorder and corruption, of incompetent judges and poor and unjust judgments. These afflictions, 'Abduh warned, not only affected the Islamic courts; they prevailed in all the courts, including the secular ones.[83]

In describing the conditions of the Islamic courts, 'Abduh observed how poor conditions impair the judgment of even upright and good judges. Because the courts were so ineffective, some of the honorable judges were forced to out-of-court reconciliation (*sulh*) in order to avoid passing unenforceable verdicts that would leave the plaintiffs without justice. However, although reconciliation worked in a few cases, most out-of-court arrangements 'Abduh observed collapsed soon after being reached.[84]

New rules for the election process and the appointment of judges to their respective seats needed to be created. Qualifications for appointment must include, other than the fundamentals of Islamic jurisprudence relating to family law, some knowledge of Islamic law regarding transactions (mu'amalat) as well as the general knowledge required of an educated person (i.e., secular forms of knowledge, such as history, geography, and mathematics) to enable courts to make better judgments that would take into account the circumstances as well as the mental and social status of those seeking out the courts. The qualifications for appointment, 'Abduh insisted, must include the requirement that judges be civil and of refined character; he also insisted on an investigation of personal conduct prior to a judge's appointment.

Other than these arrangements, 'Abduh recommended the replacement of the old cadre of jurists, trained in taqlid, with new, better qualified and educated jurists who were strongly versed in ijtihad forms of reasoning.[85] In particular, he criticized the existing policy of favoring Hanafi jurists over those from different legal schools as this practice was partial, sectarian (ta'asub), and in violation of the fundamentals of a just Islamic legal system.[86] Other than the judgeship being open equally to qualified jurists regardless of the school to which they belonged, ʿAbduh suggested a proper codification of the four schools of law.

The idea behind the codification of the shariʿa was to create a unified system of law that would govern all Egyptian Muslims alike, regardless of the school of thought they belonged to (madhab) or their social and political status. A methodical and systematic recodification of the shariʿa, ʿAbduh argued, involved what Rida later on referred to as *talfiq*, or the process of sifting through this huge legal corpus and selecting the key and essential principles (theoretical and practical) relevant to and commensurable with modern arrangements. A revised jurisprudence, ʿAbduh argued, should not be founded on the doctrines and rulings of only one of the legal schools, even at the risk of angering Hanafi jurists (the dominant legal school in Egypt). It would be wrong at this point in time to favor one school over another.[87]

To have the Hanafi as the dominant legal school and to have each judge trained in only one of the four schools he also considered as divisive and ineffective, especially as it created a patchwork of judicial rulings antithetical to the functioning of a modernizing society. A codified generalized Islamic legal system, ʿAbduh stressed on many occasions, was indispensable because the current multifaceted and varied system of laws was not only inefficient but unjust, leading to arbitrary judgments. The shariʿa in its present state, he argued, was too huge and complicated for most judges to master because the corpus consisted of not just the four schools of law, but also the variant methods of argumentation used in reaching a judgment. Rather than helping, this huge corpus hindered judges from reaching reasonable judgments. [88]

ʿAbduh proposed that in making their rulings, judges ought to be free to move among the four schools, basing their opinion on whichever arguments offered the strongest reasoning and the most conclusive evidence. Rather than selecting one school, a unified code would include rulings from the four main legal traditions. His proposal suggested that the choice of rulings would hence be based on reasoned argument and evidence rather than on what he considered unreasonable loyalty (taʿasub) to one's own sect. A unified system would continue to contain the differences among the four schools; however, in making a ruling, each judge would be required to ask not what school he would enforce but rather which ruling or precedent from the four schools was best applied in this particular case.[89]

Conscious of the huge effort required to codify Islamic jurisprudence, 'Abduh recommended setting up a committee comprised of the
most qualified and knowledgeable Muslim jurists and lawyers to embark
on this project of revising the legal corpus governing both civic law
(mu'amalat) and personal status. The revised laws should then be collected and published in a series of books that would constitute the final
authority on legal matters to be consulted by judges and lawyers. To properly codify the Islamic shari'a required the collective effort of knowledgeable and open-minded Muslim jurists and scholars; it was not a task, he
insisted, that could be left to the whims of the government or a foreign
colonial power, nor, for that matter, to the traditionalist old cadre of
justices.[90]

Instituting Reform Through *Fatawa*

Between 1899 and 1905, 'Abduh held the position of grand mufti of
Egypt, which allowed him to put into practice his vision of a reformed
Muslim world.[91] During his six years as grand mufti, 'Abduh delivered
close to a thousand *fatawi*, the vast majority of which addressed matters
relating to routine monetary transactions and did not represent significant departures from existing legal thought.[92] In some of these opinions,
however, 'Abduh addressed questions and concerns arising from the social
and economic restructuring of Muslim societies in general and Egypt in
particular. In what follows, I take representative samples from his fatawi
that exemplify his attempt to define new standards for Islamic social
norms and mores that would accommodate the needs in the modern context without violating the boundaries set by the Islamic tradition.

In 1899, 'Abduh delivered a fatwa addressing the role of government
intervention in regulating the economy from an Islamic legal perspective.
The opinion he delivered favored state intervention in order to create
symmetry between competing interests and as the best way to safeguard
public interest. 'Abduh justified government action on the basis of *maslaha
'amma*, an Islamic legal notion that endorses public welfare and shuns
possessive individualistic interest. This fatwa was triggered by the first
general labor strike in Egypt, which was initiated by the cigarette workers (30,000) and spilled over to other subsidiary and manufacturing

industries in support of the cigarette workers' demands for better wages, working conditions, and the right to unionize. The strike lasted over three months, beginning in December 1899 and ending on February 21, 1900. The length of the strike set off intense public debate over what became the two major, and polarized, positions: one, led by Lord Cromer, the British administrator of Egypt, advocating free enterprise and nonintervention; the other, led by 'Abduh's intellectual nemesis, Farah Antun, advocating state intervention and a welfare state system. Cromer's opinion represented the official position of the British colonial administration and was published in the pro-British newspaper *al-Muqatam*. Cromer defended laissez-faire and government neutrality by claiming that "the role of the state is to secure order and protect free industry and free labor . . . [indicating that the] government arbitrates only when conflicting sides agree to that."[93] Antun criticized the nonintervention of the colonial administration by maintaining that "free enterprise" was a screen for government protection of the interests of the capitalists and the powerful, and that when Cromer spoke of the government maintaining security and order, what he really meant was securing the order of the rich for the rich.[94] More significantly, Antun questioned whether capitalist free enterprise and the sacrosanct principle of "individualism" were even appropriate for weaker colonized economies such as that of Egypt.

In turn, the strike became the platform from which various political and national factions (both Islamic and secular) debated the uses and abuses of colonialism on Egyptian society and economy. Other leaders joined Antun's interrogation of British colonial authority and its wisdom in enforcing laissez-faire capitalism on Egypt, a poor developing nation unable to guard itself against the incursions of foreign capital that monopolized and controlled its economy. The application of the laissez-faire system in Egypt, many complained, translated simply into making the rich and the powerful, who happened to be foreigners, richer and more powerful and making the weak natives weaker and poorer.[95]

Searching for a consensus that could unify the Egyptian public against free enterprise, Antun sought out 'Abduh, the grand mufti of Egypt, for an Islamic authoritative opinion on the matter.[96] 'Abduh's response centered on two questions: (1) whether it is legitimate for the government to intervene in the economy in general, and (2) whether the government should play the arbitrator between labor and capital in this particular case. His response to the two questions was in the affirmative based on the Islamic legal view that the government is obligated to protect the public against harm posed by individual interest. The fatwa rejected outright the notion of free enterprise because, as he opined, both in principle and in spirit, Islamic jurisprudence rebuffs free enterprise and the primacy of possessive "individualism" (*istifrad*). This is how 'Abduh explained it: earlier Islamic governing bodies justified their involvement in regulating the prices of goods for the benefit of the public; so should this government intervene to regulate just wages and fair working hours. And because manufacturing industries happened to fall within the boundaries of what is identified in the Islamic legal discourse as "public duties" (*furud kifaya*),

it is commended that these industries which many of the communities depend on for their livelihood be protected against work stoppage. It is therefore the duty of the governor to intervene to prevent a work strike and ease all unnecessary hardships affecting the livelihood of these communities. . . . Therefore, if workers go on strike in industries that affect the livelihood of the surrounding communities and their strike can cause the spread of public harm, it is the duty of the government to intervene to protect the public against harm. And if the ruling finds in favor of the workers and their claim that they, for example, work beyond what is considered normal, he must oblige the factory owners to show leniency toward the workers by increasing their wages or else reduce their working hours or do both. But if he finds in favor of the employees and the fault was that of the workers, he must then oblige the workers to go back to work.[97]

Here, I want to argue, 'Abduh seems to once again draw on the prevailing Islamic legal view of "suitability" (maqsad), which construes the goal of the shari'a as the promotion of the public good to the exclusion of harm, to find an Islamic resolution to a contemporary social problem, a problem produced by modern structures and capitalist relations. Although 'Abduh ruled for government intervention to protect the public against imminent harm, he nonetheless cautioned against extremes and recommended instead a more evenhanded stance between labor and capital. In doing so, 'Abduh, in concert with the established Islamic view, was setting up the mizan analytic as the framework from within which to define a different form of Islamic governmentality. In his opinion, a governing system in the spirit of Islam aims to always seek a balanced, harmonious society where justice ('adl) and communal cooperation (*ta'awun*) prevail. Putting it differently, 'Abduh's fatwa illustrates to Muslims the feasibility of seeking political and social norms and practices from within the Islamic discursive tradition independently of Western discourses. It is clear from 'Abduh's opinion that he recommends a form of government that is very different from the one enforced by the British, thus suggesting that a government founded on the principle of public welfare might be more suitable to Islamic sensibilities and mores than a Western liberal government founded on the principle of free market economy and individualism. It must be emphasized, however, that my interpretation of 'Abduh's position differs from that reached by 'Imara (who studied and collected his works) and by other contemporary Muslim socialists (like Hasan Hanafi), who posit that 'Abduh in this fatwa demonstrates that he was on the side of a progressivist, anticapitalist and proworker state.[98] I also take issue with the extreme opposite viewpoint (held by Antun) that posits 'Abduh as an archetypal traditionalist who drew on the prevailing Islamic view of the state as an essentially despotic governing authority (*abawiya*) that regards Muslims incapable of governing themselves.

'Abduh seems to me to distance himself from both views. He did not argue that the government ought to protect the working class from capitalist power, for he stated that the government had to reflect the general interest over that of both workers and employers. This is why he made the point that although in this case the government ought to intervene on the side of the workers, in another case it might find in favor of the employers. He was hardly paternalistic, as he did not argue against the right to strike or the right to organize, which indicates his view that ordinary Muslims are quite capable of making decisions about how they want to live and, in that sense, are capable of governing themselves. On the other hand, given that particular groups in the community will not always act in the general interest, he insisted on the necessary role of government to adjudicate between and to balance these competing demands in order to identify the good of the community as a whole.

One of 'Abduh's most famous and controversial legal opinions similarly became an occasion to reorder norms and mores that would enable Muslims to function more successfully in a changed world. In this opinion, known as the Transvaal fatwa, 'Abduh rejected the established religious authority's view that Muslims would forsake their faith by embracing non-Islamic practices in a predominantly non-Muslim context. In the fatwa tradition, 'Abduh responded to three questions posed by a Muslim from Transvaal: first, whether a Muslim living in a predominantly Christian country is permitted to wear European-style attire; second, whether a Muslim is prohibited from eating meat slaughtered by Christians; and third, whether it is permissible for a (Hanafi) Muslim imam to lead public prayers for Muslims belonging to other legal schools (Shafi'i, Maliki, and Hanbali). His response to all three questions was in the affirmative, basing his opinion on the long-standing argument within the Islamic tradition that interiority and intention are the better criteria for measuring faith. I will limit my discussion to the first two responses, as the third is clear from what has been discussed earlier and is not as controversial as the other two. 'Abduh's response to the first question goes as follows:

If the person wearing a European headdress had no intention of forsaking Islam and taking up another religion, his action is not un-Islamic. And if the person wore this outfit to overcome some physical inconveniences such as protecting himself from the sun or to facilitate social or work-related contacts that are advantageous and not harmful to him, the question of undertaking another religion is not even an issue here and is therefore a void question.[99]

'Abduh's fatwa informed by the doctrine of interiority and al-Ghazali's "hermeneutics of the self," I suggest, defined a different kind of Islamic subjectivity, more in concert with the new social, economic, and political arrangements. A good Muslim, he argued, is a conscientious moral subject who depends on his own inner sense of self rather than on external appearance or apparel that expresses his religious status. He is one who employs his own reasoning to arrive at judgments instead of blindly following conventional rulings that possibly might harm him. 'Abduh, as I argued earlier, extended al-Ghazali's definition of faith as inner sincerity beyond the engagement of inner self to include the cultivation of one's conscience, of which intelligibility constitutes a fundamental part. One of 'Abduh's principal objectives, as stated earlier in this chapter, was to free the minds of Muslims from the chains of dependence on authority and to enable them instead to exercise reason when making decisions pertaining to life and religion.

The response of other Muslim thinkers to the first question of his fatwa was mixed, ranging from a total rejection by the Azhari scholars,

'Abduh's main religious opponents, to being dismissed as an unnecessary intervention in conventional matters with no legal bearing. The Azhari 'ulama who regarded the adoption of European attire by Muslims as a strong signifier of Europeanization and by implication as a weakening of an Islamic way of life based their rejection of 'Abduh's opinion on the authoritative prophetic saying *man tashabaha bi-qawmin fahwa minhum*, which roughly translated means "when one acquires the habits of others, he will invariably become one of them." This interpretation turned 'Abduh's argument on its head by presenting an inverted version of his notion of interiority.[100] The scholars of al-Azhar who clearly opposed the acquiring of European attire by Muslims, regardless of where they lived, used for their defense the Islamic position that argues in favor of exterior actions as the norm for judging a status of a Muslim, especially as it is impossible to establish what is in one's heart.

On the other hand, the Indian Muslim reformer Sayyid Ahmad Khan disagreed with the local established scholars as much as he disapproved of 'Abduh's stance. Although he dismissed the established authority as "traditionalists," he wrote off 'Abduh's opinion on the basis that it "belonged to mundane affairs since Islam did not prescribe a social dress for Muslims to begin with."[101]

'Abduh's response to the second question posed in the fatwa was even more controversial, setting off an uproar and leading many of the local Muslim scholars to consider his ruling sacrilegious and to call for 'Abduh's dismissal as a grand mufti. 'Abduh declared that it is permissible for a Muslim minority to eat meat slaughtered by the Christian majority even when the latter's slaughtering habits are different from those practiced by Muslims.[102] In his response, 'Abduh challenges the wisdom of Islamic precedence and turns directly to the Qur'an to reach the opinion that "Muslims in distant parts should follow God's Words where He says: 'And the food of those who have been given the Book is lawful for you'" (Qur'an, 5:7). 'Abduh concludes with his own interpretation: "this verse is explicit in declaring their food lawful, so long as they, in their religion, hold it to be lawful."[103] In this opinion, 'Abduh used his prerogative as a mufti and his authority to use ijtihad by transcending older precedent and going directly to the Qur'an to reach a ruling that authorized a new Islamic practice, a practice that takes into account the special needs of Muslims in the present context.

The opinion was controversial because it overturned an already well-established precedent that ruled eating meat not slaughtered according to Islamic law unlawful, thus challenging the theory of the consensual (ijma') authority, which was considered infallible by the religious establishment.[104] Brushing aside an entire body of Islamic legal opinion, including the Hanafi school to which he belonged, 'Abduh reinstated the Qur'an as the primary source of Islamic jurisprudence. As against blind obedience to old precedent (taqlid), 'Abduh instead practiced ijtihad (reasoning free from precedence) to arrive at a different reading of the very same Quranic verse on which previous legal opinions had been based. Here he reasserted ibn Taymiya's strong views that upheld the right of Muslims to go directly to the authoritative sources and challenge the primacy of the ijma' over ijtihad.

Moreover, his method of interpretation was distinctly different from the conventional exegesis practices. Instead of interpreting each particular verse and the particular circumstances in which the verse was revealed, 'Abduh treated the Qur'an as an integral whole.[105] In his interpretation of the verse, 'Abduh points out that the verse can be understood only in the context of the previous verse (verse 5:4) that lists the forbidden meats, including pork, dead animals, blood, the strangled, and meat not consecrated to God. The next, verse 6, which asks "what then is permissible?," then lists the meats that are permissible, including meats hunted by trained dogs, and is followed by verse 7, which clearly states that the food of "those people to whom the Book was given is lawful." The last verse, according to 'Abduh's interpretation, was intended to expunge doubts among the believers regarding the legal status of meats slaughtered by Christians, not because of their different slaughtering practices, but more likely because Christians upheld the belief in Jesus as God. The verse was simply intended to reaffirm the point that meat slaughtered by Christians (in spite of the conventional view) is, in fact, lawful as long as the slaughtered meat was considered legal by all Christians, clergy as well as laity.[106]

This argument set off intense opposition, led primarily by the newspaper *al-Zahir*, published by Muhammad Abu Shadi. Abu Shadi, a lawyer widely believed to be the spokesman for the khedive, was also believed to have been setting the stage to strip 'Abduh of his position as a mufti on behalf of the khedive. Whether these suspicions were well founded or not, in ten consecutive issues, *al-Zahir* attacked ʿAbduh for violating the sacro-sanct Islamic law. The first attack to appear in the paper asked, "How can that be declared lawful which God has declared unlawful?" In the final attack, entitled "Religious Declaration," Abu Shadi draws on traditional Islamic jurisprudence to conclude that ʿAbduh was engaging in an illegiti-mate exercise of interpretation not only by setting aside all previous au-thoritative legal opinions that forbade the eating of meat not slaughtered appropriately, but also by misreading the Quranic verse (5:7) that explic-itly prohibits any meat from "knocked down" animals, a common prac-tice among Christians.[107]

The fatwa, in fact, generated as much support as it set off opposi-tion. ʿAbduh received support from Muslims in and out of Egypt, most of them defending his method of setting aside older precedents for newer norms directly derived from the Qurʾan. A leading supporter of ʿAbduh in Egypt was his disciple Rashid Rida. In his journal, *al-Manar*, Rida af-firmed ʿAbduh's right to practice both *takhayur* (selection) and ijtihad, basing his argument on the Hanafi school (to which ʿAbduh belonged) and the teachings of its founder, Abu Hanifa, who said "it is not permis-sible for anyone to take our word without proving it."[108] This statement, Rida argued, clearly shows that the father of the Hanafi tradition himself rejected the practice of taqlid and the blind following of any authority without proof. Therefore, even the Hanafi school, he argued, was open to takkayur, as it recommends that Muslims follow the strongest proof given by any of the masters. Furthermore, he defended the right of ʿAbduh to ijtihad based on his role as a reformer and as one who is obligated within the Islamic tradition to interpret directly the Qurʾan to set new standards and norms as did the earlier generation of Muslims.

Conclusion

The dispute with the religious establishment over what constitutes a Muslim, on the one hand, and with European colonial discourses over what constitutes a modern subject, on the other, created a window of op-portunity for ʿAbduh to negotiate a space for the emergence of rational, disciplined, and self-governing Muslim subjects with values different from those that defined a European liberal subject. In contrast to a "good" liberal self who seeks to be self-constitutive and sovereign, valuing a selfhood that is tradition free and detached from its social roles, 'Abduh, assuming that the essence of Islamic law resides in the self, postulated a Muslim selfhood to be formed through and within the parameters of the Muslim community. Although Islamic subjectivity allowed a space for the private self, Islamic morality and law ties the subject to the community and to worldly actions. In contrast to an autonomous liberal subject predicated on the universal notion of an already preformed self (born equal, free, and rational), a Muslim self is earned, particular, and dependent on circumstance, time, and stage of moral condition for its definition.

Far from being a liberal, what 'Abduh feared most from colonial modernity was the replacement of an Islamic moral order with a liberal one founded on self-constituted subjects driven by material interests, detached from a system of ethics. What he resisted was not the modernizing features of Europe's project but its liberal secular vision grounded in the demotion of social morality and the enshrinement of individual interests as the driving social determinant. What 'Abduh rejected most was simply European secular liberalism and its promotion of individual material interests above the collective and the good of society. One might even say that one of the driving forces behind his criticism of European modernity, other than its singular vision of secularity, is the individualism central to the liberal tradition. It is these liberal views that he considered to be incompatible and even incommensurable with a Muslim context where the driving force for organizing a society is valorized through the realization of "public interest" and "public good" rather than the validation of the "possessive quality" of individualism.

Finally, as part of practicing the Islamic modern, 'Abduh's fatawa opened a space for Muslims to envision new boundaries of the public/ private domains without dismantling the role of religion as a regulator of social morality. Differently from colonial modernity, in which the private and the public are presumed as oppositional and distinct domains, the relationship of the private to the public, the sacred to the secular, in 'Abduh's discourse appears to be far more blurred and hybrid than binary and oppositional. His questioning of the universality of European (colonial) modernity, however, should not lead us to mistake him for a traditionalist, because 'Abduh resisted as forcefully the defenders of legitimate religious authority especially for valorizing unreflective beliefs and practices.

Calling them "irrational" and "traditionalists" for their inertia and habit of rule following (taqlid), 'Abduh asserted that Islamic rationality allowed for rule making (ijtihad) and on occasion even for rule breaking to safeguard the continuous growth and survival of the Islamic tradition. Rather than perceiving Islamic tradition as oppositional to modernity, 'Abduh's reform project aspired to preserve its Islamic past through the present.

Love and Marriage

He creates for you mates out of your own kind, so that you might incline towards them, and He engenders love and tenderness between you.

The Qur'an (30:21)

As an adult sane woman in full possession of myself, it is my categorical right to marry who I see fit and appropriate for me; no one can steal away or refute a juridical right granted under the Shari'a to all mature rational Muslim female subjects; this right has been bequeathed to me by God.

Safiya al-Sadat

Freedom is the ability to enjoy one's full rights without transgressing the right of others. . . . The father's rights over his offspring are not to be forfeited since the children's rights are actualized only by honoring the father's.

al-Ahram, July 23, 1904

Introduction

As argued in the previous chapter, the project of reform in Egypt, unfolding within the context of British colonialism and operating within a structure of unequal power relations, played a key role in the formation of Egyptian modernity. In carrying out this project, Muslim reformers not only engaged modes of reasoning embedded in the Islamic tradition, but also had to engage European thought and its tradition in search of this alternative to Western secularism. The outcome was a particular conception of a modern society construed from both indigenous and European traditions. A good example of this process is the way that Islamic law was reconfigured to accommodate new social realities in the domains of personal status and family relations. In contrast to the view that interprets the contemporary shari'a governing family and personal status as a premodern remnant, preserved to accommodate powerful traditional elements resisting change and modernity, I have maintained that the terms and meaning of family law and personal status were transmuted in the process of rearranging the law to accommodate changing conditions.

This chapter approaches the subject of a modern reconfiguration of the family through the story of two lovers whose marriage turned into a national cause célèbre at the turn of the century. Rather than the ordinary event it might have been, the marriage of a noble woman to a journalist of modest origins without her father's approval became a prism through which larger arguments and societal concerns about state and family, law and morality, the profane and the sacred, colonial and anticolonial politics, came to unfold. The father's legal challenge of the marriage on three grounds—the couple's social incompatibility, their violation of prevailing national and moral customs by marrying without his consent, and the husband's "dishonorable" occupation—brought forth questions of a social, political, and legal nature that transcended the private and the personal. At first sight, the case appears to be no more than a generational conflict, signifying a struggle between the old and the new, between young, educated middle-class professionals with new hopes and desires and older forces upholding long-standing norms and values. However, the case proved more complex than anticipated as it drew on sentiments transcending the simple binary of traditional and modern. As it transpired, the fate of the two lovers became contingent on a range of forces (political, cultural, and legal) all intersecting to produce an ending that was hardly predictable. The marriage, touching on many of the social concerns emerging in a society undergoing fundamental restructuring of its institutions and social arrangements, engendered an array of irresolvable and long-standing tensions relating to the peculiar character of Egyptian modern development.[1] These unresolved conflicts included such questions as how to balance duties and rights? Is moral conduct part of or separate from the law? What constitutes compatibility: class or religio-moral character? What determines compatibility: local customary conventions or positive Islamic law? How to define the relationship between a secular state and family institutions governed by the shari'a? Rather than a simple opposition between the sacred and secular, private and public, sexual and social contract, the case unfolded to reveal a much more blurred picture in which these domains crisscross one another, demonstrating how tentative and tenuous these binaries become when put into practice.

The New Woman

The social and economic restructuring of Egyptian society in the first half of the nineteenth century under Muhammad ʿAli, and in the latter half under British colonialism, dictated a rearrangement of the family that inspired the emergence of different desires and needs, especially among the rising urban middle classes. In contrast to the older arrangements, in which the father, and not the biological mother, managed the household and was in charge of disciplining its members and educating its children, the new arrangements relegated that role to mothers and wives. Women's familial role, especially in the urban areas, was then culturally associated with the womb and reproduction. But with the emergence of a national capitalist economy, the domain of men changed. Entrepreneurial men had to turn their attention more fully outward to the world of polity and economy, relinquishing their responsibilities for everyday management of the household to women. To take up their new role of child rearing and household management required women, in turn, to be educated in the latest disciplinary measures and scientific developmental theories.[2] At the same time, the logistics of the new order required the breakdown of the old homosocial domain of the harem and its replacement with the nuclear heterosexual family. Similar to what happened in Europe, the shift to a market economy and its governing laws had a direct bearing on changing attitudes toward capital investment, discouraging luxury consumption while encouraging "productive" forms of consumption and industry. With these structural and cultural changes, attitudes toward the extended household also changed, as it now came to be perceived as an unproductive obsolete consumption site. The new market economy, in other words, encouraged the adoption of social norms and worldviews more fitting to an entrepreneurial mentality. The molding of new attitudes and desires is perhaps best captured by Qasim Amin's famous but highly contested work, *Liberation of Women*, to which ʿAbduh was a principal contributor.[3] The work, which hinges on the modern idea of the family as the building block of the nation, advocated the moral and material improvement of Egyptian women as the future wives and mothers of the nation. Muslim women in their present state were in turn depicted as "ignorant and backward," and older forms of patriarchy (or male control of women through institutions of marriage, polygamy, and sex segregation) were deemed coercive and tyrannical. The book, published in 1899, was extremely controversial, and its reception was accordingly mixed. Some embraced the book as "the finest in years," hailing Qasim Amin as the liberator of women; others rejected it, accusing the author of being a "Europeanized Muslim" and by implication an ally to Lord Cromer, the British consul general. Throughout the twentieth century, the work continued to receive mixed responses. Some continued to argue that Qasim Amin simply reproduced the colonizers' views, including the notion of societal stagnation (*inhitat*), which he attributed to the degenerate state and ignorance of women. Others, including later feminists, considered him a misogynist for his "virulent contempt" of women and for blaming Egypt's state of degeneracy on women and not men.[4]

As the book's title plainly demonstrates, *Liberation of Women; and, The New Woman* was emancipationist in tone, speaking the language of "freedom," "equality," and "awakening" that mostly valorized the ideals of European bourgeois domesticity. The process of emancipating women involved dismantling old practices of arranged marriage, sex segregation, and polygamy and embracing different family values centered on love, companionate marriage, and nuclear family. As 'Abduh explained in his section on family, one of the fundamentals of companionate marriage is that partners do not commit themselves to marriage before being sure of their feelings for one another, a condition that arranged marriage—which presumes that couples do not have to know or love one another before marriage—denies and prohibits. He denounced arranged marriage on the grounds that it led to public harm, because young couples, fighting and unhappy, neglect their duties toward one another as well as toward their children. Arranged marriage was also problematic because mature and sane Muslim subjects were denied the responsibility to decide what is best for themselves. To enable the young to take up that responsibility, however, requires first the fostering of awareness and self-reflection.

Central to this strategy of awakening the younger generation, and women especially, was formal education. The authors considered formal education pivotal to lifting women from their degenerate state as well as the nation from its moral and material stagnation. Their discussion of education draws a distinction between older forms of education and modern forms of pedagogy. Whereas in the older form of education (madrassa or home education) learning was a means to a private end, in the new education, with its objective of inculcating public sociability, pedagogy aims at creating new female subjects who can be effective educators of the nation's children and loving companions of its male citizens.[5] The section on education, attributed to Qasim Amin, begins by positing the ontological question of woman's nature and in answer evokes the modern notion of a female's humanity, her separate being-ness, and her "natural" equality to men: "Who do you understand a woman to be? Like a man, she is a human being. Her body and its functions, her feelings and her ability to think are the same as a man's. She has all the essential human traits, differing only in gender."[6] Inequality between men and women of his society, as Amin also recognized, was socially constructed and historical, rather than biological and inherent: "the superior physical and intellectual strength of men can be best explained by considering the past, when for many generations men have been involved in the world of work and in the pursuit of intellectual activities. During these years, women have been deprived of all opportunities and forced into an inferior position. The few variations have been shaped by variations in time and place."[7] As a socially produced phenomenon, women's state of inferiority was therefore rectifiable through education. Education, as Amin put it, would teach women to become independent beings with "a will of their own."[8] Public education was the means toward enabling women to become self-governing, self-regulating, and productive members of the Egyptian nation. In the context of the modern world, both 'Abduh and Amin argued, the public good could be secured only by subjects capable of exercising self-control, who would be guided by an internalized moral code and who understood the connection between their own self-discipline and the achievement of a good society. From the authors' perspective, the older form of household worked in the opposite direction, relying on external coercive authority rather than on self-discipline.

It is important to note that, as in Europe, the education of women was viewed as the instrument for restructuring the domestic domain and that its emancipatory mission was limited to this function. Proposals for remodeling education were deeply gendered, drawing a firm distinction between men and women's education. Whereas men's education was meant to prepare them for tasks relating to politics, economy, and industry, women's education targeted household chores and management.[9] As explained by Amin, households could no longer sustain the disorder of the older domestic regime. Management of the family had "become a complicated art requiring numerous and different skills. A wife should, as much as possible, set up a budget for income and expenditures to avoid an imbalance in the family finances."[10] To be competent household managers, women needed a certain amount of intellectual and cultural knowledge. Reading the segments attributed to Qasim Amin, one is struck in particular by his complete and utter fascination with modern notions of discipline, order, and routine. It is within the space of an "orderly" home, he argued, that an educated mother is able to inculcate good behavior and prepare the children to become well-behaved, moral, and productive subjects. Modern forms of discipline, routine, and order in the home were conceived as inseparable from health, cleanliness, and hygiene. Egyptian women were portrayed as undisciplined and dirty, as "not in the habit of combing their hair every day . . . nor do they bathe more than once a week. They do not know how to use a toothbrush and do not attend to what is attractive in clothing."[11] Moreover, the high infant mortality rate in Egypt was also blamed on women's ignorance:

Infant mortality in Egypt is more than double that in London. . . . if the health and ill-health, life and death, of our children are connected to the way they are brought up by our women, then is it not weak-minded and foolish to abandon them to the suggestions of ignorance and leave them to their superstitions of wet-nurses and the advice of old women who do with them as they please? . . . The number of children killed by ignorant women every year exceeds the number of people who die in the most brutal wars.[12]

He attributed the absence of healthy homes to women's lack of available knowledge about hygiene and health:

Is it not a mother's ignorance of hygiene that allows her to neglect her child's cleanliness so that he is dirty and left to wander in the streets and alleys, wallowing in the dirt as baby animals do? Is it not her ignorance that allows him to be lazy, running away from work and wasting his precious time, which is his capital, lying down or sleeping or dallying even though childhood years are the years of energy, work and action?[13]

These old ineffective methods of informal child rearing should be replaced with more advanced theories of upbringing based on "correct, sound, and scientific principles," in order to create a new generation of productive men and women, with "sound judgment and knowledge" and with "refined manners and morals."[14] Children's moral, psychological, and mental development and the inculcation of self-reliance, self-discipline, and concern for the public good were now essential features of proper mothering. Within this rearranged domestic domain where mothers rule, children would come to internalize new norms and dispositions that, while remaining Islamic, would be more appropriate for their participation in this newly restructured society.

The push for rational principles governing child rearing was emblematic of the age, beginning well before and continuing after Amin.[15] Journals and newspapers of all sorts (Islamic, nationalist, secularist, and pro-British) ran articles and dedicated many pages to discussions of what it means to be a good mother, with meticulous instructions advising young women on mothering techniques and how to take proper care of their young to ensure against psychological and physical ill health. Instructive articles on how to nurse, bathe, and feed newborns were quite popular in this period. Rashid Rida's Islamic journal, *al-Manar*, for instance, published a series of articles in 1899 instructing mothers on how to care for and manage newborns. One article entitled "Child-rearing" began by putting forth the notion that physical, psychological, and mental nurturing starts from a child's day of birth. The article gives detailed instructions on breast-feeding, stressing the importance of routine and timing for disciplining both mother and infant. The author advised a new mother "to follow a strict time schedule of two hours (no less) between each feeding for a new born and gradually increasing the spacing between feedings as she sees fit."[16] The setting up of a routine time for feeding is important for the baby's psychological and physical health as well as that of the mother's, because regulated feedings foster a sense of security and order in a baby at the same time that they ease the burden of nursing unremittingly. Rida described older practices of mothering as unruly, causing more harm than good. Those ignorant women, he argued, "pick up and feed their babies upon a whimper, mistaking their cries for hunger. Suckling [to these women] is a matter of expediency; a means of silencing a crying baby."[17] These older forms of mothering, he insisted, breed demanding, unruly children who expect to get their wishes by bullying others.

Rida explicitly called on women to abandon the older practices for more efficient and scientifically based child rearing. He tackled the subject of discipline in yet another article, *al-Tarbiya al-Nafsiya* (proper psychological training), arguing that refined character is fostered by mothers who methodically and continuously commend and praise good behavior while at the same time criticizing and disciplining misbehavior. However, he instructed mothers that when disciplining their children they should reason with the children, explaining to them their wrongdoing, and to avoid older and ineffective punishments, such as beating, insulting, and swearing. Coercion does not foster refined manners; to the contrary, it instills roughness and rudeness instead of good morals.[18]

Several journals attending to the subject of women and their affairs surfaced in this period. *Majalat al-Rawi*, for instance, dedicated several issues to women's concerns and needs in a changing time. In 1888, it published a series of articles addressing the subject of love and its meaning for women. The articles supported women's right to choose their future husbands and by implication the dismantling of arranged marriage. They also advocated "the education of the genteel sex, inculcating in them the proper attitudes and morals suitable for the age" as a way of not only enabling women "to be on equal footing with their men" but also to "be supportive of them in their good and bad moments."[19] There were numerous other journals in which women writers published their concerns, including *Anis al-Jalis* (1910–22), *Fatat al-Nil* (1913–15), *Fatat al-Sharq* (1906–36), and *al-Jins al-Latif* (1908–24).[20] One of the most famous female writers of this period was Malak Hilmi Nassif (1886–1918), better known under her pen name, Bahithat al-Badiya (Intellectual of the Desolate), who published regularly in *al-Jarida*, advising women on how to improve their lot while accusing men of misogyny, cruelty, and disregard for women.[21] In contrast to Amin, she attributed the degenerative state of women to a culture that valued males over females and maintained that, save for female infanticide (a practice prohibited under Islam), contemporary culture was little different from that of pre-Islamic Egypt. She advocated change in men's cultural attitudes toward women by urging fathers to start appreciating and loving their daughters as much as their sons and to cease discriminating against female members of the family because of their sex. At the same time, she did not spare women in her criticism, for she blamed sex inequity on women's ignorance as much as on men's despotism.[22]

It is important to note that although there was a consensus among the various reformers and nationalists, including women, over the need for education and the desirability for domestic discipline and hygiene, there was less agreement among them over the question of sex segregation, veiling, and other issues regarding women's equality and freedom.[23] Tala'at Harb, a famed anticolonial nationalist and founder of Bank Misr, for instance, defended the older family arrangements, arguing that segregation and veiling were part of Egypt's national Islamic heritage and were practices to be proud of rather than to discard. Mandated by the shari'a, veiling and segregation, to Harb's mind, were markers that separated Egypt from Europe.[24] From his perspective, Amin's *Liberation of Women* was a colonial scam. Harb, nonetheless, agreed that Egyptian women needed proper education in order to fulfill their new roles as mothers and managers of the household. Not that different from Amin, he advocated for women an education that focused on religion, household management, and the latest child-rearing technologies because he considered child rearing a sacred duty required of woman.[25]

In contrast, Malak Nassif, voicing opinions of many rising middle-class Muslims, agreed that the family needed reform and called for the dismantling of polygamy and for regulation of marriage and divorce laws in order to prevent their abuse by men. She advocated companionate marriage based on love and respect between husband and wife. In contrast to 'Abduh's legalistic approach and Amin's and Harb's male-oriented discourses, Nassif spoke on behalf of women's subjective experiences and was able to articulate authoritatively the "inner" and "personal" world of females' subjugation. The daughter of a leading nationalist reformer and man of letters, Nassif, an accomplished poet, writer, and teacher, was also intimately familiar with polygamy, as she herself was married by arrangement to a man who already had a wife.[26] Her writing on the subject conveyed with literary power her own personal pain as well that of other women. Labeling polygamy "women's mortal enemy," she described the "savagery and selfishness of co-wife-ing" (*durra*), denouncing it for its evil destruction of the homes and lives of many innocent and good women.[27] In addition to her treatment of the evils of polygamy, Nassif wrote against early marriage for girls and against a disproportionate age difference between husbands and wives.[28] She regarded all these conventional cultural practices to be cruel and humiliating, dispossessing females, both young and old, of their humanity.

While presenting a strong voice for reform of family and marital relations, Nassif at the same time objected to unveiling, not because it would be "un-Islamic" as claimed by Harb, but because it was an idea imposed by men and not chosen by women. She also objected to men enforcing unveiling on a population of women who were ill prepared and unready for such a radical step. She felt that the men's response to veiling was also unreasonable, driven by the impulse to Europeanize rather than to help improve women's status. Criticizing Amin's proposition, she asked: "How can you men of letters . . . command us to unveil when any of us is subjected to foul language if she walks in the street, this one throwing adulterous glances at her and that one bespattering her?"[29] Instead, she suggested that men focus on giving "women a chance for true education and . . . to leave it up to woman to choose that which is most advantageous to her and to the nation."[30] At the same time, Nassif demanded of men that they stop lecturing and judging women and concentrate instead on improving their own moral character so that the nation as a whole could become well educated and well mannered. This, however, was not the position held by other women activists from that period. Huda Sha'rawi, an upper-class activist, identifying more closely with Europeanization, disagreed with Nassif over the issue of unveiling and was the first woman to take off her veil in public, turning unveiling into a political act of female defiance against "traditional" mores and values.[31]

It is clear that the disputations among the literati over the "woman question" centered primarily on how to draw a distinction between European and Egyptian notions of domesticity and the opportunity for Egyptians to mold their own discourse and develop their own form of domesticity drawn from their own culture and historical experience—a discourse, in other words, that marks its difference from Victorian Europe. For Harb that marker of difference was the preservation of veiling and sex segregation. Demarcating its distance from colonial modernity,

Liberation of Women, as did Bahithat al-Badiya, instead attributed Egyptian women's degenerative status to conventions dictated by custom and habits and not to Islam and its tradition, as colonial discourse claimed. The authors' intent was to free Egyptians and women from the tyranny of custom, not from Islam. Indeed, they considered breaking from the fetishism of conventions to be the pathway to Islamic revivalism and reawakening. They rejected the conventional justifications of sex segregation and arranged marriage as measures necessary to secure modesty. To rely on segregation and external control to promote modesty, they argued, was essentially non-Islamic as it implied that Muslim women and men were unable to internalize modesty and were incapable of disciplining their bodies and desires—as is required by Islam. Imposed arrangements to promote good behavior were ineffective as well, as conjugal cloistering (i.e., in the harem), they argued, promoted more corruption than good.[32] Most of the arguments (particularly ʿAbduh's) presented in favor of the new family and against the older arrangements were founded on Islamic forms of reasoning and situated within Islamic discourses. The new family, as conceived by Bahithat al-Badiya, was the vehicle for the revival of Islam and the agent for the creation of a new generation of good Muslim subjects who in the long run would regenerate the community as a whole. Starting with the family, where children get their first exposure to Islam, al-Badiyah argued that the inculcation of proper Islamic values and morality founded on equality between the sexes at this microcosmic level was the stepping-stone toward the reawakening of the community at large. From all these variant perspectives, the family (*usra*) nonetheless was the trope for the Islamic community (umma) and the nation.

In this sense, it would be wrong to conclude that these reformers, defining the family as the proper site of moral training, were in fact participating in the privatization of religion and its marginalization to the private sphere. In contrast to European forms of modernity, Muslim reformers in this period did not construe the privatization of religion as a necessary precondition for modernity, nor did they envision a separation of law from morality. Leading Muslim scholars advocated that the law governing personal status and the family continue to derive its authority form the shariʿa as a way of having religious authority extend beyond the individual and the private. That is precisely why ʿAbduh, for example, was determined that Islamic law (albeit a revised law) should continue governing the new family, because of the law's essential role in the revival of the Islamic community. Starting from the assumption that religious duties, as embodied practice, were also constitutive of social relations that are integral to daily public transactions, Muslims including 'Abduh could not have envisioned the sharp separation between the private and public domains as commonly presumed in Western modernity.

Romance and Marriage

In light of what has been discussed, I turn now to the notorious marriage of 'Ali Yusuf to Safiya al-Sadat, a case that expressed many of the ambiguities and unresolved tensions peculiar to Egyptian modern development at the turn of the century. The story of a famed journalist of humble origins and his marriage to an aristocrat against her father's will became a national scandal precisely because the arguments and concerns it generated were central to a society in the process of reconfiguring its own arrangements of family, law, societal norms, and attitudes that would distinguish it from European and colonial forms of modernity. Although the generational conflict between the old and the new played a considerable role in the case, it was not all that the case signified. The marriage transmuted into a legal case drawing in a variety of forces that defied resolution and challenged explanations founded on simplistic conceptual oppositional binaries often drawn between the modern and the traditional. It also produced an array of long-standing and irresolvable tensions between duties and rights, law and morality, and politics and culture, many of which are still current.

The scandal began in mid-July 1904, when the marriage of a prominent Muslim journalist, Sheikh 'Ali Yusuf, to a woman of nobility, Safiya al-Sadat, hit the news. The marriage took place on Thursday, July 14, and was first announced in *al-Muqatam* the following day and two days later in *al-Mu'ayid*, whose owner was the bridegroom himself. The marriage announcement in both journals was brief and withheld the name of the bride. *Al-Mu'ayid*'s published version on July 15 went as follows: "In a small ceremony this past Thursday afternoon, the owner of this journal married the daughter of the prominent notable family of 'Abdul Khaliq al-Sadat in a small ceremony that included a few family members and leading Muslim scholars."[33] On July 17, the father of the bride denounced the marriage in the newspapers *al-Ahram* and *al-Liwa*, disclaiming his approval or involvement in the event: "the announcement that the 'marriage was witnessed by a few prominent Muslim scholars and in the presence of close family members' gives the impression of our presence and consent. . . . This is a downright lie since the event took place in Sayyid Muhammad Tawfiq al-Bakri's house, without our knowledge or approval."[34] Accusing Sheikh 'Ali of kidnapping his daughter, the father brought legal charges against him.[35]

As events unfolded, the kidnapping charges turned out to be a fabrication for public consumption, for the marriage was carried out with Safiya's full consent, in the presence of and witnessed by a legal guardian, and at the residence of an equally prominent member of society, Muhammad Tawfiq al-Bakri, who also happened to be her brother-in-law, the husband of an older sister, Hafiza. And although, according to social conventions, it would have been preferable to have the father's presence and permission, Safiya, a fully grown, mentally competent woman of twenty-seven years of age, was acting within the boundaries laid down by Islamic law, including the right to marry without the father's consent.

The public reaction, however, ignored these mundane facts. Although a few came to the couple's defense, the majority fell under the spell of hearsay and tabloid tales of abduction, seduction, and vice. The father's accusations of kidnapping did not help, for many a journalist holding one grudge or another against Sheikh 'Ali Yusuf took this opportunity to get back at him by feeding their newspapers' gossip columns with lurid news of the couple, who came to exemplify the corruption and moral collapse of the society. 'Ali Yusuf was especially demonized in the tabloids for marrying above his class and for dishonoring a notable landed family. Denouncing the marriage for its transgression of normative cultural boundaries, some journals placed the blame on Europeanization (taghrib) and the importation of foreign attitudes. *Majalat al-Shabab* (The Journal of Youth), for one, deplored the marriage for violating Islamic morals and national customs as well as for setting a bad example for Egyptian youth. In a sensationalist style, the newspaper depicted the bridegroom as a predator, and his bride, a victim: "a rogue who corrupted a gullible young woman, belonging to one of the oldest most reputable Muslim families in the East," forcefully taking her "to a stranger's house to marry her without her father's presence or consent."[36] In these tabloids, Safiya was depicted as innocent, young, and seducible rather than as whom she really was—a mature woman willingly defying her father's wishes.

Initially, *al-Liwa*, the mouthpiece of the ultranationalist leader Mustafa Kamil, took a neutral tone toward 'Ali Yusuf and his marriage but, for unclear reasons, became much more critical of him as the events took an unanticipated and surprising course. Although it did publish the father's denunciation of the marriage, the journal, nonetheless, published a letter on July 20 (without revealing the name of its author) that denied the father's accusation of kidnapping and disclosed that for some time now 'Ali Yusuf had been in negotiation with the father over the date for the marriage, but that the father kept delaying the matter by making excuses of inappropriate timing every time a date was discussed; this forced the couple, after waiting for so long, to marry somewhere else and without his approval. The point of the letter was to disclose the father's prior knowledge of the couple's engagement and intent to marry and his refusal to take the matter seriously.[37] On another occasion, *al-Liwa* hinted that several family members and friends, even the khedive himself, had approached the father on occasions on behalf of the two lovers, but with little success.[38]

As it turned out, Safiya and 'Ali Yusuf had been informally engaged for some years before their actual elopement and that her father had actually introduced them. The first time they met, according to one story, was over the phone. In the last week of December 1900, the father, 'Abdul Khaliq, anxious to find out whether the new moon had appeared (an indication of the beginning of Ramadan), asked his daughter Safiya late that night to call *al-Mu'ayid* for information, and by pure coincidence, 'Ali Yusuf, who happened to be in the office that night, answered the phone; Safiya then supposedly fell under the spell of his "enchanting voice and magical words."[39] Others tell a different story—that Safiya met 'Ali Yusuf for the first time at one of the many social events she attended in the company of her father.[40] Apparently, her father had chosen Safiya to be his social partner, to accompany him to all the public events he attended. The father, as the story goes, produced no sons in spite of the many wives and concubines living under his roof. And of all the offspring, his favorite was Safiya—who, in his heart, came to take the place of the son he never had. Born to one of his beloved concubines, a Circassian (Caucasian) woman enslaved during one of the Ottoman wars with Russia, Safiya was known to have both beauty and brains. Like all well-bred upper-class girls raised in the shelter of elite harems, she was educated and well versed in both French and Arabic.[41] She accompanied her father to all the high-society salons of the day, and it was in the year 1900, on one of these social occasions, that Safiya met 'Ali Yusuf. She was at the marriageable age of 23 and he, age 37, a man of great charm, wealth, and prominence.

The only drawback to their love affair was that his wealth and prestige were earned, whereas hers were inherited. Safiya had been born into the wealth and eminence of the Sharifian al-Sadat family, who claimed descent from the Prophet. Sheikh 'Ali was of humble origins, born in 1863 to simple unlettered parents from a poor rural village in Upper Egypt. His father having died when 'Ali was young, he was raised by his widowed peasant mother. Whereas Safiya's father was a notable member of the landed gentry who lived off the revenues of his estates and urban endowments, Sheikh 'Ali was a self-made man who earned his wealth and prestige by working his way to prominence as a writer in the new profession of journalism. Attending the local religious school (madrasa) in his village, Belsafura, he excelled at learning the Qur'an and like many others in this period was sent to al-Azhar to complete his higher education in Islamic studies. Coming to Cairo opened new opportunities for 'Ali Yusuf. Like 'Abduh, 'Ali Yusuf acquired his Islamic voice under the tutelage of the great reformer of that era, Jamal al-din al-Afghani. He joined al-Afghani's al-Azhar circle, which opened his eyes to the politics of Islamic reform and encouraged him to pursue his natural talent as a writer and poet. It is said that al-Afghani himself sponsored this young talent by publishing his articles in newspapers al-Afghani had either helped establish or had influenced. 'Ali Yusuf's immediate success as a writer encouraged him to abandon his studies for journalism, dedicating his pen to speak on behalf of reform and against the British occupation and colonization of Egypt.

In 1888, he published his first journal, *al-Adab*, devoted to Arabic poetry and literature. In the journal, he pointed to the importance of reviving classical Arabic language to the improvement and revival of Egyptian culture. He also dedicated many issues to discussion of public education and the role of modern pedagogy in the construction of unity and national pride. He backed Muslim reformers who endorsed the inclusion of religious studies in public schools as much as the introduction of modern subjects and sciences to al-Azhar. The journal targeted Lord Cromer's regressive educational policies and their impact on the poorer segments of society. In 1889, he published a second journal, *al-Mu'ayid*, a daily political paper to counter the influence of *al-Muqatam*, the mouthpiece of British imperial interests in Egypt. Encouraged by the khedive and leading anticolonial nationalists and Muslim reformers, *al-Mu'ayid* became popular as an anti-British, anticolonial, pro-reform paper. In its initial years, the paper targeted Lord Cromer and his British cronies in Egypt. In particular, it attacked the British for their attempts to replace classical Arabic with the Egyptian vernacular and for spreading corrupt Western practices, such as gambling, drinking, and prostitution. Subjects close to the hearts of many Egyptians nationalists and reformers were also covered, including the role of missionaries in colonization, Algeria's struggle against French colonization, the reform of al-Azhar, 'Abduh's famous response to Hanotaux, and al-Kawakibi's significant work on the nature of despotism. The "woman question" was another significant subject that the journal took up. One of the first to engage in the issue, the journal participated in discussions relating to the degenerate state of women within the family and society at large. It supported the controversial work of Qasim Amin on the liberation of women and the importance of a restructured family to the rebuilding of a modern free Egypt.[42] The reform of the family to accommodate modern conditions without abandoning Islamic values and morals was a central theme to this newspaper.[43]

In later years, as relations between the khedive and leading Muslim reformers (such as 'Abduh and Rida) and nationalists (Mustafa Kamil) faltered, the tone of the paper changed. Though maintaining its anti-British rhetoric, by the turn of the century, *al-Mu'ayid* had become the khedive's mouthpiece. This change did not endear 'Ali Yusuf to those carrying the banner of reform, including, in addition to 'Abduh, powerful political figures of the literati, such as Sa'ad Zaghlul and Lutfi al-Sayyid. Having direct access to the Royal Palace proved useful for 'Ali Yusuf's initial success as a journalist, as he got first access to the inner intrigues of the ruling class and, in particular, the political battles between the khedive and Lord Cromer. Yusuf's evolving friendship with the khedive not only facilitated his personal enrichment, but also increased his social prestige by gaining him entry to high society. In spite of all the benefits accrued, however, his personal relationship with the khedive proved in the end harmful. As a fellow traveler in the social orbit of the khedive, 'Ali Yusuf was to the public eye as depraved and as corrupt as the khedive himself.[44] By the time Yusuf's marriage took place, he had accumulated enough enemies by reason of his friendship with the khedive that his case, no longer the private matter it could have been, was turned into a public trial that engaged political conflicts with ramifications beyond what he and his circle of friends would have imagined.

On July 21, 1904, the court convened to hear 'Abdul Khaliq's case against 'Ali Yusuf. Rather than pursuing the kidnapping charges that had initiated the court case, the Khaliq's lawyer petitioned the court to void the marriage on the grounds of (1) incompatibility and (2) absence of the legal guardian, the father, from the ceremony. In response to the new charges, the defense lawyer requested more time to prepare his case. Agreeing to postpone the hearing to a later date, the presiding judge, Ahmad Abu Khutwa, ordered, in the meantime, the legal separation of the couple (*haylulah*) and Safiya al-Sadat's removal from her husband's residence to her father's.

The order to separate the couple provoked a public split between those who thought the ruling unreasonable and those who defended it as proper and honorable. Of course, it is easy to read the split as generational between the older social forces upholding Islamic values and the younger generation of educated middle-class professionals, the "Europeanized Moslems" in the words of Lord Cromer, or those who identified with Western values and culture. But the case drew on sentiments far more complex than the simplistic counterposition of traditional versus modern, as opponents of the ruling drew on traditional as well as European ideas to contest it. Moreover, the attitudes that different groups took toward the ruling were complicated by the interplay of various elements—power, class, gender, religion, politics, and personality—in the forming of the case. For example, the meaning and implications of the separation were bound to be different in the context of a modernizing centralized state and a newly rearranged family-court system from what they had been in an earlier time and context. Whereas in past eras, court rulings were less formal and more porous, the rulings under the newly regulated courts were far more formal and were policed and enforced by designated agents of the state. At the same time, the arguments and struggles that swirled around this case were, in fact, specific to this time and particular to its context. In that sense, it would be hard to draw generalizations outside the context of colonial Egypt, a society undergoing change and still in the process of determining the norms, attitudes, and rules best suited for it in particular. Put differently, to explain the separation ruling as an expected outcome of an inherently conservative Islamic law that is particularly oppressive of women is to misconstrue the complex interplay between the old and the new, the personal and the political, the private and the public.

In response to the judge's ruling, Safiya forwarded a letter to the honorable chief of justice, Sheikh 'Abdul Rahman Afandi, appealing to him to put an end to this charade of "legal separation."[45] She stated that nothing illegal or incriminating was committed by her marriage as she was only enacting rights granted to her under the shari'a. As a mature being of sound mind, she was claiming the legal right to marry according to her choice, a "categorical right" granted to her and not to her father. As she put it:

> I would not have married the honorable 'Ali Yusuf without full knowledge in advance that he is compatible to me both personally and socially; he has both vast wealth and social prestige. As an adult, rational, and sane woman (*baligha, rashida*) in full possession of myself (*malikatun li-amri nafsi*), it is my categorical right (*haqq mutlaq*) to marry who I see fit and appropriate for me; no one can steal away (*la yumkin an yaslubhu mini ahad*) or refute a juridical right granted under the *shari'a* to all mature sane Muslim female subjects; this right has been bequeathed to me by God. I want your Honor to know further that I am happy and content with my husband and want to remain married to him. Never would I choose any other than him. I married him out of my own wishes and of my own free will.[46]

She also recorded in detail how the marriage ceremony was legally conducted and followed all the proper procedures required by the law.

The tenor of the letter was assertive but also judicious. The letter's most interesting feature is its language, which embraced modern arguments and espoused the rhetoric of rights and individualized subjectivity as understood within the modern context. In claiming a "selfhood," Safiya utilizes the expression *malika li-amr nafsi*, a term that is understood in our modern language to mean "I own myself" or "possess myself"; in other words, she was an independent female subject responsible for herself and actions and capable of making decisions independent of an authority figure, in this case her father. In the letter, Safiya, asserting her (Islamic) right to be responsible for her own actions, informs the chief justice that no wrong was done when she made that choice—she married 'Ali Yusuf out of her own free will—and that she is both happy and content with the decision. As a self-governing and self-reflective woman, she also knows what is "good" for her—a "good" she recognizes as different from that envisioned by her father. Accordingly, she has chosen what is best for her and not what is best for her father. Differentiating her subjective self (nafs) from her father allows her to take actions on her own behalf with or without his permission. Once she asserted her female subjectivity, she was able to claim her social rights, including the freedom to choose her life-long partner. The freedom to choose obviously posed a challenge to her father, who, abiding by the older family arrangements, considered it his right as her living guardian to make that choice for her. Older forms of patriarchy did not heed a female's will as a good reason for arranging a marriage, nor did older social arrangements acknowledge or consider a female's subjectivity as a given right to own and act upon independent of her social obligations toward her family and community. Besides reclaiming a new selfhood, Safiya's understanding of a good marriage as a "companionate marriage" founded on love and compassion was also a rejection of an arranged marriage in which a husband and wife, as Amin described disapprovingly in *Liberation of Women*, "commit themselves to a contract by which they must completely blend their two lives, without having had a chance to become acquainted."[47] The old family arrangements were now construed by Safiya and her generation as a problem produced by a coercive patriarchal authority that ignored the wishes and desires of both men and women of marital age. Arranged marriage, conceived of as a remnant of old oppressive practices, needed now to yield its ways to newer social arrangements with newer forms of selfhood and marital relations.

However, although these features could also be found in the ideal of the modern family as inspired by Europe and the Victorians, the language adopted by Safiya in her letter signified more of a mutation of the received European notion of the family than a mirror image of it. Her discourse constructed a vision of family that was specific to Egypt, contingent on

Islam and its laws and not on Europe and its secular discourse of rights. In her appeal to the chief justice, Safiya reclaimed rights that are "categorically" granted to females under Islamic law and not by secular laws authorized under colonialism. She retrieved them as "bequeathed rights granted by God," rights that the judge himself should oblige rather than deny. Similarly, one must not construe her desire to marry someone she loved as a sign that she embraced liberal individualism or its notion of individual preferences, which, according to Alasdair MacIntyre, "is held to provide by itself sufficient reason for acting so as to satisfy them."[48] Rather than the liberal self with its reference to oneself and where it is the individual qua individual who reasons, in her case, it was Safiya qua Muslim who reasons. Unlike the liberal self of "I want," Safiya did not consider herself the final authority on the question of her rights and desires because her "goods," as she explained, were instead bounded by God's injunctions. And her rights as a female Muslim were instead grounded in an Islamic discourse rather than in universal human rights principles.

On the touchy question of "disobeying her father and legal guardian," Safiya in the same letter to the chief justice disclosed a personal dilemma—her father's despotic character and his habitual disregard for his daughters—a matter that is regarded unfavorably in the tradition. In the letter, she informed the judge of her father's tyranny and of his "reputation for rejecting well-suited marriage proposals, thwarting his daughters' chances of marriage and happiness."[49] Safiya was rather clever to alert the chief justice to her father's abuse of his obligations as a guardian because of an already existing precedent within the Islamic tradition on this precise question. As explained by Rashid Rida in *al-Manar*, al-Sadat did indeed transgress his authority as both a father and a legal guardian. Although Rida did not name the father directly, his analysis explicitly indicts the father for violating his daughter's rights as granted to her under law when he obstructed her chances for happiness. The "rules regulating family relations," according to Rida, "are meant to instill harmony among its members, males and females, as well as protect the dignity and honor the humanity of its members. To breach these rules violates the *shariʿa* and causes public harm."[50] The article delineates the role of a legal guardian and his responsibilities as stipulated by the four legal schools. Although there is a consensus stipulating that under normal circumstances the presence of a legal guardian in a marriage is obligatory and that no marriage is considered valid without the consent of a legal guardian, the four schools, nonetheless, do put limits to the power of the legal guardian or father by making this obligation conditional on the woman's consent.[51] They also forbid a legal guardian from obstructing a mature sound-minded woman's decision or from overriding her right to accept what she believes to be a suitable marriage offer.[52] And in the case of a guardian's "muscling his power" to obstruct a woman's wishes, the Hanafi legal school gives a woman of sound mind "the right to marry herself off, without her guardian's permission, to whomever she considers compatible to her."[53] As explained by Rida, Safiya, a mature woman of sound mind, was justly claiming the right to marry herself off as granted to her under the Hanafiya by which Egypt abided. From Rida's perspective, Safiya's declaration to the chief justice of doing no wrong was reasonable and justifiable. Her father's claim that she violated her duty to him as his daughter had no grounding, because by the standards laid out in the four legal schools, familial obligations are reciprocal in nature and not a one-sided despotic arrangement—regardless of the fact that they have tended to take this form in customary convention. The father has obligations toward his daughter, which would include protecting and supporting her quest for happiness. By standing in her way to happiness, the father had accordingly relinquished his obligations toward her and, in so doing, relieved her of any legal or moral duty to obey his wishes.

As the story unfolds, it becomes apparent that the problems encountered by 'Ali Yusuf and Safiya were not the first in that family. As the daughter of Safiya and 'Ali revealed many years later, Safiya was not alone the day she eloped. Another of her sisters joined in her escapade and was married that same day to the nephew of Muhammad Tawfiq al-Bakri without her father's knowledge or permission.[54] Even al-Bakri himself seemed to have faced the same obstacles when he wished to consummate his marriage to Safiya's older sister, Hafiza. The father tried to prevent them from marrying even though he had officially accepted an engagement dowry of 250 dinars from al-Bakri.[55] Because, in that instance, the father eventually conceded under pressure from friends and powerful members of the community, 'Ali Yusuf had hoped to eventually win the father's acceptance of his engagement to Safiya. In a letter dated in 1901, a year after Safiya and Yusuf met, he retells the story of Hafiza and Tawfiq al-Bakri's difficulties to discourage Safiya from elopement to her aunt's home. Reluctant to participate in a radical act bound to bring shame and dishonor to the family, he urged waiting as the wiser course. Agreeing with Safiya that her father's house was "a prison with steel bars," he did not fail to remind her at the same time that those "bars were already broken down by her older sister, Hafiza, whose act paved the path for her and her other sisters to follow."[56] But three years of waiting for the father to relent seemed to drain even 'Ali Yusuf's patience. With Safiya turning twenty-seven, they eloped to marry with the father's full knowledge but without his consent.

In pressing her case, Safiya did not rely exclusively on the Hanafi school. She also sought out arbitration, as recommended by the other legal schools. In his *al-Manar* article, Rida referred to this outside authority as a *hakim*, a term in Arabic that connotes a third-party arbitration. Safiya and 'Ali sought out family members and close friends to arbitrate on their behalf but also to no avail. In the final analysis, arbitration failed even though it was evidently exercised by the khedive and by the brother-in-law, Muhammad Tawfiq al-Bakri, who eventually housed the marriage at the expense of creating a rift between himself and his father-in-law. According to the published letter that appeared in *al-Liwa*, after Muhammad al-Bakri's interventions failed, he warned the father of the lovers' intent to elope and to marry at his home. The letter disclosed that as a last effort, a Muslim scholar and a friend of the family, Sheikh Muhammad Radi, was sent to warn the father about the couple's decision to marry with or without his approval.

The couple appeared to have a strong case: they had done all within their power to do right by the father, and the marriage apparently proceeded according to the terms laid down by the law. Yet, events did not run in their favor; instead, the outcome turned against them, contingent on a range of unpredictable and unforeseeable forces.

One of these factors was the government's decision to defy the court's order of separation. Powerful segments within the government that disapproved of the court ruling ordered the governor of Cairo not to comply. Following the court hearing, *al-Muqatam*, Cromer's mouthpiece, revealed the colonial authority's dissatisfaction and its intent to ignore the order. At the same time, Safiya, rejecting the validity of the ruling, refused on her own accord to move out of her husband's residence. Explicating her noncompliance with the separation, Safiya wrote to the presiding judge, Abu Khutwa, that because she was not present at nor represented (by a lawyer) in the hearing, his ruling had no legal validity to constrain her actions. Her refusal to leave her husband's home required under the new colonial regime that the government take action to enforce the ruling. But the adminstration's noncompliance with the ruling complicated matters even more for the couple as the case metamorphosed into a power struggle between the shari a courts and the government. Its further politicization, as we will see, turned it from a simple case of a family dispute into a much broader conflict involving the khedive, Lord Cromer, and various national political factions, with each exploiting different facets of the case to push their own political agenda.

For the first time, the khedive found himself fighting on the same side as his archenemy, Lord Cromer. Yet the motives of the two men were quite different. Lord Cromer construed the marriage as a manifestation of the liberalization of Egyptian society and as a sign of the breakdown of tyrannical Islamic patriarchy and Islamic traditional values. Cromer's quintessential Victorian and paternalistic views utilizing "the language of feminism in the service of its assault on Islam and its culture" charged Islam with being the principal culprit responsible for women's oppression in Egypt. In *Modern Egypt*, Cromer lays the blame on Islam when he claims that the "failure of Islam as a social system was first and foremost due to its treatment of women. The degradation of women from an early age has eaten into the whole system of Islam. Whereas Christianity teaches respect for women, Islam degraded them."[57] The only hope for the progress of Egypt, as he saw it, was for the Egyptian to "be persuaded or forced into imbibing the true spirit of western civilization."[58]

The Royal Palace, on the other hand, was motivated by the khedive's personal loyalty to his confidante and political ally, 'Ali Yusuf, the sheikh who dedicated—or sacrificed—his journalistic skills by defending the khedive against his enemies.[59] The government's push to ignore the court order created a deep rift between the administration and the courts, one that proved too costly for the newlyweds, even though, in the short run, the backing of the two powers, the khedive and Cromer, resonated with hope. The government's defiance of the court ruling created a public uproar led by the Chief Justice of Egypt himself, Sheikh 'Abdul Rahman Afandi. In a written statement, he reprimanded the government for transgressing the court's authority. As the "law stands above the government," the government was obligated to execute the law, not ignore it. What is remarkable about the statement is its implicit secular inflections by a Muslim jurist occupying the highest judicial position in the country. In ordering the government to obey the law, he did not invoke religious authority; instead, he drew on secular sensibilities and on the idea of the independence of the courts as integral to new forms of governance and to the notion of civil order. Not only did his statement presume the separation of the two powers (the judicial from the political); it also disclosed fear for "the independence of the law and its courts" from the abusive power of the state. In the statement, the chief justice ordered that the presiding judge, Abu Khutwa, suspend indefinitely all hearings regarding the case until the separation order was properly executed. Calling for what one might refer to today as an "act of civil disobedience," the chief justice threatened to shut down all the courts under his command if the government continued to defy the court order.[60] The threat to suspend court activities forced the government's hand. Conceding defeat, the government enforced the separation by ordering Safiya out of her husband's residence. She, in turn, defied the government and refused to return to her father's home. This potential crisis between the courts and the government was averted only with the personal intervention of a prominent societal figure and a trusted friend, Sheikh al-Rafiʿi, who offered to temporarily house Safiya at his private residence until the case was legally resolved.[61] With all sides agreeing to this informal arrangement, Safiya moved into al-Rafiʿi's residence.

With these events unfolding, public opinion became more and more polarized. Safiya's refusal to obey the court was regarded by many as a violation of conventional norms and as an abuse of her obligations. The government's response politicized the case further as various political factions (nationalist and otherwise) began to exploit the events to push forward their own political agendas. *Al-Liwa*, the mouthpiece of the National Party, took this as an opportune moment to attack both the khedive and British colonial policies in Egypt. ʿAli Yusuf became the pawn in Mustafa Kamil's political campaign. His *al-Liwa* staged the most malicious attacks on ʿAli Yusuf and by implication on those who supported him. Maligning him for self-aggrandizement and corruption, *al-Liwa* accused the sheikh of betraying public trust and dishonoring the nation. Rather than "craving for respectability and good morals, ʿAli Yusuf craved after money and beauty."[62] In addition, Mustafa Kamil accused the sheikh of conspiring with the local authorities to defy the court's ruling and by implication undermine the authority of the shariʿa.[63] In its campaign, the journal solicited and published letters from the public that denounced the sheikh's behavior. In response, *al-Muʾayid* ran several articles by ʿAli Yusuf under the headline "Our Affair and the Sadat [Family]," retelling his side of the story and blaming al-Sadat himself for forcing the lovers to take such a radical action. In these articles, Yusuf pointed out the father's dishonesty and shady dealings (e.g., accepting the dowry and money gifts) with the sheikh. In regard to the court ruling, though commending the judge for his vast knowledge of the law and his celebrated impartial judgments, ʿAli Yusuf doubted the legality or the wisdom of his last ruling, describing it as essentially an "emotive, non-rational and reactive response."[64]

Even *Al-Ahram*, known for its Francophile leanings, ran an article on the subject of "freedom," which indirectly criticized the couple for abusing their right to freedom and the father for violating his obligations as a parent. Real freedom, the editorial argued, is never absolute and is not supposed to transgress the rights of others; freedom is not "casting off modesty or absolute indulgence where a subject is free to do as he or she pleases. . . . Instead, freedom is the ability to enjoy one's full rights without transgressing the right of others. . . . The father's rights over his offspring are not to be forfeited since the children's rights are actualized only by honoring their father's."[65] At the same time, parents have to respect the wishes of their grown-up children. In fact, as most parents know, a priest or sheikh, in concert with local custom, can marry consenting adults without the parents' approval. The only condition is to notify the parent beforehand. Just as individual rights are not absolute, the obligation of honoring the father is also not absolute. As called for by both the Christian and the Islamic traditions, the abuse of power by the father or guardian puts limitations on the extent of his authority.[66]

Al-Manar, the journal that spoke on behalf of Islamic reform, responded to rising public concern by engaging Islamic arguments on the matter. Under the title "Guardianship and the [Question of] Compatibility in Marriage" Rida explained *al-kafaʾa* in marital relations to mean compatibility in religion and morals and not of ancestry and social descent.[67] The hadiths (prophetic sayings) he presented, all authentic, argued for religious and moral compatibility as the keystone for a well-matched harmonious marriage and familial affinity. Yet, as he pointed out, the customary practice among Egyptians had been to wrongly favor lineage over faith and good conduct. In a didactic style, he criticized the established Muslim scholars for misleading the public and legitimizing social lineage under the auspices of less authoritative and suspect prophetic sayings. It is obvious from his interpretation of the tradition that Rida was condemning the old guard, of notables, old scholarly families, and high society, who derived their power from inherited wealth and blood ties. The Sunna, he pointed out, is clear on this issue because it differentiates between compatibility in affluence (the ability to provide equivalent livelihood) and family descent. Although affluence is necessary for a harmonious marriage, bloodline is not. Additionally, while the Sunna regards compatibility in religion, morals, and wealth between the two families necessary for marriage, correspondence in occupation is different from correspondence in wealth, as it is not easy to judge compatibility between occupations. Standards of worth apply differently to different occupations; moreover, occupations and their worth do change from one society to another and from one time to another, including today. Thus, to establish worth or excellence in an occupation is to also judge each vocation in its particular time and context.[68] In his discussion of occupation as a measure of social status, Rida was defending the professions arising out of a new capitalist economy, including the profession of journalism, which was his own. Concluding his article, Rida remarked that a learned man (a quality required of all journalists), in his opinion, was more than "qualified to marry a woman of high nobility even when his social origins were humbler and inferior to hers," because "to be educated and erudite is far more honorable and commendable than being born into nobility."[69] Again, one can presume that Rida here was responding to the father's unjust attack on journalism as an unworthy and lowly profession.

In contrast to those found in other journals, Rida's arguments were didactic and less partial, as he seriously engaged Islamic discourses in an attempt to find answers for these new emerging concerns. It is clear that his position was in sympathy with the act itself (if not necessarily with the actors) by demonstrating how their marriage complied with the spirit of the shari'a. But to his surprise and the surprise of many, the court and its presiding judge thought otherwise.

The Court Ruling

On August 1, the court reconvened to discuss the case. The father's lawyer once again requested the abrogation of the marriage for the following reasons:

1. Social incompatibility, because the father, 'Abdul Khaliq, a nobleman and descendent of the Prophet Muhammad, had been shamed and disgraced by the marriage of Sheikh 'Ali Yusuf, a man of modest origins, to his daughter.
2. Violation of prevailing customs and Islamic law, as the marriage had taken place in the absence of the bride's father, her legal guardian.
3. 'Ali Yusuf's socially ignoble occupation as a journalist had brought shame to a Sharifian family of al-Sadat's social caliber.

The court turned to 'Ali Yusuf's lawyer for a response. To the first question posited by the court, as to "whether shaykh 'Ali Yusuf transgressed proper moral conduct and national customs by marrying above his class," the lawyer retorted: "we are here to adjudicate a legal matter, your Honor, not a moral one"; the court simply ignored him.[70] I want to suggest that the lawyer's response—that his client should be judged on whether he broke the law and not on whether his conduct was immoral or offended national customs—assumes and acts upon the colonial notion of a natural separation of law and morality, a position clearly not accepted by either the court or by prevailing customs, nor even by the new standards laid out by the reformists. The Islamic reformist discourse, as one recalls, was, in fact, insistent on not separating morality and the law in the same manner as did Europe, and that is precisely what distinguished its discourse of modernity from the European colonial one. Not surprisingly, the argument of the separation was ignored by all parties because it fell so far outside the parameters of the discourse.

In response to the question of "evidence of 'Ali Yusuf's occupation and level of education," the defense lawyer responded: "he studied at al-Azhar but did not earn his degree," leaving al-Azhar to pursue "the esteemed occupation" of journalism for its "laudable role in educating and guiding the public on issues of great importance—morally, politically and socially." Defending his client's occupation as an honorable profession in spite of its newness, the lawyer stressed that journalism "confers on journalists the utmost of principles by way of education and good morals."[71]

Returning finally to the issue of ʿAli's social compatibility—his modest social origins—the lawyer stunned the court by presenting a document tracing ʿAli Yusuf's "genealogical descent back to the honorable family of Hasan bin ʿAli, the son of the revered ʿAli bin Talib, the cousin and closest companion of the Prophet," as evidence of his noble descent. Its intent was to void the "social incompatibility clause" by proving that socially ʿAli Yusuf was on equal footing with the al-Sadat family, not only in wealth but also in lineage. Like Safiya's father, ʿAli Yusuf claimed to be a *sharif* and a registered member in *naqabet al-Ashraf*, the Guild of Nobles (with irony, the literal modern translation of naqabat al-asharaf is the union of nobles).[72]

Once this was disclosed, according to public accounts, mayhem broke out in the courtroom with each side slandering the other. Of course, the tabloids and gossip columns had a field day covering all the details of their smear campaigns, including the father's lawyer maligning ʿAli Yusuf as a foreigner (*ajami*), a non-Arab, a Christian, and a Shiʿa. The intention of making such a claim was to prove that a non-Arab of Christian origin (Copt), as all indigent Egyptians were before the coming of Islam, could not be a true descendent of Quraysh, the honorable Arab tribe of ʿAli and the Prophet. In fury, the sheikh's lawyer ridiculed ʿAbdul Khaliq al-Sadat's claim of blue blood, claiming him to be as much of an imposter, for his grandfather, as evidenced by the famous and reliable historian of that period, al-Jabarti, was born to a slave of unknown origin.[73] One could read the slandering campaign as the tabloids did or take them more seriously as expressions of changes in attitudes and norms. One could possibly read the sheikh's doubts about al-Sadat's honorable descent as a likely challenge to older forms of social hierarchy and family households that consisted of slaves, concubines, and wives and where the rules of descent were much less formal and more flexible, in contrast to a modern new family, where property and paternity are established through more clearly delineated laws and rules regulating descent, kinship, and inheritance. After two weeks of hearing witnesses from both sides, the judge ruled the marriage void on the grounds of incompatibility, as accorded by *ʿurf*, or custom.[74] In spite of the defense's effort to prove Sheikh Yusuf of noble origin, the judge was not convinced and ruled to revoke his marriage to Safiya on the grounds of their social incompatibility. As the judge explained, whereas under custom "wealth and affluence are championed as the utmost of worthiness, poverty is the greatest of disgrace."[75] The father's witnesses proved without a doubt that the marriage to 'Ali Yusuf would indeed bring harm to the family of al-Sadat. 'Ali Yusuf, although matching the father's wealth, did not match his prestige or social class. His was earned and theirs was inherited. In accord with custom, "an individual living off inherited landed wealth and family endowments (*waqf*) is regarded as the most honorable and worthy of all occupations but not those who earn their prosperity through hard work and the effort of their labor."[76] In regard to the question of nobility, the court found in favor of al-Sadat, who provided conclusive evidence of his lineage and against the sheikh, who lied and conjured up the evidence of his noble descent. With regard to his occupation as a journalist, the court found Yusuf to be, contrary to his lawyer's claims, "an unprincipled mercurial journalist," who "persistently changed his stance in the service of those he wanted to please. He unjustly campaigned against prominent public figures in the name of 'public interest' but kept quiet on issues when his voice was most needed, just so that he could protect those in power."[77] 'Ali Yusuf, the court maintained, "has dishonored an honorable vocation by exploiting its pages to promote his own interests and no one else's."[78]

The judge's ruling, considered severe and highly opinionated, caused anxiety among those who read his judgment as more oratorical than legal. *Al-Manar*, for one, reported: "the ruling took the majority of the population of Egypt by surprise. Some criticized the judge's rhetoric as speechifying rather than lawful."[79] Most important, the ruling skirted the issue of the validity of the marriage and of Safiya's legal right as a mature woman no longer needing her father's protection or approval. To others, it was apparent that the principal force driving the decision was blatantly political rather than legal; it was not the marriage as much as 'Ali Yusuf's journalistic conduct (and by implication, his relationship with the khedive) that was put on trial.[80]

Additionally, conjuring up a fake document to claim 'Ali Yusuf's equality with the old and well-known privileged family of al-Sadat seemed to be the straw that broke the camel's back. Not standing up for the social rights of an emerging middle class (of which he was one) and caving in to the pressures of a declining landed class's claim that blood ties and inherited wealth were still a justifiable basis for social power proved detrimental to Yusuf's case and marriage. By not questioning the older structures, as he and his lawyer did initially, he seemed to abandon the claims of his own class and along with it their support. This is not to mention the fabrication of his own descent, which proved to many that he was indeed a rogue and unworthy of trust.

Ultimately, and by all accounts, it was 'Ali Yusuf's close relationship with the khedive that proved to be his Achilles heel. The government's defiance of the separation ruling, which was read as overriding the rule of the law and as a mark of the khedive's personal allegiance to 'Ali Yusuf, did not endear him to many, including the supreme justice and the presiding judge, both of whom took the government's act, backed by the Palace, as a challenge to their authority. 'Ali Yusuf's long history of political intrigue with the khedive, who was known for pitting political factions against one another to advance his own interests, led his case to become a channel for various groups to air their political frustrations. In his early career, the khedive had shown signs of promise in defying British colonial rule over Egypt. After his inauguration, the khedive, a young man aspiring to establish his independence from the British, gathered around him the support of Egyptian young reformers and nationalists as a way of cementing his power against the British. Initially, the khedive backed many of the projects proposed by nationalists and reformers, including 'Abduh's proposal to reform al-Azhar. By the time of 'Ali Yusuf's case, however, many among the Egyptian literate middle class and national reformers had lost faith in the khedive's ability to challenge the British. In addition, the khedive's political conspiracies alienated him from leading national figures, whereas 'Ali Yusuf's unconditional support of the khedive's policies was read as betrayal of their causes. Like other reformers, 'Abduh had broken with both the khedive and Yusuf after earlier being politically allied with them. As explained earlier, the khedive himself brought 'Abduh into al-Azhar to lead the reform of the institution. But as soon as 'Abduh's reform program at al-Azhar was under way, the khedive, under the influence of or in alliance with the nationalist Mustafa Kamil (Abduh's political enemy), threw his support instead to the old guard of al-Azhar, who were plotting to remove 'Abduh from his position and undermine the influence of the board. 'Ali Yusuf initially played neutral but eventually came on board to support the khedive (and

Mustafa Kamil) against 'Abduh. Yusuf's journal, *al-Mu'ayid*, retracted its
support of 'Abduh as the presiding leader of al-Azhar, claiming that his
reform program was too radical. 'Abduh's relationship with the khedive
worsened once 'Abduh refused to give in to the khedive's demands to buy
endowment (waqf) land, which 'Abduh considered illegal. At this point,
the khedive turned against 'Abduh, accusing him of selling himself to
Cromer's camp and for betraying the trust of the Royal Palace.[81]

Some found 'Abduh's complete silence over the issues raised by 'Ali
Yusuf's court case troubling. After all, he was the mufti of Egypt when
the case unfolded, and more significantly, he himself was the leading
spokesman for the restructuring of the family that encouraged companionate marriage and called for the right of men and women to choose
their marriage partner. Some explained his silence as abstention from the
unscrupulous politics surrounding the case. The latter explanation was
confirmed by a recorded conversation between Rida and 'Abduh immediately after the court hearing was concluded. In their exchange, 'Abduh
endorsed Rida's interpretation of compatibility by saying, "I totally agree
with your article on the question of compatibility that appeared in *al-
Manar* and was reprinted in *al-Mu'ayid*." When asked to remark on 'Ali
Yusuf's belief that the mufti was the mastermind behind the judge's ruling against him, 'Abduh's response was condemning of both sides. It went
as follows: "in so far as Sheikh 'Ali and Sadat's characters are concerned, I
am of the opinion that these two are indeed compatible, not in honor but
in disgrace."[82]

One can perhaps draw on Rashid Rida's analysis to postulate
'Abduh's likely opinion on the matter. In spite of 'Ali Yusuf's betrayal of
'Abduh, as conveyed with all its unpleasant details in *al-Manar*, Rida
took the higher ground in his coverage and analysis of 'Ali Yusuf's case.
From his earliest interventions, Rida saw the importance of the case to lie
beyond the personal narrative of 'Ali Yusuf's marriage and to implicate
larger societal attitudes and responses to the unavoidable rearrangement
of the Egyptian family structure. This was the concern, as he implied,
that occupied a larger space in the Egyptian public mind than mere petty
infighting between two families. Rida's comments on the subject were
neither sensationalist nor condemning. Instead, the case presented an opportunity to discuss the possibilities for female rights within the Islamic
discourse and to engage that discourse on the meanings of compatibility

as a way of arriving at a definition more suitable to modern middle-class values and desires. The social and economic restructuring of Egyptian society throughout the nineteenth century called for different family norms—standards that inspired new desires and tastes, especially among the urban and literate middle classes. Rida argued that the subject of compatibility was not governed by 'ibadat (rules of worship prescribed by God) but was a matter of mu'amalat (or rules regulating people's daily activities and transactions), and because all relational transactions belonged to the sphere of public interest intended to safeguard people against harm, the rules governing these transactions were governed in the final analysis by man-made laws arrived at by analogy (*qiyas*, or inductive reasoning common to Islamic rationality) and as such are liable to change over time and under new circumstances.[83] It is important to note here that Rida took this position not because he was at heart an emancipationist but because he considered the older arrangements to be no longer suitable or compatible with modern sensibilities or the expectations required of a modern Muslim subject, including making rational decisions and taking responsibility for one's own life. In this sense, Rida, as one would assume of 'Abduh as well, did not see any fundamental contradiction between an Islamic way of life and modern subjectivity.

Although the court's ruling favored the father, a representative of the old and disintegrating upper class, it is best not to approach the ruling as a manifestation of traditional against modern, reactionary against progressive ideas and forces. Rather, the ruling showed several interesting features that offer a window onto the complexity of the interpretation of Islamic family law and balancing rights with duties. In asserting the father's authority over his daughter, the ruling appeared to support those who thought the father was practicing his proper obligation toward her, because he would not assent to a marriage that was socially inappropriate for her. In this sense, the ruling could be understood as affirming "traditional" forms of obligation over modern individual rights, a nonindigenous notion imported from Europe. Yet, in the first instance, Safiya asserted her right to marry without her father's consent as based in Islamic law. It appears that the court accepted this argument, as it was never addressed in the decision. Instead, the judge based his ruling on a more open-ended feature of the law, that of customary ('urf) law and specifically on the issue of compatibility. By taking this tack, the judge avoided engaging with a clear-cut law that would support her central legal claim to an absolute right given to her under the shar‘.

No one—neither the general public nor the contending parties nor commentators such as Rida—ever questioned whether compatibility was a legitimate question to bring to court or for the judge to rule on. Rather, there was disagreement about how to define compatibility, an elusive notion that escapes fixed legal definition. This ambiguity allowed questions of "public welfare" (maslaha) and morality to become part of the legal discourse. The father argued that social compatibility was defined by conventional customs in which descent was primary. However, in addition to relying on traditional notions of nobility and birth, he also questioned the moral status of ‘Ali Yusuf's profession. Rida, on the other hand, not only defended journalism but, more important, argued that compatibility should refer first and foremost to religious and moral compatibility. The judge took the middle road when reaching his ruling on compatibility. The ruling was not a matter of simply supporting the father as much as making the point that when considering compatibility, customary conventions or ‘urf (as a legitimate source of the law) have to be taken into account. At the same time, as is clearly evidenced from his statement, in his ruling the judge took even more seriously the question of morality as a constitutive feature of compatibility. ‘Ali Yusuf's incompatibility was decided primarily on the basis of his character, and he was judged as a fraudulent individual not only for contriving his noble descent but, more important, for his deceitful and dishonorable political stands. It was his character that was put on trial rather than his marriage.

Conclusion

Both father and husband continued their fight. ‘Ali Yusuf appealed to a higher court and presented the same defense once again; once again he lost. In the meantime, Safiya, refusing to return to her father's residence, remained at the home of Sheikh al-Rafi‘i, even though she was no longer a welcomed guest.[84] Safiya was eventually forced to return to her father's home, but, according to a rumor circulating at the time, only after a private conversation with none other than Lord Cromer himself, who promised to intervene on her behalf. Soon after the public storm was over, the father did indeed give in to his daughter's wishes to marry 'Ali Yusuf, his humble origins notwithstanding. Once the story of the two lovers and their violation of customary norms had been erased from public memory, their class differences slowly seeped back into their lives. Hints of dissatisfaction began to emerge in the gossip columns, disclosing stories of an unhappy wife, frustrated with a husband unable to keep up with her social responsibilities and demands. Many read his risky ventures to accumulate more wealth and power as his way of attempting to live up to his wife's unreasonable expectations. These attempts, however, backfired. In 1907, his heavy investment in an unstable real estate venture cost him the larger portion of his wealth, deepening the gap in their social status. Described as a broken and poorer man, 'Ali Yusuf in 1912 resigned his position as a journalist to take up the traditional and more respectable position of heading al-Wafa'iya, a Sufi order to which the Sadat household was known to have belonged and controlled.[85] His bid for social respectability was cut short by his unexpected death less than a year later.

The debates about love and marriage that swirled through Egyptian society offer us a window on the struggles and tribulations of a society undergoing change. What should be clear from this analysis of the various forces in play around the contested case of 'Ali Yusuf's marriage to Safiya is that the different actors were engaged in creating a new discursive reality in an open-ended process. This process belies the dominant scholarly interpretations of this period and of reformers such as 'Abduh who engaged in the debates. Rather than participating in a process shaped fundamentally by dichotomized polarities—liberal versus traditional, modern versus premodern, secular versus religious—the individuals and groups who acted in these events did not understand or make their choices in dichotomous terms, nor for that matter did their actions necessarily correspond with their intentions. Rather than choosing an ideological position and acting accordingly, the actors involved in responding to day-to-day realities on the ground found themselves shifting positions that in many ways defied simple causal explanations. Rather than being driven by consistent ideological polarities, actions and ideas were shaped through a process of negotiation and compromise, as actors sought to make sense of the new world they inhabited.

From this analytical perspective, we can see new Islamic arrangements in the making, constructed through a social process rooted in a particular time and place. The fluid meanings that were given to moral obligations, legal precedents, family forms, and so forth were neither "European" nor "traditional." Various actors in fact failed to carry out their "prescribed" roles as reformers or as traditionalists. So it was possible for a secularist newspaper to speak for traditional obligations of a patriarchal family, while an Islamic reform journal defended the individual rights of a daughter, but within a new Islamic discursive framework. Neither can we read from this case that politics trumped religion and that reformers were cynically manipulating Islamic language to accomplish a political agenda. A judge who was known as a Muslim reformer ruled in favor of the father on the "traditional" ground that social compatibility is necessary to marriage. Yet, in his ruling, he judged 'Ali Yusuf to be incompatible with his wife's family not because of his profession per se, but because he had behaved dishonorably by harnessing the power of his pen to the particular interests and political ambitions of the khedive. In this interpretation, the judge was transmuting an older meaning of honor based in familial connection into a new definition focused on individual responsibility and truthfulness. This case presents an illuminating moment in Egypt becoming modern. It also demonstrates that history in the making is a complex interplay of different elements rather than a contest determined by a rigid clash of pregiven principles in which one or the other must conquer.

6

Conclusion

> Show me just what Muhammad brought that was new and there you will find things only evil and inhuman, such as his command to spread by the sword the faith he preached.
>
> Emperor Manuel II Paleologus, 1391

The description of Islam as "evil and inhuman" was quoted by Pope Benedict XVI in a lecture, "Faith, Reason and the University—Memories and Reflections," delivered a day after the fifth anniversary of September 11. Explicating the essential differences between Christianity and Islam, the pope once again endorsed the view of Islam as nonrational and chronically violent. In contrast to a "humane Christian" faith where God acts in accordance with reason, explained the pope, an absolute transcendental God distances Islam from reason, making it more prone to violence.[1] The pope's remarks, while stunningly bigoted, were neither surprising nor unprecedented. As various scholars in the field have already noted, the deep-seated loathing of Islam has a long-standing history, one rooted in an orientalist discourse founded on the oppositionality of East and West and premised on the notions of an inferior irrational religious East and a superior rational West. As its most celebrated critic, Edward Said, pointed out, this varied body of knowledge produced under imperial Europe was "not an airy European *fantasy* about the Orient but *a created body of theory and practice*," which after many generations had become "an accepted grid for *filtering* through the Orient into *Western consciousness*."[2] It was a grid, in other words, that became operational for writers of all persuasions, left or right, scholarly or nonscholarly.

As it happens, the pope's remarks echo arguments made by the nineteenth-century French orientalist M. Gabriel Hanotaux, whose popular writings on the deficiencies of Islam precipitated similar waves of anger among Muslims and a fiery response by the subject of our study, the renowned Muslim reformer Muhammad 'Abduh. Reiterating a claim similar to the pope's, Hanotaux, in an attempt to justify European colonization over a century earlier, attributed Europe's advancement to a humane Christian faith and Muslims' "backwardness" to a despotic, antihumanist Islam. The distinction he drew between Christianity and Islam centered on the way in which the two faiths conceptualized their gods: Whereas an immanent God in Christian human life allowed for the emergence of free will and reason in Christianity, an all-powerful transcendental God in Islam precluded both. As the two faiths materialized over time, these defining doctrinal features produced two distinct and essentially opposed cultures: self-reliance and independence in Christian Europe and dependence and submissiveness in the Muslim East. To repair the rift created by such views, Hanotaux then (as the pope now) assured his Muslim audience of his good intentions and respect for Islam and his mere desire to seek dialogue with Muslims. Speaking on behalf of his Muslim brethren, 'Abduh then questioned Hanotoux's bigotry and historical amnesia, reminding him of the evils the Crusades and Spanish Inquisition committed against Muslims and Jews and of the intolerance Christians demonstrated toward one another in Counter-Reformation Europe.[3] In the same way, Muslims today, sensing a touch of insincerity in the pope's expressions of regret and desire to "work together," reprimanded him for confining his apology to the reaction to his words rather than the words themselves.

It seems as if little has changed since the nineteenth century, when Western discourses at the height of Europe's imperial power came to characterize Islam as inherently "antihumanist," "nonrational," and inimical to modernity.[4] The pope's negative depiction of Islam, which many defend today as justifiable, signifies not just an overwhelming ignorance of and prejudice against Islam but, far more significantly, the continual potency of these views in present-day discourses in spite of the demise of colonialism.[5] Orientalist scholars of Islam, from the colonial period through to the 1970s, persistently attributed the failure of the Muslim world to modernize to Islam's antihumanist, nonrational essence.[6] Advocating post-Enlightenment values—the hegemonic analytic then—the old scholarship attributed the problems in modern Islam to its antihistorical, illiberal propensities. In contrast to a West that broke with its deceptive, tyrannical past by embracing science, secularism, and historical progress, the Muslim world instead continued to seek the truth by constantly looking backward in time.[7]

Muslims' disinclination toward rationality is claimed to have originated in early Islam (3rd century A.H./7th century A.D.) and is specifically traced back to the conflict between religion (Muslim theologians and jurists) and reason (rationalists and philosophers), which resulted in the defeat of rationalism and in the triumph of traditionalism. The termination of rationalism in Islam is a prevalent and a highly cherished theme among early orientalists. It is also a highly problematic construct because it has been derived by analyzing arguments that have been largely abstracted from their contexts and studied in isolation from the system of thought and practices in which they are embedded. This modern dichotomous construct of reason and religion, to put it differently, was to a significant degree imposed by earlier scholars upon their subject matter. Religion in premodern Muslim societies, very much as in medieval Europe, was characteristically not a separate segregated aspect of life but the mode in which every aspect of life, theological and otherwise, was related to the divine. By projecting back on the past concepts extraneous to that past, Western scholars were bound to come up with highly dubious conclusions. One obviously misleading inference was to reduce an extraordinarily complex disputation between two rival claims within the Islamic tradition to a mere cast of mind. A second problem is that by detaching arbitrarily the parts from the whole, orientalist scholars were blind to the processes through which these "philosophical" methods of reasoning came to be absorbed and integrated into the Islamic language and idiom. To put the point in a different way, Islamic "theology" prevailed, as recent scholars have shown, not by the rejection of logic but by integrating logic into its arguments, thus strengthening the theologians' claims against those of their rivals. By redefining logical reasoning (i.e., syllogism) in Islamic terms, Muslim scholars were able, in other words, to transcend limitations and provide solutions for defects within the tradition without dismantling it.[8]

The dichotomy between religion and reason is also extended to explain the present. The "triumph of theology" over "Hellenic philosophy," according to the master orientalist H. A. R. Gibb (who himself was a Romantic and a critic of the iron-clad positivistic rationalism), not only confined rationality in medieval Islam but shaped the formation of the modern Muslim mind as well. It is no accident that Muslim modernists, such as al-Afghani and Iqbal, he argued, would be drawn to the nonrational and the romantic in European thought; their "intuitive" "atomistic" mind compelled them in that direction.[9] In contrast to Europe, where the revolt against reason and objective standards was offset by "scientific and historical thought," such countervailing currents were almost absent in the Muslim world. The atomistic Arab mind distrustful of "all abstract or a priori universal principles" is what modern Muslims have inherited culturally, thus making their endeavor to modernize not just unsuccessful but often pointless. To demonstrate the point, Gibb offers the example of the nineteenth-century Muslim rational "pragmatist" Muhammad 'Abduh and his attempt to separate religion from politics, which came to no avail. 'Abduh's break from his romantic mentor, al-Afghani, Gibb pointed out, failed because it lacked appeal among the main body of Muslims, both conservative (theologians) and lay modernist (apologists): conservatives rejected it "as they rejected almost all Muhammad 'Abduh's ideas—a priori and on principle" as un-Islamic, and the "modernists, who claim to be his followers, did not understand it and . . . fell back upon Jamal al-din's activism,"[10] which Gibb described as a "revolutionary theocratic impulse."[11] In the long run, rather than rehabilitating Islam, 'Abduh's reform ideas engendered "the emergence of a new fundamentalist school calling themselves 'salafiya' or upholders of the tradition of the father of the Islamic church."[12] One cannot help but recall Vatikiotis's account of 'Abduh's vain quest for a humanist Islam and his assessment that Islam's antihumanist, nonrational intrinsic qualities would impede its reformation to fit with a secular humanist and rational modern world.[13]

The perception of Islam as adverse and unreceptive to modernity has its genesis in yet another popular theme that intertwines with Islam's antihumanist propensity: the theocratic, despotic character of Islam. The fusion of religion and state, an intrinsic feature of Islamic culture, once again makes Islam irredeemable for modern times. This fusion originated with the Prophet, who was the first to install a theocratic Islamic state in seventh-century Arabia when he combined both these powers in his own hands. In contrast to Christianity, which "renders unto Caesar what is Caesar's and unto God what is God's," the despotic theocratic nature of Islam leaves Islamic "civilization" inhospitable to secular democratic and political rights, values that are intrinsic to modernity. This is not an unfamiliar theme even today, where the rampant violence in the contemporary Muslim world is constantly ascribed to a despotic Islam and to "fundamentalist" Muslims' rejection of secular democratic institutions and practices founded on the separation of state and religion and universal individual rights. Samuel Huntington's popular "clash of cultures" proposition, for instance, rests on the notion of Islam as the archenemy of Western democracy and freedom. In his influential 1998 book, *The Clash of Civilizations*, he suggested what many earlier Western orientalists had already reiterated, that the fundamental source of conflicts in the modern world is cultural, not economic or political.[14] The gist of his argument in the case of Islam goes as follows: the lack of core cultural values that produced democracy in the West—that is, the separation of secular and religious authorities, the rule of law, representative government, civil liberties, and individual rights—account for the current rift between the Islamic and Western civilizations today.[15] As this "fault line" between the Judeo-Christian and Islamic civilizations has been in existence for over 1,300 years, the prospect of it declining soon is also unlikely. The concept of the clash of civilizations, as Huntington himself notes, is really not his own but borrowed from its true champion and present-day leading orientalist, Bernard Lewis. In "Rage of Muslims," his famed article in the *Atlantic Monthly*, Lewis argued strongly that the history of the Mediterranean was and still is torn by two monolithically opposed powers: a Western Judeo-Christian world confronting an aggressive and hostile Islamic world unwavering in its quest to conquer and convert the West. The conflict is ancient, going back to the birth of Islam as a contender to Christianity. Lewis explicitly rejects the notion that current hostilities are driven by imperial policies and interests pursued first by Europe and more recently by the United States. Instead, he places the onus of the "conflict of civilization" on Islam and on "Islamic fury" against a West that has surpassed Islam as a civilization. The present political conflicts are explained as merely psychological, caused by "a feeling of humiliation—a growing awareness, among the heirs of an old, proud, and long dominant civilization, of having been overtaken, overborne, and overwhelmed by those whom they regarded as their inferiors."[16] Lewis's article came to gather a much wider audience after it was picked up and popularized by Huntington and following the ghastly events of September 11, which helped to bolster his views and embolden him to promote a more aggressive campaign recommending preemptive attacks against Islamic and Arab regimes that he considered dangerous and unreceptive to U.S. (and Israeli) interests in the region. With his views gaining wide appeal, leading journals, including the *Wall Street Journal* and the *Washington Post*, solicited Lewis's opinions on Middle Eastern matters. Lewis, reports William Dalrymple in the *New York Review of Books*, "used the attack on the World Trade Center to encourage the US to attack Saddam Hussein, implicitly making a link between the al-Qaeda operation and the secular Iraqi Baathist regime, while assuring the administration that they would be fêted by the populace who 'look to us for help and liberation' and thanked by other Muslim governments whose secret 'dearest wish' was an American invasion to remove and replace Saddam."[17] He justified his calls for military action by citing the so-called fact that Muslims abhor weakness and comprehend none other than the language of "brute force."[18] As the leading hired consultant and advisor to the Bush administration, it is not surprising that "the Lewis doctrine, in effect, had become US policy," as conveyed by the *Wall Street Journal*.[19]

Huntington and Lewis's views of an innate civilizational conflict founded on an inherently violent Islam and a culture that is in essence antithetical to the core of Western democracy, humanism, and modernity are not value free nor are they harmless, as attested by the wars being waged globally today under the United States' lead. Both Lewis's and Huntington's framework assumes that Islamic civilization is essentially static. The implications of these two ideas would include such inferences as the following: that Islam will always be counter to modernity; that the enmity is perpetual because Islam will not change, thereby deflecting any responsibility for the conflict from the West; and that there is no possibility of peaceful coexistence, in spite of the historical evidence to the contrary.[20] Recently, an increasing number of academic publications have appeared that explain the conflicts ravaging the Middle East today in terms of cultural wars. A reviewer of Vali Nasr's *The Shia Revival: How Conflicts with Islam Would Shape the Future* reaffirms Nasr's claim that an age-old animosity between Islam's two major sects, the majority Sunni and the minority Shiʿa, which dates from 632 A.D., is the primary cause for the violence consuming the Middle East and especially Iraq today.[21]

The "clash of civilizations" notion would be a matter only for scholarly dispute were it not invoked to serve as justification for the various conflicts of the late twentieth century, whether in Afghanistan, Iraq, Somalia, Lebanon, or Palestine, or for that matter when it is called upon to validate the barbaric acts of "ethnic cleansing," as it was in Serbia and Croatia, among other places.[22] Had the "clash of civilizations" not been given credibility in the West, the wars or crimes committed in its name would have been understood for what they really are, rather than as the natural manifestation of a long-standing cultural war between two opposed worlds, one Muslim, the other not.

The premise of the clash of civilizations, both in its older and newer form, is ideological and prescriptive rather than descriptive or historical. Serious scholarly accounts of Islamic–Christian encounters, as William Dalrymple's review article in the *New York Review of Books* documents, point in the opposite direction, describing porous borders across religious differences and complex commercial and trading relations as well as the formation of political alliances and exchanges of knowledge. Rather than the common story of "conversion by the sword," the historical accounts on the first wave of Islamic expansion convey the Arabs more as (for lack of a proper term) "liberators" rather than as "invaders," who freed the indigenous population of Copts and Syriacs from the discriminatory policies imposed by a "despotic" Byzantine Church.[23] Recent archeological excavations from the Umayyad period verified these accounts when they uncovered sites revealing vast expansion in church-building accompanied by a similar growth in the making of Hellenic mosaics, signaling a state of religious and cultural tolerance as well as economic prosperity for the non-Muslim indigenes.[24] There is also Nabil Matar's meticulous scholarship on later periods that provides a serious challenge to the clash of civilizations theory, demonstrating the intermingling of Christians and Muslims, exchanging both goods and knowledge, and conclusively concluding that the encounters between the two worlds were not exclusive to the battlefield. In addition, Matar's *In the Lands of the Christians: Arab Travel Writings in the Seventeenth Century* refutes Bernard Lewis's claim of Muslim disinterest in and apathy toward Europe and Christianity, documenting to the contrary a Muslim curiosity in Christendom that was equal to that of Europe.[25] There are also other historical accounts that pose a challenge to the foundational premise on which this theory of clash of civilizations rests.[26] The most significant example is that of Islamic Andalusia, which despite its constant frontier battles with Christian Europe became renowned for creating a model of a pluralist culture, one unparalleled in the history of Christian Europe.[27]

Many of the contemporary scholars writing on Islam are, in fact, ardent critics of the *Clash of Civilizations* and of the cultural wars waged in its name by the United States to stave off the Islamic fundamentalist peril. Yet, many of these critics remain caught in the binary constructs that are central to the orientalist scholarship they criticize by continuing to invoke humanistic, secularist, and tradition-free post-Enlightenment assumptions to evaluate modern Islamic thought and politics. The result, this self-reflexive, theoretical genre of postorientalist and postmodernist scholarship, continues to be encumbered by a notion of religion informed and shaped by the modern experience of Western societies. Although the larger body of this postorientalist literature represents a theoretically ambitious attempt to break the barrier of the "difference" between East and West by combining a more hermeneutical approach of understanding with postmodernist critiques, many of these authors nevertheless end up terminating any serious dialogue with Muslims who challenge and critique Western categories and their practices.[28] In this literature, Western categories (like secularism, democracy, and individualism) are never questioned, leaving them to operate as given truths rather than concepts with history and meaning. One inevitable outcome of this is that the West once again is left as the unacknowledged benchmark for evaluating modern Islam and Islamists. By uncritically embracing the Western humanist tradition, the larger body of this scholarship—rather than escaping the simplistic binarism of the "for" or "against" of earlier scholarship—is led to side with the moderates who accommodate democratic and modern values over and against the unapologetic "fundamentalists" who do not. Finally, by collapsing modernity with secularism, radical Islamists are explained primarily as "epiphenomenal of social upheaval," a reaction to social and economic predicaments, a purely political phenomenon that draws on Islamic symbols and imagery to enflame the passions of the alienated and the disenfranchised.[29] This interpretation ignores the Islamists' far-reaching critique of the functioning of Western modern societies and dismisses the importance of their vision of a society infused with Islamic ethics and practices. Although it is understandable to fear the violence and the repression of militant Islam, to treat the ideas of the movement as appealing to predominantly irrational sentiments limits Western scholars' ability to understand what makes these movements so compelling.

This conceptual problem has also limited the revisionist scholarship on Islam that rejects orientalist depictions of modern Islam as nonrational and backward looking. This is unfortunate, because postorientalist writers might have opened up possibilities for understanding Islamic tradition in its own terms. For example, the new scholarship challenges the orientalist construction of Islamic movements as rooted in tradition, arguing that Islamic movements, both radical and moderate, are produced by modern politics and circumstances and are, in effect, modern. Bruce Lawrence contends that "without modernity there are no fundamentalists, just as there are no modernists."[30] Rather than being fixated on creating their authentic past, Islamists claim ancient roots only for modern institutions and practices, and in so doing, they have invented a new tradition, one that is only mythically related to the original. A strong proponent of this view is the sociologist of Islam Sami Zubaida, who demonstrates that the nation-state and its agencies are assumed in most modern Islamic reform thought, including that of radical Islamists, like Khomeini and Qutb, and moderate reformers like 'Abduh. Their social and political ideas have little to do with Islamic heritage, for they ignore the accumulated body of Islamic discourses, deriving their justification directly from their rereading of the two fundamental sources, the Qur'an and the Sunna. In contradistinction to the traditional orientalist view, Zubaida suggests that the idea of the fusion of state and religion is not inherent to Islam but is a modern invention that represents "a departure rather than a continuity with Islamic political traditions or precepts."[31] The Islamic government of Khomeini (*Wilayat al-Faqih*), according to Zubaida, is a modern invention because "its credibility and 'thinkability' are facilitated by the conditions of the modern state and politics. What makes Khomeini's theory plausible is the idea of the people as a political force which can effect revolution and transformation."[32] Not only does this new interpretation challenge the orientalists' views on the inseparability of state and religion in Islam; it also questions their depictions of Muslims as submissive and passive. The populist nature of the Iranian Revolution, led by the Shi'a clerics, bazaar merchants, and other traditional social groupings, demonstrates the existence rather than the absence of a civil society, one capable of rallying massive popular support not only to contest state authority but also to overthrow it.[33]

Through a close reading of *Wilayat al-Faqih*, Zubaida offers us a rather engaging rendition of how much Khomeini's discourse presumes Western concepts and practices, even though the language of the doctrine "is conducted exclusively in terms of traditional Islamic discussions with hardly any reference to Western or Western-inspired politico-ideological notions."[34] Even the Quranic concept of "the people" (*al-nas*), which Khomeini invoked to awaken the Iranian masses, is impregnated with social and political meanings that are completely indebted to the modern nation-state, to political sovereignty and mass politics, and hardly at all to the original generic term of people as "collectivities."[35] Yet unlike other "fundamentalists" such as the Muslim Brothers, who reject modern political thought but adopt elements of it "clothed in Islamic terms," Khomeini "makes no claims or references to Western thought—he writes as if it does not exist."[36]

One can see the appeal as well as the usefulness of the notion of "invented tradition" to revisionists who want to scrutinize simplistic constructions of Islam as irrational, scriptural, and tradition-bound by demonstrating to the contrary that Islamists are in fact "highly flexible, remarkably innovative, and cavalier toward hallowed tradition."[37] Though providing a more dynamic and complex picture of Islamic reform movements, the notion of tradition here remains problematic. Conceptually, to posit a new Islam that has ruptured completely from its past and its discursive tradition retains the premise that a tradition is an unchanging, immutable essence. It also reads any change within the tradition as a departure from its founding doctrines rather than as a necessary condition in a discursive tradition constituted of historically extended discourses. When Islamists like Khomeini or Qutb seek the past, it is because they are searching to achieve discursive coherence by referring the present to an authoritative corpus that entails an effective assessment of that past. By locating their arguments within the tradition, they are not cynically manipulating the past but relating the tradition to the present. At the same time, engaging the tradition, as I have argued in the body of this work, does not exclude its transformation in the process of its reconfiguration. In other words, changes do not necessarily mean a rupture from the tradition, especially when Islam is approached as a discursive tradition rather than as a fixed, unchanging set of beliefs and practices. From this conceptual approach, the categories of "authentic" and "invented" traditions obscure more than illuminate contemporary Islamic reformers and their movements.

Ironically, the same dichotomous categories of authentic and invented traditions were also employed by orientalist scholars (albeit differently) to question the legitimacy of modernizing Islamic reformers of earlier eras. For instance, these scholars regarded any modernization of Islam to be simply a betrayal of its original essence. But rather than targeting the "fundamentalists" of today's scholarship, orientalists reserved their criticisms exclusively for "liberals," such as ʿAbduh, al-Afghani, Iqbal, and educated lay Muslims, whom they labeled as "modernists." They frowned upon these Muslims for wanting to invent a liberal humanist Islam while at the same time continuing to seek out knowledge in (medieval Islamic) books rather than in free inquiry. The outcome, they argued, was paradoxical, for the great majority of conservative traditional theologians, recognizing that a liberal humanist Islam is a mere distortion of true Islam, rejected the modernizers' ideas. The modernists, on the other hand, created an imaginative reconstruction of Islam along Western liberal lines in the name of preserving the religion, all the while claiming that they were being true to the spirit of Islam and the teachings of the Prophet Muhammad. The disastrous result was that neither group could "really 'rethink' the religious content of Islam in any profound sense."[38] Writing in the 1960s, Malcolm Kerr expressed this view when he admonished ʿAbduh for thinking he could construct a liberal humanist Islam out of medieval Islamic theology and for misleading Muslim reformers (such as Rashid Rida) who

proclaimed it their objective to make these [Islamic medieval] doctrines serve as such a basis in the modern age. For this purpose, they thought it worthwhile to recast them in a more modern image (emphasizing, for example, their flexibility, utilitarianism, and compatibility with certain institutional landmarks of European liberalism), proclaiming at the same time that they were returning to the original purity of what Islamic teaching had been before it was corrupted by tyranny and ignorance.[39]

'Abduh's aversion to breaking free from the tradition, asserted Kerr, was costly to the modern revivalist movement, because his thought ended up providing "a better basis for apologetics and polemics than for social reform and cultural rebirth."[40]

In fact, the theme "to modernize Islam is to betray it" was quite popular among early scholars, especially among those who studied nineteenth- and early twentieth-century reformers.[41] The most famous work is Albert Hourani's seminal and authoritative *Arabic Thought in the Liberal Age*, published in 1962 and still today one of the most frequently quoted works in the field.[42] Hourani uncritically embraced and elaborated on the orientalist notion of the invention of a modern fictitious liberal Islam.[43] As noted earlier, Hourani blamed 'Abduh for stripping Islam of its authentic tradition by conjuring new liberal meanings and illegitimately attaching them to Islamic concepts and practices, giving them meanings that they simply were never intended to have. Hourani disavowed some of his views in later years, acknowledging his error for "laying too much emphasis upon ideas which were taken from Europe, and not enough upon what was *retained*, even if in a changed form, from an older tradition."[44] In spite of his recanting, the invention of a new Islam remains one of the most popular notions in revisionist historiography.

In sum, regardless of how very different and oppositional their representations of Islam, both the old and new historiography continue to be plagued by a shared understanding of tradition as a fixed essence as well as a mutual utilization of dichotomous categories counterposing the rational to the irrational, the modern to the antimodern. This difficulty becomes even more obvious when the new historiography attempts to explain "fundamentalism" as a modern phenomenon.

Though acknowledging that modernity is the necessary condition for contemporary revivalist Islamic movements, this scholarship defines the "fundamentalists" as "modern" but not as "modernists" because their goal is ultimately to install theocratic, repressive, and antimodernist regimes. In *Defenders of God*, Bruce Lawrence states that fundamentalism, "as a psychological mindset and a historical movement, is shaped by the modern world." However, fundamentalists are "bifurcated between their cause and their outcomes; they are at once the consequence of modernity and the antithesis of modernism."[45] They are driven by "the hatred, which is also the fear, of modernism."[46] As against modernists, fundamentalists tend "to divide consciousness into two categories: objective givens and ideological variables. They posit a constant tension between the former and the latter, between modernization and modernism."[47] Even as they embrace modernization (material structures and technological innovations), fundamentalists reject modernism and its manifested ideologies (e.g., autonomy and social justice). Although fundamentalism is a revolt against the Enlightenment and the values it produced, fundamentalists nonetheless employ modern technologies and material resources for "the purpose of promoting a vision of divine restoration."[48]

The political scientist Bassam Tibi agrees with Lawrence for he sees the danger of Islamic fundamentalism as lying in its inclusion of modern science and technology and its exclusion of the secular techno-scientific culture that accompanies it.[49] In his various works, Tibi attributes the rise of fundamentalism in the Middle East to the decline of the nation-state and the political vacuum it engendered in the Arab world after the humiliating military defeat of 1967 at the hands of the Israelis. The fundamentalists in their revolt against "epistemological imperialism of the west" are characterized by Tibi as "neither religious traditionalists nor modernists" but as having their "own version of modernity as well as their own troubles with its [Islamic] civilizational project."[50] The principal interest of fundamentalists in modern Western technology, he explains, is driven by their desire to establish a theocratic Islamic state, one that would refute democratic values and renounce human rights. As a reactive political movement that hides under the guise of religion, fundamentalism is to be feared more than earlier Islamic movements because today's fundamentalists' connection with modernity is through the development of modern military technology.[51] Although Tibi acknowledges that such extremists are but a minority in the Muslim Arab world, his broad assertions that "in Islam, there is no cultural understanding of individualism, and thus no concept of individual rights," that "the requirements for successfully promoting democratization are virtually absent in Islamic civilization," and that Muslim rulers are "hateful despots" tend to conflate Islam with fundamentalism anyhow.[52]

More subtly, Zubaida proposes that semantically speaking, all modern Islamists, both moderate and radical, are fundamentalists because they all derive their "ideologies" directly from the original sources, the Qur'an and the Sunna. Yet, they do not produce one homogenous ideology as claimed by classical orientalists. Some, like 'Abduh, interpret the two authoritative sources to advance European-inspired institutions and practices "clothed in Islamic terms," whereas others, like Khomeini, go back to these sources to deligitimate all that is Western as "westoxification." Nonetheless, Zubaida concludes, as did Lawrence, that radical Islamists—like Qutb, who provided the ideological foundation for extremist groups such as the Jama'at al-Muslimin (Society of Muslims)—are not clearly modern because they renounce "the political idiom of the modern nation-state . . . in favor of a universalist project based on faith."[53] Their antimodernist stand is explained by Zubaida as reactive and defensive, as exemplified by the Islamists' antiwomen stance: "The insistence on the Quranic penal code and on the restriction on women are emotionally and symbolically potent proclamations of cultural identity and antagonism to the Westernized sectors of society who have betrayed this heritage."[54]

Some contemporary scholars contest fundamentalism as a concept and doubt its applicability to militant Islam. "Fundamentalism," they say, obfuscates rather than enhances our understanding of modern Islam, precisely because, as John Esposito explains, "fundamentalism" is "too laden with Christian presuppositions and western stereotyping."[55] He and others question the validity of transferring a term invented by a North American Protestant movement in the 1920s to Islamic movements that emerged in the 1960s in response to the failed attempt of secular nationalist regimes to modernize and to defend against Israel's military expansion. Esposito prefers the more neutral idiom of Islamic revivalism, *al-Sahwa al-Islamiya*, as used by Islamists.[56] Ervand Abrahamian agrees with Esposito that the term is not only confusing but also "downright wrong."[57] Abrahamian rejects the category altogether because unlike radical Islamists, American fundamentalism intended to "save souls," not society. Khomeinism, by contrast, is a political movement "predominantly and primarily concerned with sociopolitical issues—with revolution against the royalist elite, expulsion of the western imperialists, and mobilization of what it terms the *mostazafin* (the oppressed) against the *mostakberin* (oppressors)."[58] That is why Abrahamian favors the term *populism* over *fundamentalism* because it captures far more accurately Khomeini's political ploy of mobilizing the "common people" by employing "charismatic figures and symbols, imagery, and language that have potent value in the mass culture."[59]

Although it is indeed legitimate to reject fundamentalism as a relevant analytical category, to claim that the core concern of such Islamists as Khomeini and Qutb to be essentially "temporal and political" is to suggest that these groups are either inadvertently duplicitous or outright fraudulent for using, in the words of Beinin and Stork, "the Quran, the hadiths . . . and other canonical religious texts to justify their stances and actions."[60] And although it is as legitimate not to deny the social and economic issues that factored into the making of these movements, to understand them simply as political movements reacting against a modernizing state and its rationalizing policies of economy and society is to bring forth yet another conceptual problem encumbering this literature.[61] By stripping them of their Islamic claims not only does this body of literature make these Islamists culpable of duplicity; it also rebuffs the validity of their critique of modernity precisely because it is Islamic. Just because their Islamic moral and social vision of the future is not commensurable with liberal humanism should not by any means make their criticisms less powerful or less valid than those put forward by Western poststructuralists and postmodernists, those Enlightenment critics whose ideas happen to inform our contemporary scholarly analysis. Furthermore, to deny Islamic criticisms of secular modernity is once again to set up Western secular humanism as the single authoritative source for adjudicating difference in the public sphere. Granted, we might not find the Islamists' views on modernity palatable or their vision of the future agreeable. However, to deny rather than engage their criticisms because we happen to dislike their views fails to practice the pluralism and tolerance that the liberal tradition preaches. Excluding those who are not secularists only breeds intolerance and dogmatism and an environment that creates rather than alleviates conflicts.[62]

Although the new scholarship on Islam has moved leaps and bounds beyond orientalism, its analysis continues to be plagued by what Michel Foucault termed the "blackmail of the Enlightenment," the coercive choice between "simplistic and authoritative alternatives: you either accept the Enlightenment and remain within the tradition of its rationalism (this is considered a positive term by some and used by others, on the contrary, as a reproach); or else you criticize the Enlightenment and then try to escape from its principles of rationality (which may be seen once again as good or bad)."[63] Although no one can deny the historical effect and efficacy of the Enlightenment or its transformative power, a problem arises when we come to see our relationship to the Enlightenment as one of "faithfulness to [its] doctrinal elements" rather than as one of a "permanent reactivation of an attitude—that is, of a philosophical ethos that could be described as a permanent critique of our historical era."[64] What Foucault posits here is that rather than being seduced by the alternatives of being "for" or "against," it might be more useful to seek ways to escape this dichotomy by cultivating an "ethos" or an attitude that understands the ambiguous and the paradoxical in modernity. Clearly, to transcend these foundational dichotomies, as he also recognized, is not easy, as it requires more than the cultivation of an attitude. It involves power, which tragically continues to favor those who are unwilling to concede.

Notes

CHAPTER 1: THE ISLAMIC REFORM TRADITION

1. Throughout this book, the term *modern* is used without qualification for descriptive convenience only, not because I am proposing that there is a singular definition for the modern or that there is a multiplicity of modernities.

2. Aspects of the orientalists' view of Islam and Muslim reformers are discussed in Chapter 6.

3. For 1960s critiques of orientalist scholarship, see the Marxist Anwar 'Abdel Malek, "Orientalism in Crisis," *Diogenes* 44 (1963): 103–40; and the Arab nationalist A. L. Tibawi, "English Speaking Orientalists," *Islamic Quarterly* 8 (1964): 25–45. The turn toward a more leftist critique from a political economy perspective is apparent in Joe Stork, *Middle East Oil and the Energy Crisis* (New York: Monthly Review, 1975).

4. Edward Said, *Orientalism* (New York: Pantheon, 1978), 2–3. Said defined an orientalist as "anyone who teaches, writes about, or researches the Orient"; he defined orientalism as "a style of thought based on ontological and epistemological distinction made between the 'orient' and (most of the time) the 'Occident,'" and as the "corporate institution of dealing with the Orient—dealing with it by making statements about it, authorizing views of it, describing it, by teaching it, settling it, and ruling over it: in short, *Orientalism* as a Western style for dominating, restructuring and having authority over the Orient." The impact of Said's powerful critique extended beyond the field of Middle Eastern studies to generate entirely new academic disciplines questioning the assumptions and history of this hegemonic discourse and its relation to imperial powers, in both the colonial and neocolonial periods. For more on Said and his impact, see Robert Young, *White Mythologies: Writing History and the West* (New York: Routledge, 1990), 126, 127–40.

5. Political economy came to replace modernization and cultural essentialism in the field of Middle Eastern studies following acceptance of the arguments Said set forth in *Orientalism*. The scholars who founded and write for the journal *Middle East Research and Information Project* (*MERIP*) are strongly representative of this change. Other broad political economy approaches include Alan Richards and John Waterbury, *A Political Economy of the Middle East: State, Class,*

and Economic Development (Boulder, CO: Westview Press, 1990); and Roger Owen, *The Middle East in the World Economy, 1800–1914* (London: Methuen, 1981). On the subject of colonialism and national revolutions, see, among others, Eric Davis, *Challenging Colonialism: Bank Misr and Egyptian Industrialization, 1920–1941* (Princeton, NJ: Princeton University Press, 1983); Judith Tucker, *Women in Nineteenth-Century Egypt* (Cambridge: Cambridge University Press, 1985); Juan Cole, *Colonialism and Revolution in the Middle East: Social and Cultural Origins of Egypt's Urabi Revolt* (Princeton, NJ: Princeton University Press, 1993); Kenneth Cuno, *The Pasha's Peasants: Land, Society, and Economy in Lower Egypt* (Cambridge: Cambridge University Press, 1992).

6. A sample of the historiography influenced by the linguistic turn and postmodernist critiques include Michael M. J. Fisher and Mehdi Abedi, *Debating Muslims: Cultural Dialogues in Postmodernity and Tradition* (Madison: University of Wisconsin Press, 1990); Timothy Mitchell, *Colonising Egypt* (Cambridge: Cambridge University Press, 1988); Lisa Wadeen, *The Ambiguities of Domination: Politics, Rhetoric, and Symbols in Contemporary Syria* (Chicago: University of Chicago Press, 1999); Khaled Fahmy, *All the Pasha's Men: Mehmed Ali, His Army, and the Making of Modern Egypt* (Cambridge: Cambridge University Press, 1997); Aziz al-Azmeh, *Islam and Modernities* (London: Verso, 1993).

7. See Charles Hirschkind, "What Is Political Islam?" *Middle East Research and Information Report* 205 (1997): 12–15.

8. On Said's intellectual contradictions, see Young, *White Mythologies*, chapter 7. Young attributes the methodological tension in *Orientalism* to Said's commitment to the Enlightenment project of modernity and, particularly, to its humanist stance. In contrast to Said's mentor, Foucault, who "attacked the human as an explanatory or experiential category," Said's humanist stance, particularly "his fidelity to independent critical consciousness and the common enterprise of promoting the human community," as Young keenly points out, have often led Said to "characterize the reality of the East according to the terms of the universalist claims of European high cultures, [so that] his analysis comes to seem remarkably close to an Orientalist work itself" (131–32). For other critics, see Aijaz Ahmad, "Orientalism and After: Ambivalence and Metropolitan Location in the Work of Edward Said," in *In Theory* (London: Verso, 1992).

9. Young, *Mythologies*, 127. Differing from Said's other critics, Nadia Abu El-Haj in "Edward Said and the Political Present," *American Ethnologist* 32 (2005): 538–55, does not regard his humanism as a contradiction but as a deliberate conscious choice that he made as a political actor. Although she herself is not a humanist, she interprets Said's humanism as a sign of intellectual maturity rather than as one of inconsistency because his approach to theory is "synthetic" rather than "dogmatic." Said, as she points out, has consciously drawn "on different theorists to do very specific intellectual and political work" (547).

10. Besides his fierce critique of the author as an agent of change, Foucault described humanism as a set of themes that are too diverse, inconsistent, and value-laden to make sense as an axis for thought. See Michel Foucault, "What Is Enlightenment?," in *The Foucault Reader*, ed. Paul Rabinow (New York: Pantheon, 1984), 43–44. Contemporary critics of humanism built on this critique to show that Christian humanism as a seventeenth-century theme was closely related to Europe's secularization process, one that involved the redefinition of Christianity as private belief and the reassignment of its role away from the domain of the public and political. The secularization of Europe is itself historical and the product of particular, largely conflictual circumstances (i.e., the religious wars of the sixteenth and seventeenth centuries), which eventually fashioned Europe's modern trajectory as one that circumscribed religion to the private sphere. By the nineteenth century, humanism had acquired a different meaning as it came to include the post-Enlightenment idea of (progressive) history, one associated with the notion of human self-development and self-perfection (i.e., the birth of the modern secular subject). On the subject of secular humanism and the development of the normative modern subject, see Talal Asad, *Formations of the Secular* (Stanford, CA: Stanford University Press, 2003). For a trenchant critique of the liberal tradition from a philosophical and conceptual perspective, see Alasdair MacIntyre, *Whose Justice? Which Rationality?* (Notre Dame, IN: University of Notre Dame Press, 1988). For a critique of liberalism and its entanglement with colonialism, see Uday S. Mehta, *Liberalism and Empire: A Study in Nineteenth-Century British Liberal Thought* (Chicago: University of Chicago Press, 1999).

11. MacIntyre, *Whose Justice?*, 12.

12. Talal Asad, "The Idea of an Anthropology of Islam," Occasional Papers Series, Washington, DC: Georgetown University, Center for Contemporary Arab Studies, 1986, 14.

13. Other recent scholars on Islam have been influenced by critics of humanism and this revisionist historiography. Leading among them are Saba Mahmood, *Politics of Piety: The Islamic Revival and the Feminist Subject* (Princeton, NJ: Princeton University Press, 2005); and Charles Hirschkind, *Ethical Soundscape: Cassette Sermons and Islamic Counterpublics* (New York: Columbia University Press, 2006); Muhammad Qasim Zaman, *The Ulama in Contemporary Islam: Custodians of Change* (Princeton, NJ: Princeton University Press, 2002).

14. MacIntyre, *Whose Justice?*, 345.

15. P. J. Vatikiotis, "Muhammad Abduh and the Quest for Muslim Humanism," *Islamic Culture* 31 (1957): 109–26.

16. A critic of orientalists and an enlightened Muslim scholar, Fazlur Rahman in *Islam and Modernity* (Chicago: University of Chicago Press, 1984) posits that "all fundamentalists, like the Wahhabis and subsequently their neofundamentalist

successors such as the Ikhwan, have just said this, namely, that Muslims must go back to the original and pristine Islam; yet they have been arrested at a certain point. Again, the Muslim modernist has also explicitly held that Muslims must go back to the original and pristine Islam; yet they have come up with certain doctrines that both the fundamentalist and the conservative have failed to recognize as Islamic—indeed, as anything but Western, that is un-Islamic" (142).

17. This is where I want to distinguish my work from a number of significant works that have illuminated various aspects of Islam but have not grasped the coherence of Islamic concepts as principles of an ongoing Islamic tradition. These works include J. Esposito, *The Islamic Threat: Reality or Myth?* (Oxford: Oxford University Press, 1999); Dale F. Eickelman and James Piscattori, *Muslim Politics* (Princeton, NJ: Princeton University Press, 1996); John Voll, *Islam, Continuity and Change* (Syracuse: Syracuse University Press, 1994); Natana J. Delong Bas, *Wahhabi Islam: From Revival and Reform to Global Jihad* (Oxford: Oxford University Press, 2004).

18. A useful analysis of *tajdid* and *islah* can be found in John O. Voll, "Renewal and Reform in Islamic History: Tajdid and Islah," in *Voices of Resurgent Islam*, ed. John Esposito (Oxford: Oxford University Press, 1983), 32–45; see also Fazlur Rahman, "Revival and Reform in Islam" in *Cambridge History of Islam*, ed. P. M. Holt, K. S. Lambton, and B. Lewis (Cambridge: Cambridge University Press, 1970), 2:632–42.

19. Abdelkarim Soroush, *Reason, Freedom, and Democracy in Islam* (Oxford: Oxford University Press, 2000), 31. Soroush, trained in Islamic hermeneutics and Western philosophy, draws a distinction between Revelation and people's understanding of it: Revelation is constant and free from culture; Islamic knowledge is variable and changing and prone to cultural change. As human knowledge, Islamic knowledge is defective and is always in need of improvement. See 26–30.

20. On al-Jahiz's stagist conceptualization of Islamic history, see Fahmi Jad'an, *Usus al-taqaddum 'inda mufakiri al-Islam* (Amman, Jordan: Dar al-Shuruq, 1988), 28–99. On this notion of retreat and looking backward as essentially Islamic, see the following works by Moroccan scholar Muhammad 'Abid al-Jabiri: *Bunyat al-'aql al-'arabi: Dirasah tahliliya* (Dar al-Bayda', Morocco: Markaz al-Thaqafi al-'Arabi, 1986); and *Iskhaliyat al-fikr al-'arabi al-mu'asir* (Dar al-Bayda', Morocco: Mu'assasat Bansharah li-tiba'a wal-nashr, 1989).

21. The fifth principle of the Mu'tazila is based on the Quranic verse instructing followers to "promote the good and abstain from evil." Al-Jahiz was especially condemning of the Ummayads and their dynasty for bringing the Muslim community to the brink of collapse.

22. Al-Ghazali, *Deliverance from Error: al-Munqith min al-dhalal and Other Relevant Works of Al-Ghazali*, trans. Richard Joseph McCarthy (Louisville: Fons

Vitae, 1999), 117. Al-Ghazali's most celebrated multivolume work is *ihya´ ´ulum al-din* [*The Revival of Islamic Religious Sciences*]. This is not to claim that al-Ghazali was the first to develop this concept but to say that he is one of the greatest of that era to have practiced it.

23. Fazlur Rahman, *Islam* (New York: Anchor Books, 1968), 109. A recent and fascinating postmodern rendition of al-Ghazali is Ebrahim Moosa's *Ghazali and the Poetics of Imagination* (Chapel Hill: University of North Carolina Press, 2005). Moosa convincingly challenges the mainstream view that presents Ghazali as a pragmatist taking the middle road. Instead, Moosa brilliantly exposes how Ghazali, through a Persian-Arab notion of *dahliz* (a threshold position), created a "liminal space between the inside and the outside, a space that sublimated his own location and thinking . . . in a world of heterogeneous knowledge and subjectivities" (30). On Ghazali and other medieval Muslim thinkers' reasons for and contribution toward the Islamization of Greek philosophy, see the pioneering work of Wael Hallaq, *A History of Islamic Legal Theories* (Cambridge: Cambridge University Press, 1997).

24. The most famed among them, besides ibn ´Abdul Wahhab, are Shah Wali Allah of India (1703–62), ´Uthman ibn Fudi of West Africa (1754–1817), Muhammad ´Ali al-Sanusi of North Africa (1787–1859), and Muhammad al-Shawkani (1760–1834). For more on eighteenth-century reformers, see Ahmad Dallal, "The Origins and Objectives of Islamic Revivalist Thought," *Journal of the American Oriental Society* 113 (1993): 341–59. According to Dallal's forthcoming work, "Islam Without Europe: Tradition of Reform in 18th Century Islamic Thought," reformist ideas did not originate in the eighteenth century; there were several important reformers in the seventeenth century as well, including al-San´ani. See also Voll, *Islam, Continuity and Change*; Judith Tucker, *In the House of the Law: Gender and Islamic Law in Ottoman Syria and Palestine* (Berkeley: University of California Press, 1998); Wael Hallaq, *Authority, Continuity, and Change in Islamic Law* (Cambridge: Cambridge University Press, 2001); Rudolph Peters, "Ijtiahd and Taqlid in 18th and 19th Century Islam," *Die Welt Des Islam* 20 (1980): 131–45.

25. Muhammad al-Shawkani's *al-Qawl al-mufid fi adillat al-ijtihad wal-taqlid* (Beirut: Dar al-kitab al-libnani, 1991) is a long diatribe against taqlid and in favor of ijtihad.

26. The theory of the infallibility of the consensus (ijma´) of early authorities and scholars was introduced into the Islamic discursive tradition in the third century A.H. (ninth century A.D.). It was in this period that the idea of consensual authority came to represent the Sunna of the living community and ijtihad became a subsidiary notion to ijma´. All Muslims either of that generation or after did not accept this view. A leading figure who strongly contested it was ibn Taymiya, who defended the right of Muslims to go directly to the primary

authoritative sources and challenged the primacy of ijma' (consensus) over ijti-had. Not surprisingly, his ideas became the touchstone for many Muslim reform-ers from the eighteenth century on. The most illuminating works that challenge the Orientalist claim that the door of ijtihad was closed from the ninth century on are Hallaq, *History of Islamic Legal Theories*, and Baber Johansen, *Contingency in a Sacred Law: Legal and Ethical Norms in Muslim Fiqh* (Leiden, the Netherlands: J. Brill, 1999).

27. In the introduction to *Nayl al-awtar*, al-Shawkani states that ibn Taymiya's Hanbali grandfather, known for his strong arguments in favor of ijtihad, has be-come "a source-book for the majority of the *'Ulama* when they are in need of finding a legal proof—especially in this region and in these times; upon this sweet spring, the eyes of original thinkers collide with one another and the steps of in-vestigations vie with one another in entering its gates. It has thus become a resort for thinkers whither they repair and a haven for those who wish to flee the bonds of slavish and blind acceptance of authority." Rahman, *Islam*, 241–42.

28. Soroush, *Reason, Freedom, and Democracy*, 28.

29. Ibid., 27. Muhammad Iqbal (1877–1938) was one of the most prominent Muslim thinkers of the Indian subcontinent and one of the two founding fathers of modern Pakistan. Not only a philosopher and Muslim reformer, he was also a poet who attempted to reconcile Western philosophy and Islamic knowledge. His best-known work is *The Reconstruction of Religious Thought* (Lahore: Sh. M. Ashraf, 1958).

30. Soroush, *Reason, Freedom, and Democracy*, 27–28. The notion of being "conscripted" is taken from Talal Asad, "Conscripts of Western Civilization," in *Dialectical Anthropology: Essays in Honor of Stanley Diamond*, vol. 1, *Civilization in Crisis*, ed. Christine Gailey (Tallahassee: University Press of Florida, 1992), 335–51. See also David Scott, *Conscripts of Modernity: The Tragedy of Colonial Enlighten-ment* (Durham, NC: Duke University Press, 2004).

31. One cannot help but notice how this notion of the right to interpret is now the practiced norm among the piety movements spreading throughout the Muslim world today.

32. According to tradition, as the anthropologist of Islam Brinkley Messick points out, the Prophet was ordered to "recite," and hence the "Qur'an, an ex-tended 'recitation' was received by him, and then orally reconvened in this way to his companions. As the Qur'an circulated in the world, recitations were re-peated and memorized, the text was preserved in human hearts and, eventually, a discursive style was in place." See Messick, *Calligraphic State: Textual Domi-nation and History in a Muslim Society* (Berkeley: University of California Press, 1993), 4.

33. Ibid., 22–25.

34. There are four main legal schools within Sunni Islam: Hanafi, Maliki, Shafi'i, and Hanbali. The Hanbali school is identified within the tradition as the strictest of the four and is accordingly described in contemporary scholarship as either "conservative" or "reactionary." The majority of the population of Najd belonged to the Hanbali school.

35. The Wahhab clan was of bedouin ('Arab) descent, with a genealogical lineage that went back to the ancient tribe of Tamim, who gradually settled down to become villagers and farmers but continued to be governed by tribal customary tradition. For a lengthier description of the tribes and tribal life, see A. M. Vasilliev, *The History of Saudi Arabia* (London: Saqi Books, 2000), 29–63.

36. 'Uthman ibn 'Abdallah ibn Bishr, *'Unwan al-majd fi tarikh najd* (Riyad: matba'at al-malik 'Abdul 'Aziz, 1982), 1:90.

37. Ibid., 50, 62. According to ibn Bishr, the grandfather's most renowned work, *al-Manasik*, is on the rites of pilgrimage.

38. Sulaiman was no slouch either, for he became a qadi, following in the footsteps of his father. Although he initially joined forces with the opposition against ibn 'Abdul Wahhab's call for tawhid, he later joined his brother, according to najdi sources.

39. In a letter addressed to one of the older brothers, the father says: "I discovered that he had reached maturity before completing his 12th year. I felt that he was ready to take his place in the congregational prayer, so I brought him forward because of his knowledge of Islamic precepts. I found a wife for him in that year after he reached maturity. He then asked me for a permission to go to the Sacred House of God in Mecca to perform his pilgrimage. I granted his request and assisted him to achieve his goal." See Husain ibn Ghannam, *Kitab rawdat al-afkar wal-afham li-murtad hal al-imam wa-ti'dad ghazawat dhawi al-islam* (Bombay: al-matba'a al-mustafawiya, n.d.), 81. This work was later revised and edited by Nasir al-din al-Asad under the title *Tarikh najd* (Cairo: Dar al-shuruq, 1985). All references made by ibn Ghannam here are from the edited version.

40. Translated quote taken from Hamid Algar, *Wahhabism: A Critical Essay* (Oneonta, NY: Islamic Publication International, 2002), 6.

41. Ibid. See also al-Sayyid Dahlan, *al-Durar al-saniyah fi-al-radd 'ala-al-wahabiya* (Cairo: Dar Jawami al-Kalam, 1980), 147–48.

42. Ibn Ghannam, *Tarikh Najd*, 81–82. See also Natana J. Delong-Bas, *Wahhabi Islam: From Revival and Reform to Global Jihad* (Oxford: Oxford University Press, 2004), 18–20.

43. His biographers mention the names of the following scholars as influencing the teaching of ibn 'Abdul Wahhab: 'Abdullah ben Ibrahim al-Saif of Medina, Muhammad al-Majmu'i al-Bisri, and Shihab al-din al-Musli, the qadi of Basra; Hasan al-Islamboli of Basra; Zein al-din al-Maghribi; and Hasan al-Tamimi.

44. Ibn Bishr, '*Unwan al-majd*, 1:35; Vassiliev, *History of Saudi Arabia*, 65.

45. Muhammad Hayat al-Sindi was the teacher of other famed reformers from the eighteenth century, the most prominent among them the Indian Muslim revivalist Shah Wali 'Allah (1703–62).

46. Ibn Bishr, *Tarikh najd*, 36. Al-Sindi's most famous works are *al-Iqaf 'ala sabab al-ikhtilaf* and *Irshad al-nuqqad ila taysir al-ijtihad*. The first of these works addresses his critical views on the fanatic adherence to the four schools, while the second treatise calls on his contemporaries to validate the technique of rigorous reasoning (ijtihad). It is in his third work, *Tuhfat al-an'am fi al-'amal bi-hadith al-nabi*, that al-Sindi criticizes taqlid or consensual precedence as the only valid form of reasoning. He suggests going back to the methods of reasoning adopted by the early generation (*salaf*), in which the Sunna (hadith) was regarded above "opinion" (*al-'amal bil-sunna wa-taqdimuha 'ala al-ra'iy*). That is why he was considered one of the leading revivalists of hadith studies in the eighteenth century. See ibn al-Makarim al-Qasi al-Kittani, *fihris al-faharis*, 1:1271; Muhammad Hamid al-Fiqqi, *Athar al-da'wa al-wahhabiya* (Cairo: matba'at al-sunna al-muhamadiyya, 1938), 43.

47. *Ahl al-kitab wal-sunna* refers to the consensus (*ijma'*) of the community as represented by the four schools of thought.

48. al-Fiqqi, *Athar al-da'wa*, 43; Amena Muhammad al-Nassir, *al-Shaykh al-imam Muhammad ibn 'Abdul Wahhab wa-manhajuhu fi-mabahith al-'aqidah* (Cairo: Dar al-shuruq, 1983), 36,

49. The record of his travels is contested. Although most of the conventional scholarship reports that ibn 'Abdul Wahhab traveled far beyond Basra to Baghdad, Hamadan, Isfahan, Damascus, and Cairo, the *najdi* sources according to local scholars make the claim that his travels terminated in Basra. The source of confusion, they contend, is a document located in the British Museum in London under the title *lam' al-shihab fi sirat Muhammad ibn 'Abdul Wahhab*, author unknown. Most of the the works of the early orientalists, including *Arabia*, the travel narratives of John Philby, refer to and base their account on this document alone. Some Arab scholars and travelers in the region make similar claims, founded on the same source; one such example is Amin al-Rihani, *Tarikh najd al-hadith wa-mulhaqatuhu* (Beirut: Dar Rihani, 1954). In contrast, most najdi sources, which include the two most reliable biographers on Muhammad ibn 'Abdul Wahhab, ibn Ghannam and ibn Bishr, affirm that his travels never went beyond Basra. Both biographers, for example, report that he was thrown out of Basra by those who opposed his call for tawhid. His plan to travel to Damascus was abandoned after he was robbed on the way. See ibn Ghannam, *Tarikh najd*, 83. The local scholars that uphold this position are Nasir al-din al-Asad, the editor of ibn Ghannam, *Tarikh najd*; and Al-Nassir, *al-Shaykh al-imam Muhammad*, 30–32.

50. Ibn Bishr recalls that his own teacher, the jurist 'Uthman b. Mansur al-Nasiri, recounted to him that al-Majmu'i's sons were also renowned for their uprightness as well as their mastery of tawhid studies, which they learned from their father. *'Unwan al-majd*, 1:8.

51. Ibid. The Iraqi Muslim scholar al-Alusi, writing in the latter part of the nineteenth century, reports differently, making the claim of conflict and exchange of heated arguments between the father and the son over the latter's views. Mahmud Shukri al-Alusi, *Tarikh najd* (Cairo: Maktabat madbuli, n.d.), 108.

52. For soon after ibn 'Abdul Wahhab and his ally, the emir 'Uthman ibn Mu'ammar, began to implement their reform plans, opposition cropped up. The cutting of sacred trees and the razing of tombs over the graves of saints and patrons (*awliya'*) and the destruction of other revered sites angered many of the tribes inhabiting the region. The tribes, by refusing to pay their tribute to the emir, forced him to sever relations with ibn 'Abdul Wahhab. ibn Ghannam, *Tarikh najd*, 84–85.

53. For more on this topic, see Delong-Bas, *Wahhabi Islam*, 34–37. See also Chapter 2. Central Najd in the first decade of the eighteenth century was made up of three tribal rival forces, each centered around a cluster of villages and a number of oases: Riad, Dari'ya, and 'Uyaina, each headed by a tribe of nobility. Bitter rivalry, both internal among the ruling families themselves and external between these rival forces, was not untypical in this period. For more information, see Vassiliev, *History of Saudi Arabia*, esp. 29–64.

54. Delong-Bas, *Wahhabi Islam*, 35. The military campaigns led by the sons of ibn Sa'ud succeeded in establishing the first Sa'udi dynasty that became closely associated with his movement. Ibn Sa'uds effectively extended their control beyond Najd to Hijaz, Oman, Bahrain, Basra, and farther. Once they captured the two holy towns, Mecca (in 1803 A.D.) and Medina (in 1806 A.D.), they severed relations with the Ottoman sovereign in Istanbul, forbidding the Porte's pilgrimage caravans from entering the holy towns. In response, the Ottomans prompted Muhammad 'Ali, ruler of Egypt, to send his army to crush the religious "insurrection" labeled Wahhabism. The first Saudi dynasty, defeated in 1818 at the hands of a modernized, better-equipped Egyptian army, was to be resurrected under the tutelage of the British in the aftermath of World War I in the of form the present Kingdom of Saudi Arabia.

55. Ibid., 39–40; see also al-Nassir, *al-Shaykh Muhammad ibn 'Abdul Wahhab*, 227.

56. Delong-Bas, *Wahhabi Islam*, 35.

57. Ian Hacking, "Making Up People" in *Reconstructing Individualism: Autonomy, Individuality and the Self in Western Thought*, ed. Thomas C. Heller, D. Wellbery, and M. Sosna (Stanford, CA: Stanford University Press, 1986), 231. Hacking's main argument is that concepts are neither natural (fixed) nor totally invented

(human constructs) but are part of a process that takes place in time. The analysis and description of this process is therefore historical in character. For elaboration, see I. Hacking, *The Social Construction of What?* (Cambridge, MA: Harvard University Press, 1999).

58. As ʿAbduh put it, "it was only those men who are of the lower classes and the poor who shared their meals with their children and wives." Rashid Rida, *Tarikh al-uztaz al-Imam al-shaykh Muhammad ʿAbduh* (Cairo: Matbaʿat al-manar, 1931), 1:13. It is unfortunate that ʿAbduh never completed his autobiography as it sheds an interesting light on his personal life within the context of a changing society.

59. As many historians have already argued, the shift toward a cash-crop economy in the Delta in particular started long before the arrival of Muhammad ʿAli but was accelerated under his rule. For further discussion on the agrarian change, see Cuno, *The Pasha's Peasants*; and Peter Gran, *Islamic Roots of Capitalism in Egypt, 1760–1840* (Syracuse: Syracuse University Press, 1998).

60. ʿAbduh's life narrative was published in Rida, *Tarikh al-imam*, 1:20–27. In regard to his father compelling him to go back to his studies, ʿAbduh said the following: "after forty days into my marriage came my father and forced me to go back to Tanta to complete my studies. After I protested, argued against and refused his demand, I had no choice but submit to him." Ibid., 1:21.

61. After he fled the second time, ʿAbduh described his adventures as follows: "the young lads of the village where most of father's maternal uncles resided were very pleased to see me because of my reputation in horsemanship and target-shooting"; for weeks he was more than happy to oblige them. Ibid., 1:21.

62. Ibid., 1:21–22. As described by Rida, sheikh Darwish was more of a mystic than a trained Muslim scholar. He was inducted into the Shazilaya Sufi order during his travels in Tripoli, Libya.

63. Ibid., 1:23. See also Albert Hourani, *Arabic Thought in the Liberal Age* (London: Cambridge University Press, 1962), 131. This inspiration was not instantaneous; it took a while before ʿAbduh began to show interest and read on his own volition, ask questions, and make comments. Initially he resisted his teacher by throwing away reading assignments or else abandoning his lessons altogether once his youthful friends called on him to join them in their accustomed games.

64. Under the influence of Sufism, which he learned from sheikh Darwish, ʿAbduh lived the life of an ascetic Sufi, wearing rough garments, fasting in daytime, and spending his nights praying, reciting the Qurʾan, and meditating.

65. Rida, *Tarikh al-imam*, 1:24.

66. The new order created under Muhammad ʿAli's rule gave primary attention to the modernization of the army, which in turn meant, as Marsot explains, developing and expanding a program of education in terms of staff college, engineering corps, medical surgeons and veterinary surgeons. Schools were opened in

Egypt and educational missions sent abroad to learn technology, not only in the field of military science but in other fields as well. Thus the army became the impetus for a wide programme of education of a new secular nature. It was not that the new administration wished to educate Egyptians in the abstract; it was simply that they saw the necessity for importing technology, and education was the only way to do it. See Afaf Lutfi al-Sayyid Marsot, *A Short History of Egypt* (Cambridge: Cambridge University Press, 1985), 56.

67. Rida, *Tarikh al-imam*, 1:26.

68. Vasilliev, *History of Saudi Arabia*, 29–63. According to Vasilliev, Arabian tribes were socially stratified into (1) camel breeders, a group from which the tribal nobility and ruling elite came and who later on settled and acquired an agricultural livelihood; (2) sheep herders; (3) settled peasants who worked the land as sharecroppers; and (4) slaves. Ibid., 40–51.

69. Sources record the father's loss of job after the death of the ruler of 'Uyaina, 'Abdallah Muhammad Mu'ammar, who was replaced by his grandson Kharfoush. The new ruler dismissed ibn 'Abdul Wahhab's father from his position because of some sort of disagreement, the nature of which has not been disclosed by the sources. After his dismissal, ibn 'Abdul Wahhab's father was obliged to leave. See ibn Bishr, *'Unwan al-majd*, 1:10–11.

70. Jonathan Sheehan, "Enlightenment, Religion, and the Enigma of Secularization," *American Historical Review* 108 (October 2003): 1070.

71. Scholars who refer to 'Abduh as a liberal include Hourani, *Arabic Thought in the Liberal Age*; Rahman, *Islam and Modernity*; and Hamilton A. R. Gibb, *Modern Trends in Islam* (New York: Octagon Books, 1972).

CHAPTER 2: RETHINKING ORTHODOXY

1. The most recent serious and thorough investigation of ibn 'Abdul Wahhab is Natana J. Delong-Bas's *Wahhabi Islam*. Her attempt to historicize the reformer and his movement through a close interrogation of his work was in turn viewed by some reviewers in the field as biased and unobjective for presenting a sympathetic reading of the reformer. Another recent essay with "little liking or sympathy" is that of Hamid Algar's *Wahhabism*.

2. Hamilton A. R. Gibb, *Modern Trends in Islam* (New York: Octagon Books, 1978), 27.

3. Ibid., 26–27.

4. Algar, *Wahhabism*, 45–46. According to Algar, it was not until the 1960s that a closer connection between the two movements emerged with the likes of Sayyid Qutb (d. 1966), who, following the path of ibn 'Abdul Wahhab, began to prescribe the present condition of Muslims as one of *Jahiliya*, denoting a state of

"ignorance" equivalent to that of a pre-Islamic Arabian society. Like ibn 'Abdul Wahhab, Qutb, according to Algar, became intolerant of Muslims who disagreed with his views.

5. Ibid., 3–4.

6. Ibid., 14.

7. Henri Laoust, *Les schismes dans l'Islam* (Paris: Payot 1965), 321–32; and *Essai sur les doctrins sociales et politiques de Taki al-din Ahmad b. Taymiya* (Le Caire: de l'Institut français d'archéologie orientale, 1939), 514–20. Although dismissive of ibn 'Abdul Wahhab, Laoust was a great admirer of ibn Taymiya's thought and especially what he understood as ibn Taymiya's notion of mercy with its origins in the Platonic notion that evil is a contingent act and not an essential feature of God's creation and that it is through his Mercy that God protects his creation from evil.

8. W. Montgomery Watt, *Islamic Philosophy and Theology* (Edinburgh: Edinburgh University Press, 1962): "Its clearest dependence on ibn Taymiya is in its attack on the cult of saints and in its general insistence on a return to the purity of original Islam. For the most part it is concerned largely with externals, like much of Islamic religious thought. It shows no interest in the methodology of ibn Taymiya" (145).

9. Central to Hezbollah's conceptualization of defensive jihad is this notion of martyrdom, which the organization considers a *wajib shar'i* (religious obligation), one that entails the willingness to fight and die for God's cause. As a Shi'a group, Hezbollah's notion is seen as a reenactment of Imam Husayn's martyrdom in Karbala, which "serves as an exemplar of defensive *jihad* and a model of self-sacrifice." Amal Saad-Ghorayeb, *Hizbullah: Politics and Religion* (London: Pluto Press, 2002), 127.

10. Ibn 'Abdul Wahhab cites several hadiths, including the following: "No one should wish death, nor call for it before its due date. For once one dies, her good deeds get suspended. The longer the faithful lives, the more rewards he earns." Another: "Ye, Prophet of God, Who in your opinion is the most righteous? His response: "one who is righteous and lives long." See "Rules on Suicide" (*ahkam tamanni al-mawt*) in *Mu'allafat al-Sheikh al-Imam Muhammad ibn 'Abdul Wahhab: Al-Fiqh* (Riyad: Jami'at al-imam Muhammad ibn Sa'ud al-islamiya, 1976), v. 2:3–5. On "Rules on Jihad" (*Kitab al-Jihad*), he states three conditions when jihad is required: (1) when two enemy forces meet one another, (2) when an enemy invades a country and its people are required to defend it, and (3) when called by the imam to fight. Ibid., 1:371–75. In all three conditions, he considers jihad to be *fard kifaya* (public obligation) rather than *fard 'ayn* (individual).

11. See Stephen Toulmin, *Cosmopolis: The Hidden Agenda of Modernity* (Chicago: University of Chicago Press, 1990); Mary Poovey, *A History of the Modern*

Fact: Problems of Knowledge in the Sciences of Wealth and Society (Chicago: University of Chicago Press, 1998); Michel Foucault, *The Order of Things: An Archeology of the Human Sciences* (New York: Vintage Books, 1994).

12. An excellent study on memory is Mary Carruthers, *The Book of Memory: A Study of Memory in Medieval Culture* (Cambridge: Cambridge University Press, 1999). Her thesis is that although the conception of the activity of intellect and thought are strikingly different between the modern and the medieval, the idea of creativity itself has remained essentially the same. Both, according to her, express intricate reasoning and original discovery. Carruthers also challenges the idea of "the rise of literacy" and the distinction that often is drawn between "oral" and "literate" societies. Learning by hearing and reciting aloud, she argues, should not be confused with ignorance of reading and illiteracy. The privileging of memory in certain cultures should be addressed independent of "orality" and "literacy" as these terms came to be defined in the social sciences of today. It is misleading "to speak of literary culture as a version of literacy at all[;] the reason is that this concept privileges a physical artifact, the writing-support over the social and composition by an author and its reception by an audience" (11).

13. Ibid.

14. Carl Brockelmann, *History of the Islamic Peoples*, trans. Joel Carmichael and Moshe Perlmann (New York: Capricorn Books, 1960), 353.

15. In the definition and analysis of Islamic concepts and words, I consulted the following Arabic classical dictionaries: al-Raghib al-Asfahani (d. 1108 or 1109 A.H.), *al-Mufradat fi-gharib al-Qur'an* (Beirut: Dar al-ma'arifa, n.d.); Muhammad ibn Mukarram ibn Manzur (1232–1311 A.H.), *Lisan al-'Arab* (Beirut: Dar Sader, 1990); and Edward William Lane (1801–1876 A.D.), *Arabic-English Lexicon* (Beirut: Librairie du Liban, 1980). As defined by Lane, *khalal fi al-din* refers to laxity of religion. The word *khalal* literally means "defective, faulty, and unsound." Another term used often to indicate corruption and laxity is *t'atil al-din*. *T'atil* in Arabic means void, vacant, or neglected; or the leaving of a thing unattended.

16. In the Islamic literature, the umma is commonly referred to as *ummat al-nabi* and sometimes as *al-umma al-muhamadiyya*. It is important to note that the concept of an existing umma is taken for granted by Muslims. The umma is a representative of a divinely sanctioned moral community. It is within the space of a moral community that rational discussion and criticism take place and where power is exercised and punishment enforced.

17. In fact, many of the modernists draw a similarity between ibn Taymiya's disrupted context after the Mongol invasion and their own.

18. Al-Jlayned, *Dar' ta'arud al-'aql wal-naql li-sheikh al-islam ibn Taymiya* (Cairo: Matabi' al-ahram al-tijariya, 1988), 42–56; F. Rahman, *Islam*, 132–34.

19. This doctrine transformed the notion of a transcendental God in orthodox tawhid into union with God (the Arabic term *tawhid* means both "regarding something as one" and "unification of something with something else"). In his doctrine of Unity of Existence, as Rahman explains in the following quote, ibn 'Arabi posited the theory that "Absolute Reality is transcendent and nameless and that its only attribute is self-existence. But this Absolute, by a kind of propulsion or process of 'descent' and 'determination', develops a state of being wherein it becomes conscious of its attributes, knowledge, power, life, creativity, etc. These attributes of perfection, however, exist only in its mind or consciousness. But it is also these attributes which constitute the stuff from which the world is made. The 'creation' of the world is nothing but the projection of these attributes from the Divine Mind outward into 'real existence' which is nothing but the existence of the Absolute himself" (Rahman, *Islam*, 175). Ibn 'Arabi also elaborates on the notion of prophecy, which he claimed is premised on the notion of the "perfect" man or saint. Instead of the orthodox view on prophecy, which is careful to emphasize the externality of the prophet's revelation in order to safeguard God's otherness, ibn 'Arabi made the claim that the oneness of the divine was realizable only through the oneness of the perfect man or perfect saint with God. Every prophet, he postulated, was a perfect man, and in his absence, a perfect saint (*qutb*) may take his place. Virtually every individual, from the perspective of this claim, has the potential of becoming the perfect man or saint and of attaining oneness with God. It is only when the oneness of the perfect man is realized, ibn 'Arabi states, that the multiplicity of the real world becomes illusory and the oneness of God himself is realized. For more on this subject, see Marshall Hodgson, *Venture of Islam* (Chicago: University of Chicago Press, 1974), 2:241–44.

20. Some view ibn Taymiya's work as "a synthesis or conciliation" of the three approaches that dominated religious knowledge then: that of the speculative theology which accentuated reason (*aql*), the traditionalist which highlighted hadith (*naql*) and Sufism with its stress on the will (*irada*). His doctrine "provides authority, within the framework of Holy Writ and of tradition, for the widest possible scope in the personal interiorization of religion." See "Ibn Taymiya" in *The Encyclopedia of Islam* (Leiden, the Netherlands: Brill, 1960), 954.

21. Messick, *Calligraphic State*, 17–18, 25.

22. In unraveling *Kitab al-tawhid* I relied on *fath al-majid li-sharh kitab al-tawhid*, both the shortened as well as the longer version published in two volumes that include commentary and elaboration on the text by his grandson, a scholar and revivalist in his own right, 'Abdul Rahman ibn Hasan ibn Muhammad ibn 'Abdul Wahhab. The shorter version is *Kitab al-tawhid* (Beirut: Dar maktabat al-hayat, n.d.); the longer version is *Fath al-majid li-sharh kitab al-tawhid* (Beirut: Dar al-samiy'i, 1415 A.H., 1944). 'Abdul Rahaman ibn Hasan ibn Mu-

hammad ibn ʿAbdul Wahhab was raised by his grandfather after his father died when he was a child. He was taught by famous Muslim scholars and went to al-Azhar in Cairo, where he studied under the famous Muslim historian and scholar Abdul Rahman al-Jabarti. After the destruction of the Saudi dynasty at the hands of the Egyptian army, he and his family sought residence in Egypt for a while and returned later on to Arabia.

23. Reminiscent of ibn Taymiya's doctrine of tawhid, ibn ʿAbdul Wahhab explains in a letter (no. 7) addressed to ʿAbdallah ibn Sahim, a critic, that "*tawhid* is of two kinds: *tawhid al-rububiya*, to recognize that God is the Creator (*mutafarid bil-khalq*). . . . [This] acknowledgement while essential does not necessarily guarantee a man's entry to *islam* (*la yudkhil al-rajul fil-islam*) since most created beings do recognize this truth. . . . What guarantees a man's entry to *islam* is *tawhid al-uluhiya*, or the worship of the One God (ʿ*ibada*)." Ibn Ghannam, *Tarikh najd*, 278.

24. For a discussion of the difference between "freedom from" and "freedom to" in Western liberalism, see Isaiah Berlin's famous essay, "Two Concepts of Liberty," in *Four Essays on Liberty* (London: Oxford University Press, 1969).

25. ibn Taymiya, *al-ʿUbudiya* (Beirut: Dar al-kutub al-ʿilmiya, 1981), 22.

26. As Talal Asad explains, the Islamic notion of slave that describes man's relation to God is distinctively different from God the father in the Christian tradition or the concept of the covenant with God in the Judaic tradition. In fact, Islamic literature constantly draws on this distinction whenever discussing Islamic monotheism and its notion of tawhid. See Asad, *Genealogies of Religion: Discipline and Reasons of Power in Christianity and Islam* (Baltimore: Johns Hopkins University Press, 1993), 221–22.

27. Wahhab, *Kitab al-tawhid*, 10.

28. The concept of virtue employed here draws on Alasdair MacIntyre's definition and on the link he makes between virtues and practices by pointing out that it is impossible to write the history of a practice without a history of virtues and vices. As he explains, virtue is "an acquired human quality the possession of which tends to enable us to achieve those goods which are internal to practices and the lack of which effectively prevents us from achieving any such goods." See Alasdair MacIntyre, *After Virtue: A Study in Moral Theory* (Notre Dame, IN: University of Notre Dame Press, 1984), 191.

29. Wahhab, *Kitab al-tawhid*, chap. 1, 5–10.

30. A key to MacIntyre's understanding of virtue is the inseparability of a historical moral identity and a social identity: "I am never able to seek for the good or exercise the virtues only qua individual. This is partly because to live the good life concretely varies from circumstance to circumstance even when it is one and the same conception of the good life and one and the same set of virtues which are embodied in a human life." This is the case because "the self cultivates

its moral identity in and through its membership in communities such as those of the family, the neighborhood, the city and the tribe; it does not entail that the self has to accept the moral limitations of the particularity of those forms of community." See *After Virtue*, 220, 221.

31. It is a given that surrendering (*islam*) to God entails practicing the pillars (*arkan*) of Islam: prayer, fasting, *zakat* (almsgiving), pilgrimage.

32. Ibn Kathir, *Tafsir al-Qur'an al-'azim* (Beirut: Maktaba al-'asriyya, 1993), 3:33–39. A caveat should be noted: I use ibn Kathir's *Tafsir* because ibn 'Abdul Wahhab mentioned ibn Kathir's name on several occasions and not the names of other exegetes.

33. al-Ghazali, *On Disciplining the Soul*, trans. T. J. Winter (Cambridge: Islamic Text Society, 1995), xxv.

34. To make a stronger claim for tawhid, ibn 'Abdul Wahhab refers to other Quranic verses in support of his claim, including the following verses from *surat al-an'am*: "Say: Come, I will recite unto you that which your Lord hath made a sacred duty for you: that ye ascribe no thing as partner unto Him and that ye do good to parents, and that ye slay not your children because of penury—We provide for you and for them—and that ye draw not nigh to lewd things whether open or concealed. And that ye slay not the life which Allah hath made sacred, save in the course of justice, This He hath commanded you, in order that ye may discern" (6:152). "And approach not wealth of the orphan save with that which is better, till he reach maturity. Give full measure and full weight, in justice. We take not any soul beyond its scope" (6:153). "And (He commandeth you, saying): This is My straight path, so follow it. Follow not other ways, lest ye be parted from His way. This hath He ordained for you, that ye may ward off (evil)" (6:152).

35. By upholding the position that iman and *islam* are single and identical, the Mu'tazila is also saying that works are themselves acts of faith.

36. There is an irony in this, as the Mu'tazila sect is greatly admired by Western scholarship for its "rationalism," not its "extremism," which is clearly displayed in this position, for the implications of it are grave once it is translated into practice—as grave, one might perhaps add, as what ibn 'Abdul Wahhab and his so-called contemporary followers have been accused of.

37. L. Gardet, "iman" and "islam" in *Encyclopedia of Islam* (Leiden, the Netherlands: Brill, 1950–), 3:171–74; 1170–75.

38. In response to the question of whether *islam* is the same as *iman*, ibn 'Abdul Wahhab says, "*islam* is the outer action, while *iman* is inner action [*fal-islam al-'amal al-zahira, wal-iman al-'amal al-batina*]. . . . *Iman* is higher than *islam* . . . but the truth of the matter is that *iman* truly necessitates *islam* [*al-iman yastalzim al-islam qat'an, wa-'amma al-islam fa-qad yastalzimuhu wa-qad la-yastalzimuhu*]." This is quoted from *al-mas'ala* (no. 15) in ibn Ghannam, *Tarikh najd*, 446.

39. Most Hanbalis, ibn ʿAbdul Wahhab concluded, base their analysis of faith with some variation on Ahmed ibn Hanbal's principal explanation that "faith is utterance (*qawl*), act (*amal*) and right intention (*niyya*)." In the Musnad, ibn Hanbal also defines the difference between *islam* and *iman* as follows: "Islam is external, faith belongs to the heart." See Ahmed ibn Hanbal, *Al-Musnad* (Misr: Dar al-maʿarif, 1990).

40. T. Asad, *Formations of the Secular*, 90.

41. Wilfred Cantwell Smith demonstrates in *Faith and Belief* (Princeton, NJ: Princeton University Press, 1974), 35. See also chapter 1, especially 9–10. The term *belief* as explained by W. C. Smith is not in reference to Christian belief, for he also would maintain that even in the context of Christianity, *faith* is a more appropriate term to employ than *belief*. See also W. C. Smith, *On Understanding Islam* (The Hague: Mouton, 1981).

42. Smith, *Faith and Belief*, 44–45.

43. The term *khuduʿ* connoting surrendering and submitting *islam* is also part of what it means to be a muʾmin. See ibn Manzur, *Lisan al-ʿArab*.

44. W. C. Smith, *Faith and Belief*, 43.

45. L. Gardet, "ikhlas" in *Encyclopedia of Islam*, 1159–. Gardet and Laoust argue that ikhlas, as a quality of inner excellence, is a notion that emerged out of the Sufi tradition and was later integrated into the dominant Sunni discourses by such prominent theologians as al-Ghazali and ibn Taymiya. But in Sufism, the notion of ikhlas, as a necessary stage in the soul's search for union with God, refers primarily to inner purity and not outer activity. This is what ibn ʿAbdul Wahhab was critical of, the favoring of inner faith over outer conduct. This separation between inner faith and outer action is what caused the deviation from the true path of religion. See his treatise "*Usul al-iman*" in *Muʾallafat al-Sheikh al-Imam Muhammad ibn ʿAbdul Wahhab*, 1 (Riad: Jamiʿat al-imam Muhammad ibn Saʿud al-Islamiyya, 1976), in which he maintained that the absence of ikhlas is what differentiates a Muslim from a kafir.

46. Ibn ʿAbdul Wahhab, *Kitab al-tawhid*, chap. 5: 38–39.

47. This position is implied when Smith compares Christianity and Islam and tries to draw out the differences between them. Whereas on the one hand, the expression of faith in Christianity is primarily doctrinal and intellectual, faith in Islam is "felt rather as primarily a moral command: The oneness of God is less a metaphysical description than an ethical injunction. Since the Qurʾan is fundamentally a moral orientation, it is law and not theology that is encouraged." He contends that theology (*ilm al-kalam*) in Islam is "peripheral, dispensable and even suspect." Whereas in Christianity, theology, being influenced by Greek philosophy, "has played and continues to play a quite dominant role in Christianity; intellectual expression of the faith has by many been considered the chief expression." W. C. Smith, *Faith and Belief*, 17; *On Understanding Islam*, 240–41. Implicit

in this interpretation is the view that Islam is more pragmatic and practical and hence less intellectual than Christianity, which tends to be doctrinal and theological. This interpretation, I suggest, is problematic because it assumes a duality that is inapplicable and inappropriate to premodern times, Islamic or Christian. This criticism is best illuminated in the work of Alasdair MacIntyre, *Whose Justice?*, and Mary Carruthers, *The Book of Memory: A Study of Memory in Medieval Culture* (Cambridge: Cambridge University Press, 1990). The latter work describes how the process of writing and thinking, being fundamentally memorial and not documentary, involved the training of the whole body—body, soul, and mind. In this manner, the creative process differs from our modern comprehension of it as a mental exercise that involves the making of detached doctrinal statements. Carruthers describes how Thomas Aquinas's creativity involved deep concentration "often approaching a trance-like state in which he did not feel physical pain" (6). Later on she explains how "medieval *'cogitatio'* translates . . . not as our phrase of 'reasoning out' (with its emphasis on logical connections) but as a process of 'mulling over,' a process that depends heavily on free association and one's 'feeling for' a matter" (200–201).

48. It is of importance to recognize that the separation of thought and feeling or "reason" and "faith" is currently questioned even in the West. See William E. Connolly, *Why I Am Not a Secularist* (Minneapolis: University of Minnesota Press, 2000).

49. Lane, in the *Arabic-English Lexicon* (7:2554), defines qalb as the endeavor to understand. He gives the example of *'afa'al al-qulub* (acts of hearts) as meaning "the operations of the mind." In *Lisan al-'Arab* (1:687) qalb refers to both *al-fu'ad* (heart) and *al-'aql* (mind), *liman kana lahu qalb* refers to *al-'aql*, and *wa-ma qalbuka ma'ak* means *ma-'aqluka ma'ak*. Linguistically, qalb is the pith of the palm tree and symbolizes purity, essence, and sincerity.

50. Wahhab, *Kitab al-tawhid*, 38–39. The interpreted Quranic verses by ibn Kathir are as follows: "and who give whatever they (have to) give with their hearts trembling at the thought unto their Sustainer they must return" (17:59–60). Wahhab elaborates on the notion of ikhlas in *al-Durar al-Sunniyya fi al-ajwiba al-najdiya* (Saudi Arabia: Dar al-ifta', 1965), 2:42–44.

51. *Ihsan* is defined by Lane as "contra to *isa'a* (harm) and as different from *in'am*, in being to oneself and as surpassing *'adl*, inasmuch as it means giving more than one owes," whereas "the latter mean[s] . . . giving what one owes and taking what is owed to one." Ikhlas also means to "assert oneself to be clear of believing in any beside God, which is a sign of soundness of *iman* and *islam* together: and as denoting watchfulness, and good obedience, and as meaning the continuing in the right way and following the way of the righteous." See Lane, *Arabic-English Lexicon*, 2:570.

52. Ibn Kathir, *Tafsir al-Qur'an al-'azim* (Beirut: Dar al-andulus li-tiba'a wal-nashr, 1966), 3:234.

53. Ibid.

54. On the definition of kufr and hypocrisy, see *Lisan al-'Arab* (5:146–149); *Mufradat fi-gharib al-Qur'an* (433–435). Ibn 'Abdul Wahhab discusses the dangers of hypocrisy under "*kufr al-nifaq*" in his treatise *Kashf al-shubuhat* in *Mualafat al-shaykh al-imam Muhammad ibn 'Abdul Wahhab* (al-Riad: Jam'iat al-imam Muhammad ibn Saud al-Islamiyya, 1976), 1:153–81.

55. Ibn 'Abdul Wahhab's chronicler, ibn Ghannam, reports that the practice of revering saints was not limited to those long dead. In *Kitab al-tawhid*, ibn 'Abdul Wahhab addresses this issue in chapters 10 and 11, 59–66. In the first, entitled "On slaughtering for other than God's sake," he explains why it is improper to pray to anyone other than God and to slaughter animals to any other than him, by recounting the following hadith: "In his *sahih*, Muslim relates from 'Ali (raa) the following: 'the Prophet of God (saas) gave me four judgments: Abomination to him who slaughters in the name of anyone other than Allah! Abomination to him who curses his parents! Abomination to him who shelters the perpetrator of a crime! Abomination to him who unjustly alters the borders of landed properties'" (60).

56. In chapter 4, ibn 'Abdul Wahhab discusses how the donning of Sufi garments or chains for the prevention or cure of affliction is a small shirk, for such acts are signs of a duplicitous divided self, of one who claims to trust in God but who in practice trusts others (idols and things) over God. One of the hadiths he recounts goes as follows: "the prophet saw a man carrying a garment which he claimed protected him against fever; that he tore it to pieces recalling the verse: 'most of them believe in God and still practice *shirk*.'" He also criticizes the common practices of theurgy, talismans, and bewitchment among his community by recounting hadiths that confirm these practices as forms of shirk, for they are testimony to a refusal to exercise those virtues that promote the good of the community (*Kitab al-tawhid*, 29–32).

57. Ibid., 45.

58. Ibn Ghannam, *Tarikh najd*, 15. Ibn 'Abdul Wahhab makes reference to the famed blind man in *Kitab al-tawhid* (28). Ibn Ghannam also reports other tales, including the following: "a male date palm at the little town of al-Fida' was sought by women who had waited in vain to be wedded, they would embrace the trunk of the tree and cry out 'o male palm of the palms, I desire a husband before I become barren' (*ya fahl al-fuhul, uridu zawjan qabla al-haul*)."

59. *Amana* comes from the root *amn*, which means to safeguard against harm. *Amn* is also the opposite of fear (*khawf*), *amana* is the opposite of khiyana, betrayal or breach of trust (in God). See *Lisan al-'Arab* (13:23–24); *al-Mufradat fi*

gharib al-Qur'an (52). See also ibn 'Abdul Wahhab, *Kitab al-Tawhid*, in particular, the addendum attached to chapter 9, 57–58.

60. Delong-Bas, *Wahhabi Islam*, 27–29.

61. The question of women's vulnerability came up in ibn 'Abdul Wahhab's discussion of female slaves. In fact, he rejected Islamic consensus, which permits men to have sexual intercourse with female slaves. Instead, as Delong Bas argues, he interpreted the Quranic verse of "what they possess by their right hands" (76:29–30) not to mean having sexual access to slave women since allowing men to engage in lowering and debasing slave women to the status of prostitutes is categorically forbidden as stated by the following Quranic verse: "Do not compel your young women into prostitution" (24:33) (Delong Bas, *Wahhabi Islam*, 130–31).

62. I say "for the most part" because of abrogation, that is, when one Quranic verse repeals another. The same approach applies to hadith. In the latter, prophetic reports are probed and scrutinized on the basis of the authenticity of the transmitters and the modes of their transmission. This process of probing led in turn to the classification of these reports in accordance with their epistemic value. See Wael B. Hallaq, *A History of Islamic Legal Theories: An Introduction to Sunni Usul al-fiqh* (Cambridge: Cambridge University Press, 1997).

63. Ibn 'Abdul Wahhab also cites another hadith by ibn 'Abbas, who reported that the prophet condemned women visiting the graves and also condemned the men who set up a mosque and lights over them. Ibn 'Abdul Wahhab, *Kitab al-tawhid*, 21, 103.

64. Ibn 'Abdul Wahhab recognizes that when *Bani umayya* incorporated 'Aisha's quarter into the mosque, it was not intended for the exaltation of the Prophet but merely to expand the space surrounding the mosque.

65. Muhammad ibn Sulaiman al-Madani (d. 1799 A.D., a leading Shafi'i scholar in Medina, wrote a two-volume *al-Fatawa*, refuting Wahhabism, as recorded by Ayyub Sabri Pasha in *Wahhabism and Its Refutation by Ahl as-Sunna* (n.p.), 14–15, 18–20. A. Sabri Pasha (d. 1890 A.D.) was an official Ottoman historian who wrote extensively on and against the Wahhabiya movement. *Wahhabism and Its Refutation* is a collection of excerpted works of Muslim scholars, both contemporaneous and later, who refuted ibn 'Abdul Wahhab.

Ibn 'Abdul Wahhab refutes the claim of visitations and offerings to the dead on two accounts: first, it is founded on weak hadith (*burhan da'if*), and second, this claim has already been rejected by *ijma'* (consensus) by the four theological schools.

66. Hasan Khuzbak, "al-nuqul al-shar'iya fi al-radd 'ala al-wahabiya," 208. Khuzbak's response was published as an addendum (184–235) to Sulaiman ibn 'Abdul Wahhab's response to his brother in an edited work by Muhammad 'Abdul Wasif titled *al-Sawa'iq al-ilahiyya fi al-radd 'ala- al-Wahhabiya* (al-Qahira: Matba'at al-kamal, 1923). This edition of *al-Sawa'iq* is comprised of other re-

sponses as well, including the response on the practice of "invocation" titled "Risalah fi hukm al-tawassul" (65–183), by the Sheikh of al-Azhar, Muhammad Hussein Makhluf.

67. Abu al-ma'ali Mahmud Shukri al-Alusi, *Ghayat al-amani fi al-radd 'ala al-Nabahani* (al-Iskandariyya: Dar ihya' al-sunnah al-nabawiyyah, 1971), 36.

68. Wali Allah, *Hujjat allah al-balighah* (al-Qahira: Dar al-turath, 1978).

69. Sulaiman ibn 'Abdul Wahhab, *al-Sawa'iq al-ilahiyya fi al-radd 'ala-al-Wahhabiya*, 8, 14, 16.

70. There are some among the Muslims that reject *shafa'a* (intercession). The *khawarij* rejected it outright because they believed that any sinner who entered hell was there to stay. The Mu'tazila rejected it on behalf of a grave sinner, in particular. On the subject of the various schools and their doctrinal differences, see Muhammad Abu Zahra, *Tarikh al-madhahib al-islamiyah* (al-Qahira: Dar al-fikr al-'arabi, 1963).

71. According to the hadith, the Prophet says, "those are the worst of all men: When a righteous member of their group dies, they build a church over his grave and set up all kinds of images of him therein. They combine the two evils of worshipping at the grave and setting up images." Ibn 'Abdul Wahhab, *Kitab al-tawhid*, 98; see also chapters 12–19.

72. Ibid., 93–96.

73. Wahhab, *Kashf al-shubuhat*, 165–66.

74. Muhammad Hussain Makhluf's *Risalah fi hukm al-tawasul bil-anbiya' wal-awliya* appeared as an addendum in Sulaiman ibn 'Abdul Wahhab's *al-Sawa'iq al-ilahiya fi al-radd 'ala- al-Wahhabiya* (see note 67). Although Makhluf was not a contemporary of ibn 'Abdul Wahhab, he nonetheless articulates well the position of the opposition.

75. To say "intercede for me, ye prophet of God, or to say I entreat ye to plead for me on the Day of Judgment" is a practice that is permitted, according to Makhluf, on the basis of the following Quranic verse: "Pray for me and I will respond." Makhluf, *Risalah*, 75–86.

76. Ibid.

77. "Beseeching the assistance of another, is intended by God to create the incentive in the slave of God to do good and for his slaves to share in the act of doing good . . . as is stated in the Quranic verse: 'And never let your hatred of people who would bar you from the Inviolable House of Worship lead you into the sin of aggression: but rather help one another in furthering evil and enmity'" (5:2). Makhluf, *Risalah*, 86.

78. Algar, *Wahhabism*, 82. The appendix consists of different responses by Muslims opposed to the Wahhabi movement. One of these responses is a translation of al-Ghita's treatise.

79. Ibid., 83.

CHAPTER 3: AN ISLAMIC RECONFIGURATION OF COLONIAL MODERNITY

1. Quoted in Brian R. Clack, *An Introduction to Wittgenstein's Philosophy of Religion* (Edinburgh: Edinburgh University Press, 1999), 52. To Wittgenstein, religion is not about speculative thought, it is more about emotions and passions, and religious life is not about the acceptance of a doctrine but about *works.* See also Norman Malcolm, *Wittgenstein: A Religious Point of View?* (Ithaca, NY: Cornell University Press, 1993).

2. This is how a respected postorientalist sociologist in the field delineates the difference between what is and what is not fundamentalist:

Abdu is not normally identified as a fundamentalist but rather as a liberal reformer with a nineteenth-century faith in progress through the enlightenment. The major contrast between Abdu and, say, the Muslim Brotherhood is his liberalism with regard to the application of Islamic law, particularly elements of the penal code and the restrictions on women. . . . What underlies the difference between Abdu and later fundamentalists are their different attitudes to European ideas and models: whereas for Abdu Europe, the oppressor, was at the same time the model for progress and strength, for the latter fundamentalists the West was both oppressive and culturally threatening. . . . While Abdu is clearly not a fundamentalist in the current sense, his construction of the "sacred history" as a model for the modern state was a very important episode in the quest for this Islamic state.

Sami Zubaida, *Islam, the People and the State: Essays on Political Ideas and Movements in the Middle East* (New York: Routledge, 1989), 45–46.

3. P. J. Vatikiotis, "Muhammad ʿAbduh and the Quest for a Muslim Humanism," *Islamic Culture* 31 (1975): 126.

4. Ibid.

5. Ibid., 115.

6. Ibid., 116. According to Vatikiotis, the obstacles that prevent Islam from becoming humanist are (1) the "closeness between the spiritual and temporal, and more so, the political"; (2) the sanctity of the Sacred Law, a shariʿa "codified thousands of years ago into a *corpus juris* of lasting value, and defying change"; and (3) the "ever present anti-rational disposition of orthodoxy as well as the average Muslim" that eventually compelled ʿAbduh to insist "on the return to the true religion as the only source of power" (116).

7. Although the field celebrates the death of orientalism, recent events in the Western hemisphere, including the pope's remarks on the antihumanist nature of Islam, demonstrate strongly the persistence and potency of these categories of analysis in contemporary Western discourses. See Chapter 6.

8. Albert Hourani, *Arabic Thought in the Liberal Age, 1798–1939* (Cambridge: Cambridge University Press, 1983), 144.

9. Ibid., 143.

10. ʿAbduh's ingenious religiosity is evidenced by the following: "Cromer thought he was really an agnostic, and Blunt recorded in his diary 'I fear that he has as little faith in Islam . . . as I have in the Catholic Church.' In the same way some of his Muslim critics hinted that he was not scrupulous in performing his religious duties as a Muslim, even that of regular prayer." Hourani, *Arabic Thought*, 141.

11. Ibid., 144 [emphasis is mine].

12. Evelyn Baring Cromer, *Modern Egypt* (New York: Macmillan, 1916), 2:229.

13. The "invented tradition" as an analytical category is commonly identified with the English Marxist historian E. Hobsbawm, who popularized that term in *The Invention of Tradition*, ed. Eric Hobsbawm and Terence Ranger (Cambridge: Cambridge University Press, 1988).

14. See Albert Hourani, "How Should We Write the History of the Middle East?" *International Journal of Middle East Studies* (*IJMES*) 23 (1991): 125–36; Donald M. Reid, "Arabic Thought in the Liberal Age Twenty Years After," *IJMES* 14 (1982): 541–57.

15. Hourani, *Arabic Thought*, 138.

16. Reinhardt Koselleck, *Futures Past: On the Semantics of Historical Times*, trans. Keith Tribe (Cambridge, MA: MIT Press, 1985).

17. On the history of nineteenth-century Egypt, see Afaf Lutfi al-Sayyid Marsot, *Egypt and Cromer: A Study in Anglo-Egyptian Relations* (New York: Praeger, 1969); Afaf Lutfi al-Sayyid Marsot, *Egypt in the Reign of Muhammad ʿAli* (Cambridge: Cambridge University Press, 1984); Juan Cole, *Colonialism and Revolution in the Middle East: Social and Cultural Origins of Egypt's ʿUrabi Revolt* (Princeton, NJ: Princeton University Press, 1993).

18. I depend largely on two sources that collected ʿAbduh's works: (1) Muhammad Rashid Rida's three-volume collection, *Tarikh al-Imam Muhammad ʿAbduh*, hereafter cited as *Tarikh al-Imam*. The collection includes, in addition to ʿAbduh's writing, Rida's running commentaries on contemporary events, which I found not only amusing, but extremely useful for shedding light on ʿAbduh's writings and activities, as well as the political intrigues and social and cultural attitude of that period; and (2) *al-Aʿmal al-kamilah lil-Imam Muhammad ʿAbduh*, compiled and edited by Muhammad ʿImara (al-Qahira: Dar al-shuruq, 1993), 5 vols., hereafter cited as *Aʿmal kamilah*. All translations are mine except when acknowledged.

19. The Syrian Muslim reformer Rashid Rida was a student in this circle who later followed ʿAbduh to Egypt, where he began to work closely with him and to promote and publicize his ideas in his journal, *al-Manar*.

20. The term *taghrib* comes from the stem *gharb* or west.

21. ʿAbduh's criticism of taqlid was located in the works of ibn Taymiya and ibn al-Qayim, while his definition of orthodoxy drew on al-Ghazali.

22. Quoted from Charles Adams, *Islam and Modernism in Egypt* (New York: Russell & Russell, 1968), 130.

23. The notion of din as embodied practice, commonly translated as "religion" does not have the same meaning as the term *religion* in modern Western Christian traditions. Within the Islamic tradition, the notion of din correlates to conduct or a course of action; thus, the word *habitus* conveys more accurately the Arabic meaning of din than does *religion*. *Dana bil-islam*, according to *Lisan al-Arab*, is for one to become obedient to Islam, while din signifies an active commitment to obedience through the enactment of certain practices and rituals.

24. This is contrary to Rahman's analysis that 'Abduh, following in ibn 'Abdul Wahhab's footsteps, wanted to liberate Islam from all medieval works. Neither of these authors proposed to do so. In his article "Jurists and Jurisprudence," 'Abduh, in fact, deals specifically with this matter by scolding his contemporaries for following outdated works like *al-tanweer* (Illumination) and *al-kinz* (the Treasure) and not *al-Zayla'i*, a medieval Hanafi jurist, in matter of law. See 'Abduh's "al-Fiqh wal-fuqaha," in *A'mal kamilah*, 3:213. In regard to ibn 'Abdul Wahhab, see Chapter 2.

25. 'Abduh, *A'mal kamilah*, 4:393; see also Muhammad Asad, *The Message of the Qur'an* (Lahore: Matba'at Jawahar ul-Ulum, n.d.), 34, n. 137. Volumes 4 and 5 of *A'mal kamilah* are dedicated to 'Abduh's tafsir or interpretation of the Qur'an.

26. The translated quote was taken from Adams, *Islam and Modernism*, 130. See also 'Abduh, *A'mal kamilah*, 3:395, 396–97.

27. See Indira Falk Gesink, "Chaos on Earth: Subjective Truths Versus Communal Unity in Islamic Law and the Rise of Militant Islam," *American Historical Review* 108 (2003): 718–20.

28. Wael Hallaq, *Authority, Continuity, and Change in Islamic Law* (Cambridge: Cambridge University Press, 2001), 85.

29. Ibid., 103.

30. Ibid., 85. Five classifications of analytical categories evolved in the process of creating a positive legal knowledge: ijtihad, *takhrij, tarjih,* taqlid, and *tasnif.*

31. Ibid., 113.

32. 'Abduh, "Fiqh wal-Fuqaha'," in *A'mal kamilah*, 3:212–15.

33. Ibid., 3:212.

34. Ibid.

35. Ibid., 3:213.

36. Ibid.

37. Ibid., 3:214. On encounters between al-Anbabi and 'Abduh, see Rida, *Tarikh al-Imam*, 1:426, 450, 944. Confirming the ignorance of Azhari scholars, Rida recalls his visit to al-Azhar to see al-Anbabi, where he came across some of

al-Anbabi's friends, including Sheikh al-Zawahiri, who upon Rida's disclosure that he was from Mount Lebanon turned to his friends in ignorance to ask where Mount Lebanon was, in the east or in the west. Ibid., 411.

38. Hallaq, *Authority, Continuity, and Change*, esp. chapters 6 and 7.

39. In *Tafsir juz' 'amma*, 'Abduh makes his case for ijtihad as a duty of every rational believer. Muhammad 'Abduh, *Tafsir juz' 'amma* (al-Qahira: Muhammad 'Ali Subayh, 1967), 169.

40. 'Abduh, "fiqh and al-Fuqaha," in *A'mal kamilah*, 3:214.

41. 'Abduh, *A'mal kamilah*, 4:7. Al-Shatibi is mentioned several times in 'Abduh's work, which clearly indicates that he utilized al-Shatibi's notion of maslaha and *istislah*. 'Abduh listed al-Shatibi's work on fiqh as required reading for students seeking higher education in dar al-'Ulum, al-Azhar among others.

42. Ibid., 7–12. In the "Introduction to the Exegesis of the Qur'an," 'Abduh presents his rationale for reinstating the Qur'an as the primary source and his reasons for interpreting the Qur'an anew.

43. This was an argument utilized by many of the eighteenth-century revivalists, including ibn 'Abdul Wahhab and al-Shawkani. See Chapters 1 and 2.

44. 'Abduh, *A'mal kamilah*, 4:9. He reiterates the same argument in his commentary on *surat al-fatiha*: "the Qur'an should be the source (*asl*) to all the Islamic legal schools (*madhahib*). These schools should refer to and seek answers in the Qur'an rather than the other way around where the Qur'an becomes a tool for them to justify and rationalize their dogmatic doctrinal positions. I want the Qur'an to be the primary source and not an auxiliary, to be the judge and not the one to be judged [*kitab allah matbu' la tabi'; hakim la muhkamun 'alayhu*]." Ibid., 22–25.

45. 'Abduh, *A'mal kamilah*, 3:214–15. Many historians attribute the economic crisis of the 1870s to excessive expenditures incurred primarily in the building of the Suez Canal. See Afaf Lufti al-Sayyid-Marsot, *A Short History of Modern Egypt* (Cambridge: Cambridge University Press, 1985), 96–100.

46. Hallaq, *A History of Islamic Legal Theories*, 112.

47. Ibid. On Shatibi, see esp. chapter 5, "Social Reality and the Response of Theory," 162–206.

48. Mizan, according to al-Ghazali, is integral to justice. It defines the normative character of God's wisdom as is indicated in the following Quranic verse (5:7–9): "We have sent you the Book and the Balance, that people may act with justice." Al-Ghazali, *al-Qistat al-mustaqim: al-mawazin al-khamsa lil-ma'arifa*, ed. Mahmud Beijo (Dimashq: al-Matba'a al-'ilmiya, 1993), 19–27.

49. The middle-of-the-road rule is founded in Aristotle's notion of the golden mean, with the difference that whereas the Greeks considered the "good" as natural, for Muslims the "good" is divinely driven. Al-Ghazali Islamicized Greek philosophy and blended it into the Islamic belief system. For more on al-Ghazali, see

Mohammad Sharif, *Ghazali's Theory of Virtue* (Albany: State University of New York Press, 1975); al-Ghazali, "The Rescuer from Error," in *Medieval Islamic Philosophical Writings*, ed. Muhammad ʿAli Khalidi (Cambridge: Cambridge University Press, 2005), 59–99.

50. The middle, or wasat, is further demonstrated in the Qurʾan (17:29): "Make not thy hand tied to the neck, nor stretch it forth to its utmost reach, so that you become blameworthy and destitute." It is also demonstrated in verse 25:57, which states, "Those who, when they spend, are not extravagant and not niggardly but hold a just [balance] between the two [extremes]"; and in verse 7:31, "Eat and drink, but waste not excess, for God loveth not wasters," and in the prophetic saying "the best in all things is the mean." See also al-Ghazali, *al-Qistat*.

51. Marshall G. S. Hodgson, *The Venture of Islam: Conscience and History in a World Civilization* (Chicago: University of Chicago Press, 1974), 2:180–92; Rahman, *Islam*, 109–11. For a new and refreshing look on al-Ghazali and his contribution to the Islamic tradition and his relevance to the modern period, see Ebrahim Moosa's recent study, *Ghazali and the Poetics of Imagination* (Chapel Hill: University of North Carolina Press, 2000).

52. Entitled "Face to Face with Islam and the Muslim Question," the article made its first appearance in a French journal, *Journal de Paris*, in 1900. A version of this essay was translated into Arabic and published in the Egyptian newspaper *al-Muʾayid*, which supported the Islamists and was owned by Sheikh ʿAli Yusuf. The translated version angered many Muslims in Egypt and beyond, generating a heated debate among Europeans, Europeanized Arabs, and Muslim modernists over the nature of stagnation (*inhitat*) and its causes.

53. Charles Adams, *Islam and Modernism in Egypt* (New York: Russell and Russell, 1968), 86–87; see also ʿAbduh, *Aʿmal kamila*, 3:263–64.

54. ʿAbduh wrote six essays on the subject: the first three appeared in *al-Muʾayid* and responded to Hanotaux's first two essays. The other three were in response to Hanotaux's interview with the Francophile Egyptian newspaper *al-Ahram* (conducted by Bishara Taqla, the editor) in which Hanotaux had disputed ʿAbduh's first response to him, which also appeared in *al-Ahram*. The six essays and Hanotaux's articles and interviews were compiled along with four pieces from his "Theology of Unity" (*risalat al-tawhid*) and were published in a book under the title *Islam and the Reply to Its Critics* [*al-islam wal-radd ala muntaqiduha*] in 1924. In the first response, ʿAbduh notes that Hanotaux's articles were meant to inform French colonial policies in Algeria and their other Muslim colonies. See also ʿAbduh, *Aʿmal kamilah*, 3:217–51; Rida, *Tarikh al-Imam*, 2:400–468.

55. For background information on ʿAbduh's response to Hanotaux, I suggest reading Rida, *Tarikh al-Imam*, 1:799–802.

56. An example of this racialist binary analytic is Lord Cromer's *Modern Egypt*, and a strong critique of it is Edward Said's *Orientalism* (New York: Pantheon Books, 1978).

57. "Islam, Muslims and Colonialism" is the first of the essays in a series of responses to Hanotaux. See 'Abduh, *A'mal kamilah*, 3:222–26.

58. Ibid., 249–50. "Muslim Stagnation and Its Causes" is the fifth essay in this series.

59. Ibid., 250.

60. Translation quoted from Charles Adams, *Islam and Modernism*, 89. 'Abduh here is mocking the rulers of Egypt as well as the Ottoman Porte. In the debates on the nature of Muslim stagnation, many, including Islamists, have attributed the decline of Muslims to the Ottomans.

61. 'Abduh, "Muslim Stagnation," in *A'mal kamilah*, 3:250.

62. Ibid., 3:248. 'Abduh makes the point that the revivalist movement started in the mid-eighteenth century, with Muslim reformers appearing in India, Afghanistan, Arabia, and Africa as well as other regions of the Muslim world. Each of these movements defined its goal as the moral reformation of the Muslims in spite of the difference in their approaches regarding the cure (3:247).

63. Ibid., 247–48.

64. See al-Kumi, *al-Sahafa al-Islamiyya fi misr* (al-Mansura: Dar al wafa', 1992), 183. On Farah Antun's motives and politics, see Rida, *Tarikh al-Imam*, 1:805–16.

65. 'Abduh, *A'mal kamilah*, 3:264, 310. In response, 'Abduh cited the two Quranic verses (2:257; 18:29) that he interpreted as forbidding Muslims to combine the two authorities together for fear of coercion.

66. Ibid., 3:308–9.

67. Ibid., 3:308.

68. Ibid., 3:307–9.

69. On the religious wars and the decline of ecclesiastical power in Europe, see Owen Chadwick, *The Reformation* (Baltimore: Pelican Books, 1964), esp. 316–20, 325–47, 375–405.

70. Despite the intense doctrinal disagreements among Muslims, these did not translate into violence and wars among them:

Who ever heard of a war between the early salafi movement and the Ash'ariya despite the deep disagreement among them, or between *ahl al-sunna* and the Mu'tazila despite the irreconcilable differences in their creeds? Moreover, we never heard of Muslim philosophers becoming a sect or ever entering into a violent war between them and the others. Yes, we know of the *Kharajities* and the war against them and the *Qaramita* sect and the war against them, too. These wars, however, were politically and not doctrinally driven, they held particular views on political sovereignty, and their wars against the caliphs were not over creed but over politics and their desire to overtake political power.

See *A'mal kamilah*, 3:267.

71. *A'mal kamilah*, 3:353–54.

72. 'Abduh goes through the history of the Spanish inquisition and discusses torture and the burning alive of those condemned as a habitual practice by the Roman Catholic Church in the fifteenth and sixteenth centuries. He discussed the Turin meeting in 1502 and how the Church declared as apostates anyone interested in the philosophical writings of ibn Rushd. He mentions the forced conversions of Jews and Muslims to Christianity and the intolerance of the Church to beliefs and practices other than its own. He gives many historical examples to substantiate how the Church, contrary to Antun's description, was intolerant of scientific knowledge, including medicine and astronomy, among others. Even the Protestant reformist movement demonstrated its intolerance to philosophy: Luther damned Aristotle and his writings, and Calvin, though less vocal in his condemnation of Aristotle, considered him an apostate, as did Luther. In contrast, the medieval Muslim jurists and scholars regarded Aristotle with great respect and considered him their "principal teacher." The Protestant movement was as intolerant of science and learning as was the Catholic Church. It was, after all, a religious movement aiming to reform the Church, not to find an alternative to the religion. See *A'mal kamilah*, 3:286–93.

73. See *American Historical Review* 108 (2003): 1058–1104. Dror Wahrman's "Review Essays: God and the Enlightenment" introduced Sheehan's "Enlightenment, Religion, and the Enigma of Secularization," and Dale Kley's "Christianity as Casualty and Chrysalis of Modernity: The Problem of Dechristianization in the French Revolution." These two articles clearly demonstrate that secularization in the Western hemisphere has never in practice fully separated religion from politics or other social spheres, thus making the point that secularization is neither self-evident nor universal. As Sheehan argues, "religion has never been left behind, either personally or institutionally. Instead it has been continually remade and given new forms and meanings over time. Thinking more carefully about religion is a fundamental step in understanding both the Enlightenment and the enigmas of secularization" (1072).

74. On this discussion, see John McManners, *Church and Society in Eighteenth-Century France* (New York: Oxford University Press, 1998); Jonathan Clark, *English Society, 1600–1832: Religion, Ideology, and Politics During the Ancien Regime,* 2nd ed. (Cambridge: Cambridge University Press, 2000); Hent De Vries, *Philosophy and the Turn to Religion* (Baltimore: Johns Hopkins University Press, 1999); B. W. Young, "Religious History and the Eighteenth-Century Historian,"

Historical Journal 43 (September 2000): 857; Talal Asad, *Formations of the Secular: Christianity, Islam, Modernity* (Stanford, CA: Stanford University Press, 2003); Rajeev Bhargava, ed., *Secularism and Its Critics* (New York: Oxford University Press, 1998); Philip Hamburger, *Separation of Church and State* (Cambridge, MA: Harvard University Press, 2002).

75. Rida, *Tarikh al-Imam*, 1:425.

76. Afaf Lutfi al-Sayyid Marsot, "Modernization Among the Rectors of al-Azhar, 1798–1879," in *Beginnings of Modernization in the Middle East: The Nineteenth Century*, ed. William R. Polk and Richard L. Chambers (Chicago: University of Chicago Press, 1968), 275.

77. Brinkley Messick, *The Calligraphic State*, esp. chapter 1, on the genealogy of the text; Timothy Mitchell, *Colonising Egypt* (Cambridge: Cambridge University Press, 1988), 80–94.

78. 'Abduh was not alone in this judgment; many of his generation called for similar reforms. Their anger at the condition of al-Azhar was voiced in journals that included *al-Manar, al-tankit wal-tabkit, al-uztadh*, and *al-Mu'ayid*, among others. For more information on the reform of al-Azhar and the newspapers that covered this topic, see Kumi, *al-Sahafa*, 15–100, 147–55.

79. Rida, *Tarikh al-Imam*, 1:527.

80. Ibid., 1:133–34.

81. For more information on the internal politics of al-Azhar, see A. Chris Eccel, *Egypt, Islam, and Social Change: Al-Azhar in Conflict and Accommodation* (Berlin: Klaus Schwarz, 1984), 168. Before the 1870s, resolution of conflicts, as reported by Ali Mubarak Pasha, was left for the sheikhs of the arcades or sheikh al-Azhar to resolve. Only when these conflicts exceeded the settlement of the al-Azhar were government agencies called upon (*muhtasib*).

82. When appointed for the job, 'Abduh enjoyed the full support of the khedive, 'Abbas Hilmi, but their cordial relationship ended in 1894, and the khedive withdrew his political backing of 'Abduh, turning against 'Abduh and supporting his enemies, the old guard. In 1899, for instance, the khedive backed the appointment of Salim al-Bishri as the rector of al-Azhar. A defender of the status quo, al-Bishri made sure that those reforms passed while 'Abduh was in charge were shelved and made inactive. He also suspended the annual student examination introduced during 'Abduh's tenure. All these political intrigues are recorded in detail in Rida, *Tarikh al-Imam*, 1:426, 487–95.

83. 'Abduh, *A'mal kamilah*, 3:195, 197. Although 'Abduh used caution when seeking the support of the state, he was constantly caught in the intrigues and political rivalries between the khedive and the British administration, sometimes unintentionally. For instance, when he lost the backing of the khedive and was pressured to resign his position at al-Azhar, he received the backing of the more powerful Lord Cromer, who rejected his removal, leading many (including

Azhari scholars) to conclude that 'Abduh was no more than an agent of the British and an endorser of their project.

84. Rida, *Tarikh al-Imam*, 1:425. This was based on a personal conversation between Rida and 'Abduh, as recorded by Rida.

85. The three distinguished Azhari members on the council representing the different madhahib or legal schools were Salim al-Bishri, a Maliki; Hasan al-Marsafi, a Shafi'i; and Yusif al-Nabulsi, a Hanbali. Rida, *Tarikh al-Imam*, 1:425–27.

86. Hassuna al-Nawawi (1838–1924) became rector following the resignation of al-Anbabi in 1895 and after assisting him for a year or so. A Hanafi reformer, al-Nawawi taught at al-Azhar in the *Dar al-'Ulum* (School of Social Sciences) and the School of Business Administration (*madrasat al-idara*), later to become the School of Law (*madrasat al-huquq*). Aware of the difficulty of teaching conventional fiqh, he composed a simplified version of Hanafi fiqh (the Ladder to Those Who Seek Guidance) for students not trained or in training to acquire knowledge in traditional fiqh. In 1897, al-Nawawi was appointed mufti of Egypt and as a result came to occupy the two most powerful Islamic posts, the rector of al-Azhar and grand mufti of Egypt, until his dismissal by the khedive four years later. Like 'Abduh, he was dismissed for challenging the khedive's power by claiming that the khedive was not above the law and had to abide by its rules. The conflict arose when the khedive tried to appoint lawyers from the national courts to serve in the shari'a courts, thus overriding the authority of the grand mufti of Egypt. Al-Nawawi was reappointed rector of al-Azhar in 1907 and resigned in 1909. See Jakob Skovgaard-Peterson, *Defining Islam for the Egyptian State: Muftis and Fatwas of the Dār al-Iftā* (Leiden, the Netherlands: Brill, 1997), 111–15.

It is worth noting that al-Nawawi, like other Muslim reformers of his age, including al-Abbasi al-Mahdi and 'Abduh, ended up being alienated from the khedive who initially backed their efforts in the hope of enhancing his secular power and not because of a genuine commitment to Islamic reform. In other words, these reformers were bound to clash with the khedive once he tried to undermine the changes attempting to enhance Islamic authority rather than to diminish it.

87. For more, see Rida, *Tarikh al-Imam*, 1:432–33, 440–43, 446–65. As an outcome of these changes, the students in the first four years of training were forbidden from reading glossaries and super-commentaries (*hawashi*) and after that were only allowed to read limited commentaries with their master teachers; reading glossaries, however, required special permission from the council. See *Fatawa al-Islamiya min dar al-ifta' al-Misriya* (Cairo: wizarat al-awqaf, al-majlis al-a'la lil shu'un al-islamiyya, 1980), 7:361; also Skovgaard-Peterson, *Defining Islam*, 119.

88. On detailed information of the modernization of al-Azhar, see Eccel, *Egypt, Islam, and Social Change.*

89. One spokesman against the reform of al-Azhar was Sheikh al-Buhayri, who in a heated argument disputed ʿAbduh's views on al-Azhar by reminding him that the institution continued to produce men with keen intellect and considerable knowledge, ʿAbduh among them. The argument went as follows: Al-Buhayri asked ʿAbduh, "Do you not know that you are an Azhari, and yet you have ascended to where you are on the stairs to knowledge and have become a brilliant scholar?" ʿAbduh's responded: "If I have a portion of true knowledge, as you mention, I got it through ten years of sweeping the dirt of Azhari knowledge from my brain and to this day it is not as clean as it should be." Eccel, *Egypt, Islam, and Social Change*, 157.

90. Rida, *Tarikh al-Imam*, 1:502. Rida describes al-Sharbini as a leading scholar in al-Azhar, known for his piety and disdain for worldly matters, until his co-optation by the khedive, who offered him the rectorship of al-Azhar (1323 A.H./1905 A.D.) with the condition that he put a halt to the reforms introduced by ʿAbduh (501, 512).

91. Rida, *Tarikh al-Imam*, 1:503.

92. Ibid., 1:506. ʿAbduh's response to Sharbini was anonymous.

93. Ibid., 1:507. I took the liberty of translating the term *funun* in the original as secular modern subjects because it captures best Sharbini's references to ʿulum al-aʿsur (modern sciences) and *umur al-dunya* (worldly or secular matters), which he accused ʿAbduh of introducing to al-Azhar.

94. Ibid., 1:508.

95. In a public gathering of the sheikhs at the palace, ʿAbduh denounced the khedive for recommending the name of a sheikh, a favorite of the khedive, for the assignment of the "robe of honor" because it infringed on the regulations governing these assignments as prescribed by the advisory council. He asked the khedive to either amend the regulations to empower him with that right of assignment or else to abide by the principles laid down by the regulations. Later on, the advisory council, under the influence of ʿAbduh, turned down the candidate suggested by the khedive, intensifying the animosity of the khedive toward ʿAbduh. Rida, *Tarikh al-Imam*, 1:497, 500. The periodicals that voiced the opinions of those who criticized the reform policies of ʿAbduh were *al-Muʾayid* as well as the nationalist newspaper *al-liwa*.

96. The quote is taken from Mahmudul Haq, *Muhammad ʿAbduh: A Study of a Modern Thinker of Egypt* (Aligarh: Institute of Islamic Studies, 1970), 75.

CHAPTER 4: GOVERNABLE MUSLIM SUBJECTS

1. T. Asad, *Formations of the Secular*, 225. In the chapter titled "Reconfigurations of Law and Ethics in Colonial Egypt," Asad criticizes the new scholarship in Islamic studies for mistakenly assuming that "modernity introduced subjective

interiority into Islam, something that was previously absent," because "subjective interiority has always been recognized in the Islamic tradition—in ritual worship (*'ibadat*) as well as in mysticism (*tasawwuf*)." Ebrahim Moosa in *Ghazali and the Poetics of Imagination* demonstrates more extensively the emergence and development of interiority and subjectivity in Islam, starting with al-Ghazali.

2. The concept of "civil" is meant to signify orderly and educated, an understanding equated with "civil society," a seventeenth- and eighteenth-century notion that describes an ordered regulated society as a condition required of a modern society. See Raymond Williams, *Keywords* (New York: Oxford University Press, 1976), 57; M. Foucault, *The Order of Things*.

3. Skovgaard-Peterson, *Defining Islam*. Although extremely informative and illuminating, the author nonetheless maintains that Abduh's Islamic subjectivity is a novel notion and a natural and necessary outcome of modernity.

4. The question of what constitutes knowledge is a contested issue within the tradition. In contrast to the Ash'ariya and other strains within the tradition, the Mu'tazila, while arguing that knowledge is objectively verifiable, acknowledged that disagreement about the source of knowledge is probable but not what constituted knowledge itself. See Moosa, *Ghazali and the Poetics of Imagination*, 250. See also Marshall Hodgson, *Venture of Islam*, 2:315–444; and Rahman, *Islam*, 97–181.

5. Such a virtuous state, as al-Ghazali explains, is reached only by the privileged. That is why there are different degrees of virtuosity that a Muslim subject can attain, according to which he will be rewarded in the afterlife. The relationship of body and soul does not abide by the Platonic dualism of body versus soul. To al-Ghazali, although there is tension between the two, it takes a dialogical rather than an oppositional form of expression. For more information on Islamic "hermeneutics of the self and subjectivity," see Moosa, *Ghazali and the Poetics of Imagination*, 209–36.

6. Ibid., 214.

7. Ibid., 219.

8. Ibid.

9. Skovgaard-Peterson, *Defining Islam*, esp. 119–33.

10. 'Abduh, *A'mal kamilah*, 4:9, 51.

11. Ibid., 4:52. 'Abduh's reformulation of free will and rational judgment are founded on the concepts of the Mu'tazila. 'Abduh's reliance on the Mu'tazila did not spare them his criticism for he denounced them and the other mahdhib (legal schools) of factionalism and sectarianism. He distinguished between healthy disputation—as active dialogical engagement with one another had been the practice of early master jurists—and harmful dissension (*tashayyu'*) and sectarianism where each sect came to "patronize and adhere to its own understandings and where each sect became partial to its own and when disputes arise, each sect would accuse the other of intolerance and partisanship. It is this dissension among

the sects that led to the weakening of Muslims and their eventual decline. Rather than engaging one another and debating each other, each sect kept to itself, thus ending any form of intelligent discussion and open debate."

12. Within al-Ghazali's analytic, the good Muslim is one who strikes a state of equilibrium between the inner truthful self (nafs, or soul) and an outer body and action. To attain that good, a Muslim has to seek the middle way (wasat) between these two extremes. To bring a body or soul to a healthy and a balanced state therefore requires a prescription of the opposite of what the soul or body is suffering from. It is only through the simultaneous training of the body, mind, and emotions that a balance is possibly attained. Al-Ghazali considered training and disciplining the soul/mind as a constant process, ensuring a cure when the soul/mind is sick and sustaining it when it is healthy. To be good, a Muslim has to continuously make the effort to seek out this state of balance; therefore, a good Muslim is always one in the making or in the process of becoming. On this question, see M. Sharif, *Ghazali's Theory of Virtue*; Moosa, *Ghazali and the Poetics of Imagination*, chapter 9, 240–60.

13. On Ghazali's dialogic of the inner and outer and soul and body, see Moosa, *Ghazali and the Poetics of Imagination*, 221–32.

14. 'Abduh, *A'mal kamilah*, 3:350. 'Abduh addressed the subject of civility and the practice of disciplining mind and body in an article entitled "*Malakat and 'adat*," in Rida, *Tarikh al-Imam*, 2:181–93.

15. 'Abduh, *A'mal kamilah*, 4:396; Muhammad 'Abduh, *Tafsir juz' 'amma*, 169.

16. One cannot help but notice the similarities between 'Abduh and ibn 'Abdul Wahhab's explanations of prayer and its goal in inculcating the virtue of piety.

17. 'Abduh referred to the term *malaka* in describing the acquisition of good virtues or bad vices in human behavior. In "Philosophy of Pedagogy," he says: "All human virtues (*al-malaka al-fadila*) are but a balance between two extremes. When one extreme outweighs the other, a state of imbalance permeates, leading to a state of depravity (*malaka al- radhila*) and to the breakdown of the good and happy life both in this world and the after." See *Tarikh al-Imam*, 2:5.

18. On al-Ghazali, see Moosa, *Ghazali and the Poetics of Imagination*; Rahman, *Islam*, 108–14; and Henry Corban, *History of Islamic Philosophy* (London: Kegan Paul, 1996), 179–86.

19. It is important to note here that the term *reason* is qualified because it connotes a different form of reasoning than the universal, transhistorical Reason implied in European modern thought. It refers more to what the philosopher Stephen Toulmin, in *Cosmopolis: The Hidden Agenda of Modernity* (Chicago: University of Chicago Press, 1990), refers to as practical reasoning or a contemplative form of reason, which is more particular and relative rather than universal.

20. The Mu'tazila (1st century A.H./8th century A.D.) claim that reason is an equal source with revelation in ascertaining truth was a response to and a rejection of *al-Jabriya*, a predeterminist tendency that appeared in the same period. It would be wrong to portray the Mu'tazila rationalists as "free thinkers" or "pure rationalists" as they confined their understanding of 'aql in terms of its relation to nass or Revelation. Rahman, *Islam*, 88–89. In an earlier version of the Theology of Unity, 'Abduh supports the Mu'tazila's claim that the Qur'an was created rather than eternal, a position that stressed the importance of human reasoning in establishing the truth. This claim was dropped from later editions, which is read by Kerr and Hourani as a sign of 'Abduh's eclecticism. I am more of the opinion that it was dropped for tactical reasons, as 'Abduh continued to stress rationality as an essential feature of his revivalist project. Hourani, *Arabic Thought*, 142.

21. Rahman, *Islam*, 99–104. Many recent scholars, following in the footsteps of Hourani and Kerr, conclude that 'Abduh was eclectic for his tendency to draw on all different Islamic schools of thought within the tradition rather than restrict himself to one school and one point of view. My point all along is that what he drew on were arguments within the tradition that seemed relevant to his time regardless of the school. This is a method that he had reflected upon and consciously arrived at, as is evidenced in his practice of *takhayur* and talfiq, discussed later in this chapter. His approach of picking and choosing from within the tradition without abiding to one particular school of thought is clearly stated in his confrontation with his nemesis from al-Azhar, 'Ilish, which I quoted in the introduction to Chapter 3 for the purpose of highlighting his method of reasoning.

22. The terms *fiqh al-nafs*, *tafqih*, and *faqqaha* as connoting interior active discernment are taken from Moosa, *Ghazali and the Poetics of Imagination*, 238–40. As Moosa points out, al-Ghazali used the terms of *fiqh batin* for inner discernment and *fiqh zahir* for external law.

23. Rida, *Tarikh al-Imam*, 1:974–77. It is ironic that the same verse was used by al-Afghani on many occasions to suggest a reform program very different from 'Abduh's.

24. The idea of relating education and Islamic pedagogy to raising a new generation of ethically responsible and independent individuals was made on several occasions and in other contexts. See 'Abduh's series of articles on religious pedagogy and education that appeared in *al-Waqa'i al-misriya* in 1880 and 1881, including "al-'Adala wal-'ilm" [Justice and knowledge], "Al-Tarbiya fil-madaris wal-makatib al-amiriya" [Pedagogy in public and Ottoman school systems], "Ma howa al-faqr al-haqiqi fil Bilad?" [The real causes of poverty in Egypt], and "Ta'thir al-ta'lim fil-din wal-'aqida" [The impact of education on religion and theology]. All of these articles were republished under the heading "Islah Mashru' al-tarbiya fi-misr" [The project of reforming education in Egypt] in 'Abduh, *A'mal kamilah*, 3:109–48. In these articles, 'Abduh criticized the schools, the

plight of teachers, the methods of instruction, and the new educational programs that were created by the Department of Education. To improve education, he proposed the surveillance of schools through a special agency that would inspect the schools on a regular basis. He was quite concerned about the courses being taught and the textbooks being used, suggesting again that a committee of experts be formed to look into such matters.

25. The idea of a public school system coincided with the creation of the first Egyptian Parliament in 1866. *Majlis al-nuwwab*, or the Consultative Chamber of Deputies, took seriously the subject of public education and the need for a literate public as a precondition for the creation of a political community able to participate in elections. In 1867, the chamber recommended the founding of primary schools in each and every province in Egypt and in the major large towns. Admission was to be free for all, regardless of social or religious status. The implementation of the plan was handed over to 'Ali Mubarak, the minister of education, who in turn set up an advisory committee, made up of both Muslim scholars and notables, charged with developing a comprehensive plan for the creation of a centralized system of public education. The following year, the chamber implemented the recommendations of the committee with the passage of the Primary School Law of 1868. See Fritz Steppat, "National Education Projects in Egypt Before British Occupation," in *The Beginnings of Modernization in the Middle East*, 288–89.

26. As Leila Ahmed points out, "With the British Occupation, which began in 1882, the thrust toward educational expansion generally, including girls' education, slowed down. The finances of the country improved, and the British Administration expended some of the increased revenues on irrigation and other projects, deliberately keeping down expenditure on education for both financial and political reasons, even though the demand for education was steadily intensifying. . . . The British did little to meet this growing demand; rather they introduced measures to curb it." See Leila Ahmed, *Women and Gender in Islam: Historical Roots of the Modern Debate* (New Haven, CT: Yale University Press, 1992), 137.

27. Ibid.

28. 'Abduh, *A'mal kamilah* 3:81–82, 119–20; 2:178–179.

29. See the article "Ma howa al-faqr al-haqiqi fil bilad?" in 'Abduh, *A'mal kamilah*, 3:45–51, where he describes the state of agriculture as one suffering from low levels of productivity due to the absence of specialized experts: "our agriculture is antiquated [because] no one among us is capable of coming up with new and better methods to increase the output of crops, decrease hardships and facilitate better working conditions [for the peasantry]" (46). See also the series of short articles under the subheading *Ta'lim awlad al-fuqra'*, in *A'mal kamilah*, 2:172–82.

30. This quote comes from a speech ʿAbduh delivered as mufti on the occasion of the opening of a school by the Islamic Benevolent Society in al-Mahala al-Kubra, which was published in *al-Manar*, vol. 7 (1322 A.H.), and republished in Ridaʾs *Tarikh al-Imam*, 1:743. The Islamic Benevolent Society was founded in 1892 by rich Muslim notables and social leaders who were looking for an alternative to private missionary schools and public secular schools. ʿAbduh was one of the founders and one of its most illustrious and active members. In 1900, he was elected president of the society, a position he held until his death. The Benevolent Society was mainly created to open special schools for orphans and poor children; but as Rashid Rida pointed out, the school in Mahala al-Kubra was founded primarily for the children of the rich and hence included in its educational program the teaching of a foreign language, which was not offered in the other schools belonging to the Benevolent Society. Rida, *Tarikh al-Imam*, 1:744 footnote 1.

31. ʿAbduh, *Aʿmal kamilah*, 4:9. At the same time, it is equally the duty (*fard kifaya*) of those in charge of interpreting the Qurʾan to make it accessible to the public by avoiding obscure language and redundant semantics. Ibid., 13.

32. ʿAbduh, *Tafsir juzʾ ʿamma*, 168; see also Hourani, *Liberal Thought*, 148.

33. C. B. Macpherson, *The Political Theory of Possessive Individualism* (Oxford: Oxford University Press, 1962), 3. Individualism in the liberal tradition, as the political theorist and critic of liberal theory C. B. Macpherson explains, lies in its "possessive quality," where the individual is conceived of "as essentially the proprietor of his own person or capacities, owing nothing to society for them" and where "the individual is seen neither as a moral whole, nor as part of a larger society but as an owner of himself," and "the society becomes a lot of free equal individuals related to each other as proprietors of their own capacities and of what they have acquired by their exercise. Society consists of relations of exchange between proprietors."

34. ʿAbduh, "al-Wataniya" (Nationalism), in *Aʿmal kamilah*, 1:318–21.

35. Ibid., 319. I felt that the best term to express his notion of *iʿtidaalan fil-tasawurrat* to mean a more balanced worldview.

36. Rida, *Tarikh al-Imam*, 2:469–72.

37. In this period, the Charitable Muslim Societies began to run their own elementary schools geared mostly for the socially disadvantaged and the poor, which included those who were unable to pay the school fees instated under the British administration in the public school system. In his speech, ʿAbduh remarked that these schools were established as an alternative to the public and missionary schools and hoped that they would become the model for the public educational system in general. See Rida, *Tarikh al-Imam*, 2:470–72.

38. Ibid., 2:469–70.

39. Ibid., 2:470.

40. Ibid.

41. Ibid. He stressed that women have as much right as men to have access to education, both religious and worldly. These rights have been granted to them by God (471).

42. Ibid., 2:471.

43. It is important to note that these views were not simply those of 'Abduh alone but were held and propagated by many of the lesser-known Muslim intellectuals and reformers of this age. One of the most prolific Muslim writers and critics of this period was 'Abdallah al-Nadim, who used his two journals, *Majallat al-tankit wal-tabkit* (July–October 1881) and *Majallat al-Ustadh* (August 1892–July 1893) to disseminate his ideas on reform. Another, as mentioned earlier, was Sheikh 'Ali Yusuf of the newspaper *al-Mu'ayid*; as well as Ibrahim al-Muwaylihi of *Misbah al-Sharq* and Rashid Rida of *al-Manar*, which was the principal journal to popularize Abduh's ideas via Rida's commentaries on these ideas. For others, see al-Koumi, *al-sahafa al-islamiya* (al-Mansura: Dar al-Wafa li-tiba'a wal-nashr, 1992); Ahmad Amin, *Zu'ma' al-islah fil-'ahd al-hadith* (Cairo: Matba'at lajnat al-ta'lif wal-tarjama wal-nashr, 1948).

44. These articles were collected and published under the title *al-murshid al-amin lil-banat wal-banin* [The proper guide for girls and boys]. Others, including 'Ali Mubarak (1824–93), supported women's education and their right to seek knowledge and work outside the home, although Mubarak believed their primary task to be housewives and mothers. On 'Ali Mubarak, see Amin, *Zu'ma' al-islah fil-'ahd al-hadith*, 186–204.

45. 'Abduh, "al-Zawaj" [Marriage], in *A'mal kamilah*, 2:70.

46. Ibid.

47. Ibid., 2:74.

48. Ibid., 2:71.

49. Ibid., 2:75.

50. Ibid., 2:72–73.

51. Ibid., 2:73.

52. Ibid.

53. Ibid.

54. Ibid.

55. Ibid.

56. Ibid., 2:73–74.

57. Ibid., 2:74. 'Abduh articulates an independent thinking woman as follows: *imra' a taht hukm 'aqliha*. According to Ahmed, "the first public school for girls was a primary school established in 1873, followed by a secondary school in 1874. By 1875, out of the 5,362 attending students, 890 of them were girls. The thrust of public education slowed down with British occupation." Ahmed, *Women and Gender in Islam*, 138.

58. Because love is intrinsically possessive (*hub al-ikhtisas*), it is impossible, 'Abduh says, to equally love more than one person at the same time. 'Abduh, *A'mal kamilah*, 2:83.

59. The quote is from 'Abduh's "fatwa fi-ta'adud al-zawjat" [fatwa on polygamy], in *A'mal kamilah*, 2:91.

60. Ibid., 2:84.

61. Ibid., 2:76–81.

62. 'Abduh, "Ta'adud al-zawjat" [Multiple wives], in *A'mal kamilah*, 2:83.

63. Ibid., 2:86.

64. In his interpretation of the Quranic verse "and not to display their charms [in public] beyond what may [decently] be apparent therefore" (24:31), Muhammad Asad says that the *Khimar* refers "to the headcovering customarily used by Arabian women before and after the advent of Islam. According to most of the classical commentators, it was worn in pre-Islamic times more or less as an ornament and was let down loosely over the wearer's back; and since, in accordance with the fashion prevalent at that time, the upper part of a woman's tunic had a wide opening in the front, her breasts were left bare. Hence, the injunction to cover the bosom by means of a *khimar* . . . [which is] meant to make it clear that a woman's breasts are *not* included in the concept of "what may decently be apparent" of her body and should not, therefore, be displayed." M. Asad, *The Message of the Qur'an*, 538–39, n. 38.

65. 'Abduh, "al-Talaq" [On divorce], in *A'mal kamilah*, 2:114–26.

66. Ibid., 2:122.

67. Ibid., 2:117.

68. The quote is taken from Qasim Amin's *Liberation of Women and the New Woman*, trans. Samiha Sidhom Peterson (Cairo: American University in Cairo Press), 96. The section on the family, marriage, and divorce is written by 'Abduh. See also the Arabic equivalent in 'Abduh, *A'mal kamilah*, 2:122.

69. Amin, *Liberation of Women*, 90; 'Abduh, *A'mal kamilah*, 2:123.

70. Amin, *Liberation of Women*, 90–94; 'Abduh, *A'mal kamilah*, 2:118–20.

71. 'Abduh, *A'mal kamilah*, 2:126.

72. New amendments that delineated and consolidated these rulings were introduced in the Code of 1909–10, 1913, and 1930. Divorce reform legislation was instated in 1920 and amended in 1929, thus recognizing the right of women to divorce on the basis of maltreatment, desertion, contagious disease, and the failure of their husbands to provide support (*nafaqa*). Other addendums were added in the following years. Many of these reforms were justified under the Islamic legal doctrine of *takhayur*. See J. N. D. Anderson, "Recent Development in Shari'ah Law III," *Muslim World* 41 (1952): 113–30.

73. As stated earlier, by the 1860s, with its coffers empty and in heavy debt to European capital, Egypt was forced to set up the Caisse de la Dette Publique, an

institution made up of the four chief European bondholding countries (England, France, Italy, and Austria). In addition, two controllers, one French and one English, were appointed to the treasury to supervise state revenue and expenditure. Under the Dual Control system, as it came to be popularly known, Egypt virtually lost its autonomy as the Europeans were given the legitimacy to actively intervene in the internal affairs of the country. Al-Sayyid-Marsot, *A Short History*, 74–75.

74. For further information on the change in the legal system in Egypt, see Skovgaard-Peterson, *Defining Islam*, 57–63; Farhat Ziyadeh, *Lawyers, the Rule of Law and Liberalism in Modern Egypt* (Stanford, CA: Hoover Institution Publication, 1968), 9–30; Nathan J. Brown, *The Role of the Law in the Arab World: Courts in Egypt and the Gulf* (Cambridge: Cambridge University Press, 2007), esp. chap. 2, 23–61.

75. Although Egyptian judges sat on the benches of the mixed courts, only European judges had the authority to rule. The Egyptian government had no authority over these courts. In Lord Cromer's description, the courts were "not under the effective control of any legislation. . . . The judges of the Mixed Courts are practically a law unto themselves." Cromer, *Modern Egypt*, 319.

76. Nathan Brown rightly suggests that the Egyptian elite, including pious Muslims, not the Europeans, were the ones to initiate modernizing the shariʿa courts by codifying and centralizing the legal system in Egypt. Yet, he gives the impression that the Egyptian elite, believing the *shariʿa* not open to modernization, opted out by the adoption of the European legal system. As with Hourani, Brown considers talfiq or "the method of selecting doctrines from various schools of law and seeking to reconcile the *Shariʿa* with modern sensibilities . . . eclectic at best and incoherent at worst." Nathan Brown, "Law and Imperialism: Egypt in Comparative Perspective," *Law and Society* 29 (1995): 118, 119. For a more thorough critique of this literature, see T. Asad, *The Formations of the Secular*, esp. chap. 7, 205–57.

77. When ʿAbduh addressed this issue, he conceived of the shariʿa as governing more than personal matters, thus hoping to extend the shariʿa to cover other matters relating to social transactions, such as contracts. Skovgaard-Peterson, *Defining Islam*, 64.

78. ʿAbduh, "Taqrir islah al-mahakim al-sharʿiya" [Report on reforming the shariʿa courts], in *Aʿmal kamilah*, 2:213–91.

79. ʿAbduh, *Aʿmal kamilah*, 2:216.

80. Ibid., 2:217.

81. Ibid., 2:219–20. The report states that most of the complaints and criticisms from judges and commoners targeted primarily the scribes, who were "barely literate and have minimal knowledge of the law." Due to their poor qualification, they often wrote terms that were inappropriate and confusing, thus hindering a fair judgment. ʿAbduh recommended creating new rules and educational standards for the employment of scribes.

82. ʿAbduh also points out that many of the scribes in the provinces combined farming with scribing, which contributed to a high rate of absenteeism, especially in farming seasons—hence his suggestion that scribes be hired as full-time employees of the state and be paid higher wages (2:220).

83. ʿAbduh, *Aʿmal kamila*, 2:221–24. ʿAbduh described the conditions of the mixed and national courts as follows: "many of the judgments reached by the Civil and Mixed courts defied what any person would consider reasonable or fair, and not simply because they contradicted Islamic law. We all watched and witnessed—the government was not blind to this—as these blunders and injustices were committed by these courts as well" (221).

84. Ibid., 2:221.

85. He recommended that the search board that considers applicants consult with and seek out *mashyakhit al-Azhar* for names of qualified and upright jurists who had been trained within the analytical framework of ijtihad rather than taqlid.

86. ʿAbduh, *Aʿmal kamila*, 2:222–23.

87. Ibid.; see also Rida, *Tarikh al-Imam*, 1:615–16.

88. Rida, *Tarikh al-Imam*, 1:616. Since the four legal schools have no fundamental differences in their opinions, ʿAbduh did not see the necessity of having one school dominate the legal system. Objecting to the dominance of the Hanafiya in Egypt, he called for all four schools to be equally utilized by judges when dispensing justice.

89. ʿAbduh, *Aʿmal kamilah*, 2:223.

90. Rida, *Tarikh al-Imam*, 1:613. It would be possible to unify the system because the differences among the four schools related to interpretive man-made law (*furuʿ*) derived from usul, the foundational or theoretical principles that govern jurisprudence.

91. *Fatawi* (sometimes referred to as fatawa) are legal opinions passed by a mufti; they are authoritative but not binding. A mufti is consulted on all issues relating to Islamic jurisprudence or rules that define how Muslims should conduct themselves in their daily activities, including civil and religious matters. A mufti therefore must master both aspects of Islamic jurisprudence, usul al-fiqh (theoretical foundations or principles of Islamic jurisprudence) and the furuʿ (branches of the law), in contrast to a judge for example who needs proper knowledge only of the branches of law. For more detail, see Brinkley Messick, *The Calligraphic State*; and Muhammad Khalid Masud, Brinkley Messick, and David S. Powers, *Islamic Legal Interpretation: Muftis and Their Fatwas* (Cambridge, MA: Harvard University Press, 1996), chapter 1.

92. ʿImara, the editor of *Aʿmal kamilah*, classified ʿAbduh's fatawa in three different categories: (1) close to 80 percent addressed matters relating to waqf

(religious endowment), inheritance, lease, rent, mortgage, and economic concerns; (2) over 100 fatawa related to issues of the family, including matters of matrimony, divorce, and alimony for child care; and (3) 29 fatawa related to criminal matters, such as killing and retaliation. See *A'mal kamilah*, 2:483–501, 693.

93. *A'mal kamilah*, 1:126.

94. Farah Antun argued that security in the vocabulary of Cromer's administration meant (1) defending order in the streets against workers' attacks, (2) protecting the factories against workers' attacks, and (3) protection of strikebreakers from the striking workers. Antun bluntly stated that the present government objected to mandatory arbitration because it was protecting the interests of business and capital and was not neutral. *A'mal kamilah*, 1:125–28.

95. For a fuller description of the debates and context, consult 'Imara's comments in *A'mal kamilah*, 1:124–31.

96. Ibid., 1:127. At the same time that debate over the strike was consuming the Egyptian nationalists and intellectuals, a similar strike by Algerian port workers against their French colonial bosses took place, which led to similar debates in France over whether the government should intervene to protect labor. A French economist recommended state intervention and the government's role as an arbitrator following the Islamic shari'a, which advocates government arbitration between the employer and employees. Once this French article came to Farah Antun's attention, he realized that he could gain support for the opposition by putting the question to the mufti.

97. Ibid., 1:130.

98. Ibid., 1:132.

99. Ibid. *A'mal kamilah*, 2:508–9. On 'Abduh's fatawa and their societal impact, see Jakob Skovgaard-Peterson, *Defining Islam*, 119–33.

100. Rida, *Tarikh al-Imam*, 1:717.

101. Mahmudl Haq, *Muhammad 'Abduh: A Study of a Modern Thinker of Egypt* (Aligarh: Institute of Islamic Studies, 1970), 55 n. 2. Although this was a mundane issue in earlier contexts, Islamic attire has acquired immense political significance in the contemporary period, resulting in a prolific discourse over what constitutes Islamic dress. Whether 'Abduh's fatwa was the first to set a precedent in and of itself might be an interesting question to explore.

102. The difference was that Christians first strike the animals with an ax and then proceed to slaughter them, and they never pronounce the *tasmiya* (or the saying of "In the name of God, God is Great") as Muslims do.

103. 'Abduh, *A'mal kamilah*, 2:509.

104. As a matter of fact, consensus is not even followed by all four schools. The Hanbali school in principle did not consider consensus infallible and insisted on the right to ijtihad as a necessary measure for the survival of the tradition.

This, however, does not mean that taqlid was not commonly practiced within the school, but it does mean that its rationale for ijtihad became available for later-generation scholars within and outside the school to draw on.

105. Muhammad Ibrahim Sharif, *Itijahat al-tajdid fi-tafsir al-Qur'an al-Karim fi-Misr* (Cairo: Dar al-turath, 1982), 131, 147–68; Skovgaard-Peterson, *Defining Islam for the Egyptian State*, 126–27.

106. Wael Hallaq's work demonstrates that this method of exegesis was not new and was substantially utilized by the fourteenth-century Andalusian jurist Abu Ishaq al-Shatibi (d. 790 A.H./1388 A.D.). Recognizing the failure of the Islamic law in meeting the social and economic needs of his age, al-Shatibi, like ibn Taymiya before him, defended the right of Muslims to ijtihad and, in a similar fashion to the modernists and ibn Taymiya, reasserted the self-sufficiency of the Qur'an, thus rejecting the view of the conventional leadership of his age that "the Sunna offers substantive addition to the Qur'an." See Wael Hallaq, "The Primacy of the Qur'an in Shatibi's Legal Theory" in *Islamic Studies Presented to Charles J. Adams*, ed. Wael Hallaq and Donald P. Little (Leiden, the Netherlands: Brill, 1991), 69–90.

107. For complete coverage of the arguments made by the opposition, see Rida, *Tarikh al-Imam*, 1:668–74; Skovgaard-Peterson, *Defining Islam*, 124–27.

108. Rashid Rida here was attempting to undermine the conventional leadership's reaction to 'Abduh's criticism of the infallibility of consensus by demonstrating that the practice of ijtihad and takhayur was not confined to a minority tendency within the Islamic tradition, represented by ibn Taymiya and his student ibn al-Qayim, but was a common practice among the founders of the legal schools, including that of the official Hanafi school at this time. Rida, *Tarikh al-Imam*, 1:706–7.

CHAPTER 5: LOVE AND MARRIAGE

1. These long-standing tensions continue to manifest themselves in contemporary Egypt. One of the most famous cases was that of Nasr Hamid Abu Zeid, who published a "literary criticism of the Qur'an" and was accused of heresy for historicizing the Qur'an. He was found by the Islamic family court to be an "unfit husband" to a Muslim woman, thus forcing the separation between him and his wife. I am saying here not that this problem of establishing the boundary between the secular and the sacred is particular to Muslim societies such as Egypt but that these boundaries are tested differently in different societies, including the United States (cf. the question of abortion).

2. For an analytically informed article on this topic, see Afsaneh Najmbadi, "Crafting an Educated Housewife in Iran," in *Remaking Women: Feminism and Modernity in the Middle East*, ed. Lila Abu-Lughod (Princeton, NJ: Princeton University Press, 1998), 91–125.

3. Many scholars, including Muhammad 'Imara, who collected 'Abduh's massive work, acknowledge that *The Liberation of Women* was the outcome of a collaboration between 'Abduh and Amin. 'Abduh wrote the chapters relating to the family and the shari'a, while Amin discussed education and women's role in the building of the nation. See 'Imara's comments in 'Abduh's *A'mal kamilah*, 1:262–66; and Ibrahim 'Abduh, *tatawwur al-nahdha al-nisa'iya fi-Misr* (Cairo: Maktabat al-Adab, 1945), 252, 274–75.

4. See Ahmed, *Women and Gender*, 157, and more generally chapters 7, 8, and 9, for a good summary and analysis of the debates and politics regarding the "woman question" during colonial Egypt. On this topic, see also Margot Badran, *Feminists, Islam, and Nation: Gender and the Making of Modern Egypt* (Princeton, NJ: Princeton University Press, 1995), esp. the introduction and part I, 3–74.

5. The following quote from Amin's *Liberation of Women and New Woman* explains his views on the difference between old and new education: "Women do not attain the desired level of intellectual development simply by learning to read and write and studying foreign languages. She must also develop an understanding of history and learn the principles of the natural and social sciences, which will enable her to grasp the central laws that influence the universe and the human condition" (67).

6. Amin, *Liberation of Women and New Woman*, 11.

7. Ibid.

8. This is how Amin put it: "A woman needs to be educated so that she can have understanding and a *will of her own*. . . . At present whenever we think of a woman, we assume that she has a guardian who administers all facets of her life" (ibid., 13; emphasis added).

9. At the same time, it would be misleading to read Amin's position on women's education as a sign of insincerity, as the notion of equality and liberation as used and understood by Amin and others of his period, despite maintaining gender difference, did empower women by enabling them to seek out and act on their interests and desires in a fashion not available to them earlier. At the same time, their emancipation (as that of women in the West in that same period) was bounded by rules and regulatory policies dictated under this new gender regime. The discourse of emancipation opened up opportunities for women (including Nassif and Nabawiya Musa) to challenge the gendered nature of education by contesting its limitations on women even though they, too, did not envision opening education to women beyond the profession of teaching. It is important to note that some women and men (e.g., Mustafa Kamil) did contest putting limitations on the level of education for women. See Nabawiya Musa's autobiography, *Tarikhi* (al-Qahira: Multaqa al-mar'a wal-zakira, 1999), which describes her life-long struggle against an educational system that she experienced as biased and unjust to women.

10. Amin, *Liberation of Women and New Woman*, 23.

11. As quoted in Ahmed, *Women and Gender*, 157. This obsession with cleanliness associated with bathing and combing and brushing one's teeth was uttered by many besides Amin, including the popular woman writer Malak Nassif. For an illuminating study of hygiene and modern forms of mothering, see Omnia el-Shakry, "Schooled Mothers and Structured Play: Child Rearing in Turn of the Century Egypt," in *Remaking of Women*, 126–70.

12. Amin, *Liberation of Women and New Woman*, 48, 66. He estimated that 30 percent of Egyptian women die during childbirth and attributed this high rate to lack of strong, healthy constitutions, especially among urban women.

13. Amin, *Liberation of Women and New Woman*, 27.

14. Ibid., 28.

15. On the discourse of domesticity and the manuals that popularized rational management of the household, see Beth Baron, *The Women's Awakening in Egypt: Culture, Society, and the Press* (New Haven, CT: Yale University Press, 1994).

16. *al-Manar* 2, no. 9 (1899): 90–92.

17. Ibid., 91.

18. Ibid., 140–43. Proper child rearing was also a topic central to Amin's *Liberation of Women and New Woman*. He addressed the need for proper psychological training in the section entitled "Woman's Obligation to Her Family" (161–78).

19. Sami Aziz, *al-Sahafa al-misriya wa-mawqifuha min-al-ihtilal*, 290.

20. Ibid., 295; Ahmad, *Women and Gender*, 172.

21. Against the wisdom of many of my respected colleagues who transcribed bahithat al-badiya as the "Seeker in the Desert," I have taken the liberty to translate it as the "Intellectual of the Desolate," a bleaker term perhaps but one that captures more profoundly her personal and public struggles as a female Muslim subject.

22. Bahithat al-Badiya, *al-Nisa'iyat* (Cairo: Dar-al-huda, 1919), 66–75. In particular, see the articles entitled "Men's Vices," in which she addresses the three vices of men: "Avariciousness," "Despotism," and "Contempt for Women." Women's vices included distrust, unreasonable jealousy, anger, and squandering (see pp. 52–66).

23. See Ahmed, *Women and Gender*, esp. chaps. 8 and 9; Badran, *Feminists*, esp. the introduction and chap. 1; and Judith Tucker, *Women in Nineteenth-Century Egypt* (Cambridge: Cambridge University Press, 1985).

24. Tal'at Harb, *Tarbiyat al-mar'ah wal-hijab* (al-Qahira: Matba'at al-turki, 1899), 34–40. The book was in defense of the old arrangements and against what he considered to be the British and Amin's plans to Europeanize Egypt and its culture. See also Juan Cole, "Feminism, Class and Islam in the Turn of the Century Egypt," *IJMES* 13 (November 1981): 387–407.

25. Cole, "Feminism, Class and Islam," 402–4.

26. Malak Hilmi Nassif was a product of the modern educational system, a graduate of the Saniya Teacher Training College, where she later taught. She mastered both Arabic and French. She was married at the age of 21 to an enlightened and learned tribal chief, 'Abdul Sattar al-Basil, from the region of al-Fayyum Oasis in Lower Egypt. Nassif, some sources claim, came to realize that he already had a wife only after her marriage. Her father, Hifni Nassif, was trained at al-Azhar at the same time as 'Abduh. He was a famous literary figure and a leading member of al-Umma Party, a moderate nationalist party sympathetic to the project of modernizing Islam. See the introduction to Bahithat al-badiya, *al-Nisa'iyat*, 9–19; Margot Badran and Miriam Cooke, eds., *Opening the Gates: A Century of Arab Feminist Writing* (Bloomington: Indiana University Press, 1990), 136–38, 227–39; Ahmed, *Women and Gender*, 171–75, 177–85.

27. "It [*co-wife*] is a terrible word—my pen almost halts in writing it—women's mortal enemy . . . how much evil brought and how much innocents sacrificed and prisoners taken for whom it was the origin of personal calamity? Bear in mind as you amuse yourself with your new bride you cause another's despair to flow in tears . . . and children whom you taught to sorrow, weep for her tears. . . . You hear the drums and pipes [at a wedding] and they hear only the beat of misery." Quotes taken from Ahmed, *Women and Gender*, 182, 180; see also Nassif's article on polygamy in Bahithat al-Badiya, *al-Nisa'iyat*, 41–44.

28. She wrote a series of articles entitled "Marriage," "Polygamy," and "Age of Marriage." See Bahithat al-Badiya, *al-Nisa'iyat*, 36–49.

29. Quote from Ahmed, *Women and Gender*, 180.

30. Bahithat al-Badiya, "To Veil or Not to Veil," in *al-Nisa'iyat*, 24–29; the translated quote was taken from Ahmed, *Women and Gender*, 180–81.

31. Huda Sha'rawi, *Harem Years: The Memoirs of an Egyptian Feminist (1879–1924)*, trans. and ed. Margot Badran (London: Virago, 1986); see also Ahmed, *Women and Gender*, 185–87.

32. See Amin, "Education and Seclusion," in *Liberation of Women and New Woman*, 179–98; Bahithat al-Badiya, *al-Nisa'iyat*, 24–29.

33. Hilmi al-Namnam, *'Ali Yusuf wa Safiya al-Sadat* (al-Qahira: Mirit lil nashr wal-ma'lumat, 2001), 12.

34. Ibid.

35. On July 20, *al-Ahram* reported the charge of kidnapping made by al-Sadat. See al-Namnam, *Yusuf wa Safiya*, 14.

36. 'Abd al-Latif Hamzah, *Adab al-maqalah al-sahafiyah fi-Misr* (al-Qahira: Dar al-fikr al-'arabi, 1955), 4:116.

37. The letter, if one is to guess, likely came from the brother-in-law, as it disclosed details that only a close member of the family would have access to. The

letter revealed that Muhammad Tawfiq al-Bakri informed the father in advance of their intent to elope in order to convince the father to make up his mind by either accepting or rejecting the marriage. Another Muslim scholar and a friend, Sheikh Muhammad Radi, was sent to inform the father of their impending marriage to no avail. See al-Namnam, *Yusuf wa Safiya*, 13–14.

38. *Al-Liwa* reported that the khedive himself tried to put pressure on the father to concede to the marriage but met with no success. Al-Namnam, *Yusuf wa Safiya*, 13.

39. Ibid., 69.

40. Hamzah, *Adab al-maqalah*, 4:115.

41. In fact, she was better versed in French than Arabic. Her letters to Yusuf demonstrate that her written Arabic was elemental (*rakik*) in contrast to his poetic and moving love letters. He, on the other hand, had no knowledge of French. See Namnam, *Yusuf wa Safiya*, 65–66.

42. Sami ʿAbdul Aziz al-Kumi, *al-Sahafa al-Islamiyyah fi Misr fil qarn al-tasiʿ ʿashr* (al-Mansura: Dar al-Wafa li-tibaʾa wal-nashr, 1992), 44–61.

43. The paper was popular and had relatively wide circulation, reaching its highest sales in 1904 due to the court case brought against him and his wife, Safiya. Ibid.

44. Rida, *Tarikh al-Imam*, 1:594–95, 721.

45. The language and content of the letter suggest that it was authored by ʿAli Yusuf himself. The letter demonstrates both sophistication and knowledge of Islamic art of argumentation that Safiya, with her French training, would have been less capable of composing. This, however, should not by any means deny that the letter is a genuine expression of her sentiments.

46. Al-Namnam, *Yusuf wa Safiya*, 17.

47. Quoted from Amin, *Liberation of Women and New Woman*, 77. The quote is ʿAbduh's and belongs to the section he wrote on the family which addressed marriage, polygamy, divorce, and the veil, 76–101; see also Chapter 4.

48. MacIntyre, *Whose Justice?*, 339.

49. Al-Namnam, *Yusuf wa Safiya*, 18.

50. *Al-Manar* 7 no. 12 (August 28, 1904), 462. Rida stipulates that because the purpose of marriage is to solidify relations between families on the basis of respect and love, the Islamic tradition does not encourage a woman to choose her husband against her guardian's will as it will produce animosity and hatred among families. By the same token, it is reasonable to expect of the legal guardian or father that he follow the daughter's wishes and desires in a marriage and not stand in her way of happiness because it, too, will lead to harm and unhappiness.

51. For the sake of comparison, Muhammad ibn ʿAbdul Wahhab, who considered protection of women the responsibility of men, denied a woman under all

circumstances the right to marry herself. But although he agreed that a guardian or father is necessary for a marriage to be valid, at the same time, he stipulated that marriage would be invalid when contracted by a father or a guardian without consent, particularly of minors, be it a male or a virgin female. Objecting to the Shafi'i and Maliki schools, which gave the father the right to compel his daughter into marriage, Wahhab forbade this practice. He also commended the consummation of marriage only after a female minor has reached maturity and not before. He differentiated between the guardian's role of contracting a marriage, which he considered a procedural matter, and a female's consent to marry as an absolute right. See Ibn 'Abdul Wahhab, *Mu'allafat al-Shaykh al-Imam Muhammad ibn Abdul Wahhab* (al-Fiqh), 1:644–51.

52. *Al-Manar* 7, no. 12 (August 28, 1904): 457–62.

53. Ibid., 462. Rida used the Arabic term *'addalah* (the active verb *'adal*) to signify a guardian's obstructive despotic power, a term derived from the phrase "brawny muscle," thus associating older forms of patriarchal power with coercive masculinity.

54. See al-Namnam, *Yusuf wa Safiya*, 28.

55. The acceptance of a dowry is traditionally considered a formal sealing of the arrangement.

56. Al-Namnam, *Yusuf wa Safiya*, 148. It is clear from the letter that Safiya's mother was aware and accepting of the relationship and most likely knew of the elopement but did not stop it. In most of his letters to Safiya, Yusuf sends personal greetings to the mother.

57. Ahmed, *Women and Gender*, 152; see also Omnia el-Shakry, "Schooled Mothers," 127–70.

58. Ahmed, *Women and Gender*, 153.

59. It was a well-known fact by then that the khedive depended heavily on the advice of 'Ali Yusuf to the point that the khedive would not take up any policy or make any decision without first running it by the sheikh.

60. The threat for a general strike was reported in Hamzah, *Adab al-maqalah*, 118; al-Namnam, *Yusuf wa Safiya*, 20, reported only the suspension of the court hearing the case.

61. The tabloids claimed that Safiya moved to al-Rafi'i's residence to sneak 'Ali into the house at night in defiance of the court order. The lovers did indeed correspond daily, sending letters back and forth through the help of two European sisters employed in the household of al-Rafi'i. The head of the household knew of these activities and complained of its social inappropriateness and fired the maids. Hamzah, *Adab al-maqalah*, 119–20.

62. Al-Namnam, *Yusuf wa Safiya*, 30.

63. Ibid., 19.

64. Ibid., 21. Al-Muwaylihi, another journalist with a personal grudge against 'Ali Yusuf, took this opportunity to mock the sheikh in his journal, *Misbah al-Sharq*, by naming 1904 the "Year of Compatibility!"

65. *Al-Ahram*, July 29, 1904.

66. Ibid.

67. *Al-Manar*, June 30, 1904, 381–83. Ibn 'Abdul Wahhab, too, affirmed that from the perspective of the Islamic tradition, only the status of being a Muslim, rather than social prestige, skin color, or tribal affiliation, matters in marriage. But he does mention that neither a guardian nor the woman have the right to invalidate a marriage if the man is of a higher social status than the woman, as the marriage would be considered an improvement of her social status. For the difference on the question of suitability and marriage between 'Abduh's time and that of ibn 'Abdul Wahhab, see ibn 'Abdul Wahhab, *Mu'allafat al-Shaykh al-Imam Muhammad ibn 'Abdul Wahhab* (al-Fiqh), 1:145.

68. "Al-Awliya' wa-al-kafa'a fil-azwaj" [Guardians and compatibility in marriage], *al-Manar* 7 (August 13, 1904), 383.

69. Ibid., 384.

70. Hamzah, *Adab al-maqalah*, 120.

71. Ibid., 121.

72. *Al-Ahram*, August 1, 1904.

73. Ibid.; al-Namnam, *Yusuf wa Safiya*, 32–34.

74. 'Urf, or custom, played a marginal role in the early formation of legal thought of the four schools of law. Custom was incorporated into the law in the twelfth century A.D. only on a case-by-case basis. It became acknowledged as part of the law in the sixteenth century as long as these rulings did not disturb the postulates and basic assumptions of legal Islamic theory. The authoritativeness of custom as a legal source became more of a normative practice after the eighteenth century, following its justification within the tradition by the Muslim scholar ibn 'Abidin. See Hallaq, *Authority, Continuity, and Change*, 217–35.

75. Al-Namnam, *Yusuf wa Safiya*, 38; *al-Ahram*, August 6, 1904, 22.

76. Al-Namnam, *Yusuf wa Safiya*, 39.

77. Hamzeh, *Adab al-maqalah*, 121.

78. Ibid.

79. Rida, "Qaddiyat al-Sadat wa Sahib al-Mu'ayid" [The court case of al-Sadat and the owner of al-Mu'ayid], *al-Manar* 7, no. 11 (August 13, 1904), 440.

80. The exception was *al-Liwa*, which complimented the judge as a defender of Islam and its culture, using such inflammatory statements as "long live justice, long live the shari'a . . . hurray to the judge . . . all you Muslims . . . go kiss his hands." Al-Namnam, *Yusuf wa Safiya*, 43. It is important to note that Mustafa Kamil is described by mainstream scholarship as a "secular" nationalist.

81. In an article 'Abduh wrote on Muhammad 'Ali, the great grandfather of the khedive and the founder of that dynasty, he was critical of the view that presented Muhammad 'Ali as reformer and father of modern Egypt. He disapproved of the ruler's many policies, especially his military campaign against the Wahhabiya movement on behalf of the Ottoman sultan. He condemned the idea of Muslims fighting other Muslims. 'Abduh, *A'mal Kamilah*, 1:851–58.

82. 'Abduh, *A'mal kamilah*, 3:137.

83. Rida, "al-Awliya' wal-kafa'a" [Guardians and Suitability], *al-Manar*, 7 (1904): 383. *Masail al-mu'amalat* are governed by customs arrived at by analogical reasoning; they are meant to protect public interest and lessen dangers that threaten them.

84. A-Rafi'i appealed to the chief justice to order her removal from his house because, he claimed, Safiya refused to obey the rules governing his household and continued to see and correspond with 'Ali Yusuf. Al-Namnam, *Yusuf wa Safiya*, 26–27.

85. Hamzah, *Adab al-maqalah*, 115.

CHAPTER 6: CONCLUSION

1. As Karen Armstrong wrote in *The Guardian* (September 18, 2006), the pope's remarks were neither neutral nor historically correct, and the "Muslims who have objected so vociferously to the Pope's denigration of Islam have accused him of 'hypocrisy', pointing out that the Catholic church is ill-placed to condemn violent jihad when it has itself been guilty of unholy violence in crusades, persecutions and inquisitions and, under Pope Pius XII, tacitly condoned the Nazi Holocaust." Available at http://www.guardian.co.uk/commentisfree/story/0,,1874786,00.html.

2. Edward Said, *Orientalism*, 19. Norman Daniel's *Islam and the West: The Making of an Image*, 3rd ed. (Oxford: Oneworld Publications, 1997), discusses how anti-Muslim sentiment was initially grounded in a Christian ethos. The development of the Trinity as a doctrine was central to the emergence of "misconceived" perceptions of Islam because the theological proof of the Trinity rested on rejecting Islam as a legitimate rival religion, especially because Islam rejects outright the foundational assumption of Jesus as God's son. Proving Islam as phony and its prophet as a fake and a charlatan was a necessary step toward establishing the truth of the early Church's own doctrinal claims. Starting in Christian Europe, the construction of these "hostile medieval themes on Islam," Daniel says, was "to continue into the future so powerfully as to affect many generations, even up to the present time" (307), albeit it with a difference, I would suggest. The continuity between the medieval and European perceptions of Islam is quite obvious, but the context in which these perceptions functioned and their implications

differed. In contrast to that found in the medieval period, modern discourse on Islam is more political than theological or doctrinally founded and by implication far more instrumental to the colonization and forceful secularization of the Muslim world. As a body of knowledge, this modern discourse, which Said named *orientalism*, was closely tied to the rise of Europe as a colonial power informing its policies and practices.

3. For more on ʿAbduh and Hanotaux, see Chapter 3.

4. In the October 19, 2006, issue of the *New York Review of Books*, Robert F. Worth, in his laudable review of Lawrence Wright's *The Looming Tower: al-Qaeda and the Road to 9/11*, reduces the radicalization of the Islamist Sayyid Qutb (1906–66), who many, including the two authors, consider to be the father of the contemporary jihadist movement, to his exposure to and hateful experience with free liberal American women during his two-year visit to the United States in the 1950s: "Qutb was deeply disturbed by encounters with young women with forthright liberal views. . . . Like his ideological descendents in al-Qaeda, he came to hate the United States because it stood for the modern way of life that was drawing people from his native country away from the kind of theocratic state he envisioned, . . . in which conservative Islamic values would be imposed on all aspects of life" (14). This psychological ahistorical explanation of Qutb's views is proliferating in the media nowadays. Anyone and everyone proclaim their expertise on Islam, and on Qutb in particular. The fact that a leading Muslim feminist in the United States, Amina Wadud, refers to and situates her argument for women's equality in Qutb's Quranic commentary clearly indicates that Sayyid Qutb's writing is far more complex than its presentation in Western media. See Amina Wadud, *Qurʾan and Woman*.

For a more nuanced reading of Qutb, I suggest Ibrahim Abu Rabi's *Intellectual Origins of Islamic Resurgence in the Modern Arab World* (Albany: State University of New York Press, 1995), chapters 4–6. For an excellent critique of the theoretical foundation of Qutb's critics, I recommend Roxanne L. Euben, "Comparative Political Theory: An Islamic Fundamentalist Critique of Rationalism," *Journal of Politics* 69 (February 1997): 28–55.

5. In his usual condescending and abrasive style, the patriotic journalist Thomas Friedman in an op-ed piece endorsed the pope's unapologetic criticism of Islam and Muslims, reading it as a sign of respect rather than as an insult to Islam. He commended the pope for approaching Muslims as equals, as rational human beings, and for not fearing their irrational violent response: "The Pope was actually treating Islam with dignity. He was treating the faith and its community as adults who could be challenged and engaged. That is a sign of respect." Insulting, says Friedman, is the "kid-gloves view of how to deal with Muslims . . . [that] goes like this: 'hushhh. Don't say anything about Islam! Don't

you understand? If you say anything critical or questioning about Muslims, they'll burn down your house.'" "Islam and the Pope," *New York Times*, September 26, 2006.

6. Orientalist scholars, as Said rightly points out, differed in their representation of Islam from one period to another, from one country to another, and from one person to the next. Despite the difference, there exists a latent conception of Islam (inferior and irrational), which they all shared.

7. It is important to note that these themes remain quite popular in the academy today, including among leading contemporary scholars, such as Aziz al-Azmeh, who incorporate this notion of "Muslims as backward looking" into their analysis of modern Islamic movements. In *Islams and Modernities* (London: Verso, 1993), al-Azmeh constantly bemoans Islamists (and Arab nationalists) for their irrational attachment to the past and constant search for an absolute authentic essence, leading them in effect to live in denial of the present (reality) and the future (progress). See especially chapters 1–3.

8. See Wael Hallaq, *Authority, Continuity, and Change*; Baber Johansen, *Contingency in a Sacred Law: Legal and Ethical Norms in Muslim Fiqh* (Leiden, the Netherlands: Brill, 1999).

9. Hamilton A. R. Gibb, *Modern Trends in Islam*, especially 1–14. On the attraction of the Romantic movement for Muslims, Gibb says: "The resemblance between the intuitive bent of the Arab and the Muslim mind and the Romantic currents in European thought is certainly a very close one, and this may (I believe) explain the rapidity with which the Romantic tendencies in Western thought spread among the educated classes in Islam" (110).

10. Ibid., 29.

11. Ibid., 27.

12. Ibid., 29. On the theme of an atomized Muslim/Arab mind and psychologically impaired Arabs, see Fouad Ajami, *The Arab Predicament: Arab Political Thought and Practice Since 1967* (Cambridge: Cambridge University Press, 1981), which was reissued in 1992; and especially Raphael Patai, *The Arab Mind* (New York: Scribner, 1973), reissued in 1983 and 2002 (New York: Hatherleigh Press). Patai's work includes a chapter on Arabs and sex, which theorizes that Arab men (as homophobics) would do anything rather than be sexually humiliated in public. This is a cultural image that came to inform policies and practices especially in Israel and now in the United States, the most recent example being the torture of Iraqi prisoners at Abu Ghraib prison. For more information on this particular topic see Seymour Hersh's "Torture at Abu Ghraib," in *Chain of Command: The Road from 9/11 to Abu Ghraib* (New York: Harper Perennial, 2004), 1–67.

13. See Chapter 3.

14. Samuel Huntington's *The Clash of Civilizations and the Remaking of World Order* (New York: Simon and Schuster, 1998) first appeared in the form of an article in *Foreign Affairs* titled "The Clash of Civilizations?" (Summer 1993) that was later expanded into a book in response to the positive reaction it received in the United States as well as globally. This, however, does not mean that there were no critics. For strong critiques, see Edward Said, "The Clash of Definitions," and Roy Mottahedah, "The Clash of Civilizations: An Islamist Response," both reprinted in *The New Crusades: Constructing the Muslim Enemy*, ed. Emran Qureshi and Michael Anthony Sells (New York: Columbia University Press, 2003), 68–87, 131–52; see also Amartya Sen, *Identity and Violence: The Illusion of Destiny* (New York: Norton, 2006).

15. It is important to note that Huntington does not limit his discussion to Islam and the West but categorizes the world along so-called civilizational lines that closely follow religious divisions. Western civilization is contrasted not only to the Islamic but also to the "Buddhist civilization" and the "Hindu civilization," among others.

16. Bernard Lewis, "The Roots of Islamic Rage," *Atlantic Monthly* 266 (September 1990): 47–66. The article was reproduced in Bernard Lewis, *From Babel to Dragomans: Interpreting the Middle East* (New York: Oxford University Press, 2005).

17. William Dalrymple, "The Truth About Muslims," *New York Review of Books* 51 (November 4, 2004). Available at http://www.nybooks.com/articles/17516.

18. Ibid.

19. Ibid.

20. Qurshi and Sells, *The New Crusades*, 5.

21. Irshad Manji, review of *The Shia Revival*, by Vali Nasr, *New York Times Book Review* (August 13, 2006). See also Vali Nasr, *The Shia Revival: How Conflicts with Islam Would Shape the Future* (New York: Norton, 2006); Efraim Karsh, *Islamic Imperialism* (New Haven, CT: Yale University Press, 2006). Maureen Dowd, a liberal *New York Times* journalist and a strong critic of the Iraqi war and of George W. Bush's policies both on the home front and internationally, reasserts the same view in an op-ed piece, declaring that the war in Iraq, even with the latest "surge" policy, is ultimately not winnable because of this raging religious war between Shi'a and Sunni that has been going on for the last thirteen centuries. For an even more inventive version of the same theory, see Ronald Inglehart and Pippa Norris, "The True Clash of Civilization," *Foreign Affairs* 135 (March–April 2003): 62–70, in which they propose that Huntington was only half right because the cultural fault line is not about democracy per se but about sex. Although Muslims want democracy, they are opposed to extending it to women and gays.

22. The ethno-religious purification conducted by Serb and Croat religious nationalists against Bosnian Muslims was explained by Huntington as a civilizational clash, an argument that implicated Muslims for fighting "a bloody and disastrous war with Orthodox Serbs and [for] hav[ing] engaged in other violence with Catholic Croatians" at a time when "Serbia was descending, with the complicity of its intellectuals and Church leaders, into a mass psychology of war and hate." Qureshi and Sells, *The New Crusade*, 9.

23. Dalrymple, in "The Truth About Muslims," *New York Review of Books* 51 (November 4, 2004), cites Richard Fletcher's *The Cross and the Crescent: Christianity and Islam from Muhammad to the Reformation* (New York: Viking, 2004).

24. Dalrymple cites Michele Piccirillo, "The Christians in Palestine During a Time of Transition: 7th–9th Centuries," in *The Christian Heritage in the Holy Land*, ed. Anthony O'Mahony (London: Scorpion Cavendish, 1995); M. Piccirillo, *The Mosaics of Jordan* (Amman, Jordan: American Center of Oriental Research, 1993). On the relations of Venice to the East in the age of the Crusades, see Deborah Howard, *Venice and the East: The Impact of the Islamic World on Venetian Architecture, 1100–1500* (New Haven, CT: Yale University Press, 2000).

25. Lewis's main argument rests on the idea that Muslims' lack of curiosity about the Christian world and that culture caused them to fall behind in both learning and technology, which eventually led to their decline as a civilization. As Dalrymple notes in "Truth About Muslims," his review of Nabil Matar's *In the Lands of the Christians: Arab Travel Writing in the Seventeenth Century*, Matar directly counters Lewis's idea that Muslim interest in the West really began in earnest in the nineteenth century. Here a succession of previously unknown seventeenth-century travel narratives unfold in English translation, with Arab writer after writer describing his intense interest in and excitement with Western science, literature, music, politics, and even opera." Matar's two other works, *Islam in Britain, 1558–1685* (Cambridge: Cambridge University Press, 1998), and *Turk, Moors, and Englishmen in the Age of Discovery* (New York: Columbia University Press, 1999), convey amiable relations between Muslims and Britons in the sixteenth and seventeenth centuries. Matar tells of Queen Elizabeth's request for the naval support of the Ottoman sultan Murad against the Spanish Armada in the mid-1580s. Of all the European countries, Britain seemed to have enjoyed the most extensive trade with Muslim lands in this period.

26. George Makdisi's work on medieval Muslim–Christian encounters is among the earliest to challenge the culturalist theory of the clash of civilizations. See *The Rise of Humanism in Classical Islam and the Christian West* (Edinburgh: Edinburgh University Press, 1995); *The Rise of Colleges: Institutions of Learning in Islam and the West* (Edinburgh: Edinburgh University Press, 1981).

27. On Islamic Andalusia, see Maria Rosa Menocal, *The Ornament of the World: How Muslims, Jews, and Christians Created a Culture of Tolerance in Medieval Spain*

(Boston: Little, Brown, 2002); see also Richard Fletcher, *Moorish Spain* (Berkeley: University of California, 2006).

28. Nilüfer Göle, "Secularism and Islamism in Turkey," *Middle East Journal* 51 (Winter 1977): 50. See also Michael M. J. Fischer and Mehdi Abedi, *Debating Muslims: Cultural Dialogues in Postmodernity and Tradition* (Madison: University of Wisconsin Press, 1990); and Sami Zubaida, "Islam, the State, and Democracy: Contrasting Conceptions of Society in Egypt," *Middle East Research Information Project* 179 (November–December 1992): 2–10.

29. As Euben put it, "Fundamentalism as epiphenomenal . . . reinforce[s] the impression that the growing appeal of fundamentalism owes little to its own inherent power as a moral ideal." See Euben, "Comparative Political Theory," 30.

30. Bruce Lawrence, *Defenders of God: The Fundamentalist Revolt Against Modernity* (Columbia: University of South Carolina Press, 1995), 2.

31. Sami Zubaida, *Islam, the People and the State*, 3, 6. There are also others who invoke the notion of invention, such as Indira Falk Gesink, "Chaos on Earth," *American Historical Review* 108 (June 2003): 710–33.

32. Zubaida, *Islam, the People and the State*, 18.

33. On the populist nature of the Iranian Revolution, see Evrand Abrahamian, *Khomeinism: Essays on the Islamic Republic* (Berkeley: University of California Press, 1993); Juan Cole and Nikki Keddie, eds., *Shi'ism and Social Protest* (New Haven, CT: Yale University Press, 1982).

34. Zubaida, *Islam, the People and the State*, 13.

35. Ibid., 22–23.

36. Ibid.

37. Abrahamian, *Khomeinism*, 17.

38. H. A. R. Gibb, *Modern Trends in Islam*, 71. The most pernicious study on Muslim reformers, however, was produced by Elie Kedouri in *Afghani and 'Abduh: An Essay on Religious Unbelief and Political Activism in Modern Islam* (London: Cass, 1966). In this polemical essay, Kedouri's intention was primarily focused on discrediting and exposing these two reformers as, he claimed, two deviously duplicitous ambitious political men who disguised their politics under the mantle of Islam.

39. Malcolm Kerr, *Islamic Reform: The Political and Legal Theories of Muhammad Abduh and Rashid Rida* (Berkeley: University of California Press, 1966), 12.

40. Ibid., 105.

41. See Charles Adams, *Islam and Modernism in Egypt*; Nikki Keddie, *An Islamic Response to Imperialism: Political and Religious Writings of Sayyid Jamal al-Din al-Afghani* (Berkeley: University of California Press, 1993).

42. Donald M. Reid, in "Arabic Thought in the Liberal Age Twenty Years After," *IJMES* 14 (1982): 541–57, calls *Arabic Thought in the Liberal Age* a masterpiece and documents its continuous influence among contemporary writers.

43. Hourani modestly acknowledged *Arabic Thought in the Liberal Age* as merely "an extended footnote to Gibb's *Modern Trend of Islam.*" See Hourani's "How Should We Write the History of the Middle East?" *IJMES* 23 (1991): 128.

44. Ibid., 125–36. See also Donald M. Reid's article, "Arabic Thought in the Liberal Age Twenty Years After."

45. Bruce Lawrence, *Defenders of God*, 2. Fundamentalists are modern, Lawrence says, because "fundamentalists, like other moderns, recognize that the world in which they strive to locate their deepest identity is constantly shifting, that there is an unbridgeable gap between who they are and where they want to be" (1).

46. Ibid., 6.

47. Ibid., 2. Borrowing the elusive definition of modernism from Marshal Berman, Lawrence asserts that fundamentalists are not modernists precisely because "to be a modernist is to make oneself somehow at home in the maelstrom, to make its rhythms one's own, to move within its currents in search of the forms of reality, of beauty, of freedom, of justice" (1–2).

48. Ibid., 1, 8.

49. Bassam Tibi, "The Worldview of Sunni Arab Fundamentalists: Attitudes Toward Modern Science and Technology," in *Fundamentalisms and Society: Reclaiming the Sciences, the Family, and Education*, ed. Martin E. Marty and R. Scott Appleby (Chicago: University of Chicago Press, 1997), 73–102.

50. Ibid, 79.

51. Ibid. Tibi puts it this way: "fundamentalist Muslims are dramatically exposed to modernity in the guise of arms technology and see it as both the symbol and substance of the threatening Muslim" (81).

52. Bassam Tibi, *The Challenge of Fundamentalism: Political Islam and the New World Disorder* (Berkeley: University of California Press, 1998), 91, 191, 177. A critical review of this work is Tarif Khalidi, *Journal of Palestine Studies* 28 (Summer 1999): 104–5.

53. Zubaida, *Islam, the People and the State*, 53. See also Nikki Keddie, *Modern Iran: Roots and Results of Revolution* (New Haven, CT: Yale University Press, 2006); Gilles Kepel, *Muslim Extremism in Egypt: The Prophet and the Pharaoh* (Berkeley: University of California Press, 2003); Olivier Roy, *The Failure of Political Islam* (Cambridge, MA: Harvard University Press, 1998).

54. Zubaida, *Islam, the People and the State*, 46. In a similar vein, Gilles Kepel's key point in *Muslim Extremism* is that the radical zealots of Egypt are reacting more to poverty than to a true desire to establish an Islamic state.

55. John Esposito, *The Islamic Threat: Myth or Reality?* (New York: Oxford University Press, 1995), 6.

56. Ibid. See also Dale Eikelman and James Piscatori, *Muslim Politics* (Princeton, NJ: Princeton University Press, 1996); John Voll, *Islam, Continuity and Change.*

57. Abrahamian, *Khomeinism*, 13. Abrahamian gives eight different explanations as to why we should reject the term *fundamentalism*, including that mentioned in the text (13–17).

58. Ibid., 16–17.

59. Ibid., 17. There are also others who present a much drier account in contrast to the gripping account presented by Abrahamian. See Joel Beinin and Joe Stork, eds., *Political Islam: Essays from Middle East Report* (Berkeley: University of California Press, 1997); Alan Richards and John Waterbury, *The Political Economy of the Middle East* (Boulder, CO: Westview Press, 1990); Saad Eddin Ibrahim, "Anatomy of Egypt's Militant Islamic Groups," *IJMES* 12 (1980): 42–53.

60. Beinin and Stork, "On Modernity: Historical Specificity and International Context of Political Islam," in *Political Islam*, 3. The exact quote goes as follows: "We term the movements examined in this volume 'political Islam' because we regard their core concerns as temporal and political. They use the Qur'an, the hadith . . . to justify their stances and actions. They do so in all sincerity. . . . But today's Islamist thinkers and activists are creatively deploying selected elements of the Islamic tradition, combined with ideas, techniques, institutions and commodities of the present and recent past, to cope with specifically modern predicaments."

61. Some scholars attribute the rise of fundamentalism to the failure of modernization. B. Lawrence, for example, maintains that Islamic fundamentalism is a "historical accident," one that "arose as a response to the failure of Muslim nationalisms. Had the transition from dependence to independence worked as its advocates thought it should, there would have been no Islamic fundamentalism, or at most it would have been a modest movement. . . . Instead, independence proved a severe disappointment to most Muslims." Lawrence, *Defenders of God*, 190, 201.

62. On the intolerance of secularism, see the inspiring work of William E. Connolly, *Why I Am Not a Secularist*.

63. Michel Foucault, "What Is Enlightenment?" in *The Foucault Reader*, 43. In this essay as well as in others, Foucault is critical of the "facile confusion between humanism and Enlightenment." As he explains, Enlightenment as a "a set of events and complex historical processes" that express transformation in social and political institutions, forms of knowledge, and technological mutation, among other things, is entirely different from humanism as "a set of themes "tied to value judgments, [which] have obviously varied greatly in their content, as well as the values they have preserved . . . [and] as humanistic themes [they] are too supple, too diverse, too inconsistent to serve as an axis for reflection" (43–44).

64. Ibid., 42. For illuminating critiques of colonial Enlightenment, see David Scott, *Conscripts of Modernity: The Tragedy of Colonial Enlightenment* (Durham, NC: Duke University Press, 2004); Dipesh Chakrabarty, *Provincializing Europe: Postcolonial Thought and Historical Difference* (Princeton, NJ: Princeton University Press, 2000).

Bibliography

ʿAbd al-Baqi, Muhammad Faud. 1991. *al-Muʿjam al-mufahris li-alfath al-Qurʾan al-Karim*. Beirut: Dar al-maʾrifah.

ʿAbdel Malek, Anwar. 1963. "Orientalism in Crisis." *Diogenes* 44: 103–40.

ʿAbduh, Ibrahim. 1945. *Tatawwur al-nahdha al-nisaʾiya fi-Misr*. Cairo: Maktabat al-adab.

ʿAbduh, Muhammad. 1931. *Tarikh al-Imam Muhammad ʿAbduh* [Life and history of Muhammad ʿAbduh]. 2 vols. Comp. and ed. Rashid Rida. Misr: Matbaʿat al-manar.

———. 1964. *The Theology of Unity* [*Risalat al-tawhid*]. Trans. Ishaq Musaʿad and Kenneth Gragg. London: George Allen & Unwin.

———. 1967. *Tafsir juzʾ ʿamma*. Cairo: Muhammad Ali Subayh.

———. 1992. *Risalat al-tawhid*. Introduced and commented on by Shaykh Hussayn Yusuf al-Ghazal. Beirut: Dar ihyaʾ al-ʿulum.

———. 1993. *al-ʿAmal al-kamilah lil-Imam Muhammad ʿAbduh* [The complete works of Muhammad ʿAbduh]. 5 vols. Comp. and ed. Muhammad ʿImara. Cairo: Dar al-shuruq.

———. 1994. *Risalat al-tawhid*. Introduced and commented on by Muhammad ʿImara. Cairo: Dar al-shuruq.

Abrahamian, Evrand. 1993. *Khomeinism: Essays on the Islamic Republic*. Berkeley: University of California Press.

———. 1978. *Iran Between Two Revolutions*. Princeton, NJ: Princeton University Press.

Abu El-Haj, Nadia. 2005. "Edward Said and the Political Present." *American Ethnologist* 32, no. 4: 538–55.

Abu-Lughod, Lila, ed. 1998. *Remaking Women: Feminism and Modernity in the Middle East*. Princeton, NJ: Princeton University Press.

Abu Rabiʿ, Ibrahim M. 1996. *Intellectual Origins of Islamic Resurgence in the Modern Arab World*. Albany: State University of New York Press.

Abu Zahra, Muhammad. 1958. *Usul al-Fiqh*. Cairo: Dar al-fikr al-arabi.

———. 1963. *Tarikh al-madhahib al-Islamiyah* [History of the Islamic legal schools]. Cairo: Dar al-fikr al-arabi.

Adams, Charles. 1968. *Islam and Modernism in Egypt.* New York: Russell & Russell.

Ahmad, Aijaz. 1992. *Theory: Classes, Nations, Literatures.* London: Verso.

Ahmed, Leila. 1992. *Women and Gender in Islam: Historical Roots of the Modern Debate.* New Haven, CT: Yale University Press.

Ajami, Fouad. 1981. *The Arab Predicament: Arab Political Thought and Practice Since 1967.* Cambridge: Cambridge University Press.

Algar, Hamid. 2002. *Wahhabism: A Critical Essay.* Oneonta, NY: Islamic Publication International.

Alusi, Mahmud Shukri al-. n.d. *Tarikh Najd.* Cairo: Maktabat Madbuli.

Amin, Ahmad. 1948. *Zu'ma' al-islah fil-'ahd al-hadith.* Cairo: Matba'at lajnat al-ta'lif wal-tarjama wal-nashr.

Amin, Qasim. 1992. *The Liberation of Women; and, The New Woman.* Trans. Samiha Sidhom Peterson. Cairo: AUC Press.

'Aqqad, Abbas Mahmoud al-. 1962. *Muhammad 'Abduh: 'abqariy al-islah.* Cairo: Nahdhat Misr lil-tiba'a wal-nashr.

Asad, Talal. 1986. "The Idea of an Anthropology of Islam." Occasional Papers Series. Washington, DC: Georgetown University, Center for Contemporary Arab Studies.

———. 1992. "Conscripts of Western Civilization." In *Dialectical Anthropology: Essays in Honor of Stanley Diamond,* Vol. 2, ed. Christine Gailey, 333–51. Gainesville: University Press of Florida.

———. 1993. *Genealogies of Religion: Discipline and Reasons of Power in Christianity and Islam.* Baltimore: Johns Hopkins University Press.

———. 2000. *The Formations of the Secular.* Stanford, CA: Stanford University Press.

Aziz, Sami. *al-Sahafa al-misriyah wa-mawqifuha min-al-ihtilal al-inglizi.* Cairo: Dar al-kitab al-'arabi, 1968.

Azm, Sadiq al-. 1981. "Orientalism and Orientalism in Reverse." *Khamsin* 8: 5–26.

Azmeh, Aziz al-. 1993. *Islams and Modernities.* London: Verso.

Badran, Margot. 1995. *Feminists, Islam, and Nation.* Princeton, NJ: Princeton University Press.

Bahithat al-Badiya. 1919. *Al-Nisa'iyat.* Cairo: Dar-al-huda.

Baron, Beth. 1994. *The Women's Awakening in Egypt: Culture, Society, and the Press.* New Haven, CT: Yale University Press.

Beinin, Joel, and Joe Stork, eds. 1997. *Political Islam: Essays from Middle East Report.* Berkeley: University of California Press.

Bernstein, Richard J. 1992. *The New Constellation: The Ethical-Political Horizons of Modernity/Postmodernity.* Cambridge, MA: MIT Press.

Bhargava, Rajeev, ed. 1998. *Secularism and Its Critics.* Oxford: Oxford University Press.

Bourdieu, Pierre. 1990. *The Logic of Practice.* Trans. Richard Nice. Stanford, CA: Stanford University Press.

Brown, Daniel. 1996. *Rethinking Tradition in Modern Islamic Thought.* Cambridge: Cambridge University Press.

Carruthers, Mary. 1990. *The Book of Memory: A Study of Memory in Medieval Culture.* Cambridge: Cambridge University Press.

Carter, Stephen. 1994. *Culture of Disbelief.* New York: Anchor Books.

Chadwick, Owen. 1964. *The Reformation.* New York: Pelican Books.

Chakrabarty, Dipesh. 2000. *Provincializing Europe: Postcolonial Thought and Historical Difference.* Princeton, NJ: Princeton University Press.

Clack, Brian R. 1999. *An Introduction to Wittgenstein's Philosophy of Religion.* Edinburgh: Edinburgh University Press.

Cole, Juan. 1981. "Feminism, Class and Islam in Turn-of-the-Century Egypt." *IJMES* 13, no. 4: 387–407.

———. 1993. *Colonialism and Revolution in the Middle East: Social and Cultural Origins of Egypt's Urabi Revolt.* Princeton, NJ: Princeton University Press.

Cole, Juan, and Nikki Keddie, eds. 1982. *Shi'ism and Social Protest.* New Haven, CT: Yale University Press.

Connolly, William E. 1999. *Why I Am Not a Secularist.* Minneapolis: University of Minnesota Press.

Corban, Henry. 1996. *History of Islamic Philosophy.* London: Kegan Paul.

Cromer, Evelyn Baring. 1916. *Modern Egypt.* 2 vols. New York: Macmillan.

Dahlan al-Sayyid, Ahmad ibn Zayni. 1991. *Al-Durar al-saniyah fi-al-radd 'ala-al-wahabiya.* Cairo: Dar al-ghad al-arabi.

Dallal, Ahmad. 1995. "The Origins and Objectives of Islamic Revivalist Thought." *Journal of Oriental and American Studies* (February 1).

Dalrymple, William. 2004. "The Truth About Muslims." *New York Review of Books* 51, no. 17.

de Certeau, Michel. 1984. *The Practice of Everyday Life.* Trans. Steven Randall. Berkeley: University of California Press.

de Vries, Hent. 1999. *Philosophy and the Turn to Religion.* Baltimore: Johns Hopkins University Press, 1999.

Eccel, Chris A. 1984. *Egypt, Islam, and Social Change: Al-Azhar in Conflict and Accommodation.* Berlin: Klaus Schwarz.

Eikelman, Dale, and James Piscatori. 1996. *Muslim Politics.* Princeton, NJ: Princeton University Press.

Esposito, John. 1995. *The Islamic Threat: Myth or Reality?* Oxford: Oxford University Press.

Euben, Roxanne L. 1997. "Comparative Political Theory: An Islamic Fundamentalist Critique of Rationalism." *Journal of Politics* 69, no. 1: 28–55.

Fahmy, Khaled. 1997. *All the Pasha's Men: Mehmed Ali, His Army, and the Making of Modern Egypt.* Cambridge: Cambridge University Press.

Fatawa Islamiya. 1980. Vol. 1. Cairo: wizarat al-awqaf, Dar al-Ifta.

Fiqqi, Muhammad Hamid al-. 1983. *Athar al-da'wa al-wahhabiya.* Cairo: matba'at al-sunna al-muhamadiyya.

Fisher, Michael M. J., and Mehdi Abedi. 2001. *Debating Muslims: Cultural Dialogues in Postmodernity and Tradition.* Madison: University of Wisconsin Press.

Fletcher, Richard. 2004. *The Cross and the Crescent: Christianity and Islam from Muhammad to the Reformation.* New York: Viking.

Foucault, Michel. 1973. *The Order of Things: An Archeology of the Human Sciences.* New York: Vintage.

———. 1977. *Power/Knowledge: Selected Interviews and Other Writings, 1972–1977.* Ed. Colin Gordon. New York: Pantheon Books.

———. 1984. *The Foucault Reader.* Ed. Paul Rabinow. New York: Pantheon.

———. 1988. *History of Sexuality.* 3 vols. New York: Vintage Books.

———. 2006. *The Hermeneutics of the Subject: Lectures at the College de France, 1981–1982.* Trans. Graham Burchell. New York: Picador.

Gesnick, Indira Falk. 2003. "Chaos on Earth." *American Historical Review* 108, no. 3: 710–33.

Ghazali, Abu Hamid ibn Muhammad. 1993. *al-Qistat al-mustaqim: al-Mauazin al-Khamzah lil-ma'arifah fil-Qur'an* [The straight path: The five keys to Quranic knowledge]. Ed. Mahmoud Bijou. Damascus: al-Matba'a al-'ilmiya.

———. 1995. *On Disciplining the Soul and on Breaking the Two Desires.* Trans. T. J. Winters. Cambridge: Islamic Text Society.

———. 1999. *Deliverance from Error* [*al-Munqidh min al-dhalal*]. Annotated and translated by Richard Joseph McCarthy. Louisville: Fons Vitae.

Gibb, Hamilton A. R. 1972. *Modern Trends in Islam.* New York: Octagon Books.

Göle, Nilüfer. 1977. "Secularism and Islamism in Turkey." *Middle East Journal* 51, no. 1.

———. 1997. *The Forbidden Modern: Civilization and Veiling.* Ann Arbor: University of Michigan Press.

Gran, Peter. 1998. *Islamic Roots of Capitalism in Egypt, 1760–1840.* Syracuse: Syracuse University Press.

Hacking, Ian. 1995. *Rewriting the Soul: Multiple Personalities and the Sciences of Memory.* Princeton, NJ: Princeton University Press.

———. 1999. *The Social Construction of What?* Cambridge, MA: Harvard University Press.

———. 2002. *Historical Ontology.* Cambridge, MA: Harvard University Press.

Hallaq, Wael. 1997. *History of Islamic Legal Theory: An Introduction to Sunni usul al-fiqh.* Cambridge: Cambridge University Press.

———. 2001. *Authority, Continuity, and Change in Islamic Law.* Cambridge: Cambridge University Press.

Hamburger, Philip. 2002. *Separation of Church and State.* Cambridge, MA: Harvard University Press.

Hamzah, ʿAbd al-Latif. 1955. *Adab al-maqala al-sahafiya fi-Misr.* Vol. 4. Cairo: Dar al-fikr al-ʿarabi.

Haq, Mahmudal. 1970. *Muhammad ʿAbduh: A Study of a Modern Thinker of Egypt.* Aligarh: Institute of Islamic Studies.

Hirschkind, Charles. 2006. *Ethical Soundscape: Cassette Sermons and Islamic Counterpublics.* New York: Columbia University Press.

Hobsbawm, Eric, and Terence Ranger, eds. 1988. *The Invention of Tradition.* Cambridge: Cambridge University Press.

Hodgson, Marshall G. S. 1974. *The Venture of Islam: Conscience and History in a World Civilization.* Vol. 2. Chicago: University of Chicago Press.

Hourani, Albert. 1983. *Arabic Thought in the Liberal Age, 1798–1939.* Cambridge: Cambridge University Press.

———. 1991. "How Should We Write the History of the Middle East?" *IJMES* 23: 125–36.

———. 1991. *Islam in European Thought.* Cambridge: Cambridge University Press.

Huntington, Samuel. 1998. *The Clash of Civilizations and the Remaking of World Order.* New York: Simon and Schuster.

Ibn ʿAbdul Wahhab, Muhammad. 1974. *Masaʾil al-jahiliya.* Introduced by Mahmud al-Alusi. Cairo: al-Matbaʿa al-Salafiya wa-Maktabatuha.

———. 1976. *Muʾallafat al-Shaykh al-Imam Muhammad ibn Abdul Wahhab.* 5 vols. Riyad: Jamiʿat al-Imam Muhammad ibn Saʿud al-Islamiyah.

———. 1979. *Kitab al-tawhid: Essay on the Unicity of Allah or What Is Due to Allah from His Creatures.* Trans. Ismail al-Faruqi. Beirut: I.I.F.S.O.

———. 1986. *Kitab al-tawhid.* Comp. and ed. Ahmad Muhammad Shakir. Beirut: Alam al-Kutub.

———. n.d. *Kitab al-tawhid.* Edited and annotated by ʿAbdul Rahman ibn Hasan ibn Muhamdad ibn ʿAbdul Wahhab. Beirut: Dar maktabat al-Hayat.

Ibn ʿAbdul Wahhab, Sulaiman. 1975. *Al-Sawaʿiq al-ilahiyah fi-al-radd ʿala-al-wahabiyah.* Istanbul: Maktabat Ishiq.

Ibn Bishr, Uthman ibn ʿAbdallah. 1982. *ʿUnwan al-majd fi tarikh Najd.* 2 vols. Comp. and ed. Abd al-Latif ibn ʿAbd Allah al-Shaykh. Riyad: Matbaʿat al-malik ʿAbdul ʿAziz.

Ibn Ghannam, Hussain. 1985. *Tarikh Najd.* 2 vols. Comp. and ed. Nasir al-Din al-Asad. Beirut: Dar al-shuruq.

Ibn Kathir, Abu al-fida Isma'il. 1993. *Tafsir al-Qur'an al-'Azim.* 4 vols. Beirut: al-Maktaba al-asriyah.

Ibn Manzur, Jamal al-din Muhammad bin Mukaram. 1994. *Lisan al-'arab.* 15 vols. Beirut: Dar Sader.

Ibrahim, Saad Eddin. 1980. "Anatomy of Egypt's Militant Islamic Groups." *IJMES* 12: 42–53.

Iqbal, Muhammad. 1958. *The Reconstruction of Religious Thought in Islam.* Lahore: Sh. M. Ashraf.

Jad'an, Fahmi. 1988. *Usus al-taqadum 'ind mufakiri al-ilsam fil-'alim al-arabi al-hadith* [The concept of progress in Islamic thought and in the modern Arab world]. Cairo: Dar al-shuruq.

Johansen, Baber. 1999. *Contingency in a Sacred Law: Legal and Ethical Norms in Muslim Fiqh.* Leiden, the Netherlands: Brill.

Karsh, Efraim. 2006. *Islamic Imperialism.* New Haven, CT: Yale University Press.

Keddie, Nikkie. 1983. *An Islamic Response to Imperialism: Political and Religious Writings of Sayyid Jamal al-Din al-Afghani.* Berkeley: University of California Press.

———. 2006. *Modern Iran: Roots and Results of Revolution.* New Haven, CT: Yale University Press.

Kedouri, Elie. 1966. *Afghani and 'Abduh: An Essay on Religious Unbelief and Political Activism in Modern Islam.* London: Cass.

Kepel, Gilles. 2003. *Muslim Extremism in Egypt: The Prophet and the Pharaoh.* Berkeley: University of California Press.

Kerr, Malcolm H. 1966. *Islamic Reform: The Political and Legal Theories of Muhammad Abduh and Rashid Rida.* Berkeley: University of California Press.

Koselleck, Reinhardt. 1985. *Futures Past: On the Semantics of Historical Times.* Trans. Keith Tribe. Cambridge, MA: MIT Press.

———. 2002. *The Practice of Conceptual History: Timing History, Spacing Concepts.* Trans. Todd Samuel Presner et al. Stanford, CA: Stanford University Press.

Kumi, Sami Abdul Aziz. 1992. *Al-Sahafa al-islamiya fi Misr fil qarn al-tasi' 'ashr* [Islamic press in nineteenth-century Egypt]. al-Mansura: Dar al-Wafa li-tiba'a wal-nashr.

Kurzman, Charles. 1998. *Liberal Islam: A Sourcebook.* Oxford: Oxford University Press.

Lawrence, Bruce. 1995. *Defenders of God: The Fundamentalist Revolt Against Modernity.* Columbia: University of South Carolina Press.

Lewis, Bernard. 2005. *From Babel to Dragomans: Interpreting the Middle East.* Oxford: Oxford University Press.

MacIntyre, Alasdair. 1984. *After Virtue: A Study in Moral Theory*. Notre Dame, IN: University of Notre Dame Press.

———. 1988. *Whose Justice? Which Rationality?* Notre Dame, IN: Notre Dame University Press.

———. 1990. *Three Rival Versions of Moral Inquiry: Encyclopaedia, Genealogy, and Tradition*. Notre Dame, IN: Notre Dame University Press.

Macpherson, C. B. 1962. *The Political Theory of Possessive Individualism*. Oxford: Oxford University Press.

Mahmood, Saba. 2005. *Politics of Piety: The Islamic Revival and the Feminist Subject*. Princeton, NJ: Princeton University Press.

Makdisi, George. 1981. *The Rise of Colleges: Institutions of Learning in Islam and the West*. Edinburgh: Edinburgh University Press.

———. 1995. *The Rise of Humanism in Classical Islam and the Christian West*. Edinburgh: Edinburgh University Press.

Malcolm, Norman. 1993. *Wittgenstein: A Religious Point of View?* Ithaca, NY: Cornell University Press.

al-Manar. 1898–1904.

Masud, Muhammad Khalid, Brinkley Messick, and David S. Powers, eds. 1996. *Islamic Legal Interpretation: Muftis and Their Fatwas*. Cambridge, MA: Harvard University Press.

Matar, Nabil I. 1998. *Islam in Britain, 1558–1685*. Cambridge: Cambridge University Press, 1998.

———. 1999. *Turks, Moors, and Englishmen in the Age of Discovery*. New York: Columbia University Press.

———, ed. and trans. 2003. *In the Lands of the Christians: Arab Travel Writing in the Seventeenth Century*. New York: Routledge.

Meaning of the Holy Qur'an. 1995. Translation and commentary by 'Abdullah Yusuf 'Ali. Beltsville, MD: Amana Publications.

Mehta, Uday Singh. 1999. *Liberalism and Empire: A Study in Nineteenth-Century British Liberal Thought*. Chicago: University of Chicago Press.

Message of the Quran. 1980. Translated and explained by Muhammad Asad. Gibraltar: Dar al-Andalus; London: Brill.

Messick, Brinkley. 1993. *The Calligraphic State*. Berkeley: University of California Press.

Mitchell, Timothy. 1988. *Colonising Egypt*. Cambridge: Cambridge University Press, 1988.

———, ed. 2000. *Questions of Modernity*. Minneapolis: University of Minnesota Press.

Moosa, Ebrahim. 2000. *Ghazali and the Poetics of Imagination*. Chapel Hill: University of North Carolina Press.

Musa, Nabawiyah. 1999. *Tarikhi*. Cairo: Multaqa al-mar'a wal-zakira.

Namnam, Hilmi. 2001. *'Ali Yusuf wa Safiya al-Sadat.* Cairo: Mirit lil nashr wal-ma'lumat.

Nasr, Vali. 2006. *The Shia Revival: How Conflicts with Islam Would Shape the Future.* New York: Norton.

Patai, Raphael. 1973. *The Arab Mind.* New York: Scribner.

Peters, Rudolph. 1996. *Jihad in Classical and Modern Islam.* Princeton, NJ: Markus Wiener.

Piccirillo, Michele. 1995. "The Christians in Palestine During a Time of Transition: 7th–9th Centuries." In *The Christian Heritage in the Holy Land,* ed. Anthony O'Mahony. London: Scorpion Cavendish.

Qureshi, Emran, and Michael A. Sells, eds. 2003. *The New Crusades: Constructing the Muslim Enemy.* New York: Columbia University Press.

Rahman, Fazlur. 1968. *Islam.* New York: Anchor Books.

———. 1970. "Revival and Reform in Islam." In *The Cambridge History of Islam,* Vol. 2, ed. P. M. Holt, A. K. S. Lambton, and B. Lewis, 632–42. Cambridge: Cambridge University Press.

———. 1984. *Islam and Modernity.* Chicago: University of Chicago Press.

Reid, Donald M. 1982. "*Arabic Thought in the Liberal Age* Twenty Years After." *IJMES* 14: 541–57.

Rejali, Darius M. 1994. *Torture and Modernity: Self, Society, and State in Modern Iran.* Boulder, CO: Westview Press.

Richards, Alan, and John Waterbury. 1990. *A Political Economy of the Middle East: State, Class, and Economic Development.* Boulder, CO: Westview Press.

Roy, Olivier. 1998. *The Failure of Political Islam.* Trans. Carol Volk. Cambridge, MA: Harvard University Press.

Saad-Ghorayeb, Amal. 2002. *Hizbullah: Politics and Religion.* London: Pluto Press.

Sadowski, Yahya. 1993. "The New Orientalism and the Democracy Debate." *MERIP* (183).

Said, Edward. 1978. *Orientalism.* New York: Pantheon Books.

Sayyid Marsot, Afaf Lutfi al-. 1968. "Modernization Among the Rectors of al-Azhar, 1798–1879." In *Beginnings of Modernization in the Middle East: The Nineteenth Century,* ed. William R. Polk and Richard L. Chambers. Chicago: University of Chicago Press.

———. 1969. *Egypt and Cromer: A Study in Anglo-Egyptian Relations.* New York: Praeger.

———. 1985. *A Short History of Egypt.* Cambridge: Cambridge University Press.

Scott, David. 2004. *Conscripts of Modernity: The Tragedy of Colonial Enlightenment.* Durham, NC: Duke University Press.

Scott, David, and Charles Hirschkind, eds. 2006. *Powers of the Secular Modern: Talal Asad and His Interlocutors.* Stanford, CA: Stanford University Press.

Sen, Amartya. 2006. *Identity and Violence: The Illusion of Destiny.* New York: Norton.

Shakry, Omnia. 1998. "Schooled Mothers and Structured Play: Child Rearing in Turn of the Century Egypt." In *Remaking Women: Feminism and Modernity in the Middle East*, ed. Lila Abu-Lughod, 126–70. Princeton, NJ: Princeton University Press.

Sharif, Mohammad. 1975. *Ghazali's Theory of Virtue.* Albany: State University of New York Press.

Sharif, Muhammad Ibrahim. 1982. *Itijahat al-tajdid fi-tafsir al-Quran al-Karim fi-Misr* [New approaches to the interpretation of the Qur'an in Egypt]. Cairo: Dar al-turath.

Shawkani, Muhammad ibn Ali. 1932. *Kitab Durar al-nadid fi-ikhlas al-tawhid* [The cult of saints and true tawhid]. Yemen: Attiya Muhammad al-Kitbi.

———. 1991. *al-Qawl al-mufid fi-adillat al-ijtihad wal-taqlid* [Useful words on ijtihad and taqlid]. Beirut: Dar al-kitab al-libnani.

Sheehan, Jonathan. 2003. "Enlightenment, Religion and the Enigma of Secularization: A Review Article." *American Historical Review* 108, no. 4: 1061–80.

Skovgaard-Peterson, Jakob. 1997. *Defining Islam for the Egyptian State: Muftis and Fatwas of dar al-ifta'.* Leiden, the Netherlands: Brill.

Soroush, Abdolkarim. 2000. *Reason, Freedom, and Democracy in Islam.* Trans. and ed. Mahmoud Sadri and Ahmad Sadri. Oxford: Oxford University Press.

Steppat, Fritz. 1968. "National Education Projects in Egypt Before British Occupation." In *Beginnings of Modernization in the Middle East: The Nineteenth Century*, ed. William R. Polk and Richard L. Chambers. Chicago: University of Chicago Press.

Tibawi, A. L. 1964. "English Speaking Orientalists." *Islamic Quarterly* 8: 25–45.

Tibi, Bassam. 2002. *The Challenge of Fundamentalism: Political Islam and the New World Order.* Berkeley: University of California Press.

Toulmin, Stephen. 1990. *Cosmopolis: The Hidden Agenda of Modernity.* Chicago: University of Chicago Press.

———. 2003. *The Uses of Argument.* Cambridge: Cambridge University Press.

Tucker, Judith E. 1985. *Women in Nineteenth-Century Egypt.* Cambridge: Cambridge University Press.

———. 1998. *In the House of the Law: Gender and Islamic Law in Ottoman Syria and Palestine.* Berkeley: University of California Press.

Van Kley, Dale K. 2003. "Christianity as Casualty and Chrysalis of Modernity: The Problem of Dechristianization in the French Revolution: A Review Essay." *American Historical Review* 108, no. 4: 1081–1105.

Vassiliev, Alexei. 2000. *The History of Saudi Arabia.* London: Saqi Books.

Vatikiotis, J. 1957. "Muhammad Abduh and the Quest for a Muslim Humanism." *Islamic Culture* 31: 109–26.

Voll, John. 1994. *Islam, Continuity and Change in the Modern World.* Syracuse: Syracuse University Press.

Von Grunebaum, Gustave E. 1964. *Modern Islam: The Search for Cultural Identity.* New York: Vintage Books.

Wadeen, Lisa. 1999. *The Ambiguities of Domination: Politics, Rhetoric, and Symbols in Contemporary Syria.* Chicago: University of Chicago Press.

Wadud, Amina. 1999. *Qur'an and Woman: Reading the Sacred Text from a Woman's Perspective.* Oxford: Oxford University Press.

Williams, Raymond. 1976. *Keywords.* New York: Oxford University Press.

Young, Robert. 1990. *White Mythologies: Writing History and the West.* New York: Routledge.

Zaman, Muhammad Qasim. 2002. *The Ulama of Contemporary Islam: Custodians of Change.* Princeton, NJ: Princeton University Press.

Zubaida, Sami. 1989. *Islam, the People and the State: Essays on Political Ideas and Movements in the Middle East.* New York: Routledge.

———. 1992. "Islam: The State and Democracy: Contrasting Conceptions of Society in Egypt." *MERIP* 179: 2–10.

Index

'abd (slave of God), 39, 42, 62–63, 64, 221n26

'Abduh, Muhammad, 6–7; al-Azhar reform and, 99–108, 182–83, 237n89; 'aql (reasoning) and, 72–73, 110, 114–15, 117; attack of, on jurists and scholars, 79–85; critique of taghrib and secularism, 90–99, 189; on education (al-taʿlim wal-tarbiya), 119–27, 240–41n24; on family, marriage and divorce, 128–43; fatawa of, 143–50; free will and, 113, 238–39n11; ijtihad and, 72–73, 78, 80–81, 83–84, 110, 148–49, 152, 231n39, 248n108; *Islam and Christianity and Their Respective Attitudes Toward Learning and Civilization*, 91; *Islam and the Reply to Its Critics*, 90–91, 232n54; life narrative of, 19–24, 216nn60–61, 216nn63–64; mean between taqlid and taghrib and, 72, 77–87, 107; mizan and, 86–90; as Muslim reformer, 71–72, 77, 90, 150; political rulers and, 94, 102, 121, 233n60; revivalism of, 70–71, 73, 94–95, 233n62; social setting and, 10–13, 27–29; subjective interiority and, 110–19, 238n3; tajdid project of, 73–77; taqlid and, 72–73, 76, 149, 152; *The Unity of Theology*, 78, 240n20; viewed as eclectic, 69, 229n10, 240nn20–21; viewed as humanist, 6, 66–70, 191, 198–99

Abrahamian, Evrand, 201, 262n57

Abu Hanifa (founder of Hanafiya legal school), 150. *See* also Hanafi legal school

Abu Khutwa, Ahmad, 169, 175–76

Abu Shadi, Muhammad, 149–50. See also *Zahir, al-*

Adab, al (dicourse of ethics), 59, 105, 111

'adl (justice), 13, 87, 116, 146

adultery. *See* zina

Afandi, 'Abdul Rahman, 170, 175–76

Afghani, Jamal al-Din al-, 23–24, 31, 75–76, 119, 167, 191, 198

Ahmed, Leila, 241n26, 243n57, 249n4, 250n11

Ahram, al-, 75, 153, 165, 177, 232n54

Algar, Hamid, 31; *Wahhabism*, 217n1, 217–18n4

'Ali, Muhammad, 23, 75, 127, 215n54, 216n59, 216–17n66, 255n81

'alim. *See* 'ulama

al-kafa'a (compatibility), 177–80, 183–87

almsgiving. *See* zakat

Alusi, Mahmud Shukri al-, 59

'amal (sing.)/Aʿmal (pl.)(practices and deeds), 45–49, 51–53, 125, 223n39

Amin, Qasim, 133; *Liberation of Women*, 155–59, 161, 163, 249n3, 249n5, 249n8; new woman and, 155–64

Anbabi, al-, 83, 230–31n37, 236n86

anti-humanism, Islam and, 1, 66, 68, 90–91, 189–91, 228n7

Antun, Farah, 91, 95, 99, 144, 146, 234n72, 247n94

apostasy. *See* kufr

ʿaql (reasoning), 38; ʿAbduh and, 72–73, 110, inner self and 114–15, 117, 122, 125, 240n20

aqwal (pl.) (utterances), 46–48; deeds and, 53, 57, 223n39

Aristotle, 87

Asad, Muhammad, 244n64

Asad, Talal, 3–4, 49, 139, 221n26, 237–38n1

asceticism. *See* ʿilm al-tasawwuf

Ashʿariya, 48, 86–88, 101–2, 107, 113, 238n4, 233n70

asl (source), 11, 231n44. *See also* usul

associationism. *See* kufr; shirk

ʿAttar, Hasan al-, 100

Azhar, al-, 21–23, 75, 80–83; curricula at, 103–5, 236n87; internal politics at, 102–7, 235–36nn81–83, 236n86; reform movement at, 99–108, 179, 182, 235n78

Bahithat al-Badiya, 160–63, 250nn21–22. *See also* Nassif, Malak Hilmi

Bakri, Muhammad Tawfiq al-, 165, 173–74, 252n37

balance. *See* mizan

Benedict XVI (pope), 188–89, 255n1, 256–57n5

bidʿa (sing.)/bidaʿ (pl.) (innovations), 17, 33, 56, 58, 63, 88–89, 94

binary constructs: 19, 27, 35, 90–91, 117–18, 154, 195; modern vs. traditional, 1–3, 5–7, 27–28, 32, 56, 73, 90–99, 151, 188–91; reason vs. belief, 190–91

Bishri, Salim al-, 106, 235n82, 236n85

Brockelmann, Carl, 32, 35

Caisse de la Dette Publique, 138, 244–45n73; Dual Control and, 245n73

Carruthers, Mary, 33–34, 219n12, 224n47

child rearing, 133, 159–61, 250n18

Christianity, compared to Islam: faith and, 91, 223–24n47; intolerance and, 92–97; monotheism and, 45; religion and, 230n23; religious wars and, 97, 233–34n70; theocracy and, 93, 96–97; view of God and, 188–89, 192, 194–95

Clash of Civilizations, The (Huntington), 192–93, 258nn14–15; challenge to theory of, 194–95, 259n22, 259n25

colonialism. *See* imperialism

colonial modernity, reconfiguration of, 67–108; al-Azhar reform and, 99–108; critique of taghrib and secularism and, 90–99; mean between taqlid and taghrib and, 77–86; tajdid and, 73–77; Western view of ʿAbduh and, 67–70

community. *See* moral community; umma

consensus. *See* ijmaʿ; taqlid

courting practices, ʿAbduh on, 130–31

courts, reforming Islamic family, 136–43. *See also* shariʿa

Cromer, Evelyn Baring, Earl of, 70, 156; ʿAbduh and, 106, 229n10, 235–36n83; contested marriage and, 174–75, 185; education and, 120–21, 168; on Egyptian legal system, 245n75; labor strike and, 144, 247n94

cult of saints, 14–16, 26, 32, 35–37, 41–43, 52, 55–66, 225nn55–56, 226n65

dahliz (liminal space), 211n23. *See also* Ghazali, Abu Hamid ibn Muhammad, al-

Darwish, shaikh, and ʿAbduh, 21–23, 216n62

Delong-Bas, Natana J., 18, 54, 226n61, 217n1

din (Islam/religion), 35, 38, 56, 79, 230n23

divorce: ʿAbduh's views on, 134–36; reform, 244n72

documentary cultures, 12, 33–34.
  See also Carruthers, Mary
durra (co-wife-ing). *See* polygamy

economy: 'Abduh's fatwa on, 143–46;
  impact of market, 155
education: al-Azhar reform and,
  99–108; ethics, 111; judicial system
  and, 140, 245n81; men's, 158; women's,
  157–58, 161, 249nn8–9. *See also*
  tarbiya
education systems, Egyptian, 119;
  commoners and, 121–24; missionary,
  120; public, 120–22, 241n25; religious, 120
Egypt: agrarian change in, 20, 216n59;
  education in, 11, 23, 100, 119–27,
  216–17n66; European imperial power
  in, 23, 74–75, 120–21, 241n26; labor
  strikes in, 143–45, 247n94, 247n96;
  legal systems in, 137–43, 244–45n73,
  245nn75–77; long-standing tensions
  in, 154–55, 248n1; print culture in, 11;
  social and economic restructuring of,
  20–23, 27–28, 100, 216n59, 216–
  17n66; woman question in, 155–64,
  168
Enlightenment, 2–3, 22, 49, 68, 73–74,
  95, 98; post-Enlightenment and, 190,
  195, 200, 208n7, 209n10, 228n2;
  blackmail of, 202–3, 234n73,
  262n63
ethics (adab and 'ilm al-akhlaq), 111;
  "hermeneutics of the self" and,
  110–13, 147, 239n12
Europeanization, 77–78. *See also*
  taghrib

fada'il (virtues), 238n17; as acts of
  worship, 43–47, 60; and fiqh (law),
  111; interiorized, 111, 238n5
fadila. *See* fada'il
faith, 115; coercion and, 95–96;
  interiority of, 89; vs. belief, 49–50.
  See also iman

family: 'Abduh's views on, 127–43;
  morality and, 127–28, 156; nuclear,
  155
fard 'ayn (individual duty), 10–11, 32,
  212n31; 'Abduh and, 123–24; ibn
  'Abdul Wahhab and, 32–33, 218n10
fard kifaya (public duty): 'Abduh and,
  83, 85, 123, 145; ibn 'Abdul Wahhab
  and, 218n10
fasad (moral corruption of the community), 8, 15, 35–36, 41, 48, 134, 163–65,
  219n15
fatawa/i (legal opinions), 80, 246n91;
  'Abduh's, 119, 143–50, 246–47n92
fatwa. *See* fatawa/i
fiqh (legal doctrine), 12, 85, 86, 111–12, 113;
  fiqh al-nafs (self-intelligibility), 109,
  116–17, 147; usul al-fiqh, 38, 103,
  246n90. *See also* shari'a; Hallaq, Wael
Foucault, Michel, 2–3, 115, 202–3,
  208n8, 209n10, 262n63
fundamentalism, Islamic, 209–10n16;
  defining features of, 67–68, 228n2;
  and modernity, 199–202, 261n45,
  261n47, 261n51, 262nn60–61;
  modernization vs. modernism and,
  200; modern politics and, 196–97,
  201–2; negative Western views of,
  195–96, 260n29; rejection of
  terminology of, 201–2, 262n57

Ghazali, Abu Hamid ibn Muhammad,
  al-, 84, 86–87, 211nn22–23, 231n48,
  240n22; "ethics/hermeneutics of the
  self" and, 110–13, 116, 147, 238n5,
  239n12; Greek philosophy and, 8–9,
  88–89, 231–32n49
Gibb, Hamilton A., 31–32, 191, 257n9
golden mean, 231n49. *See also* mizan
graves, visitation of, 56–61, 226n63.
  See also cult of saints

habitus, 111, 116, 230n23. *See also*
  malaka
Hacking, Ian, 19, 215–16n57

Hadith, 9, 13, 1, 32, 41–43, 58, 60,
61–62, 65, 79, 80, 82, 84, 105, 134,
177, 202. See also Sunna
Hallaq, Wael, 83, 86, 248n106; Author-
ity, Continuity, and Change in Islamic
Law, 81
Hanafi legal school, 15–16, 141–42, 147,
149–50, 213n34, 248n108
Hanbali legal school, 15–16, 32, 48,
213n34, 223n39, 247–48n104
Hanotaux, Gabriel, 91, 189, 232n54;
"Face to Face with Islam and the
Muslim Question," 232n52
Harb, Tala'at, 161, 250n24
Hezbollah, defensive jihad and, 218n9
Hilmi, 'Abbas (khedive), 106, 235–
36nn82–83, 236n86, 237n90, 237n95;
Yusuf and, 168–69, 175, 182–83,
253n59;
Hourani, Albert, 73, 240nn20–21;
Arabic Thought in the Liberal Age,
69–70, 199, 260h61nn42–43
humanism: 'Abduh and Islamic, 6,
66–70; Foucault and , 209, 262n63;
Said and, 3, 208nn8–9; secularization
and, 195, 209n10, 262n63; Western
liberal, 1–3, 5–7, 27–28, 73, 56,
90–99, 193, 195, 202, 208. See also
anti-humanism, Islam and
Huntington, Samuel, The Clash of
Civilizations, 192–93, 258nn14–15;
challenges to theory of, 194–95,
259n22, 259n25

'ibada (bond/worship), 40–47, 49, 64,
184
ibn 'Abdul Wahhab, Muhammad,
6–7, 30–66, 114; cult of saints and,
16–17, 26, 36–37, 55–66, 225nn55–56,
226n65; fada'il and, 43–47; ijtihad
and, 16, 37; Kitab al-tawhid, 36,
40–41, 52, 62, 225nn55–56; life
narrative of, 13–19, 213n43, 214n49,
215n52, 221n22; marriages, families
and, 252–53n51, 254n67; scholastic

disinterest in, 30–35; social setting
and, 10–13, 24–27; tajdid and,
35–36; taqlid and, 16, 37; tawhid
and, 14–15, 17, 26, 36–46, 221n23,
222n34; view of iman and islam of,
47–55, 223n45
ibn 'Abdul Wahhab, Sulaiman, 13–14,
60–61, 213n38
ibn 'Ali, Sulaiman, 13, 213n37
ibn al-Qayim, 16, 60
ibn 'Arabi (Unity of Existence), 39,
220n19. See also Sufism, monistic
ibn Bishr, Uthman ibn 'Abdallah,
14–15, 17
ibn Ghannam, Hussain, 225n55
ibn Hanbal, Ahmed (founder of the
Hanbaliya school), 48, 223n39
ibn Hasan Khuzbak, Hasan, 58–59
ibn Kathir, 51–52, 224n50
ibn Rushd (Averroes) 95, 234n72
ibn Sa'ud, Muhammad, 17–18, 25,
215n54
ibn Sulaiman, 'Abdul Wahhab, 13–14,
213n39
ibn Sulaiman, Ibrahim, 13
ibn Taymiya, 9, 16, 31–32, 37, 38–40, 42,
60, 218nn7–8, 219n17, 220n20;
critique of monistic Sufism of, 37–40;
ijtihad and, 9, 16, 211–12nn26–27
ihsan (giving more than one owes),
51–52, 224n51
ihya' (revival), 7–9. See also tajdid;
reform, Islamic
ijma' (authorized consensus), 80, 107,
149, 211–12n26, 214n47, 247–48n104
ijtihad (reasoning independent of
precedent), 9; 'Abduh and, 72–73, 78,
80–81, 83–84, 110, 148–50, 152,
231n39, 248n108; Hanbali school and,
247–48n104; ibn 'Abdul Wahhab
and, 16, 37; Islamic courts and, 141,
246n85; revivalists and, 9, 211n24
ikhlas (devotion), 51–53, 223n45, 224n51
ikrah (coercion), 95–96
'Ilish, Muhammad, 80, 101–2, 107

'ilm al-akhlaq (ethics), 111. *See* also
    fada'il
'ilm al-kalam (speculative theology),
    38–40, 105, 116, 223–24n47
'ilm al-tasawwuf (asceticism), 21
iman (faith),43, 46–53, 60, 222n35
'Imara, Muhammad, 146, 246–47n92,
    249n3
imperialism: current hostilities and, 192,
    200; dichotomization of East and
    West and, 2; in Egypt, 23, 74–75,
    120–21, 241n26
individualism, possessive, 143 145,
    242n33. *See also* istifrad; Liberalism,
    individualism in
inhitat (stagnation), 156, 232n52
Invented tradition, 70, 196–98, 201,
    229n13
islah (reform), 7–9, 35, 46. *See also*
    tajdid
Islamic movements, 2, 6 197–98;
    modern politics and, 196–97, 201–2;
    Western views of, 2–3, 32. *See also*
    fundamentalism, Islamic
islam (submission), 40–48, 222n31;
    iman and, 47–48, 222n35,
    222–23nn38–39
istifrad (individualism), 145, 151

Jabarti, Abdul Rahman al-, 221n22
Jahiz, al-, 8, 210n21
Jami'a al-'Uthmaniya, al-, 91, 95.
    See also Antun, Farah
jihad, 17–18, 218nn9–10
judh (effort), 45, 49
jurists, 81–82, 141–42, 246n85

kafir (sing.), 50, 223n45
Kamil, Mustafa, 166, 168, 176–77,
    182–83, 249n9, 254n80
Kerr, Malcolm, 87, 198–99, 240nn20–21
khalal fi al-din (religious defects), 35–36,
    219n15. *See also* tajdid; reform,
    Islamic
Khan, Sayyid Ahmad, 148

khedive. *See* Hilmi, 'Abbas
khimar (headcovering extended over
    the torso), 244n64
Khomeini, Ayatollah 196–97, 201
kuffar (pl.) (rejectors of God), 59–60
kufr, 43, 50, 52, 60

Laoust, Henri, 31–32, 218n7, 223n45
law. *See* fiqh; shari'a; 'urf; usul: al-fiqh
legal opinions. *See* fatawa/i
legal schools, 213n34; at al-Azhar, 102–3;
    Islamic courts and, 141–42, 246n88.
    See also madhahib
Lewis, Bernard, 192–93; refutation of,
    194–95, 259n25
Liberalism, 4–5, 88, 118, 146, 198;
    'Abduh and, 28, 74, 91, 124; human-
    ism and, 3, 73, 90, 202; individualism
    in, 124, 126, 172, 196, 242n33; judicial
    systems and, 137, 139; liberal subjects
    of, 109–10, 112, 113, 118, 150–51;
    secularism and, 91, 126, 129; subjec-
    tive interiority and, 109–12, 117–18; as
    a tradition, 5, 74, 110, 117, 128, 151,
    202
Liwa, al-, 165–66, 174, 176–77, 252n38,
    254n80
logocentrism, 12, 22, 100
love and marriage, 172, 153–87;
    contested marriage and, 164–87;
    new woman, 155–64. *See also* mahaba

MacIntyre, Alasdair, 3–5, 88, 221–
    22n30, 221n28.
madhahib (the four Islamic legal
    schools), 81, 231n44, 236n85
mahaba (love), 128, 131, 244n58
mahakim ahliya, al- (national courts),
    138, 245n75
Maliki legal school, 136, 213n34, 253n51
majallah (Ottoman), 138–39
Makhluf, Muhammad Hassain, 63–64,
    227n77, 227nn74–75
malaka (habitus), 111; Abduh and, 116,
    239n17

Manar, al-, 125, 150, 159, 172, 177, 181, 183, 235n78, 243n4. *See also* Rida, Mohammad Rashid

marriage: arranged, 129–30, 156, 163, 171; companionate, 128–31, 156, 171; compatibility and, 177–78, 183–87; contested, 164–85; polygamous and monogamous, 131–33

maslaha (public good), 86, 157, 185; 'Abduh and, 123–24; labor strikes and, 143–45; polygamy and, 131–33; vs. individualism, 151

Matar, Nabil, *In the Lands of the Christians*, 194–95, 259n25

Matn (sing.). *See* mutun

mazalim, al (nonreligious grievance courts), 137–38

mean (balance), 72, 87. *See also* middle-of-the-road rule; mizan; wasat

memory cultures, 12, 33–34, 100, 219n12, 224n47

Messick, Brinkley, 12, 41, 212n32

millet (non-Muslim courts), 137

mizan (mean), 72, 86–90, 107, 231n48. *See also* middle-of-the-road rule; wasat

modernism, fundamentalists and, 199–201, 261n45, 261n47, 261n51

modernity, 207n1; 'Abduh's view of, 28, 71–72, 112, 116, 151; coercive universalization of European, 98–99; Muslim views of, 6, 10, 110, 112–19, 163–65, 179, 202; Western definitions of, 1–3, 27–28, 68, 89–90, 195, 202.

modesty, 128, 133–34, 244n64. *See also* piety

monotheism: Christian compared to Islamic, 45, 47. *See also* tawhid

Moosa, Ebrahim, 111, 211n23, 238n1, 240n22; *Ghazali and the Poetics of Imagination*, 109, 111

moral community, 7, 28–29, 38–40; fada'il (virtues) and, 43–46, 221–22n30; Muslim subjects and,112–14, 118, 124–26; tawhid and, 41–46

morality: families and, 127–28, 137, 163, 185; privatization of, 126. *See also* husn al-khulq; ta'addub

mu'amalat (rules regulating daily lives), 184, 255n83

Mu'ayid, al-, 92, 168, 183, 232n52, 232n54, 235n78, 237n95, 243n43; contested marriage and, 164, 177, 252n43

Muqatam, al-, 144, 164, 168, 174

Mu'tazila, 88, 210n21, 222n36, 227n70, 233n70; 'Abduh and, 110, 117, 238n4, 240n20

Muwahidun, al- (Unitarians), 17. *See also* Wahhabi movement

Nadim, 'Abdallah al-, 243n43

nafs (inner self/soul), 109, 114, 239n12; fiqh al- (self-intelligibility), 109, 114–17, 147; Muslim women and, 171

naql (Revelation), 38, 101

Nasr, Vali, *The Shia Revival*, 193

Nassif, Malak Hilmi, 160–63, 250n11, 251n26, 251n27

nass (revealed knowledge), 73, 117, 240n20

nationalism: failure of, 200, 262n61. *See also* wataniya, al-

Nawawi, Hassuna al-, 103, 106, 236n86

niqab (veiling), 133, 161–62

niyya (intention), 47–48, 59–60, 223n39; attire and, 147; divorce and, 134

Official Gazette (al-Waqai' al-misriya), 75

Orientalism: conception of Islam in, 2–3, 32–33, 68–71, 73, 188–91, 199, 207–8nn4–5, 228n7, 255–56n2, 257n6; critique of reformers by, 198–99, 260n38; Wahhabi movement and, 31; *Orientalism* (Said), 2–3, 207n4, 208n8

orthodoxy, rethinking, 30–66; 'Abduh and, 72, 74, 77–78, 99–100, 107–8,

229n21; cult of saints issue and, 55–66; making of a good Muslim and, 47–55; mizan and, 86–90; monotheism and, 36–43; power and, 72, 89, 108, 113; reconfiguration of, 108; reform and tajdid and, 35–36; virtue and, 43–47

patriarchy, 156, 171, 253n53
pedagogy, 114–15, 119–27; women and, 157
piety, 45, 59, 123; movements, 212n31. *See also* mu'min; taqahqur
polygamy, 128, 131–34, 156, ; Nassif on, 161–62, 251n27
post-orientalism, 70, 195–201
prayer, 82, 116, 239n16
Prophet, humanity of, 62
public good. *See* maslaha
public obligation. *See* fard kifaya

qalb (heart/conviction), 47, 51, 224nn49–50; interiority and, 114–15
qanun (Ottoman imperial law), 137
qawl. *See* aqwal
Qur'an (Revelation), 7, 9, 11; 'Abduh and, 84, 86, 148–49, 231n42, 231n44; commands of, 43–45; marriage and divorce in, 128–30, 132
Qutb, Sayyid, 196, 201, 217–18n4, 256n4

Rafi'i, Muhammad al-, 106, 176, 185, 253n61, 255n84
rahma (compassion), 128
Rahman, Fazlur, 209–10n16, 220n19, 230n24 Fazlur is the correct spelling
rationality, post-Enlightenment, 1, 32–33, 68, 73, 188–91, 199, 202; Islamic, 73, 117, 152, 240n20. *See also* reasoning, Islamic
Raziq, 'Abdul, 69
reasoning, Islamic, 5, 7, 16, 29, 73–74, 184, 190, 239n19; 'Abduh's broadening of, 123–24; Greek philosophy

and, 8, 88–89, 232–32n49; tajdid-Islah, 71; Western negative view of, 188–91, 195. *See also* 'aql; ijtihad
reasoning, Western (Christian), 29; dichotomy between religion and, 32–33, 190–91, 224n48
recitation, 12, 22, 41, 212n32; al-Azhar university and, 100–101
reform, Islamic, 1–29; al-Azhar and, 99–108, 237n89; discursive nature of, 4–7; education and, 119–27, 240–41n24; family, marriage, and divorce and, 127–36; fatawa/i and, 143–50, 246n91; impact of social settings on, 10–13; Islamic courts and, 136–43, 245nn75–77, 245–46nn81–83; reform and revival discourses in, 7–9; task of reformers in, 8, 35–36, 90, 150. *See also* islah; tajdid
Religion: dichotomous construct of reason and, 190–91; fusion of with state, 18–19, 92–99, 191–94, 196–97; interiority and exteriority of, 113–14; privatization of, 112–13, 126, 163–65; as screen for political power, 35. *See also* din
religious endowment. *See* waqf
religious wars, 97, 233–34n70
renewal. *See* tajdid
retreat. *See* taqahqur
Revelation, 210n19. *See also* naql; nass; Qur'an
revival. *See* ihya'
revivalism, 1–3, 7–9; 'Abduh and, 70–71, 73, 78, 94–95, 163–64, 233n62.
riba (usury), 85–86
Rida, Mohammad Rashid, 69, 102, 150, 229n19, 230–31n37, 237n90, 242n30, 243n43, 248n108; patriarchal power and, 172–73, 253n53; *Tarikh al-Imam*, 229n18; women, marriage and, 159–60, 174, 177–78, 183–85, 252n50
Romantic movement, 191, 257n9
ruqqy (advancement), 11, 71

Sadat, Abdul Khaliq al-, 166–67, 169, 177, 181
Sadat, Safiya al-, contested marriage of, 153, 164–86, 252n41, 253n61
Said, Edward, 188, 255–56n2, 257n6, 258n14; humanism and, 3, 208nn8–9; *Orientalism*, 2–3, 207n4, 208n8
Saif, 'Abdullah ibn Ibrahim al-, 15
Salafiya movement, 31, 191, 233n70
Sa'udi dynasty, 215n54
scholarship/scholars, Muslim, 4–9, 34, 37. *See also* 'ulama
sciences, modern: 'Abduh, education and, 122, 241n29; Islamic knowledge and, 76, 110, 238n4
scribes, 140–41, 245–46nn81–82
sectarian loyalty. *See* ta'asub
secularism, 28, 68–69, 89, 'Abduh critique of, 90–99; equating modernity with, 68–69, 117, 190, 195, 202
self: divided, 225n56; ethics/hermeneutics of the, 110–13, 147; Muslim modern, 110, 151; Muslim women and, 170–71; Western vs. Islamic views of, 44, 50, 151, 221–22n30. *See also* nafs
sex segregation, 128, 133–34, 156, 161–63
shafa'a (intercession), 61–65, 227n75, 227nn70–71, 227n77
shafaqa (caring mixed with awe), 52
Shafi'i legal school, 89, 213n34, 253n51
shahada, 41, 44, 47–48, 60
Sha'rawi, Huda, 162
Sharbini, 'Abdul Rahman al-, 104–6, 237n90
shari'a (Islamic law), 12, 29, 37, 38–40, 136, 154 ; 'Abduh and reform of, 135–43, 245nn76–77, 245–46nn81–83; family law, 163–64, 172–73, 252–53n51; women and, 128, 131, 170–72, 181
Shatibi, Abu Ishaq, al-, 80, 84, 86, 231n41, 248n106
Shawkani, Muhammad ibn Ali, al-, 212n27

Sheehan, Jonathan, 26, 234n73
shi'ism, 64–65
shirk (polytheism), 14, 17, 44, 52–53, 62–63, 225n56
Sindi, Muhammad Hayat ibn Ibrahim al-, 15–16, 214n46
Skovgaard-Peterson, Jakob, 139, 238n3
slaughtering practices, 148–49, 247n102
Smith, Wilfred C., 49–51, 223n41, 223–24n47
Soroush, Abdolkarim, 7, 210n19
soul. *See* nafs
sources. *See* usul
speculative theology. *See* 'ilm al-kalam
speech, interconnected with conviction, 46–47. *See also* aqwal stagnation. *See* degeneration; inhitat
subjective interiority: 'Abduh and, 110–12, 147, 239n3; in Islamic tradition, 109–19, 237–38n1; maslaha (public good) and, 157; Muslim women and, 170–71; in Western liberal tradition, 109–12, 117–18
subjects, Muslim, 109–52; 'Abduh's fatawa and, 143–50; community and, 112, 118, 151; construction of modern, 112–19; education and pedagogy and, 119–27; family, marriage and divorce and, 127–36; judicial systems and, 136–43; subjective interiority and, 109–12
submission. *See* islam
Sufism, 9, 38–39, 88, 216n64, 223n45, 225n56; al-Ghazali and, 116–17; monistic, 37–40, 220nn19–20
suicide bombing, ibn 'Abdul Wahhab and, 32–33, 218n10
suitability, marriage. *See* tawafuq
suitability clause. *See* maqsad
sulh (out-of-court reconciliation), 141
Sunna (sayings and practices of the Prophet), 7, 11–12, 211n26, 214n46; honoring parents and, 44–45

ta'addub (moral cultivation), 111, 123
ta'asub (sectarian loyalty), 141–42
Taftazani, al-, 24, 101
taghrib (Europeanization), 72, 104, 165, 229n20; 'Abduh, taqlid and, 77–86, 107
tahdhib (disciplining), 110, 114–15, 238n12
Tahtawi, Rifa'a Rafi' al-, 100, 127
tajdid-Islah (reasoning within discursive tradition), 71
tajdid (renewal), 7–9; 'Abdul and, 73–77; ibn 'Abdul Wahhab and, 35–36
takfir (apostasy), 59–60
takhayur (selection), 150, 240n21, 248n108
talfiq (combining the doctrines of different legal schools to arrive at new rules), 142, 245n76
tankit wal-tabkit, al-, 235n78, 243n43
Transvaal fatwa, 146–50
tanzimat (Ottoman governance), 138
taqahqur (retreat from piety), 8
taqlid (consensual precedence), 9; 'Abduh and, 72–73, 76, 77–87, 107, 149, 152; Hanbali school and, 247–48n104; ibn 'Abdul Wahhab and, 16, 37; Islamic courts and, 141, 245n76, 246n85; from legal perspective, 80–82
tarbiya (education), 110, 114–15; 'Abduh on, 119–27
tasdiq (inner conviction), 110, 114–15, 117
tashayyu' (harmful dissension), 238–39n11
ta'til al-din (impaired religion), 35, 219n15
tawafuq (suitability, marriage), 130
tawakul (trust in God), 53
tawhid (oneness of God), 16, 105, 220n19; al-ilah and al-rab, 39, 41; cult of saints and, 57–58; as embodied practice, 41–42; ibn 'Abdul Wahhab and, 14–15, 17, 26, 36–46, 222n34; Sufism and, 39

theocracy: Christian, 93, 96–97; Islam as despotic, 191–94, 200
theology, 223–24n47; at al-Azhar (university), 101; speculative, 38–40, 105, 116
Tradition: definition of, 3–5, Islamic discursive 4–13, 28–29, 33–34, 38, 66; invented vs. authentic, 70, 197–98, 229n13; liberalism as a, 5, 28, ; living, 88.
Trinity (Christian), anti-Muslim sentiment and, 255n1
trust in God. *See* tawakul

'ubudiya (worship), 42–43
'ulama (Muslim scholars), 5, 11; 'Abduh and, 79–85, 100–107, 148, 237n89; ibn 'Abdul Wahhab and, 37
umma (community), 36, 44, 118, 125, 219n16
unauthorized innovations. *See* bid'a
'Urabi revolt, 75–76
'urf (customary law), 137, 180–81, 184–85, 254n74
'Urwa al-Wuthqa, al-, 76
usul (principle sources), 11–12, 231n44, 246nn90–91; al-din (theology), 38; al-fiqh (legal), 38
usury. *See* riba
utterances. *See* aqwal

Vatikiotis, P. J., 68, 191, 228n6
veil. *See* khimar; niqab
violence: Christianity and, 97, 234n72, 255n1; Wahhabism and, 30–33
virtue/virtues: 12, 29, 33–36, 42–46, 49–50, 55, 61, 82, 111, 116, 120, 123–24, 128, 221n28, 221n30. *See also* fada'il; malaka
visitation of graves, 56–61, 226n63. *See also* cult of saints

Wali Allah, Shah, 59–60, 64
Wadud, Amina, 256n4
Wahhabi movement, 26–27, 30–33, 209–10n16, 215n54, 255n81

waqf (religious endowment), 138, 181,
    246–47n92
wasat (middle way), 87, 232n50, 239n12.
    See also middle-of-the-road rule;
    mizan
wataniya, al- (nationalism), 124–25
Watt, W. Montgomery, 32
wijdan (sentiment), 114–15, 117
Wilayat al-Faqih (Khomeini), 196–97
Wittgenstein, Ludwig, 67, 228n1
women: education and, 127, 131, 157–58,
    161, 243n41, 243n57, 249nn8–9;
    household management and, 155–60;
    marriage, divorce and, 128–36,
    244n72; new, in Egypt, 155–64; rights
    of, Islam and, 127–28, 170–72, 181,
183–87, 243n41, 243n44; sex segrega-
    tion and, 133–34, 161, 163, 193;
    vulnerability of, 54, 226n61
worship. *See* 'ibada; 'ubudiya

Young, Robert, 208n8
Yusuf, 'Ali: contested marriage of,
    164–86, 252n45; khedive and,
    168–69, 175, 182–83, 232n52, 243n43,
    253n59

Zaghlul, Sa'ad, 168
Zahir, al- (newspaper), 149–50
zakat (almsgiving), 116
zina (adultery), 54
Zubaida, Sami, 196, 200–201

Cultural Memory | *in the Present*

Samira Haj, *Reconfiguring Islamic Tradition: Reform, Rationality, and Modernity*

Diane Perpich, *The Ethics of Emmanuel Levinas*

Marcel Detienne, *Comparing the Incomparable*

François Delaporte, *Anatomy of the Passions*

René Girard, *Mimesis and Theory: Essays on Literature and Criticism, 1959–2005*

Richard Baxstrom, *Wrecking Balls, Ruins, Reform: The Experience of Place and the Problem of Belief in Urban Malaysia*

Jennifer L. Culbert, *Capital Punishment and the Problem of Judgment*

Samantha Frost, *Lessons from a Materialist Thinker: Hobbesian Reflections on Ethics and Politics*

Regina Mara Schwartz, *When God Left the World: Sacramental Poetics at the Dawn of Secularism*

Gil Anidjar, *Semites: Race, Religion, Literature*

Ranjana Khanna, *Algeria Cuts: Women and Representation, 1830 to the Present*

Esther Peeren, *Intersubjectivities and Popular Culture: Bakhtin and Beyond*

Eyal Peretz, *Becoming Visionary: Brian De Palma's Cinematic Education of the Senses*

Diana Sorensen, *A Turbulent Decade Remembered: Scenes from the Latin American Sixties*

Hubert Damisch, *A Childhood Memory by Piero della Francesca*

Dana Hollander, *Exemplarity and Chosenness: Rosenzweig and Derrida on the Nation of Philosophy*

Asja Szafraniec, *Beckett, Derrida, and the Event of Literature*

Sara Guyer, *Romanticism After Auschwitz*

Alison Ross, *The Aesthetic Paths of Philosophy: Presentation in Kant, Heidegger, Lacoue-Labarthe, and Nancy*

Gerhard Richter, *Thought-Images: Frankfurt School Writers' Reflections from Damaged Life*

Bella Brodzki, *Can These Bones Live? Translation, Survival, and Cultural Memory*

Rodolphe Gasché, *The Honor of Thinking: Critique, Theory, Philosophy*

Brigitte Peucker, *The Material Image: Art and the Real in Film*

Natalie Melas, *All the Difference in the World: Postcoloniality and the Ends of Comparison*

Jonathan Culler, *The Literary in Theory*

Michael G. Levine, *The Belated Witness: Literature, Testimony, and the Question of Holocaust Survival*

Jennifer A. Jordan, *Structures of Memory: Understanding German Change in Berlin and Beyond*

Christoph Menke, *Reflections of Equality*

Marlène Zarader, *The Unthought Debt: Heidegger and the Hebraic Heritage*

Jan Assmann, *Religion and Cultural Memory: Ten Studies*

David Scott and Charles Hirschkind, *Powers of the Secular Modern: Talal Asad and His Interlocutors*

Gyanendra Pandey, *Routine Violence: Nations, Fragments, Histories*

James Siegel, *Naming the Witch*

J. M. Bernstein, *Against Voluptuous Bodies: Late Modernism and the Meaning of Painting*

Theodore W. Jennings, Jr., *Reading Derrida / Thinking Paul: On Justice*

Richard Rorty and Eduardo Mendieta, *Take Care of Freedom and Truth Will Take Care of Itself: Interviews with Richard Rorty*

Jacques Derrida, *Paper Machine*

Renaud Barbaras, *Desire and Distance: Introduction to a Phenomenology of Perception*

Jill Bennett, *Empathic Vision: Affect, Trauma, and Contemporary Art*

Ban Wang, *Illuminations from the Past: Trauma, Memory, and History in Modern China*

James Phillips, *Heidegger's Volk: Between National Socialism and Poetry*

Frank Ankersmit, *Sublime Historical Experience*

István Rév, *Retroactive Justice: Prehistory of Post-Communism*

Paola Marrati, *Genesis and Trace: Derrida Reading Husserl and Heidegger*

Krzysztof Ziarek, *The Force of Art*

Marie-José Mondzain, *Image, Icon, Economy: The Byzantine Origins of the Contemporary Imaginary*

Cecilia Sjöholm, *The Antigone Complex: Ethics and the Invention of Feminine Desire*

Jacques Derrida and Elisabeth Roudinesco, *For What Tomorrow . . . : A Dialogue*

Elisabeth Weber, *Questioning Judaism: Interviews by Elisabeth Weber*

Jacques Derrida and Catherine Malabou, *Counterpath: Traveling with Jacques Derrida*

Martin Seel, *Aesthetics of Appearing*

Nanette Salomon, *Shifting Priorities: Gender and Genre in Seventeenth-Century Dutch Painting*

Jacob Taubes, *The Political Theology of Paul*

Jean-Luc Marion, *The Crossing of the Visible*

Eric Michaud, *The Cult of Art in Nazi Germany*

Anne Freadman, *The Machinery of Talk: Charles Peirce and the Sign Hypothesis*

Stanley Cavell, *Emerson's Transcendental Etudes*

Stuart McLean, *The Event and Its Terrors: Ireland, Famine, Modernity*

Beate Rössler, ed., *Privacies: Philosophical Evaluations*

Bernard Faure, *Double Exposure: Cutting Across Buddhist and Western Discourses*

Alessia Ricciardi, *The Ends of Mourning: Psychoanalysis, Literature, Film*

Alain Badiou, *Saint Paul: The Foundation of Universalism*

Gil Anidjar, *The Jew, the Arab: A History of the Enemy*

Jonathan Culler and Kevin Lamb, eds., *Just Being Difficult? Academic Writing in the Public Arena*

Jean-Luc Nancy, *A Finite Thinking*, edited by Simon Sparks

Theodor W. Adorno, *Can One Live after Auschwitz? A Philosophical Reader*, edited by Rolf Tiedemann

Patricia Pisters, *The Matrix of Visual Culture: Working with Deleuze in Film Theory*

Andreas Huyssen, *Present Pasts: Urban Palimpsests and the Politics of Memory*

Talal Asad, *Formations of the Secular: Christianity, Islam, Modernity*

Dorothea von Mücke, *The Rise of the Fantastic Tale*

Marc Redfield, *The Politics of Aesthetics: Nationalism, Gender, Romanticism*

Emmanuel Levinas, *On Escape*

Dan Zahavi, *Husserl's Phenomenology*

Rodolphe Gasché, *The Idea of Form: Rethinking Kant's Aesthetics*

Michael Naas, *Taking on the Tradition: Jacques Derrida and the Legacies of Deconstruction*

Herlinde Pauer-Studer, ed., *Constructions of Practical Reason: Interviews on Moral and Political Philosophy*

Jean-Luc Marion, *Being Given That: Toward a Phenomenology of Givenness*

Theodor W. Adorno and Max Horkheimer, *Dialectic of Enlightenment*

Ian Balfour, *The Rhetoric of Romantic Prophecy*

Martin Stokhof, *World and Life as One: Ethics and Ontology in Wittgenstein's Early Thought*

Gianni Vattimo, *Nietzsche: An Introduction*

Jacques Derrida, *Negotiations: Interventions and Interviews, 1971–1998*, ed. Elizabeth Rottenberg

Brett Levinson, *The Ends of Literature: The Latin American "Boom" in the Neoliberal Marketplace*

Timothy J. Reiss, *Against Autonomy: Cultural Instruments, Mutualities, and the Fictive Imagination*

Hent de Vries and Samuel Weber, eds., *Religion and Media*

Niklas Luhmann, *Theories of Distinction: Re-Describing the Descriptions of Modernity*, ed. and introd. William Rasch

Johannes Fabian, *Anthropology with an Attitude: Critical Essays*

Michel Henry, *I Am the Truth: Toward a Philosophy of Christianity*

Gil Anidjar, *"Our Place in Al-Andalus": Kabbalah, Philosophy, Literature in Arab-Jewish Letters*

Hélène Cixous and Jacques Derrida, *Veils*

F. R. Ankersmit, *Historical Representation*

F. R. Ankersmit, *Political Representation*

Elissa Marder, *Dead Time: Temporal Disorders in the Wake of Modernity (Baudelaire and Flaubert)*

Reinhart Koselleck, *The Practice of Conceptual History: Timing History, Spacing Concepts*

Niklas Luhmann, *The Reality of the Mass Media*

Hubert Damisch, *A Theory of /Cloud/: Toward a History of Painting*

Jean-Luc Nancy, *The Speculative Remark: (One of Hegel's bon mots)*

Jean-François Lyotard, *Soundproof Room: Malraux's Anti-Aesthetics*

Jan Patočka, *Plato and Europe*

Hubert Damisch, *Skyline: The Narcissistic City*

Isabel Hoving, *In Praise of New Travelers: Reading Caribbean Migrant Women Writers*

Richard Rand, ed., *Futures: Of Jacques Derrida*

William Rasch, *Niklas Luhmann's Modernity: The Paradoxes of Differentiation*

Jacques Derrida and Anne Dufourmantelle, *Of Hospitality*

Jean-François Lyotard, *The Confession of Augustine*

Kaja Silverman, *World Spectators*

Samuel Weber, *Institution and Interpretation: Expanded Edition*

Jeffrey S. Librett, *The Rhetoric of Cultural Dialogue: Jews and Germans in the Epoch of Emancipation*

Ulrich Baer, *Remnants of Song: Trauma and the Experience of Modernity in Charles Baudelaire and Paul Celan*

Samuel C. Wheeler III, *Deconstruction as Analytic Philosophy*

David S. Ferris, *Silent Urns: Romanticism, Hellenism, Modernity*

Rodolphe Gasché, *Of Minimal Things: Studies on the Notion of Relation*

Sarah Winter, *Freud and the Institution of Psychoanalytic Knowledge*

Samuel Weber, *The Legend of Freud: Expanded Edition*

Aris Fioretos, ed., *The Solid Letter: Readings of Friedrich Hölderlin*

J. Hillis Miller / Manuel Asensi, *Black Holes / J. Hillis Miller; or, Boustrophedonic Reading*

Miryam Sas, *Fault Lines: Cultural Memory and Japanese Surrealism*

Peter Schwenger, *Fantasm and Fiction: On Textual Envisioning*

Didier Maleuvre, *Museum Memories: History, Technology, Art*

Jacques Derrida, *Monolingualism of the Other; or, The Prosthesis of Origin*

Andrew Baruch Wachtel, *Making a Nation, Breaking a Nation: Literature and Cultural Politics in Yugoslavia*

Niklas Luhmann, *Love as Passion: The Codification of Intimacy*

Mieke Bal, ed., *The Practice of Cultural Analysis: Exposing Interdisciplinary Interpretation*

Jacques Derrida and Gianni Vattimo, eds., *Religion*

CPSIA information can be obtained
at www.ICGtesting.com
Printed in the USA
LVOW08s1224300717
543152LV00003B/379/P